Matthew Bell is a mechanical engineer by trade but spends every spare moment writing about Sheffield United. He has edited the United fanzine, *Flashing Blade* for over twenty years and has written a weekly column in the *Green 'Un* since 1993. He was co-editor of the imaginatively titled books, *Blades Tales* and *Blades Tales 2* and has written articles for *4-4-2* magazine and the 2003 Sheffield United v Arsenal FA Cup semi-final programme. Despite all this, he says that United's results are less important than the quality of his pre-match pint.

Dr. Gary Armstrong is a Reader in the School of Sport and Education, Brunel University, London. He previously lectured in Criminology at the University of Westminster and the University of Reading. His research into sports-related matters has produced various publications including: *Football Hooligans:Knowing the Score*, *Blade Runners: Lives in Football* and *Sheffield United FC: The Biography*. Away from academe Gary Armstrong is coach of Hampstead FC Boys U-11 team and Vice Chair of the Camden Community Football and Sports Association, North London's largest youth football entity.

FIT AND PROPER?

Conflicts and Conscience in an English Football Club

By Matthew Bell
and Gary Armstrong

peakpublish

Peakpublish
An imprint of Peak Platform
New Bridge
Calver
Hope Valley
S32 3XT

First published by Peakpublish 2010

Printed in England

A CIP catalogue record for this book is available from
the British Library

ISBN: 978-1-907219-11-5
www.peakplatform.com

Matthew Bell:
In memory of Colin Bell (1926-2009), who introduced a seven-year-old to the footballing brilliance of Tony Currie. The rest, including this book, is history.

Gary Armstrong:
To Blades past and present – you make life worth living and have taught me so much.

This book is also dedicated to the long-suffering followers of Sheffield United FC (nicknamed the Blades), who turn up in their thousands despite none living long enough to see their club win anything of note. In 2007/08 the Blades had the best home attendance in English football outside the Premier League with an average of 25,648. This made them the 46th-best supported club in Europe. Their last major trophy – the 1925 FA Cup – was won some 85 years ago. Considering their support, Sheffield United are the most under-performing club in the UK. An occasional promotion to the top division of English football is soon followed by relegation. A decent cup run every decade continues to be the lot of the red and white half of the city that gave the world Association Football.

Acknowledgements

The authors are indebted to literally hundreds of sources in the making of what follows.   These informants - not always conscious that their information would one day appear in print - were variously fans of the club, writers about the club, employees of the club and on occasion sat on the board of directors of the club. Some played football for the club, others drew a wage in a variety of capacities. We thank them all but protect their identity.

Table of Contents

Preface

Preface

Some books just write themselves. This is one of them. The authors might best be considered as midwives facilitating the entry to the world of this tale that was in a sense conceived some 120 years ago. Consider us historians and not polemicists - for the most part the facts that we seek to present speak volumes without our interpretation. We wish that what follows wasn't so - it would have saved us years of research and probably made us less despairing about the nature of professional football in Britain. Many times in the course of producing this text we asked how wonderful must it be to follow a club that is well run, solvent, performs well on the pitch and has good relations with the fans that sustain it and are its life-blood. Could we hark back to a Golden Age when this was so? That depends on the individual: some readers will speak of 'that time' in the 1960s, the happy days of 1981/82 or the fun times at the end of that decade. We would venture to suggest that few readers would speak well of the way the club they support has been run over the past 30 years. The disgruntled fan is today part of the make-up of English football. The fans of Sheffield United have many tales to tell on the table of woe alongside other fans.

But alongside the tales of woe, we can brag. Sheffield hosts the world's oldest football club in Sheffield FC, formed in 1857. It is where the first rules of Association Football were formulated. It is home to two of the world's oldest sports grounds in continuous use - Bramall Lane and Hallam FC's Sandygate. The world's first cup final - the Youden Cup - was held at Bramall Lane in 1867. Eleven years later the first ever floodlit game was staged at the ground. Sheffield also boasts today of two fine, long-standing professional clubs: Sheffield Wednesday, founded in 1867, and Sheffield United, founded in 1889. Allow us to reflect on how for some 150 years the game has been variously played, supported and administered in this fine city.

Beyond boasting, allow us to explain our purpose – to chronicle the way Sheffield United Football Club has been run, particularly over the past 30 years. Integral to such an objective are two questions that we may not answer in the course of the following 300 pages. The first asks: what is a professional football club for and what is its purpose? The second seeks to address the way that those who occupied the Bramall Lane boardroom saw their sense of mission. The two questions are inseparable and might best be examined in isolation for academic purposes. However, we realise that football clubs have both material and emotional ownership. The bearers of such sentiment and structures are not always in agreement as to what is best for the club. Then again the club owners are often not in agreement themselves. And then of course there are the football players and team managers to take into consideration. This is not a topic that lends itself to easy analysis, not least because a football club does not usually have a mission statement or economic rationale. As such, those who have had the responsibility of running the club have either imposed their world view on the football entity or made up policy and strategy on the hoof.

In writing what follows we attempt to leave judgement to the reader. Had circumstances been different and monies or inheritance and legacies placed us in the hot-seat would we have done any better in charge of the club? No one will carry the two authors - Sheffield-born and decades-long followers of Sheffield United FC - around the pitch proclaiming our role in the club's footballing glory. Likewise we will never have to address the post-match disgruntled thousands in the club car park. The stories that follow are thus those of the men who tried in various ways to run a football club and in doing so make tens of thousands of supporters happy. We have to thank them for their efforts. We also hope that what follows is charitable in its sentiment.

People enjoy football for many reasons. Underlying these reasons is the generally unarticulated melancholia the game offers, alongside the moments of unrequited joy. The game is a constant reminder of what it is to be alive. It is this life-affirming struggle, usually against logic and common sense, that sustains our collective sense of belonging in the face of all that life can throw at us. The men who have taken responsibility to run football clubs carry a big burden, which is in part financial but also emotional - a lot (possibly too much) is invested by maybe too many in the game at the professional level. People want the vicarious glory that a team captain lifting a trophy brings. Football club directors are thus tasked with 'Getting It Right' and meanwhile are trusted that they won't run off with the money or bring too much shame to the name of the club by a variety of nefarious activities. The directors will forever talk about the 'business principles' (they might even mention the word 'logic') that they claim to bring to the club. However they, like the fans who pay their weekly monies to their club, have to watch a contest where success and failure is often arbitrary and dependent on a variety of factors that could not be legislated for, nor anticipated by any model of governance.

The wealth swishing around the game at the elite level in England is staggering. At the same time over half of professional clubs in the Premier League and Football League are running on empty. The boardrooms in many instances are a Fool's Paradise, containing the preposterous, the pompous and occasionally the pious. Football is collapsing under its own bloat, its moral compass is going haywire and it stares into the financial abyss. But the fans still love the spectacle and politicians still line up to be associated with the game. The aesthetic of the game is addictive and for many impossible to leave, no matter how many times football and those who run it disappoint or deceive. Quite where the game at top level will go over the next decade no one knows. Who will drive it on those journeys is a matter of conjecture. One thing is certain: there will be no shortage of men - and maybe women - who will seek to sit in the best seats of Sheffield United's Bramall Lane stadium, enjoying the status of football club director and the profile that comes with it. Such people - with a few exceptions - for the past 120 years have had local accents, albeit with tones more suited to the lounge than the tap-room. This could soon change as the forces of global financial flows see the ownership of English clubs as something highly desired by both the established capitalist nations and those whose new-found wealth seeks an easily acquired personal profile.

It wasn't until the last third of the twentieth century that football club boardrooms and the people who occupied them gained as high a profile in the media and amongst the supporters as the players and managers they employed. Prior to this period, the men who frequently waddled to games were notable in being the only ones present wearing expensive suits; for the most part these men were mysterious figures known mainly via gossip and anecdote. They did not court the media because the media had little interest in such quintessential local worthies. In some instances they even controlled the local media. For the best part of a century the media was not an issue in the game; it was unintrusive, concerning itself with reporting the facts around the football match. The men of the press had little interest in personal foibles, prurience or perversions. They presumed their readers had the same disdain for scandal.

Apart from the familial dynasties like the Hill-Woods at Arsenal and the Moores at Liverpool, who until the last two decades knew the names of more than half a dozen of the 92 league football club chairmen? They and their directors generally fitted a profile: comparatively wealthy local businessmen, often ageing, and always keen for a bit of reflected glory within their community after years of work in the offices above the factory, mill or store. They were the proverbial butchers, bakers and candlestick makers, or, in the case of Sheffield United, the timber merchants and the builders' suppliers. As Arthur Hopcraft wrote in *The Football Man* in 1968, 'Directors under the age of 45 are not common, and those under 40 distinctly rare. There is an immediate similarity in age group, worldly experience and physical look between football directors and magistrates' benches….. feet-on-the-ground citizenry, local boys made good none too early in life, no fancy talk, a bit booze stained round the edges, a high incidence of waistcoats.' A football directorship suggested a life well lived and one that had followed the straight road. Such men were generally serious and often abstemious.

It was rare that football club directors were voted out, bought out or thrown out, unless the club they were in charge of was in such dire straits that only a newcomer with access to a readier supply of cash could step in and take over. If everything went well, or even just satisfactorily, the position of football club director was usually a job for life, or at least lasted until voluntary retirement. The board of directors was seldom subject to collective abuse from the stands or terraces, even if the team was performing badly on the pitch. A rare example of supporters' agitation against the men in charge occurred at United's Bramall Lane ground after Sheffield United were relegated from the old First Division in April 1956. The match programme of the next home game told the reader of a 'ginger group' of shareholders who voiced their opposition to the board of directors at the Annual General Meeting. Such protest, however, was to no avail. At the AGM the directors were re-elected by large majorities - this restrained demonstration of opposition was confined by the formalities of structured business proceedings and was restricted to the privileged few who owned shares in the company. The protestors did not contain 'ordinary' supporters from the kop or the terrace. It was more than another decade before concerted protests emanated from such quarters. One of the first public outpourings of dissent against the United board was prompted by the sales, each for £100,000, of top scorers Mick Jones, to Leeds United, and Alan Birchenall, to Chelsea, during the 1967/68 season. The supporters on the kop, upset at the loss of the team's two best forwards, offered advice to the chairman Dick Wragg when, chanting, to the tune of the hymn *Michael, Row The Boat Ashore*, 'Send Dick Wragg to Vietnam!' That season also saw United relegated from the First Division, an outcome considered by many as reaping what the chairman had sown.

The timing of this show of anger was significant. The late sixties was the period when British society was changing (as it was throughout the USA and Western Europe), with rebellious cultures of music, student demonstrations, riots of a variety of natures and anti-war protests coming to the fore. Much of these attitudes and actions were fed by the growing influence of television that spread news around the globe like never before. It was a period of free expression, protest against privilege, and the rejection of deference. This was also the time when media interest in football and those connected with it rose phenomenally. The spotlight attracted a new breed of men, desirous of the limelight and the publicity that owning a football club would bring. One such man, who described himself as a 'sheep farmer', was Ken Bates, who in 1965 at 35 years of age bought Oldham Athletic, provoking Arthur Hopcraft to scathingly contrast him with the patrician figure of Arsenal's Denis Hill-Wood: '…. the two poles of the football director. They are, definitively, the representatives of the public school and Brick Street secondary in the boardroom, the one committed to duty, the other to opportunity.' In 2010 the Hill-Wood family are clinging on to their shares at Arsenal. Ken Bates clings on to his position of chairman of Leeds United FC as demands increase for him to reveal who really owns the club; an identity hitherto never disclosed by Bates.

To many working in high finance, purchasing a football club is a 'vanity project', which provokes the question: what makes someone want to become a director or owner of a professional football club? Apart from the handful of unscrupulous chairman who undertake various dubious financial activities, few can make money out of the task. Many are unpaid, non-executive directors who may well end up putting their own money into the club to help it out of what seem to be inevitable difficulties or to ensure that it continues to exist. That said, some individuals have taken over a club just to run it into the ground in order to sell its ground for property development. Fortunately, most directors do not have this outcome as their prime objective and most seek to neither pocket monies nor asset-strip. However, enough people exist to provide consternation and to provoke demands for football in England to attempt to put its own house in order.

The 'Fit and Proper Person Test' was introduced by the Football Association in 2004 and adopted by the Premier League and the Football League. In an attempt to keep 'dodgy' owners out of football, the 'Fit and Proper' criteria are a series of criminal offences generally involving fraud, theft or insolvency that would prevent someone sitting in the position of director at an English professional football club. The 'Test' - which is not really a test - has rarely been used to its full extent. Consequently, supporters have to trust that the (usually) men who temporarily control their club do so with honest intentions. By the middle of 2010 only one person had been deemed 'unfit' by the FA to own a football club. This was Stephen Vaughan, who in 2001 took over Chester City Football Club. In 2009 he was disqualified from being a company director after an alleged VAT fraud at Widnes Vikings, a rugby club he also owned. The disqualification forced him to stand down from Chester's board. Desperately in debt and burdened by a 25-point penalty for two offences – for being insolvent and failing to agree a Company Voluntary Arrangement (CVA) - the Chester club went out of business in early 2010, having its results expunged from the Conference league table. The club now exists as Chester FC and plays in the north-west regional leagues. A critic might argue that the 'Test' was applied too late.

There will never be a shortage of people willing to sit on the boards of football clubs. There are football supporters who hypothesise that if they came into money, say by winning the national lottery, they would buy shares in their club to gain a seat on the board. However, just as many, usually after another inept team performance or yet another headline of unrealised promises made by chairman and manager, mumble into their beer; 'They're not getting any of my cash,' certain in the knowledge that such funds would only go to waste on unnecessarily large transfer fees or impossibly high player salaries, or more recently in the belief that their monies were paying for building projects over and above footballing talent and which benefited only the bank account of the chairman. Those same supporters might then be the ones who accuse their board of 'lack of ambition' when they fail to sign players of sufficient quality to improve the team's fortunes. In truth, football club directors cannot win; few chairmen receive adulation when their team wins a trophy or gain promotions, the same men, however, usually cop the flack when the team is doing badly: 'Sack the board!' is a chant heard at grounds throughout Britain, but when did supporters last sing, 'We love you, chairman!' when their team was successful?

Most football club directors and owners have become wealthy in business outside of the game. They thus have to be far richer than the average supporter to even get a seat on the board in the first place. They ideally possess the financial wherewithal to keep a struggling club afloat or push a reasonably secure one on to greater achievement. Usually they will have been able to base their personal business decisions on matters they could control and manipulate, such as employing the right people in the right jobs, keeping a sharp eye on production costs and income flows and identifying the right market for sourcing their materials and selling their products. They would have to be willing to take advice when necessary and be ruthless with budgets and personnel when needs be. The fundamental principles of success in business similarly apply to running a football club. However, men who made their wealth in property, finance or industry usually did so without thousands scrutinising their every move or attracting constant press attention. They made or lost their monies without the burden of carrying the hopes and dreams of thousands. The emotional investment that so many put into football clubs is not found in business ventures, which exist to make profits and retain employees. Football is a business but not one that could be considered rational; fortunes can be influenced by an erroneous refereeing decision or a freak bounce of the ball. Football is unpredictable, arbitrary, and too often irrational and illogical. Outcomes are never guaranteed and the best team does not always win. Systems of play are not guaranteed to produce rewards evidenced elsewhere and those tasked with managing are not always able to replicate the success they achieved elsewhere. In truth it is all rather risky, sometimes silly, often hilariously pretentious and takes up too much time considering what else is going on in the world. But would supporters or directors want it any other way?

Chapter 1

Faith, Hope and Charity
A Football Club and the Men Who Made It

The Industrial Revolution of 19th century Britain made some men fabulously wealthy. But for the millions drawn to the newly emerging urban areas the wage-labouring rewards of industrial production provided for a life that was nasty, brutish and short. The city of Sheffield grew out of the Industrial Revolution and gave the world two things; stainless steel and football. These two inventions changed the world. The genius for such invention has been down-played in the Steel City, the commitment of its populace to hard work and physicality too often dismissed. So let us begin with both an appreciation of and thanks to the men who both invented the rules of the game of Association Football and who - often alongside running steel production and the City Council - also ran football clubs.

Charity was an underlying causation of both the first football clubs in Sheffield and indeed the game itself. Locally the first charity match played in Sheffield took place on December 28, 1881 in the Hyde Park district where Sheffield FC played Hallam FC in a match that saw gate receipts donated to local good causes. A similar fixture took place the following year. The first football match ever at Bramall Lane on December 29, 1862 saw the same two clubs play, the takings of the game being donated to the Lancashire District Fund to assist the impoverished populations of the north-west mill towns, whose trade was brought to a standstill by the absence of imported

1

cotton due to a blockade on exports arising out of the American Civil War. Over a century later football clubs would use the term 'Corporate Social Responsibility' to justify the publicity around the good causes they either funded or facilitated in a variety of ways. Giving and taking were integral to the game, but to many football enthusiasts the balance got very confused from the late 20th century onwards.

The condition of the soul of man concerned many in the era of industrialisation and urbanisation. Many thought higher than football results, whilst others at least realised the game's potential to reach people to offer a path to a better life. Preaching respect, politically conservative and prone to authoritarianism, the Methodism and non-conformist Christianity promoted and practised widely in 19th century Sheffield was to provide for generations of hard-working and uncompromising factory owners. This in turn informed a stratum below them in wealth and status but who sought nonetheless to emulate in many ways their social betters. Working on the principles of good works and charity, allied to a belief that not everything could be left to God's will, the non-conformist creed also produced many a capable trade unionist and, later, Socialists. The same conviction could also produce football activists. A distinguishing feature of such conviction was an ingrained sense of responsibility for one's conduct. Such a philosophy was often Puritan in outlook and censorious to those that did not follow the path to virtue and either the Kingdom of God or the rights of man. Applied to football in Sheffield it could be argued that such ideology sought systems and results above elaboration and artistry, and praised the sense and celebration of the collective over and above the individualist.

Such a background is important because the formation of Sheffield United FC needs to be located in the socio-political context of the social changes witnessed in 19th century Britain. In 1889, the year Sheffield United FC was formed, the gas workers had gone on strike and won their case for an eight-hour working day. This victory led to the mass unionisation of northern-based workers, a sign of rising confidence in the working-class population. Nationally, the decade from 1890 saw a rise in trade unionism and monumental industrial disputes. A class consciousness was very evident, but significantly football attracted both rich and poor. The wealthy middle-class, however, held power. The shareholders of football clubs were invariably middle-class and, in Sheffield United's case, drew their wealth primarily from manufacturing. Just a decade after its foundation, in 1899 Sheffield United FC became a limited liability company and in the ensuing share offer became owned by 422 shareholders. The shares were in part bought by existing committee people and others with modest wealth in the city. Interestingly no one had a block of shares, nor in fact did anyone have more than one. Even in the 1970s, those holding two shares did so mainly by virtue of inheritance. For some 80-plus years Sheffield United FC was owned equally by around 400 people. Sheffield United FC in origin was established as a business and, like all businesses subject to the fluctuations and vagaries of market forces, sought to make a profit for its shareholders. The change from the 1889 sporting club run by committee to that of a limited company for football and cricket took away personal liability in case of debt.

The Great and the Good

The men who founded Sheffield United FC were the great and good of what was - and remains - a very provincial city. The man who can claim credit for the football club that exists some 120 years later is Michael Ellison, who worked for the Duke of Norfolk, owner of the land upon which Bramall Lane stands today. The stadium in origin was thus a product of the largesse of one of Britain's richest men and largest landowners and the good work of Ellison, a loyal servant and devoted Catholic. That said, Sheffield United FC carries no religious connotations and has never felt betrothed to the Duke and his successors. The men best remembered for founding the football club were local and their principles grounded in locally-inspired doctrine. One such man was Sheffield-born Joseph Beckett Wostinholm. He held the position of secretary of Yorkshire County Cricket Club and became the first secretary of Sheffield United FC, having been secretary of the

3

Sheffield United Ground Committee since 1862. His task was to draw back the financial losses incurred by the cricket club that played its games in the sporting enclosure that was Bramall Lane, and then provide funds to build a new cricket pavilion. His legacy was the building of the boundary walls and the Shoreham Street enclosure. A stockbroker, chartered accountant and renowned philanthropist, Wostinholm's philosophy was rooted in the Unitarian church. His Norfolk Row offices in the centre of Sheffield hosted the meeting that formally declared a football club by the name of Sheffield United FC.

Alongside Wostinholm was another Sheffield native, Henry 'Harry' Stones. Born in 1860, Stones began paid employment at the age of 15, working his way up to become a partner in the Wostinholm and Stevenson chartered accountancy business. Initially assistant secretary to Wostinholm at Bramall Lane in 1893, Stones' significance in football pre-dated this position. Letters sent from Sheffield FC – founded in 1857 - seeking to play at Bramall Lane in early 1889 are addressed to him. This made sense; Wostinholm had little interest in football and made this fact quite evident in meetings. When the football club was formed the administrative workload doubled. Stones was thus made football club secretary, a position he held until retiring in 1898, when he was replaced by John Nicholson.

Helping in the task of building a football club was Charles Stokes, a dental surgeon and chair of the Dental Board of the city's Royal Hospital. Stokes was a renowned runner and a former player of both Christ Church FC of Heeley and The Wednesday FC, which he was instrumental in helping to found. Stokes joined the Sheffield United Ground Committee in 1875, via the Bowling Green Club, which he had originally joined in 1869. In later years he was chairman of Sheffield United FC and a one-time treasurer of Sheffield Football Association. Alongside Stokes sat William Beardshaw (known as 'Baltic' by virtue of his steel-producing factory of that name). Beardshaw had once played in a Sheffield FC v Glasgow FC game and for Sheffield United FC in a friendly match. Beardshaw assisted in the 1882 formation of the amateur midweek team drawn from the ranks of the London-based aristocracy, who took the name of Corinthians, but initially considered the nomenclature of 'The Wednesday'. Choosing to play on a Saturday, and taking the Corinthian name, they were to beat Blackburn Rovers in the 1884 FA Cup final with a team that contained two Sheffield-born players. Such men, to use common parlance, 'multi-tasked'. Capable and industrious, they were good at what they did.

Temperance of Football

The history of Sheffield football in its first 50 years is entwined with the lives of the brothers John and William Clegg. Sons of William Clegg senior, three times Mayor of Sheffield, the pair became solicitors and, whilst wealthy by local standards, were also strict Methodists and gave their time freely to good causes. William was a Liberal councillor for 40 years and council leader for 24 years. His was a career and profile matched only by his brother, John, best known by his second name Charles who, when asked about his hobbies, replied, 'the furtherance of temperance and football.' Both Cleggs were capable athletes and played local football. Both were connected to The Wednesday FC team of the 1870s, and both played for Sheffield in a game against London in 1871. The following year, Charles played for England against Scotland. They captained the two sides that played the first floodlit match at Bramall Lane in 1878 and became referees when they retired from playing. Charles Clegg held the status of the Official Receiver in Bankruptcy in Sheffield. He could run the 100-yard dash in ten seconds and was a capable quarter-mile competitor. A one-time president of the Sheffield FA, Charles became first vice president of the Football Association, then chairman in 1902. He was to keep this office and combine it with that of FA president from 1923. One commentator, describing him in 1906, stated the following: '…a warm heart, a generous mind, a winning way and an unaffected courtesy… a solid, weighty logical man… his principles are nailed to the mast… a long and wide experience in the frailties of human nature.' In appreciation of his services as chairman of the FA, Charles was knighted by George V in 1927, thereby becoming the first person ever knighted for services to football.

5

Temperate in both deed and nature, such men had time on their hands to do good deeds. Being the first boy in Sheffield to sign the 'Pledge' (pledging never to drink intoxicating liquor via a procedure prompted by the National Temperance Movement, assisted by the Methodist church), Charles Clegg was oft cited for the mantra 'No one got lost on a straight road'. His refusal to permit 'secret' and underhand payments to United players or offer inducements to them to sign from other teams, whilst admirable in spirit, made him and United (and indeed Wednesday) somewhat different to many clubs of the era. In October 1899 the ethos of the club that won a league championship and an FA Cup in 1898 and 1899 respectively was expressed in the match programme: 'In our prosperity, let us not forget in prosperity there's nothing so becomes the club as modest mildness and humility.' Whilst a big fish locally, Charles Clegg was to others a northerner from a place few from the south would deign to visit. When chosen to represent England at a game in Scotland in 1872, Clegg felt he was snubbed by his southern middle-class colleagues. He never forgot such an attitude. Reluctant to permit professionalism in the game, he nevertheless acknowledged defeat on the issue in his position at the FA and, accepting that money talked, set about trying to keep the game on the straight and narrow. This was never going to be an easy task.

Charity Begins at Home

Individuals who held status by inheritance and public office recognised the potential of football to contribute to the local, social good. The Sheffield FA began a cup tournament in 1879 for a trophy donated by local landowner the Earl of Wharncliffe, with a percentage (the precise figure never revealed) of gate receipts being given to local charities. Such largesse was necessary. Income tax was not known in these times. Communities had to fend for themselves and giving was the thing. Philanthropy built hospitals. Those with wealth had a duty to patronise. In the Sheffield context the same people who sat on committees built hospitals and colleges, and also football clubs. In November 1899 Bramall Lane hosted a game between teams described as 'Sheffield

6

Boys' and 'London Team'. Ten shillings of the gate receipts were sent to the Lord Mayor's Fund, which was to be passed on to the wives and children of 'those gallant lads', doing duty for Queen and Country in the Boer War. Monies raised around football funded both the contemplative and the infirm. In 1903 United played Wednesday and gave the gate receipts towards the building of Sheffield University. The fixture was the idea of Charles Clegg, who considered that the charitable efforts of the city's two big football clubs were paltry compared to teams of comparable and even lesser status elsewhere in the country. The Firth Building Cup of 1913, provided by the steel baron and philanthropist Mark Firth, was the product of a match played between United and Wednesday, once again to raise funds for the construction of the University in Sheffield. The following year the same fixture saw the proceeds given to the four hospitals in the city. In this pre-welfare state era, hospitals existed on philanthropy and charity and football and footballers played their part in contributions to the greater good. A pre-season competition called the Hull Hospital Cup involved teams from the Yorkshire region, the proceeds of games going towards local hospitals. In this tournament players were not paid for their services; however, the winners received a gold medal. United twice won the tournament, which ended in late 1930s. Monies raised around football were thus routinely given to local causes. At times football gave to causes of a wider nature.

Club, Country and Commitments

Sheffield United FC made a significant contribution to the First World War effort. During the course of it United had some 15 players on active service. In the carnage came dispatches from the front line that provoked pathos. A letter appeared in the United match programme of October 21, 1916 from a 'solicitor' appealing to the club to send a match ball to the front line of north-east France. For what purpose the ball was to be put was not specified. For the Sheffield men who died, and the millions of others who died alongside them, a war charity match was held at Bramall Lane on New Year's Day 1916. Another was held on Easter Monday 1917. The latter was between the Sheffield steel firm of Hadfield's and the National Projectile Factory; the gate money was given to local war charities. A further charity match at Bramall Lane aimed to raise money to buy an ambulance. The same fixture saw 5,000 cigarettes distributed to the wounded soldiers in attendance. In April 1917 a United player with five years' service by the name of Jimmy Revill was killed in action. His widow and family received £130 from the club following a benefit match held in January 1918.

Following the Great War men who were also elected councillors appeared in the United boardroom; politics were entering football in Sheffield in a more obvious manner than in previous decades. Religious worship declined after the War and a society that benefited from the 1870 Education Act began to be more critical of the established order. Football clubs had a role to play in times of economic turmoil. At a time of impending industrial conflict in the 1920s, many English football clubs had started the decade with decent incomes and modest profits. Only Blackburn Rovers and Sheffield Wednesday - both in the First Division - failed to make a profit in the 1919/20 season. Both had invested heavily in transfers in their attempts to avoid relegation. United's profit for this season was £3,521 on total gate receipts of £30,376 and after an Entertainment Tax bill of £7,020. Football at this time offered a wage comparable to that of a skilled manual worker. At the beginning of the 1920/21 season a United player received £5 weekly in his first full season, rising to an impressive £9 weekly after four full seasons of service. An international cap would bring him a further one-off payment of £6. Five years of service would bring a benefit game and entitlement to a free transfer, albeit, the programme informed fans: 'He could not, under existing laws, take his benefit and say, "Goodbye, I'm off."' Social mores accepted there were days when a player might not wish to ply his trade. FA rule number 25 stated that a player could not be compelled to play any match on Good Friday or Christmas Day. Furthermore, Sunday amateur football games were not recognised by the FA. When change to the latter procedure was mooted in December 1924, Charles Clegg, in his capacity as president of the FA, quashed the idea, stating matter-of-factly: 'Better for the country and better for the game that we should not have it.' This dismissive sentence proved a powerful rebuff to the idea of playing on the Sabbath. It was 50 years before amateur Sunday football was recognised by the FA and played in Sheffield parks and recreation grounds.

It was in the 1920s that a more realistic business ethos entered English football. Clubs needed every penny they could raise. Good business sense produced profits and profits brought footballing success. The clubs became less inclined to give money away. Charity events and football matches of the type that typified the late 19th and early 20th centuries became less necessary as a national system of assistance was begun; the concept of social security replaced the local worthies who were the 'Guardians of the Poor'. The war veterans and invalids saw society recompense those who could no longer work and earn. Footballers were no longer at the mercy of charity should they be injured. In this decade the club's jurisdiction over its players when not playing or training was troubling club officials. In 1926, in response to advances in technology and production techniques, some English clubs instructed their players not to ride the more freely available motorcycles as driver or pillion. This issue, notably of command and compulsion, was debated in the United match programme. An anonymous writer asked whether clubs had the power to specify such prohibition, concluding, 'Anything which savours undue risk might be construed into a breach of agreement.' In September of the same year the issue of players smoking tobacco was raised in the match programme. The response from the editor was that in moderation smoking did the player 'no harm', but ideally the player would refrain from smoking the day before a game and on match day. Some players a year later seemed to have progressed from mopeds and had learned to drive cars. In October 1927 the programme stated with a degree of consternation, albeit possibly over wealth-related pique rather than health-related concerns; 'At... one club we have in mind more than one player drives his own car, and drives to the ground each morning to do his training.' Players owning cars? Where would it all end? Indeed, by December 1927, United's secretary speculated on the possibility of the first £10,000 player transfer.

One could say he had little to worry about even if such a transfer was realised. That year had seen a Bramall Lane crowd over 60,000 for the visit of Wednesday and, with half the 1927/28 season gone, United's average attendance was 24,555. The clubs, however, pleaded poverty. In fact in 1928, only one third of Football League clubs claimed to be in credit; others, according to the United secretary, were existing by transfer fees, overdrafts and the largesse of creditors. The cause of the problem, in his analysis, was unusually wet weather that had reduced attendances and provoked clubs to seek alternative funds. Methods used to raise such monies included bazaars, prize draws, whist drives and even disposing their stadiums to greyhound racing promoters to capture the late 1920s wave of public interest around betting on the dogs. A somewhat remarkable statement appeared in the February 22, 1928 United programme. Commenting on football's financial woes, the secretary suggested the emergence of football-related socialism, when informing readers that, '… the opinion that the rich clubs should be taxed to help the poorer ones is gaining adherence every day.' Amongst whom such 'opinion' was raised and how it was met was not elaborated upon. Somehow this idea never caught on in English football.

By the end of the decade the men who ran the game were proud of what they had achieved and were cynical of politicians. At a football dinner held in Sheffield, Alderman Cattell toasted the Football Association and its wise government and, aware of his company, praised the FA President Charles Clegg who, in response, claimed that no game was better controlled or organised. Clegg then introduced a degree of controversy stating; 'One thing, however, I am not prepared for: that is that our game should come under the control of Government in the form of a Ministry of Sport, that those who are carrying on sport in a voluntary way are not prepared to submit themselves to any Government control.' United began the new decade with Charles Clegg as club president leading a 15-man board of directors. Two years later, however, the number was reduced. The April 1932 match programme bore a black border in commemoration of the death of club secretary, John

Nicholson, killed in a road accident outside Sheffield's Midland station on his way to join the squad for a match in Birmingham. Over 30 years of dedicated service to United died with Nicholson. The match programme days later stated; '... a white soul has gone to choir invisible... a straight, true man... if he could not speak good of a man, he never spoke ill... every future cup final day will be like a revolving tombstone to the memory.'

Nicholson had balanced the books well. United made a profit in the 1930/31 season of £1,868. The programme hinted of two clubs elsewhere 'living on the bank' with debts of £10,000. The majority of United players were paid between £5 and £6 per week; first teamers earned between £7 and £10. The recession had consequences for the playing personnel. The match programme in August 1932 explained that their failure to pay the full going rate for a first-class player was due to the world economic depression. Whether it was Wall Street or other factors that saw United sell their leading goalscorer Jimmy Dunne to Arsenal in 1932, one will never know. Responding to the supporters' reported 'fury', the United board chorused in what was to become honoured fashion that the club had to sell because they needed the money as gate income was inadequate. The club did seek financial improvements from elsewhere. That same year United were part of a Football League representation urging the Chancellor of the Exchequer to abolish Entertainment Tax because of the financial burden it was placing on football clubs. The representation was unsuccessful. Tax issues were to concentrate the minds of the men in charge of Sheffield United in a big way 50 years later.

In God We Trust?

The men who controlled United in the 1930s remained - nominally at least - guided by religious teachings. They led by example and epitomised the belief that virtue was its own reward and attempted to live – publicly at least - the unblemished life best personified by hard work and sobriety. Their financial commitment to the club was primarily one of guaranteeing loans, usually with low interest. Their return was the glory by association of any footballing triumph and the hope that on leaving the board their money would be returned. One director, Mr George Lawrence, known to all as 'Bladesman', was particularly generous. Modelling himself on Charles Clegg, Lawrence loathed gambling and was a well-known philanthropist. He funded the building of an open-air swimming pool in his home village of Hathersage, Derbyshire, and offered cash for player purchases, albeit other members of the United board refused the offer! This former newspaper seller was a self-made man who not only funded an annual pre-season day out and dinner in Hathersage for the United squad, but also, out of his own pocket, paid for a roof to be built over the Shoreham Street kop in 1936/37. He also bought Jock Dodds, United's top goalscorer in the 1935/36 season, an Armstrong Siddeley car as a show of appreciation. But God works in strange ways and Lawrence was killed during the Luftwaffe bombing of Sheffield, whilst driving to his razor blade factory (hence the nickname). Such figures were patrician but benevolent to football. Men like Lawrence, by virtue of owning businesses, had the power of employment and so could provide footballers with the promise of jobs, at times to supplement their footballing income or provide a guarantee of employment should a football career not work out. The same men could usually have a 'word in an ear' to ensure favourable conditions for their players, aspiring or departing, in a variety of circumstances, which might make the life of the players less troublesome.

Sheffield suffered terrible unemployment in the early and mid 1930s on account of the world economic slump arising out of the Wall Street Crash. The subsequent Great Depression brought unemployment, poverty and, no doubt, considerable anger. In both 1932 and 1934, to assist social harmony, Sheffield United attempted to reduce admission for the unemployed following a similar policy begun by the Rugby League; the Football League Management Committee, however, refused United permission. Also in 1934, in response to rumours that the unemployed would storm the gates at the next home game, hundreds of police surrounded the Bramall Lane ground. The club seemed to be quite paternalistic towards the unemployed in its midst, even allowing a physical training display by the unemployed under the aegis of the Yorkshire Unemployed Advisory Council before the final home game of the 1938/39 season. Unemployed leagues were organised in the middle of the decade by the local FA with the support of the local press and City Council and hand in hand with property owners. Private pitches were made available – a paternalism by those with power and money to those with neither. Such consideration for the less well off was not something typical of football or Sheffield United for the next 70 years.

Supporters' Backing

In the 1938/39 season, the club publicly recognised the loss of thousands of fans who, by virtue of new housing developments (i.e. large council estates), were moved from the back-to-back slums of central Sheffield to their new outlying dwellings. Their relocation meant that going to the match now had to include transport costs. The economic situation of the decade destroyed some League clubs and made local football prohibitive for many. In this era of recession, the Yorkshire region's coal miners were guaranteed three shifts a week. Each shift paid ten shillings. When not working, many were found in the market area of the city centre seeking daily labouring work. By 1938 things had changed. With World War II approaching, the city saw near full employment as its workforce was called upon to provide the coal and steel for armament production. With such a boom-and-bust economy it was difficult for a football club to operate, never mind make a profit. Football clubs were sensibly cautious towards their players' contracts and wages.

The 1930s also witnessed the beginning of fan activism. In November 1930 the United supporters organised themselves into a fan club. The emerging Sheffield United Supporters' Club began to advertise its existence in the match programme. The adverts informed readers of social events, which ranged from an Armistice dance to a fancy dress party to be held in the Bramall Lane cricket pavilion. The autumn of 1930 further announced whist drives, golf tournaments and the founders' ambition to achieve - by Christmas - a 500-strong membership. A year later, special trains informing of a trip to watch United play at Leicester were advertised. The United fans who made the journey walked out of the railway station in the spirit of friendship and placed a wreath at a war memorial for the Leicester fallen. Interestingly, the return train did not depart for Sheffield until 12.30am, which meant some seven hours of socialising in a distant city. Similar to the United boardroom, the Supporters' Club 1930/31 committee saw representation of local worthies. A local councillor by the name of J.T. Stokes, who was the United chairman, held the position of vice chairman of the Supporters' Club. Curiously the committee contained six women – of the three named in archives only one surname corresponds to one of the men's names listed. The honorary secretary of the club was the landlord of the Old Crown Public House on London Road, close to Bramall Lane, the premises where the Supporters' Club first met. Joining the club cost one shilling. For another shilling a member could wear the Supporters' Club badge that depicted two crossed knives and the club name – the badge differed subtly but significantly from that of the football club's. Such fans did not 'own' the club or its insignia.

Power Contests

Whilst both the local culture and social mores of this era produced many a player who was deferential towards their employers, there were always going to be exceptions. Some by virtue of their ability or character would not be told what to do. As the wider society they lived in struggled for rights of employment and improved pay, it was inevitable that such attitudes would permeate football's dressing rooms. Collective action, however, whilst the core of the culture of football when performed on the pitch, was not manifest in off-field oppositions. Many a player realised that in getting the best deal for himself he had to go it alone and negotiate with whoever seemed to hold the best opportunities. To this end United's 1930s centre forward Jock Dodds might be considered the man who facilitated an incident in the English game that changed labour relations between clubs and players forever.

Always a man looking to make a few bob, Dodds left United in 1939 for Blackpool. Whilst there he met South American footballing 'entrepreneurs' and ended up as the middle man in deals that saw England international players leaving Stoke City and Manchester United for the balmy climate of Bogota, Colombia. The monies on offer for such players was a king's ransom compared to what they received from their football club employers in Britain. Whilst the arrangement collapsed in some acrimony (and Dodds claimed to have never received his fee), the incident revealed that the worm was turning and that footballers were no longer as deferential as in previous decades. The game, whilst inherently conservative, was changing. The somewhat regal Charles Clegg had died in the summer of 1937. Some 18 months earlier, the King had died and a reserve game at Bramall Lane saw a two minutes' silence and a singing of both 'Abide with Me' and the national anthem in his honour. Many more British citizens were soon to die and the terraces of Bramall Lane were to fall silent and then be damaged irrevocably.

The New Society

Bramall Lane urgently needed rebuilding in the 1940s following extensive damage, courtesy of the German Luftwaffe's blitz on the city. The money invested in the re-building was, therefore, lost from the pot towards potential transfers and players' wages. The club had no local sugar daddy; the directors were still local businessmen and city dignitaries. Mr Senior Atkin was a silversmith, Mr Frank Copestake ran the wholesale fruit market, Mr Dick Wragg was a builders' merchant. Both Mr George Marlow and Mr Ernest Graham had held the office of the Lord Mayor of Sheffield – but this did not imply they had fabulous wealth. In the company of such gentlemen on match days were often the good men of the Sheffield Chamber of Trade and Cutlers' Company. They were dignitaries in a city not awash with money. The populace laboured hard in collective manual work. They had employment but not big incomes. Being a footballer was a good job by anyone's standards. The hotels the United squad stayed in during this decade were not always the best, but the players received, on top of their wage, a daily

15

meal after training and could look quite dapper when on their way to games in regulation blazer and slacks given to them by the club. Football still beat waking early to clock on for a minimum eight-hour day in dirty conditions. The game also offered the chance for foreign travel and meeting teams that travelled great distances to Sheffield.

Post-War attempts at producing a pan-European friendship saw Sheffield twinned with the Dutch city of Eindhoven. Matches between Select XIs representing their respective cities were annual events in the 1960s. When the Sheffield and Hallamshire FA sent a team to Holland it was fairly representative of the city, drawn from United, Wednesday and Sheffield FC. The post-War return to normality also saw the first foreign team playing United at Bramall Lane. This occurred in November 1946 on a Monday afternoon in front of 16,000 fans and saw the Swedish club Norrköping trounce United 5-2. The match programme informed readers of how '... the pupil has become virtually on a par with the master', a somewhat patronising attitude that assumed 'Johnny Foreigner' could not play the game as well as the British. The 1940s was a time of recovery for both society and football. Things had changed forever in many respects. Sheffield United was still dominated by a parochial concern and was held back by a relative shortage of stadium seating, which meant lower gate takings. They also had two boards – the football and the cricket – to make decisions. At times each contained 15 men. The opportunity to fall out and procrastinate was endless. New ideas ran up against established and eccentric attitudes. In this era Sheffield Wednesday, with Eric Taylor emerging as secretary-manager, became more influential in national football circles. Publicity conscious, Taylor was to purchase the best floodlights the game could offer at the time and was to rebuild the Hillsborough stadium. When austerity ended in the mid 1950s even those willing to spend their new-found monies at Bramall Lane could not find a seat to sit on.

Things were, however, slowly changing at Bramall Lane as the 1950s dawned. The new decade was to see the club seek a new direction and then return to what it knew best. In 1954 Joe Mercer became the first man in the managerial chair of Bramall Lane not out of the Methodist-teetotal mode. From George Waller to Reg Freeman, the United trainer-managers had been of similar disposition. In choosing Mercer, United were perhaps admitting that such men were now a rarity or an anachronism. Mercer's appointment reflected two forces in the game at the time. One was the rising power of the chairman, who was in some clubs now *primus inter pares* over his board of directors. The other was an acknowledgement that the national media could play a role in managerial selection. Mercer had finished a quite brilliant footballing career, but when approached by United was gainfully employed in his greengrocer's shop. The move for Mercer was a gamble, probably arising out of chairman Senior Atkin's friendship with a high-profile football writer. The writer was the mediator between the club and Mercer. The outcome was a new United manager who broke the mould. Appointed primarily on the say-so of Atkin, Mercer's arrival was not to the approval of all the board. This did not perturb Atkin, who celebrated his bluntness in conversation, but nevertheless hated addressing AGM audiences. With wealth founded on the cutlery and silversmith industry, Atkin was quintessentially traditional but rather eccentric in refusing to use the then recent invention of Sellotape, arguing that with string such a product was not necessary.

Having been promoted to Division One in 1953, United remained in the top flight until 1956. Relegation then saw the club recognise the need for better training conditions. In the late 1950s United took over a training area called the Ball Inn ground less than a mile from Bramall Lane. The area of land, leased by the Duke of Norfolk, was formerly the home of football played under the auspices of the Sheffield Licensed Victuallers' League and later the Sheffield Schools Association. United took over a controlling interest in the pitch and pavilion. One beneficiary was the Bramall Lane pitch, now spared the daily training sessions of its players. The matchday programme throughout much of the 1950s depicted the enclosed arena that was Bramall Lane. In keeping with tradition, Wardonia razor blades remained a dominant advertising space within. Other adverts indicated a rise in consumer power – Kenning's car wash appeared in 1953 as did coach excursions to Blackpool Illuminations. In the same year an advert appeared for the first time depicting a woman enjoying the benefits of Jubilee Stout beer. In the ground, however, the only advertising display was one on the top of the John Street stand advertising United director Arnold Laver's wood yard, which lay adjacent to Bramall Lane. As building a new society began and others enjoyed consumption on a scale not previously known, football took on a new appearance and Sheffield United sought to be part of it.

Seeing the Light?

The Bramall Lane ground changes reflected technological innovations, and with it came teams from beyond the borders of England. Floodlight pylons appeared in the early 1950s and United played a number of friendly games as a way of popularising the new technology whilst waiting for the Football League to permit floodlit matches. Thus visiting Bramall Lane in 1954 and 1955 were Hibernian, Clyde, Dundee and St Mirren from Scotland. From further afield came Esbjerg of Denmark, and the Graz Sports Klub of Austria. In 1956 the visitors were Radnicki Nis of Yugoslavia, and in 1959, Lucerne of Switzerland. The most exotic visitors of this decade, however, arrived in October 1958 when Bella Vista of Brazil played a game to allow United to demonstrate the capabilities of their floodlights. A few years earlier the Shoreham Street kop end was extended to produce what was known to regular users for the next 40 years as the 'white wall', a term used to describe a corner annexe offering an excellent view. The club could now host 35,000 spectators under cover, a fact broadcast on the programme cover throughout most of the 1959/60 season. Crowds were occasionally too large for the facilities. A United-Wednesday FA Cup quarter final in 1958 saw a temporary stand holding 3,200 erected on the cricket pitch and the crowd limited to

60,000. The game was booming, but the players were not rich. The directors could count the gate money, but where it all went has always been a mystery to Blades of this generation.

Football in this era still collected for charity and was slowly becoming more generous with those who played the game. The abolition of Entertainment Tax in 1957 saw a rise in players' wages and the sanctioning of bigger cheques for players' benefit matches. In December 1959, the United director Blacow Yates presented United's Tommy Hoyland with a £1,000 cheque for his ten years' service – the first four-figure cheque for a player's benefit in the club's history. The 1953 Christmas matchday collection was no longer for local charities but went towards the Westminster Abbey Restoration Fund. In this time of austerity cash was king; the commercial practicalities around football saw United supporters advised in a January 1953 match programme that when seeking tickets for a forthcoming cup fixture 'personal and telephonic applications will not be entertained'. One had to send a cheque or postal order and rely on the Royal Mail. Things were changing, but the legacy of the gentleman amateur player was still evident, however, when in October 1957 Sheffield FC played Queens Park of Glasgow at Bramall Lane in celebration of the 100th anniversary of the former. The special guest at the match played on a Thursday afternoon was the Duke of Edinburgh. However, a crowd of just 5,000 witnessed a 2-2 draw, probably indicating the lack of interest in the amateur game. It did not suggest a great enthusiasm for the Royal Family either.

Despite the processes of modernity that were affecting football the United directors remained parochial characters. In an unprecedented move, the 1956/57 match programme featured profiles of United's 11-man board of directors and paid officials. The language used to detail their lives and personal qualities was remarkably blunt. Two things were striking to a reader. One was the level of their involvement in local matters beyond football. The other was the longevity of their association with the club. This extended to paid officials, with two boasting an association of over 40 years. By modern standards there was a certain innocence in some of their

19

activities. Interviewed in 1999, Fred Furniss, a United player for much of the 1950s, told of some of the unusual bonuses the team received: 'When we played at Grimsby, we always got a box of kippers. When we were at Portsmouth, the director, Arnold Laver, had a farm down there and he'd call in and get us all a chicken.' But Furniss explained that the directors weren't afraid to employ more clandestine methods of distributing benefits too, stating; 'There were bungs in them days. They kept it all quiet.... some got more money on our team than others.' But even this was progress of sorts. Twenty years earlier leading scorer Jock Dodds was openly given a car; now the gifts to players consisted of kippers, chickens and under-the-table envelopes. There was also rumour of other underhand dealings. One player of the 1940s, interviewed by Gary Armstrong in 2003, claimed that a long-serving team-mate who moved on to the coaching staff after retirement only lasted so long at the club because he was the illegitimate son of a United director.

United's directors were sometimes not the most forward thinking of their era. A match programme reader could learn the opinions of Senior Atkin, the chairman of the Football Club committee. In November 1953 the programme notes informed a reader that: '… to achieve success there's no need to be ultra artistic. In the Football League's intense competition, there's no stage available for ball trickery suitable for a music hall turn.' England had recently lost 6-3 at Wembley to the trickery, artistry and tactical brilliance of the Hungarians. The United squad had travelled to Wembley to watch the match. In a fixture in Budapest a year later the score was 7-1 in favour of the hosts. This clearly annoyed Atkin who, in December 1955, wrote to BBC commentator Kenneth Wolstenholme, accusing him of bias in favour of foreign teams when commentating on matches between England and continental sides. The match programme informed a reader that: 'Atkin disagreed with Mr Wolstenholme that these foreigners were the last word in football and pointed out also that the type of football they play "is not football, as the Englishmen know it".' Regardless, Atkin opined further that, if competing in the English First Division, none of these foreign clubs would finish 'beyond mid-table'. The letter was shown by Wolstenholme to a 'leading continental club manager'. The response, passed to Atkin, stated amongst other things that they would not wish to play within a league where winning points was all that mattered at the expense of experimenting with style, adding for good measure, 'So your football has become static and it moves like a wartime convoy – at the speed of the slowest.' Some people could not see the light.

Six Figures – One Man

Joining the board in 1953 was Dick Wragg, who later in life became the first president of Sheffield United. Born in Attercliffe in 1910, Wragg once played for United's 'A' team and later Sheffield FC and Macclesfield Town. Wragg made his money from a builders' merchant business and having joined the board seemed to have kept out of the row generated by the appointment of Joe Mercer as manager. Elected to the Sheffield United Football Committee in 1955, Wragg became club chairman in August 1968. He became chairman of the FA International Committee and had a large say in the appointment of England managers. His ambition even saw him become a member of UEFA. Wragg sat in on many controversies at Sheffield United. On the 1958 retirement of Jimmy Hagan, one of United's greatest ever players, Wragg had opined to board members that he did not believe Hagan could impart football knowledge to others. Hagan's success as manager of Portuguese club Benfica proved this opinion wrong. Ten years later, Wragg was chairman when Mick Jones and Alan Birchenall were sold for £100,000 each against the wishes of the manager. However, Wragg was responsible for changing United's thinking and finances forever. He played a significant role in removing cricket from Bramall Lane and the subsequent planning of the south stand, which opened in 1975. In August 1968 Wragg was instrumental in ending the system of six separate committees at Bramall Lane, implementing instead one committee that dealt with all football issues. At national level he was part of the crisis in the England national side when, in 1977, Don Revie left the England manager's job for the more lucrative offer to manage the Kuwaiti national team.

Pipe smoking, amiable, opinionated and usually smiling, Wragg was an avuncular-looking figure, but who nonetheless wished to be addressed as 'Mister Wragg'. In the 1960s, he was genuinely trying to push United forward. To bring in more money the Bramall Lane stand was built in 1966 at a cost of £100,000. It seated 3,000 and thereby increased Bramall Lane's seating capacity by 50 per cent. To fill it and other space, the club sent out a mobile ticket office to the town of the following week's visitors. Wragg was influential in the post-1967 change of policy that recognised the limitations of relying on local-born players progressing through the ranks. He encouraged manager John Harris to spend money and look around the lower divisions and Scottish leagues. It was from Wales that Harris acquired wingers Len Allchurch and Gil Reece. The 1968 signing of 18-year-old Tony Currie from Watford may well have been attributed to Wragg. Earlier in the year, United had knocked Watford out of the FA Cup and Wragg was believed to have had an agreement with the Watford chairman to sign Currie when Watford's cup run was over. The signing produced the greatest 'flair' player in the club's history and a man who was to play for England whilst a United player. Wragg retired as United's chairman in 1974 but remained in the honorary position of president until his death in 1992 at the age of 82.

Tradition and Modernity

Adopting the slogan 'City on the Move' at the end of the 1960s, Sheffield City Council sought to sell itself and the city as a modern, go-ahead urban entity. Integral to this marketing ploy was the promotion of sport. The 1966 World Cup had put Sheffield on the map by virtue of Sheffield Wednesday's Hillsborough Stadium hosting some of the games. Wednesday had built both a magnificent cantilever stand and a new stand at the Leppings Lane end. Their ground could comfortably hold 50,000. Investment in the Bramall Lane ground was badly needed if United were to compete. The club realised that its footballing ambitions would always be thwarted by having a three-sided ground by virtue of its hosting county cricket and wished to make Bramall Lane into a conventional football stadium with stands on all four sides. There was subsequent talk of dividing the Bramall Lane land to have both a football and a cricket stadium. This was thwarted when the Yorkshire County Cricket Club representative demanded no less than a 20,000 seating capacity. At this time the United board minutes revealed the club discussing with the City Council the possibility of selling Bramall Lane in return for land in the Batemoor area on the southern boundary of the city. The talks fizzled out. The site identified was soon to house a council housing estate. United were to get rid of cricket in 1973 and immediately commenced building work on a new south stand.

Elsewhere the club sought to build bridges. From the early 1960s to the late 1970s, Sheffield United travelled globally, playing more exhibition games than any British club. These tours, which began in the 1950s, initially saw United travel no further than Holland and West Germany. Between 1953 and 1976, United played some 15 times in the Netherlands. By the 1960s, however, the club was involved on occasion in six-week tours to countries far and wide. Such travel, whilst broadening a player's horizons, brought them no extra pay beyond a £5 daily expenses allowance. One particular tournament, to the Antipodes in 1965, was called the 'BOAC tour' after the initials of a British-owned Transcontinental airline seeking to promote - in this case through football - its new long-haul flights. The airline flew the team for free, paid for their accommodation and one of their officials presented the cup won by United. The team also earned the club a £1,000 victory prize for their four-week, 11-game effort. The necessity for such exhausting tours has never been explained. Nothing exists in United's record books articulating the logic for them, or the finances involved. Almost certainly United were given these tours by the English FA at the request of their foreign counterparts. Bigger clubs than United would have taken other, less arduous, journeys. United seemed gluttons for punishing travel arrangements. One plausible explanation is that United manager, John Harris, having little personal life beyond football, could not bear the closed season. The six-week tours occupied him as much as it did the team.

In April 1959 United appointed John Harris to succeed Joe Mercer, who left for Aston Villa, claiming that such was the mindset of the board of directors United would never win anything. Harris, the 41-year-old, Glasgow-born player-manager of Chester, had a good football pedigree; his father had played for Partick Thistle, Oldham Athletic and Newcastle United before managing Swansea Town, where he had signed his son as a 15-year-old. In later years, John Harris made guest appearances with Spurs and Wolves before joining Chelsea in 1943, where he remained for 12 years. He was captain, aged 37, of Chelsea's 1954/55 league championship winning side. An abstemious figure, Harris was a bachelor, a church-going Methodist and teetotaller. He was also frugal and modest. A man of integrity, Harris would never utter a swear word and avoided the limelight. Living with his mother, who openly drank and smoked, his one passion was football. United finished fourth in Division Two at the end of his first season. The following season the club was promoted and made it to the semi final of the FA Cup. Stability helped the campaign; the six men who constituted the defence missed only four games amongst them. Whilst his predecessors had brought in many of the players that provided the backbone of his early teams, what Harris was able to do was bring out the best in them - without ever voicing a curse.

At the same time, Harris and his assistant Archie Clark were developing a good youth policy. Youngsters such as Len Badger, Reg Matthewson, Mick Jones, Bernard Shaw and Alan Woodward were drawn from South Yorkshire and came of age in 1963/64. By 1966, the United side was the youngest in its history. The captain, Len Badger, was 21 years old. Harris's 15 seasons as manager at Bramall Lane produced two promotions to the top division and five top-half finishes. Paying poor wages by the standard of the day, Harris assembled teams that, at times, played superb football much remembered by Blades fans over the age of 45. Reluctant to spend money, which no doubt pleased the board of directors, Harris made his first purchases when paying Swansea Town £12,500 for Len Allchurch and Rotherham United £15,000 for

Keith Kettleborough. The signings Harris made were usually astute and the £26,500 he paid Watford for the teenage Tony Currie in 1968 was one of the greatest steals in the history of the English game. In later years Harris seemed to favour buying experience over youth, a tactic that was to prove costly when injuries struck. Prepared to fine his players for on- and off-pitch indiscretions and sendings off, Harris believed a manager should balance the books of the club. Liking routine, Harris did not permit his players latitude when on long-distance foreign tours; he wanted them in their rooms early. When some broke curfews he would lecture them on responsibility. Finding communication with players difficult at times, and despite being loath to express humour or warmth, Harris remained a father figure to some young players, albeit a distant one. He never joined in a training session, preferring to watch, often from the back row of the Bramall Lane stand. He favoured the use of wingers and never promoted defensive play; even away from home he sought victory. Demanding 'proper trousers' and blazer and ties when on club duty, Harris enforced 'smartness' in his squad and, initially, short hair. He was, however, lenient towards genius and allowed Tony Currie to keep his flowing blond locks and wear his shirt outside his shorts. Home games invariably saw the United players meet at 11.30am at the Kenwood Hotel in the Nether Edge area and eat a steak dinner. For London games the squad stayed at the Bonnington Hotel in Bloomsbury. Because of his time at Chelsea, Harris had friends in high places and occasionally used a contact at Buckingham Palace, who provided his squad with a pre-match tour of the building. Harris was occasionally generous, albeit not with his own money. He would advise the secretary when compiling pay packets to add a few pounds into certain envelopes if he thought the player had done well the previous week. Twice moving 'upstairs' at United in 1968 and again in 1974, Harris was replaced, in the first instance, by Arthur Rowley and later by Ken Furphy. When elevated, Harris was twice given the title 'Football Executive', but was really no more than a chief scout with a grander title. His reassignment in 1974 came with a three-and-a-half-year contract, which would have taken him to his 60th birthday. He lasted less than the term of the contract and, realising he was superfluous to requirements, left United in 1977, accepting the job of chief scout at Sheffield Wednesday, where he remained for four years. Harris died in 1988.

All Bets Are Off

The reign of Harris was briefly interrupted in the late 1960s when Arthur Rowley was appointed to the position of team manager in July 1968, following United's relegation from Division One. Rowley had been a very good footballer, scoring an English record 434 league goals in his career. Retiring from playing in 1965 at the age of 40, Rowley took the manager's job at Shrewsbury Town. His move to Sheffield United came out of the blue; all he had achieved at Shrewsbury was a couple of cup giant-killing feats. With a low budget, Rowley had produced a decent team, which on its day could match the big boys. Rowley's teams played 'off the cuff', i.e. without much awareness of tactics and formation. Despite this, Rowley had a very good eye for a player and enjoyed balancing full backs with wingers. The consequence of this was exciting, high-scoring games. Rowley took the managerial position at Bramall Lane at a time when his and John Harris's duties were not clearly defined. The people Rowley had to work with were all Harris appointees. This new structure was meant to be a partnership between Rowley and Harris with a consequent restructuring of the coaching staff. Under Rowley United finished his first season ninth in Division Two.

His stay, however, was short, his departure shrouded in mystery. Rowley had an evident talent for recognising potential. He was responsible for bringing in some excellent defenders in Ted Hemsley, Dave Powell, John Flynn and Eddie Colquhoun. Disappointing results, however, saw Rowley become the first-ever Sheffield United manager to be dismissed. Almost a year to the day of his appointment, and on the day the club reported a loss on the year's workings of nearly £100,000, John Harris resumed the position of team manager. Rumours abounded as to the 'real' reason for Rowley's departure. Only weeks after his appointment his involvement with and ownership of racehorses had attracted the consternation of United chairman Dick Wragg. When a big three o'clock race was broadcast, Rowley occasionally would not appear in the dugout until ten minutes after kick-off. Players also recall uninspiring team talks that reflected a quietly spoken, and even introverted, individual. Just as significant to his departure was the fact that at the time some of the United players were in dispute with the club over a pay incentive. Such insubordination did not impress Wragg, who sacked Rowley on his return from a pre-season tour of Holland, probably for failing to quash the players' 'revolt' that had built up on the tour. Upon leaving, Rowley congratulated the 'agitators' for obtaining a better deal from the board.

New Times, New Behaviour

The willingness of some players to sell a better deal was indicative of changes in both wider society and the English game. The late 1960s footballer was more prepared than his predecessor to question those who employed and coached him. The age-long contest between employer and employee was to be played out within new boundaries.Whilst players might win the occasional battle, the outcome of the wider war was still balanced in favour of the board and those who reported to it.

The Worksop-born Mick Jones joined United as a teenager in 1962 and was sold to Leeds United in 1967 for £100,000. A furious John Harris offered his resignation over the sale. He had good reason to be angry. In his five years at Bramall Lane, Jones had finished as top scorer in three seasons and made his England debut at both Under-23 and full level. It was small recompense to manager and fans that Jones was the first United player to be sold for a six-figure sum. His departure became inevitable after the final home game of the 1966/67 season brought rumours of interest in Jones from Matt Busby at Manchester United. The close season saw Jones teamed up for the first time with Allan Clarke of Fulham in the England Under-23 team. Within two years they were together at Leeds United and formed the deadliest attacking duo in the English game. There were the usual denials before Jones left for new pastures. United officials informed the footballing world at the beginning of the 1967/68 season that Jones was not available, at any price. However, with United bottom of the table and unable to progress in a three-sided ground, the board succumbed to a £100,000 offer from Leeds; Harris's resignation offer was politely refused. Soon afterwards Alan Birchenall left United for Chelsea for a similar sum. The local media was full of indignant letters criticising United's lack of ambition and selling policy. In subsequent years this was to become a familiar refrain.

Another late 1960s advent was football hooliganism, provoking both a media and political response. What followed were Government reports and dismissive attitudes. Dick Wragg, speaking in 1968 about the recently published Harrington Report (a Government-sponsored inquiry into football hooliganism), called it 'so much nonsense' adding: 'We don't need a bunch of professors to tell us what to do about the problem of hooliganism in soccer. In fact I think the problem has been exaggerated, we don't get a lot of trouble in Sheffield.' He was in denial. Bramall Lane was the scene of dozens of outbreaks of disorder and Sheffield topped the hooligan arrest charts in this era. Such disorder continued throughout the 1970s. Sheffield had one per cent unemployment in the late 1970s and the impregnable Labour vote saw municipal socialism subsidise public transport, making the city the cheapest place in Europe in which to travel. The wider population of Britain was, like football clubs, looking for greater income. The outcome was industrial strife, which saw a three-day working week and power cuts as both the mines and electricity workers went on strike. The early 1970s saw United playing games on midweek afternoons and Saturday kick-offs moved earlier in the day to beat the dusk and avoid electricity shortages and power cuts. Prime Ministers went to the electorate asking who ruled the country - the Government or the unions? Whilst pondering the question, United fans could enter the newly-opened Bramall Lane restaurant for a pre-match three-course meal as a new bourgeoisie entered English football. As credit became available in the wider economy, a loan system for clubs to obtain players was begun in the 1969/70 season. Possibly reflecting a Methodist attitude to lending, this facility was not utilised by United until February 1975, when striker Gary Jones arrived from Bolton Wanderers. Footballers' wages continued to rise, their income assisted by television money. In 1979 the BBC and ITV signed a joint £2.3 million deal to broadcast football for the next four years. This was renewed in 1983 for £5.2 million over two years.

Money Talks

Commercial considerations saw the introduction of new football tournaments and allowed United to travel to places not previously known to English football. In 1970 Watney's brewery introduced a pre-season cup tournament open to the previous season's two top-scoring teams from each of the four divisions. Innovative in being the first English competition to decide drawn ties with penalty shoot-outs, it was also one of the first trophies to carry the name of a sponsor. Representing Division Two in 1970 were Hull City and United. Having beaten Aldershot 6-0, United lost to Derby County 1-0. Two years later United were representing Division One alongside Manchester United. Defeats of Notts County and Peterborough brought United a final against Bristol Rovers at their Eastville ground. A goalless draw meant a penalty shoot-out, which United lost 7-6.

Some away games were like none ever seen before. In 1972, a three-week tour of Zambia saw United play the national team no fewer than five times. One game attracted a crowd of 80,000 and was watched by President Kenneth Kaunda. In the mid 1970s, United played games in Algeria and Tunisia and were also to be found in Gibraltar, France, Cyprus, Poland and New Caledonia. The South Pacific trip was memorable for crossing the international dateline on June 8, giving Len Badger two birthdays. One game saw United play an Israeli XI in February 1972 and produced a memorable match programme cover the week after, showing Trevor Hockey shaking hands with the former chief of staff of the Israeli Defence Force and later Minister of Defence, Moshe Dayan. On the following Tuesday United hosted the Ukrainian team Dynamo Kiev, to whom they lost 2-1 in front of a crowd of over 18,000. Why the Ukrainians visited Sheffield for this game has never been fully explained beyond the possibility it was part of a Sheffield-Soviet trade agreement.

Whilst such games put the club in the global shop window they were not money-spinners. Thus in an attempt to boost club income beyond the turnstile-paying fans United's first souvenir shop was opened in 1971 in a terraced house adjacent to the ground. The shop was a tiny affair with part-time staff and was not open all week. It was, however, emblematic. Times were changing; the realisation that football clubs had to look beyond the turnstile for income was dawning even on United. Money-raising lotteries became part of the match-going experience. One sold at Bramall Lane titled 'Golden Goal' let fans buy a ticket, which revealed a time between one and 90 minutes. If the time of the first goal corresponded to the number on the ticket, a cash prize was won. Seeking income elsewhere, companies, public organisations and individuals could, from 1970, become match-ball 'donors' and have their names in the programme and announced to the crowd over the tannoy. The year of 1969 saw United appoint a 'Commercial Consultant', to be renamed 'Commercial Manager' six weeks later. By 1973 the commercial manager had an assistant. Then came a semantic process – the former was titled marketing executive in 1980, then later that same year commercial manager again. The post-holder then found himself holding the title of commercial director in 1982.

Other commercial schemes begun in 1974/75 saw match sponsors given advertising space in the match programme, pitch-side hoardings for their organisation and complimentary tickets for a few dozen employees in return for parting with several hundred pounds. In the 1976/77 season the United team was sponsored at £6 a point by a local trucking company. The same year saw pages of the match programme sponsored. Sartorial matters were to come second to the pursuit of new income. United's team shirt frequently changed in design, seemingly at the whim of the garment manufacturer, even losing its stripes to accommodate the name of a furniture store, as United sold the shirt to commercial sponsors. There was no pleasing some though. In January 1975, halfway through the club's most successful season since the War, United chairman John Hassall used the match programme to berate his fans, both for their lack of vocal backing and low numbers. What was stopping people flocking to Bramall Lane was something one United manager attempted to address.

The Modern Manager?

In contrast to John Harris United sought a manager who was not shy of self-promotion and who wore a tracksuit in training sessions. Upon accepting the United job in early 1974, the 41-year-old Ken Furphy sought assurance from the United board that he was not being employed to build a grandstand. Speaking in 1997, Furphy explained the conversation he had with the United chairman and secretary: 'They told me they'd got £250,000 in their account, a £500,000 deal with a supermarket behind one goal and a £250,000 deal with a petrol filling station on one corner… the stand would pay for itself.'

Six weeks after he joined United from Blackburn Rovers, the City Council refused planning permission and the development plan was in ruins. The newly-built south stand meant United had big debts. Furphy was then instructed by the board to search for players aged between 23 and 26 with a re-sale value. Forced to sell a top-class player in the shape of Geoff Salmons, Furphy brought in a few players he had known from his time at Watford and Blackburn with mixed success. Realising he needed a centre forward to replace the ageing Bill Dearden, Furphy agreed a deal in the summer of 1975 to buy Manchester City and England forward Francis Lee for £100,000. The board refused the deal, arguing that such money was not available. A few weeks later a relatively unknown Third Division forward by the name of Chris Guthrie was signed for roughly the same fee; the signing was a disaster. Furphy had bid only £40,000 for Guthrie but chairman John Hassall went over his head and negotiated the higher fee with Southend. At one time it had all seemed so right. Under Furphy United finished sixth in the First Division at the end of the 1974/75 season. Furphy was at one time manager of the England Under-23 side at the same time as managing United. Then three months into the 1975/76 season Furphy was sacked United were bottom of the league. The club was relegated and at one time went 19 games without a victory. Furphy was later to manage the New York Cosmos in the newly-established North American Soccer League. Meanwhile, Hassall found himself six years later the chairman of a football club in what was then the Fourth Division of the Football League.

One pioneering scheme that saw manager and chairman temporarily united was their attempt to appeal to a wider audience. For the conservative figure that was Furphy, the drop in attendances at the time was due to fearful parents not allowing their children to attend matches because of hooliganism. Furphy thus invited parents with children aged under 15 to attend Bramall Lane one Sunday morning to discuss plans for a young supporters' club. In April 1974 Furphy also instigated an open day at Bramall Lane; thousands of predominantly male under-15s queued in the pouring rain for the privilege of viewing the dressing rooms and watching the players train. No such insight into the club had ever been afforded young Blades. Soon after, a supporters' club for young (under-16s) United fans was established under the moniker 'EDS' ('educated, dedicated supporters'). It was a forum consisting of parents, police and a local referee. An 'EDS pen' was set aside on the Shoreham End with railings around it. Entry to the pen was only possible by showing an EDS pass, which also brought a reduction in admission. Parents volunteered to act as stewards, both at home games and aboard their dedicated coaches to away games. Their intentions were good; the EDS pen had a regular attendance of between 100 and 200 (99 per cent of them boys). The local police were enthusiastic, regarding it as an unprecedented 'success' and a 'cure for hooliganism'. Chief Inspector Mosely, the head of the force's Juvenile Bureau and Community Relations Department, saw the EDS scheme as providing young supporters with both a carrot and a stick. The 'carrots' were cheap travel, and the chance to meet United players. The 'stick' was the termination of membership for misbehaviour. After two years, the EDS membership was 4,000, none of whom had apparently committed an offence. The idea folded following the departure of Ken Furphy. The man who replaced Furphy was not the charmer his predecessor could be.

After Furphy's sacking in October 1975 United persuaded Notts County to part with their manager Jimmy Sirrel. He was to last just under two years in an appointment that proved disastrous for both parties. What United got was a man for whom the word 'dour' was invented. Scottish, Protestant, soberly dressed and with a face dominated by a large tooth, this chap was strangely enigmatic, if not photogenic. Disliking the press he chose his words carefully but could use the media to hint at problems. Days after his appointment he was a studio guest of BBC TV's 'Match of the Day' as United lost 1-0 at Queens Park Rangers. A co-guest picked out the performance of United full back Cliff Calvert, which elicited a strange and undiplomatic response of, 'Want to buy him?'

Sirrel arrived at Bramall Lane without the support of an assistant or a coach of his own. Many believed that, regardless of what he had achieved with limited resources at Notts County, he was not a manager for the top division of the English game. His early days confused the senior professionals at United. Confusion turned to ridicule and contempt within a few months. Sirrel's pre- and post-match lectures baffled everybody. His Glaswegian vernacular was difficult to understand at the best of times, but was compounded by metaphors. One long-time Blade player recalled a game memorable for the advice of Sirrel that, 'You always dress up for a fuckin' corner.' Another pearl of wisdom, which apparently saw the dressing room in tears of laughter upon his departure, was: 'I go up the hill wi' m' team and I come back wi' a headache.' Either Sirrel had to go or the players did. What happened, in his terminology, was a 'slow-motion players' revolt', which centred on confusion of instructions and contempt for training methods.

To adopt a modern-day cliché, Sirrel 'lost the dressing room'. The rot that had started under Furphy was continued. The new stand, which financially crippled the club, was essentially a shell with nothing in its innards. United were going down and Sirrel was too proud a man to seek assistance to arrest this free-fall. The club was living in a bubble of delusion following the near miss into European competition the previous season. Money remained a perennial problem for any manager at Sheffield United. Within weeks of arriving at Bramall Lane Sirrel had offered his resignation upon realising there were no funds available to him. The chairman did not help matters. In Sirrel's memory, John Hassall would greet him each day by entering his room asking, 'Who've we sold today?' Faced with this reality the solution had to be youth development. To this end Sirrel persuaded the club to buy a Victorian property in Sheffield's Nether Edge district, named Moncrieff House. This became a hostel for youth team players; at its peak some 12 players lived there. Whereas United apparently had little money to sign players, they were able to buy a large house. At one time in the 1970s United owned a number of houses in Sheffield, occupied by players, but this was probably the last time the club made such a purchase. If and when these properties were sold was not made public.

Sirrel was starved of funds as the club saved what it earned to pay off the costs of the south stand, with the further problem of falling gates due to relegation from Division One. Two players he wanted to sign - Ian Wallace of Dumbarton and Alan Hansen of Partick Thistle - were available for modest sums but the board refused his request for monies. The former went to Coventry City, then Nottingham Forest under Brian Clough for £1 million two years later. The latter signed for Liverpool and captained them to a European Cup victory. He also captained Scotland. In hindsight what were the causes of this debacle? Under Sirrel United's most expensive signing was midfielder Ian 'Chico' Hamilton, who cost £30,000 from Aston Villa. One might argue that the long-time United chairman Dick Wragg thrust his young successor Hassall into a position above his ability. Whilst a successful builder, Hassall's football knowledge wasn't thorough. His vice chairman, Maurice Board, was a stockbroker with even less first-hand knowledge of the game. Sirrel was scathing of the squad he inherited, stating when 2-0 ahead it was almost inevitable it would become a 2-2 draw. He was also scathing of the board. His departure followed a 2-1 defeat at Brighton, after which he met Hassall, to whom he stated 'I'm finished with this club.' He repeated this statement two days later in the Bramall Lane boardroom. Having got the financial pay-off he wanted from secretary Keith Walker, Sirrel got the players together and told them he was leaving. He insisted until his death in 2008 that he was not sacked. Interviewed by Gary Armstrong in 2006 Sirrel explained: 'I should have left sooner... I should have looked at the balance sheet... there were too many who wanted to piss higher than you.'

He recalled a pre-season tour of Holland when United played a game in Eindhoven, recounting the unwelcome visit the players received after the game from two travelling board members: 'There was O'Gorman, the surgeon, and a little fellow who worked for the council... this little chap I remember when I was once in the boardroom explaining something to them all and his button fell off... I'm explaining football and he's on the floor looking for a fuckin' button.' United had drawn 1-1 with PSV when into the dressing room - much to Sirrel's disgust - entered the two besuited gentlemen: 'I wouldn't talk to them about the game....fuckin' pests.' His contempt for such pundits was total. Sirrel claimed to have no good memories of Sheffield United.

The One That Got Away?

The dour Sirrel was replaced by a man his polar opposite in personality. Living up to his nickname, 'Happy' Harry Haslam arrived at Bramall Lane from Luton Town in January 1978. At Luton he had, at one time, been employed in the commercial office before moving on to scouting, then being appointed assistant manager. When Luton manager Alec Stock left in 1972, Haslam succeeded him and built a reputation for both bringing young players through and being very astute in the transfer market. Such qualities obviously appealed to a club with no money. The appointment didn't work out. United were relegated to the Third Division in 1978/79, where a good start the following season fizzled out and illness took its toll on the manager. He was to resign in early 1981 and died five years later. The club meanwhile fell into the Fourth Division on the final day of the 1980/81 season.

One tale of note of Haslam's time at Bramall Lane concerns a player by the name of Diego Maradona. Haslam had good connections in the game and employed a Uruguayan assistant by the name of Danny Bergara and an Argentinian coach named Oscar Arce. Haslam was a good friend of Tottenham manager Keith Burkinshaw and in 1978 alerted him as to the availability of Argentinian World Cup winner Osvaldo Ardiles. This player apparently could have been United's but the board could not afford the fee asked and could not pay the wages a World Cup winner could command. Meanwhile, Haslam told Burkinshaw he was going to Argentina to 'see a lad play' and if he liked him, would bring him back.

Posterity claims that the delegation from Sheffield United was offered a 17-year-old footballing boy wonder by the name of Diego Maradona. Then playing with Argentinos Juniors, Maradona had not made the 22-man Argentinian World Cup squad but was recognised as a future football genius. The story circulating for over 25 years claims that Sheffield United could have taken Maradona for somewhere around £350,000 but declined. One suggested reason was that the United board considered the price too high for an untried youngster. Another more contentious reason was that the Generals of the military Junta that governed Argentina at the time would only permit Maradona to leave upon receiving a substantial financial kick-back, which United would not pay on moral grounds. Context is everything here. United were broke and would have never paid such a sum for a player who was, in their opinion, just a boy.

They did, however, return from Argentina with one player: midfielder Alejandro Sabella, bought from national champions River Plate for a reported fee of £160,000. However, when interviewed in 2006, United's Argentinian agent Antonio Rattin (the man sent off at Wembley against England in the 1966 World Cup quarter final) insisted that the fee for Sabella was only US$60,000. The discrepancy was never explained. United hosted River Plate in a friendly at Bramall Lane a few weeks after Sabella's signing. A crowd of 22,244 turned out to see a 2-1 victory for the visitors, who included five of the World Cup-winning squad. Sabella certainly brought in the crowds; 19,012 attended his first game against Orient; 35,735 watched a League Cup tie against Liverpool weeks later. But monies accrued from such attendances were not sufficient to prevent the club's decline, supervised after Haslam's departure by no less a figure than a World Cup winner. United's first attempt at 'going global' proved a failure. As well as Sabella, also signed were another Argentinian, Pedro Verde, and a Dutchman, Len de Goey. Neither was a success.

Appointed manager in January 1981, 1966 England World Cup winner Martin Peters was an urgent replacement for the ailing Haslam. He was to resign after his 18 games saw United relegated to Division Four. His reign produced just three wins and nine defeats, the most memorable being the last match of the season at home to fellow strugglers Walsall, whose 88th minute penalty gave them the win they needed to survive, and send United down in their place. Described famously by England World Cup-winning manager Sir Alf Ramsey as 'ten years ahead of his time', Peters' managerial reign at Bramall Lane lasted less than five months and saw the club in Division Four for the first time in its history. Arriving first as a player at the end of his brilliant career, Peters was mediocre on the pitch and not up to the task as manager. Time was not on his side, both as a player, when he never got to grips with the rough and tumble of Third Division football, nor when he was in the hot-seat. His apparent silence when the regular penalty taker, John Matthews, refused to take the last-minute penalty against Walsall, which, if scored, would have saved United from relegation, spoke volumes of his leadership style. In truth Peters was never cut out for management. He was to state that teaching those who did not possess his ability was difficult. Team-mates might have found Peters difficult in return. A quiet character, he would at away games not appear with the squad until midday and would eat a lunch of prime steak, whilst those around him tucked into scrambled eggs on toast by virtue of both economy and the new dietary thinking for high-performance athletes. The smell of sizzling steak did not lead to squad harmony for those eating dry toast. Peters never tried his hand at management again.

With the election of a Tory government led by Margaret Thatcher in 1979 Britain was to change beyond all recognition over the next decade as a monetarist economic philosophy replaced the socialist ideals that had preceded it for five years. Football was to change as the promotion of individualism saw a change in both the class structure and a new attitude to debt and borrowing. There were huge consequences for the city of Sheffield and the region. Initially all was calm. The streets of Sheffield were spared the rioting by the disaffected young that characterised many major cities in England in the summer of 1981. The despair and rage notable in urban areas elsewhere was largely absent in Sheffield. Whilst sections of Sheffield youth were dominating the UK pop music charts, men steeped in masculine traditions and strength walked the city streets by virtue of the National Union of Mineworkers moving its headquarters from London to Sheffield in 1982, thereby locating itself in its heartland of membership and support. The City Council was idiosyncratic, radical and provocative. Sheffield became nationally renowned in the 1980s as the 'Socialist Republic of South Yorkshire'. But trouble was not far behind as the economics of Thatcherism devastated the city.

The industrial base of the city and region changed forever in the 1980s. The change was imposed and provoked resistance, which resulted in occasions of mass public disorder. The 13 weeks of the national steel workers' strike of 1980 resulted in 160 arrests in Sheffield. At one time 1,200 police officers were dedicated to dealing with keeping the peace. The miners' strike of 1984 lasted the best part of a year and was centred around South Yorkshire coalfields in what was probably the most bitter industrial dispute in the 20th century in Britain. The strikers and those supporting them received a multitude of injuries at the hands of riot police. There were two deaths on the picket lines. Some 1,700 strikers were arrested in the region and the policing costs for South Yorkshire were close to £40 million for the year. The dispute spilled over to football. 'Coal not dole!' stickers adorned United fans' attire, both blazer and designer-hooligan wear.

Cars carrying football fans were stopped and the occupants questioned by police, who believed they might be 'flying pickets', at the time an unlawful activity. By the end of the 1980s the manufacturing base of the city remained but with less than a third of its previous workforce. Some figures might suffice here; in 1920 steel production in the area employed 120,000 people, by the late 1990s, it was fewer than 10,000. The 56,000 employed in coal mining in 1971 declined to under a thousand in just three pits by the late 1990s. Lost with this was the long-held belief that the city's football fortunes could affect industrial production.

The tribulations of industrial capitalism brought Sheffield polarities of glut and scarcity. Economic booms and busts produced alternations between awful poverty and full employment. When the good times came they were to be enjoyed. The Empire and the war effort were good for Sheffield; the steel it produced was needed for armoury, but the big guns locally were always small businessmen, solicitors and medical men. These sober, plain-speaking individuals were devoted to good works, be it at the local football club or in their Freemason and Rotarian associations. They often boasted initials after their names, thus reassuring supporters that they were trustworthy men. A typical 1970s match programme displayed a bewildering array of directors' titles and honours: J.P.; F.C.A.; M.A.; LL.B; F.R.I.C.S.; M.I.Min.E; F.G.S.; O.B.E.; LL.D.; F.R.C.S. If their successors decades later possessed such impressive qualifications they were reluctant to disclose them in print. A sign of changing times, perhaps, when a 'nouveau middle class', for whom money was everything and with no notion of public service, came to power. When the steel and coal industries died or left the city and when local and national politicians no longer wished to subsidise ailing or non-profit-making production, Sheffield had to fight for its very survival. Some might say it lost the fight in the 1980s. The city is still seeking to establish a post-industrial identity. Whilst diminished, what remains is the passion from its populace for its two professional football clubs.

Professional football clubs were always commercial entities. The game at elite level was always a business and the pursuit of success was never free of underhand methods. Some clubs attained notoriety for certain questionable practices. For nearly a hundred years of their existence United were not one of them. Why they avoided the stigma was interesting. The answer probably lies in the demography of the city. The entrepreneurial cultures of the large insurance and banking companies bypassed the city, as did the regional media. Sheffield was never a regional centre nor was it ever renowned for its commercial acumen. This influenced its football clubs. Whilst there were fall-outs and possibly scandals throughout United's existence, such features of the boardroom were kept out of the public realm. The men who looked after the club were wealthy by local standards, but were men whose main role was to provide financial guarantees at the bank and meanwhile enjoy the reflected glory that footballing success gave them.

Things changed with the arrival at the club of Reg Brealey in 1980. He and the men who succeeded him as chairmen of Sheffield United FC had wealth hitherto never evidenced in the Bramall Lane boardroom. Brealey and his successors arrived with grandiose plans for the club. After an initial flourish the vision diminished and with it the interest of the individuals. In their attempts to make Sheffield United a footballing force, such men faced conflict and had their consciences troubled. The contest for the heart and soul of a football club from the city that gave the game to the world is still being played out.

Chapter 2

The Saviour from the East (Lincolnshire!)
Reg Brealey

Lincolnshire businessman Reginald J. Brealey was invited by Sheffield United Football Club chairman John Hassall to attend United's final game of the 1979/80 season. The fixture, in May 1980, saw United play away to recently crowned Third Division champions Grimsby Town. The invitation set in motion a chain of events that changed the club forever. In footballing terms, United were sliding, seemingly irrecoverably, downwards. Since their relegation from the First Division in 1976, the club had been burdened by financial concerns, most notably debt, a situation exacerbated by seemingly endless poor decision-making in both the boardroom and the football management side of the business.

It was not always thus. In the mid seventies the club had been in a rosy position. Following promotion to Division One in 1971 under the cautious and parsimonious management of John Harris, the Blades had survived at the top level with a surprising level of comfort and played memorable football. Harris's successor, the media-friendly and occasionally outspoken north-easterner Ken Furphy, led the club to a sixth-position finish in May 1975, its highest placing since the Second World War. Narrowly missing out on European qualification, the club was on a high. The team played attractive football, crowds averaged 24,000 and an 8,000-

seater stand almost complete, replacing the 120-year-old cricket field and an anachronistic three-sided ground. The new seating was meant to bring in undreamt of revenues. The future looked good.

The Bramall Lane home of Sheffield United FC had been, in football terms, three-sided since its inception in 1855, as a sporting (mainly cricket) arena. For over 100 years the stadium was the South Yorkshire base of Yorkshire County Cricket Club. Football followed cricket in the mid 19th century and the two sports and their representative committees lived together, albeit the relationship could be fractious. In the late 1960s some of the football board wished to claim sole use of the arena to build a stand on the fourth, open, side, making 'the Lane', as it is still known colloquially, one of the oldest sports venues in the world, a 'proper' – i.e. four-sided - football ground. In *The Official Centenary History - Sheffield United Football Club - The First 100 Years*, author Denis Clarebrough described the situation surrounding the club at the end of the 1960s: 'Development of the ground and the future of cricket at Bramall Lane had remained a bone of contention during the [1970/71] season. The City Corporation had made a feasibility study in May 1970 of the idea of a joint athletics and football stadium, which United did not favour, and in December the shareholders received a letter asking: "Do you support in principle the abolition of cricket at Bramall Lane?" The replies were 140 in favour and 208 against.'

Sentiment - so integral to sport - saw many amongst the committees of Bramall Lane in favour of cricket remaining. Economic realities, however, opposed emotion. United chairman Dick Wragg had given a graphic explanation of the club's problem: the receipts from the 42,963 spectators that attended the penultimate home game against Cardiff City in April 1971 were £11,582; a similar attendance 40 miles up the M1 at Leeds United would have brought receipts of £25,000, the reason being Leeds' Elland Road ground had far more seating accommodation, traditionally more expensive than standing areas. Leeds were in cup finals and European competitions. Things had to change if Sheffield United FC were ever to achieve anything in football. Success cost. A meeting between United directors and representatives of Yorkshire County Cricket Club in July 1971 left the cricket delegates in no doubt that their sport was entering its final days at Bramall Lane. An announcement that the playing of the summer game at the Lane was to cease was made soon after at United's Annual General Meeting. Wragg told the assembled shareholders that United could not 'maintain cricket and prosper' and that the ten-man board's decision to evict Yorkshire County Cricket Club had been unanimous. A few weeks later United gave County Cricket notice to leave.

United's *Lane Line Up* match programme of Tuesday August 15, 1972 for the home game against Leeds United featured on its front cover bold, four-centimetre high letters. A headline '£650,000 SOUTH STAND' proclaimed the cost of the proposed cantilever stand that would soon be built on what was once the cricket outfield. The accompanying story told of how Wragg and his fellow directors were to make the supporters' dream come true. The 1973 summer would be Yorkshire's final season at Bramall Lane. Construction of the new stand, Wragg added, would start 'the day after Yorkshire finish playing'. The city's daily morning newspaper the *Sheffield Morning Telegraph* produced a booklet to commemorate the termination of Yorkshire's tenure of the Lane: in *The Story of Cricket at Bramall Lane – End of an Era, 1855-1973*, *Sheffield Morning Telegraph* sports journalist Keith Farnsworth wrote; 'Mr Dick Wragg and his fellow directors of Sheffield United Cricket and Football Club, having studied the state of soccer and the role they wish United to play in the winter game, felt the time had come to build a fourth side: that is, to put up the stand on the cricket pitch. Their target for United is a place among soccer's elite. Because of the modern financial pressures in football they felt that the loss of revenue from not having a stand on the fourth side would, in the long term, be a greater burden than the cost of building one.' The directors meant well, but they had not done their sums.

The new stand proved a burden for decades. The board's admirable ambitions came crashing down within three years. The stand was under construction throughout United's tremendous 1974/75 season, which saw them finish sixth in the top division, and was opened for spectators for the first game of the following season against Derby County. The attendance was 31,316, some 9,000 higher than the previous season's average. However, costs for the construction of the stand had climbed far above the initial estimate of £650,000. Rising interest rates and booming inflation, which peaked at 13 per cent in October 1973, saw the club mount up bank borrowings. At the same time the team commenced a free-fall; the 1975/76 season was one of the worst in the club's history; relegation was inevitable long before the end of the campaign. Ken Furphy was sacked as early as October 1975 and replaced by the Scotsman Jimmy Sirrel. Despite an impressive managerial record at Notts County, where Sirrel lifted the unfashionable club from the Fourth Division to the Second in five years, the on-pitch slide could not be arrested. As the team declined so did attendances, resulting in ever-worsening financial problems. Interest charges on borrowings for 1975 amounted to £91,595. The chances of paying off the loans for the new stand seemed remote.

The following two seasons United trod water in what was then Division Two, never threatening promotion. Harry Haslam left Luton Town, where he had been a success, and took over from Sirrel early in 1978. However, the new manager's policy of selling the club's promising young players for good fees and replacing them with a mixture of veterans and unproven free transfers failed. Despite the club-record signing of Argentinian international Alejandro Sabella in 1978 United dropped further. In May 1979, for the first time in the club's history, United were in the Third Division. Matters still did not improve there. Despite topping the table in the initial stages of the 1979/80 season United slumped to a mid-table finish. To compound the situation, city rivals Sheffield Wednesday were on the rise after several years of mediocrity. The ultimate ignominy occurred when Wednesday thrashed United 4-0 on Boxing Day at their Hillsborough stadium in front of an all-time record Third Division attendance of 49,309. They were to gain promotion at the end of the season; United won just four games between January and May 1980.

These were the circumstances that led chairman John Hassall to ask the wealthy Reg Brealey to join United's board. The job of the latter was to assist with the servicing of the debt. When interviewed years later Brealey admitted to being barely interested in the role but assented to it because he was a friend of United's club secretary Dick Chester. He had previous experience as a football director, being a member of Lincoln City's board when they won promotion from the Fourth Division in 1976 under a young manager by the name of Graham Taylor. He was also ambitious and not publicity-shy. Born one of seven children, to a lorry-driver father, Brealey's education did not take him to college and he thus began his working life as a bicycle delivery boy. As a young man he joined painting contractors C.J.Else, which tendered for the job of repainting the floodlight pylons at Bramall Lane and did likewise at Lincoln City. In 1967 Brealey purchased a public house, the Finch Hatton Arms in Ewerby, Lincolnshire, and modernised it, employing a manager to run it as a 'village pub', offering the timeless pub games of darts and dominoes, with live entertainment on weekend evenings. Brealey was a man who enjoyed dipping into a diverse range of commercial interests. He also knew how to make money.

Whatever Brealey's intentions were prior to the Grimsby match, events during it made up his mind. He was so taken aback by the intensity and passion of the 4,000-strong Blades following of a bad team enduring a humiliating 4-0 defeat that he decided to accept Hassall's invitation. His appointment to the board raised barely a murmur amongst supporters. Tasked to oversee financial affairs and produce a report for Hassall on the fiscal state of the club, his conclusion described United's share capital of £20,000 as 'a ridiculous figure' for a business of such size. Brealey was to reveal that over the three years 1977-1980 the club's income had risen by 72 per cent but football expenditure had risen by 80 per cent. The bank overdraft was up by 30 per cent; other loans were 11 per cent higher. The balance sheet revealed that the club was theoretically insolvent. In 1989 Brealey wrote in *The Official Centenary History - Sheffield United Football Club - The First 100 Years* that his report to Hassall stated that; 'Short-term policies have never worked in any field of business, other than to give breathing space before the next coronary. We must have short, medium and long-term plans and the strategy must be laid out by the board.'

Arguing that the club was 'out of control', Brealey sought to increase the company's share capital to £500,000 and wanted existing directors to underwrite £300,000 of this sum. A planned new share issue would allow current shareholders to subscribe for five new £100 shares for each Original share owned. In return for their commitment, shareholders would also be offered extra privileges, including a ten-year season ticket. The new shares were issued in March 1981, with the greater part of the authorised share capital, comprising 477 Ordinary £500 shares and the conversion to £100 of the 477 Original £20 shares, being underwritten by Brealey, his companies and long-standing United director Alan Laver. Staunch Thatcherite and contributor to the Conservative party, Brealey was a proponent of the 'New-Right' philosophy of wider public share ownership. To this end he wanted supporters to purchase most of the shares but £500 per five new shares was a lot of money in 1981 in a city still trying to recover from the steelworkers' strike the year before and which had no great history of shareholding or, indeed, Thatcherite monetary policies. The take-up was far short of what Brealey anticipated. Almost by default, therefore, Brealey virtually controlled the club. A year later his position was strengthened further when shareholders at the Annual General Meeting approved another issue of 1,123 Ordinary Shares of £500 each, giving the company an authorised share capital of £1,499,660. One shareholder voiced his worry that Brealey would end up in majority control: in response Brealey stated; 'But then if you buy them, you will have control.' The shareholder in question clearly didn't buy enough of them as Brealey was subsequently left with a 76 per cent shareholding.

It was around the time of Brealey becoming the (vast) majority shareholder that he was first accused of engaging in financial chicanery. What Brealey was said to have done was not illegal but stretched the limits of financial acceptability. The *Daily Mail* financial journalist Michael Walters explained to readers the complexities of Brealey's alleged 'teeming and ladling' of his companies' funds so as to take full advantage of taxation regulations. Brealey was chairman of a company called Epicure Holdings, which had interests in buildings, hotels and property. According to Walters, the first step in Brealey's clever scheme was to not pay himself dividends due on his Epicure shareholding. This non-payment resulted in a £1 million tax-free gain to Epicure. According to Walters, Epicure used this £1 million to buy companies in Gibraltar, a British overseas territory exempt from taxes and capital gains tax. Brealey then used these Gibraltar-accrued tax savings to underwrite the issue of new shares in Sheffield United Football Club. Step four was to look at Sheffield United's £1.5 million losses, the size of which allowed him to write down the paper value of his newly acquired Sheffield United shares to £100,000. The fifth stage of the manoeuvre allowed Epicure to buy Brealey's personal Sheffield United shareholding for the written-down value of £100,000. Step six saw Epicure use its own newly-acquired shareholding in Sheffield United to set United's current losses against possible future profits.

Confused? You probably are. Simplified, the bottom line was that if Sheffield United bought a footballer, the cost of that player could be written off by the club immediately, creating a tax loss for Epicure. If a player was sold, the profit could be set against the football club's past losses, saving on possible future corporation tax. Therefore normal football club transfers in and out could be allocated to either Epicure (for purchases) or to Sheffield United (for sales) to ensure the minimisation of taxes for both companies. All rather complicated but, as Walters wrote, 'If the Brealey plan works, Sheffield United lose nothing and gain tax-free profits and powerful financial friends. Epicure lose nothing and gain a fortune in tax savings.' Whether or not Brealey actually put these complex schemes into operation was not clear, although Epicure paid United's manager Ian Porterfield's salary for the first three years of his then unprecedented ten-year contract. How Epicure Holdings and Else (1982) Ltd, the Gibraltar-based company that later took control of Brealey's Sheffield United shareholding, were connected is not known but such detail gives some idea of Brealey's penchant for employing

47

practices to minimise tax liabilities for himself and his companies. In English football Brealey was, in many respects, years ahead of the game.

Brealey's earlier report to Hassall condemned United's policy of the preceding three or four years, put in place by manager Harry Haslam, of selling young playing talent to keep the club's financial head above water. He prophetically predicted that this short-sighted plan would lead to only one thing – relegation to Division Four. In May 1981 he was proved correct as United dropped into the Football League basement for the first time in their history. In early 1981 Haslam stepped down due to ill health, but the promotion of former England 1966 World Cup winner Martin Peters from player/coach to player/manager proved a dismal failure. Hassall had made it clear he had intended to resign from the board even before the last match at home to Walsall in May 1981, which United lost 1-0 to confirm relegation. If the match had been drawn Walsall would have gone down but United's Don Givens missed a last-minute penalty. Hassall's resignation statement read; 'Although I did not pick the team nor take penalties I accept responsibility for the decline in the playing fortunes of the club.' United had fallen from the brink of European qualification to the bottom tier of the league in six years. In the weeks following Hassall's departure the club declared a loss for the year of £725,230, a huge sum at the time. Brealey was the obvious, and indeed unanimous, boardroom choice to take over the chairmanship and as time went on he became more and more involved, both professionally and emotionally.

Brealey became personally responsible for rebuilding the club at all levels. He was innovative and worked to inform the fans of his intentions. To this end he introduced the free 50,000-circulation *Blades News* newspaper in November 1981 to facilitate the dissemination of information. As well as general football matters and features on the affairs and personalities of the United team and club, *Blades News* anticipated Sunday newspaper supplements as it was also something of a lifestyle publication, including articles on fitness, fashion, travel, cars, horoscopes, entertainment and food. In Brealey's words,

Blades News would contain 'the truth, facts' and would 'dispel rumours and innuendoes that are always prevalent in the game'. It did contain truth and facts but rumour and innuendo continued around both Sheffield United and Reg Brealey.

Whilst words were fine, actions spoke louder. Martin Peters departed immediately after the club's relegation. Brealey was able to lure the young and ambitious Ian Porterfield away from Rotherham United (then two divisions above the Blades) with a lucrative contract. Porterfield, scorer of the Sunderland goal that beat Leeds United in the 1973 FA Cup final, was a former Sheffield Wednesday player who had made a success of his first managerial position at United's South Yorkshire neighbours. Brealey provided Porterfield with funds unheard of in the Fourth Division (almost £300,000) to initially buy goalkeeper Keith Waugh from Peterborough United for £90,000 before the start of the season. Shortly after the season began, former Blades striker Keith Edwards was brought back from Hull City at a cost of £100,000 and winger Colin Morris came to Bramall Lane from Blackpool in February 1982 for a similar fee. All proved crucial as United won the Fourth Division title one year after relegation. Waugh was safe in goal; Edwards, with 36 goals, was the country's leading scorer, many of them provided by the mercurial wing play of Morris. The new chairman and manager were getting on famously. In the first issue of *Blades News* Porterfield said of his appointment, 'The chairman [Brealey] spoke to me in depth for a considerable time. Obviously there were a lot of problems at Bramall Lane. I accepted the job provided the chairman agreed to let me get on with it as the Rotherham chairman had done. He impressed me with his positiveness...... he appeared to be a very sincere and honest fellow and I felt I could work well with him.'

The display of the Blades fans at Grimsby may have been the catalyst for Brealey's involvement with Sheffield United but he was now showing a similar fervour. Brealey in his early years immersed himself in United's fortunes. Some of his ideas were visionary and out of step with the generally parochial and passive football thinking evident in English football of the time. He initiated several fund-raising schemes, one of which was called the Blades Future Players Fund, which would see supporters organising events to raise money to give to the club for buying players. However, it was not particularly successful. Based at the Sportsman pub just metres off Bramall Lane, its committee of ten was chaired by former United full back and the pub landlord, Graham Shaw. The fund never raised large sums of money. The idea, however, was a commendable.

Brealey brought distinctions and gradations into United fandom by introducing categories of supporter based on wealth and age. He instigated the Executive Club for the more affluent supporters to enjoy pre- and post-match hospitality, a viewing area with padded seats, and luxury coach travel to away games. In 1984 they even chartered a plane to a match on the south coast. Brealey also formalised the Senior Blades (for the over-60s) and the Junior Blades (for the under-16s) entities. Within 18 months the Senior Blades had almost 1,000 members, the Junior Blades over 3,000. Brealey appointed Sheffield-born former international referee George McCabe as 'liaison officer' to foster relationships with young people and, according to *Blades News*, to 'encourage a sense of pride in Sheffield United Football Club'. The first issue of *Blades News* also described the formation of the fund-raising, supporter-involving and profile-heightening organisation designed to bring together previously independent bodies. Under the imaginative title B.L.A.D.E.S. 1981 Ltd ('Bramall Lane Aid and Development Enterprises') Brealey linked the Executive Club, the Travel Club, the Junior Blades and the Blades Future Players Fund, with the primary objective of projecting a positive image of the club and its supporters. Brealey used the B.L.A.D.E.S. acronym in another way too, to express concisely his desires and ambitions for the development of the club: Business/commercial, Local importance, Associations, Direction and policies, Emotions and expansion, Supporter involvement. Brealey plotted the club's future in fine detail and wanted involvement from all sectors, namely supporters, businesses and the local community.

Understanding the growing value of sporting apparel Brealey opened a souvenir shop in the south stand, replacing its predecessor, a cramped two-roomed corner terraced house on Baron Street opposite the ground, opened in 1971. He provided permanent offices in the south stand interior for the club's commercial and promotions departments. He improved the pay and conditions of both the office and ancillary staff. He stood on the terraces with the fans at both home and away matches and gave away complimentary tickets to ordinary supporters. He proposed an annual match against Sheffield Wednesday for the 'Master Cutler Cup', but his idea was rejected by Wednesday, who saw no benefit in the clubs meeting on a regular basis. He offered financial support to former players in difficulties. He recruited new, locally-born, directors in an attempt to alleviate the club's financial problems. He was the first man to use the phrase 'The Family Club' in relation to football in the UK. In the club's own booklet published to celebrate promotion from Division Four, *Sheffield United FC–Portrait of a Championship 1981/82*, he wrote; 'The creation of the image of developing a family club captured the imagination of many sectors of the community and spread to the media at large, in particular in football circles who in haste visited and enquired as to the happenings at Bramall Lane.' He appointed a club chaplain – John Smith, a Church of England vicar from a church adjacent to Bramall Lane - an idea copied by dozens of other clubs over the next decade. Continuing the religious theme, in the middle of 1985 Brealey invited the American evangelist Billy Graham to hold one if his 'Mission England' gatherings at Bramall Lane. Some 50,000 people attended the event.

His vision was also of this world and beyond the parochial. In the summer of 1984 Brealey enabled Sheffield United to become the first English club from outside the First Division to tour China. Simonds Cutting Tools, the company that sponsored United at the time and which had an office in China, helped organise the trip, while the London Export Corporation, a company that began trading in China in 1952 and which 'opened doors' in the country for Western businesses, sponsored a match in Peking (Beijing) against a local representative side in the 80,000-seater Workers' Stadium. For the game the United team wore the company's name, printed in both English and Mandarin, on their shirts. The attendance was listed as 50,000, with what was described as a 'vast audience' watching the live television broadcast. Brealey's consideration for the comforts of his players extended to paying for alternative hotel accommodation out of his own pocket after the original hotel was found not to possess air conditioning. He was also to arrange with a friend at the British Embassy to provide the team with their preferred English delicacies, such as pork pies and sausage rolls. The visit, which also included stops in Hong Kong and Sarawak, was as much about 'pressing the flesh' as football, a fact highlighted by a drinks reception at the British Embassy. In truth such football-related diplomacy was probably more important for Brealey's business world than for United: Sarawak would raise its head later in Brealey's time at Bramall Lane. Brealey also claimed to be a personal friend of the Sultan of Brunei and, in September 1983, a United youth squad visited there, playing four games against local opposition to mark the opening of the new national stadium. Functions at the British High Commission proved more propitious than the match results, a point emphasised by United's commercial manager Andy Daykin, who at the time described the tour as being 'successful on the diplomatic and social front' and who well remembers the trip for his having to drink beer from a tea pot and cup as local - Islamic - custom ostensibly prohibited liquor of any sort.

Brealey became so emotionally involved with the club and the team that once when flying back to Britain following a business meeting he asked a stewardess if she could obtain from the captain some vital information. Thinking it was regarding some business deal that Brealey was negotiating, she agreed. What he was desperate to know was the result of the Fourth Division Aldershot versus Sheffield United match. The score was 1-1. Brealey's legend grew. His aspirations were far-sighted and he had the courage and desire to bring them to fruition. Brealey had the idea of fitting out the hitherto empty shell of the south stand so that the changing rooms, offices and other facilities were among the best in the country. Former chairman John Hassall opposed the development, believing it should be phased in only when finances allowed. With Hassall out of the way Brealey pushed ahead. In November 1982 *Blades News* described the background to the south stand development, informing readers of negotiations with the Mansfield Brewery Company Ltd to enable the board to proceed with the refurbishment, which was to include a social club and 'Executive Suite'. New offices and player dressing rooms would be ready in February 1982. The players would then take the field from opposite the John Street stand dressing rooms and tunnel they had run out from for close to 100 years. Brealey's words and deeds made him unlike any previous United chairman. Much was made in the local press of the fact that he owned a helicopter, a chain of hotels and a Rolls Royce. Some issue was made of whom he thanked for such possessions - Brealey was a member of the General Synod of the Church of England. His wealth impressed the generally working class supporters of Sheffield United. He wasn't one of us – perhaps God had sent him to sprinkle moondust on the then grimy, low-income, ugly industrial city that was Sheffield.

Seeking the fans' money, Brealey offered riches in return and good players to those who had no return on their investment. In 1986 he began the Blades Revival lottery scheme. Designed to raise money to buy players, the scheme at the same time offered cash and other prizes to supporters. The Blades Revival was in reality an example of Brealey's liking for both innovation and obfuscation. He publicised the fact that he had hired the Roxy nightclub in the centre of Sheffield for an event of major benefit to the club, inviting all Blades fans to attend. However, he did not disclose what the event was going to be, thus guaranteeing a full house of intrigued supporters - there were 3,500 inside the Roxy and scores locked out. He introduced his plan, one of the first of its kind in the country, with the fanfare of an electoral campaign. His words were quasi-religious; he spoke of 'a revival of faith, hope, courage' and a 'new spirit' running the club. Supporters could sign up to pay £2 per week, half of which would go towards funding player signings, half of which would be given away as weekly prizes, the highest of which was £1000. There would also be an annual prize of £20,000. The scheme was so successful that in its first few months enough money was donated to contribute £74,800 towards the £135,000 signing of striker Richard Cadette from Southend United in the summer of 1987. Over the next twelve years a further £1,393,950 was raised to assist the purchase of some three-dozen players.

Several years afterwards United's commercial manager throughout Brealey's reign, Andy Daykin, revealed what working with Brealey was like: 'With some ideas he [Brealey] was years ahead of his time. He was like that though; always having ten ideas. Out of them one would work and could make him a fortune.' Whilst a staunch Tory, Brealey was in many ways a libertarian in social issues. Brealey foresaw the removal of the perimeter fences in front of the terraces, erected in the mid 1970s to prevent 'hooligan' movement. This was years before the 1990 Taylor Report into the Hillsborough Disaster made their removal compulsory. Brealey's desire to remove them was inspired by an incident in 1981 when a fan, having caught his wedding ring on the fence when attempting to climb over to enter the pitch, lost a finger. Believing such fencing treated people like animals, Brealey wanted them pulled down - the police, however, would not allow him to do so.

The enhancement of the 'guts' of the south stand went to schedule. In January 1982 a symbolic break with Bramall Lane's cricketing past occurred when the administrative offices moved from the cricket pavilion to the new stand. When completely finished in 1983, the south stand housed the social club, a variety of offices, directors' facilities, changing rooms, a new police office and matchday police cells. The Executive Suite dining facility was opened in January 1982 by the Lord Mayor of Sheffield, Councillor Mrs Enid Hattersley (the mother of former Sheffield Councillor and Labour Minister Roy – who was to become a director of Sheffield Wednesday FC in the 1990s). Capable of catering for more than 500 people, the suite was one of the largest banqueting facilities in Sheffield at the time. Commenting on the logic behind such a venture in *Blades News*, club secretary Dick Chester said, 'The management of the club has been dissatisfied with the facilities for supporters for some time.

The problem was how did we finance new facilities? By building the suite in its present form we were able to do two things. One, to provide the supporters of the club with social facilities better than any in the Football League and two, use these facilities seven days a week to finance the improvements. In this way we hope Sheffield United will become a seven-day-a-week place – not just a Saturday one. At United we are lucky, getting bigger gates than some First Division clubs. However, if the club is to survive and thrive then the success of the Executive Suite becomes vital, for it will become a major source of income for us.' Over the next two decades the social club became a regular pre-match meeting and drinking place for supporters as well as hosting senior citizens' lunches and bingo evenings for local residents. Within three years of its completion the Executive Suite had been host to over 200,000 customers enjoying variously, pre-match hospitality, wedding receptions and Christmas parties. Replacement facilities were provided in the new John Street stand in 1996, at which point the space in the south stand was put to alternative use.

It was early in 1982 that Brealey made the first veiled mention of what he termed his 'Great Plan'. This was to turn United's Bramall Lane ground into a multi-purpose sports stadium capable of hosting world-class events. Recognising that changing working patterns were producing greater leisure time, Brealey proposed that Sheffield United could become a sporting entity with football at its core. Netball, hockey, rounders, squash and chess for boys and girls were initially mentioned but a few months later Brealey expanded his ideas. Under the headline 'World Class Stadium Planned for Bramall Lane', *Blades News* reported a proposed £10 million multi-sports 'Bramall Centre' that would be second only to Wembley Stadium in London. The complex would be more than just a stadium; it would promote the name of the city globally, as Sheffield's cutlery had once done. Ominously Brealey was to comment: 'All we need now is a nod from the Town Hall and we go'. Club secretary Dick Chester told *Blades News* readers more about the legacy and the technology it required. Once completed it would provide 600 full-time jobs. The provision of an eight-lane athletics track would add a new dimension to

British athletics; athletes would not have to go abroad to find the perfect training conditions to break world records. The track bends would be less severe than London's Crystal Palace athletics track and would be protected by a stadium on four sides. Athletics would be just part of a multi-purpose stadium that 'would give full value to the whole family'. An artist's impression showed three sides of the ground unchanged (the south stand, the Bramall Lane end and the John Street stand) but a curved stand replaced the Shoreham Street kop end. A four-storey L-shaped hotel block was planned for the Shoreham Street/Cherry Street corner and a smaller building was to be built on the corner of Cherry Street and Bramall Lane. The hotel was to be constructed by the French Novotel company. A few years later this company built a hotel just half a mile away from Bramall Lane.

Amidst the excitement came fears amongst the supporters that the atmosphere of the kop would be destroyed by the proposed 11,000-seater 'double-decker' stand in an overall revised ground capacity of 49,000. Many were also unhappy at the prospect of watching their football from the far side of an eight-lane running track. The club was quick to try to dispel their worries, assuring supporters in *Blades News* that: 'The Kop Will Survive. The kop has been a valued friend for generations of Sheffield United teams and the bellows of encouragement from the terraces will not disappear when the £10m Bramall Centre is built. The kop will not disappear and will be retained for future generations of fans, but we will be installing seating facilities in the event of special occasions.' The concerns of kop regulars caused the club to alter its plans: there would be only 5,500 seats in the top tier and a much larger standing area below. The article further explained how: 'Sheffield United is a vital social service in the local community.' Such talk was new to both Sheffield United and English football. Everyone knew football clubs were a 'social service' in so many ways to millions but no one had ever stated as much in print.

Optimism pervaded both the fans and club employees at this time. Brealey had expansive ideas for the stadium and the team had just won a comfortable promotion from the Fourth

Division, playing exciting, high-scoring football. The loss of over £850,000 reported in the 1982 annual accounts was played down by Brealey, who insisted the club was moving forward. The chairman publicly thanked Ian Porterfield at the club's Annual General Meeting for 'his commitment to the job, his honesty and dedication, his will to succeed' and showed an insight into the requirements and desires of football fans for simple comforts that escaped many of his contemporaries. For Brealey, the proposed redevelopment was symptomatic of a club facing up to the requirements of a new generation, both in outlook and expectations. Furthermore, he recognised the possibility of the match becoming a place for the suitor, arguing that, 'Football grounds have for many years been embarrassing places to take a lady.' He was to regularly talk up the 'lady factor' and even introduced the 'Miss Sheffield United' beauty pageant - yet never once could any supporter remember him bringing his wife to a match!

Brealey was right in asserting that facilities had been appalling and female supporters neglected. He believed that football grounds should be clean and modern places where a family could share their sporting interests. He was to add, somewhat ominously, 'Your board earnestly believes in the scheme presented to the local authority, whom we feel share the same aspirations in the sporting and leisure field. Hopefully minor differences on the commercial side can be overcome to enable us together to bring a bold and imaginative scheme to fruition.' He endeared himself to supporters further, adding, 'The good side of supporters never seems to get portrayed. Only the isolated incident gets blown out of proportion. The Darlington carnival [where United won the Fourth Division championship in front of a Blades following of 10,000] with a capacity crowd sitting on the touchline, no wire cages or walls, impeccable behaviour by supporters of both teams. The humour, wit and laughter that surrounded the day….. the magnificent police who entered into the spirit of the day. All this reflects the real side of supporters but alas such pleasure is not newsworthy.' Impeccable!? Ten thousand Blades supporters, most of them the worse for drink, repeatedly invaded the pitch and intimidated Darlington players! He was right on one thing however – it was great fun!

A month later Brealey's mood changed. Sheffield City Council's Planning Authority rejected his plans for Bramall Lane. The *Sheffield Star's* headline on December 23, 1982 declared, 'BREALEY RAPS LANE PLAN VETO', and described how Brealey could not contain his bitterness at the Labour-dominated Council's decision: 'I now believe we have been led along the path into their political arena for slaughter. In the light of this, this Government should remove all authority from this Council in the interests of the community. Their misadministration is unbelievable. The scheme was changed time and again to suit their requirements. It seems they delight in destroying jobs, enterprise, killing companies and then masquerading concern. They are nothing but a bunch of cheaps.' Brealey further lamented, 'We were sold down the river.' Sheffield City Council leader and the future Home Secretary (and well-known Wednesdayite) David Blunkett hit back: 'We are actually in the business of making rational decisions and not conducting our business in the cavalier fashion which Mr Brealey has been used to in his previous dealings.' Planning Committee chairman Sheila Dootson explained that the main sticking point was the 140-bedroom hotel, which would be 'too near houses on Shoreham Street' and constituted 'a gross intrusion'. There were also worries about noise and increased traffic. Overall, the planners claimed, it would be 'a retrograde step in the regeneration of an inner-city area'. How the appearance of a luxury hotel and sports facilities the city had never had in its history would somehow frustrate 'regeneration' projects was never explained by the elected members. During the inner-city riots of 1981 Sheffield City Council – in accordance with cities up and down the UK – had opened its parks and recreational facilities to the youth of the city free of charge. The idea was to swamp such areas with coaches and youth workers to get the disaffected off the streets playing sport (and not rioting). Based on this policy, the Council's decision defied the logic of both socialist ideology and what was fashionable thinking in diversions from crime.

Brealey's response was immediate. He would appeal the decision and, if successful, would cut off all partnerships with the City Council and other UK funding bodies, proclaiming:

'This will be self-financing and they can keep their grants. How could they reject something they themselves worked on? If there are any EEC monies available we shall obviously apply but as far as grants from local government or Sports Council are concerned, we could do without them.' The appeal generated support and opposition from predictable sources. Some Shoreham Street residents were reported to be against the plan, but others in the city made their feelings known in print. Mr J.D.Arnold of Carterknowle Road, in a letter to the *Sheffield Star,* complained of the Council's 'mismanagement, stubborn, pig-headed refusal'. In another letter, Mr T.Wilson of Rundle Road expressed his 'utter disgust' at the planning authority's rejection. Trevor Wilson [probably the same person] wrote in *Blades News*; 'For anybody with the interests of United and Sheffield at heart, this scheme simply must go ahead. We are all ratepayers and have the right to expect the best and most profitable use of our assets. The refusal of planning permission for the Bramall Centre is contrary to these ambitions. The club and the architects appear to have bent over backwards to pacify any complaints that may be forthcoming from residents. I doubt if the complainants fully realise the efforts that have been made – noise levels, infringement on daylight, car parking, even down to external signposting being compatible with the surroundings. In addition, a proviso has been made in the plans for a community centre and church for use by the locals. As for the Local Authority one wonders, without delving too deeply into matters political, if, on this occasion, they are taking a wide enough view of the benefits this project would provide – namely a centre unequalled in Britain, with all its attendant kudos and publicity for the city.'

The architects of the proposed plan, Costall Roberts, took the unusual step of issuing a press statement following a late-night 'crisis meeting' with Brealey. The statement outlined the negotiations they had conducted with the Council and the Planning and Highways authorities: 'The outcome of the Planning Committee meeting is extremely embarrassing to us as a practice, so we persuaded the chairman and the board to deviate from their original path and adopt a policy of close co-ordination and link with the Council in their application to the

Department of the Environment for Urban Development Grant aid for the scheme. We were, therefore, devastated and extremely disappointed when the scheme was refused. The scheme was amended, modified, omissions made and additional facilities provided, which entailed a tremendous amount of time, effort, and indeed, substantial expense – all with a view to achieving a satisfactory design solution acceptable to the Authority. We feel compelled to say that having worked with authorities throughout the length and breadth of the country for many years, we have never experienced anything like this, following such protracted negotiations. We have now received further instructions from our client, part of which entail lodging an appeal with the Secretary of State.'

The appeal against the Council's decision was lodged at the Department of the Environment. Club secretary Dick Chester said that the club had been working on the redevelopment plans for three years and had initially approached to the city's Recreation Department to discuss a possible joint involvement. The club had sought to build a stadium that could host international events but would also be available to the community. All parties had considered this to be 'an admirable proposition'. Chester concluded by stating that of the 1,700 letters sent out to people in the area by the local authority requesting their views, only 24 written objections were received. He could then argue that well over 1,600 homes had no objection and that never in the city's history of municipal socialism had 24 objections prevented the provision of a multi-million pound sports and leisure facility.

The appeal was heard in August 1983 and the decision arrived in December. It went against Brealey and Sheffield United. The Environment Secretary admitted that the project was 'architecturally exciting' but added that it would be 'unacceptable, having an overpowering visual impact on properties'. Despondent Brealey finally admitted defeat: 'It was my ambition to see the club as one of the top ten in status, financial strength and facilities but we must now accept that, although status will always depend on the success of the club on the field, the envisaged facilities will have to remain a dream.' The development of Bramall Lane would have brought the club the financial strength to acquire the Hadfield's Sports Complex, in the Darnall area in the south-east of the city. Steel company Hadfield's had kept the sale of its sports ground in abeyance throughout the period of the Bramall Centre planning and appeal in the hope that ongoing joint facilities would have been provided for their employees plus Blades supporters.[1] Such facilities would have provided the Bramall Lane project with outdoor arenas for hockey, bowling, tennis and cricket.

The rejection of his plans had a profound effect on Brealey. A staunch Tory, Brealey always blamed the City Council's opposing political views as the reason for his scheme being turned down. The self-proclaimed 'People's Republic of South Yorkshire', which on the day of the wedding of Lady Diana Spencer and Prince Charles in 1981 flew a red flag atop Sheffield Town Hall, would have no truck with an arch-capitalist like Brealey. Brealey realised this and acted: 'I offered to resign as chairman in the belief that I was the political problem, supporting a party different from the one in power in Sheffield.' He later also told the *Sheffield Star*, 'I was warned by friends that, at the last minute, they would turn us down because their ideology differs from our own private enterprise spirit.' Many in the city believed that the ever-divisive footballing loyalties of the city were as important as political ideology. Most of the leading players at the City Council, some of whom (David Blunkett and Clive Betts, for example) went on to greater things in Tony Blair's Labour Government at the end of the century, were renowned Wednesdayites and could not bear to bring themselves to support a scheme that could lead to their beloved Wednesday being overshadowed.

The City Council's decision took on even more significance fewer than three years later. In June 1986, Sheffield, along

[1] Once one of the largest steel producers in Sheffield until it was decimated by the 1980 steel strike, Hadfield's was closed down in 1983 and its former Vulcan Road site now forms part of the Meadowhall shopping complex.

with other British cities, was invited by the British Students Sports Federation (BSSF) to bid to become the national entry to host the 1991 World Student Games, then the world's largest multi-sports event outside of the Olympic Games. In February 1987 BSSF chose Sheffield ahead of Edinburgh because, it stated, of the city's commitment to provide world-class sports facilities as part of the economic regeneration of the city: a somewhat incongruous description of the Council's ambitions, considering that they seemed intent on frustrating such a development three years earlier. Later, at a meeting in Sheffield of the Executive Committee of the *Federation Internationale Du Sport Universitaire* (FISU) the Games were awarded to the city. When the news was first announced the headlines of the local press were ecstatic: 'The greatest day in the history of Sheffield' and 'It's glory for Sheffield as a dream comes true' were proclaimed. Then came the sting in the tail. When the euphoria died down it was revealed that the City Council would have to increase household and business rates by at least nine per cent in order to pay for the construction of the facilities, the provision of accommodation, transport for the competitors and officials and the hosting of the Games themselves. Millions of pounds of local taxpayers' money was therefore to be spent building the Don Valley Stadium in Sheffield's post-industrial East End and completely refurbishing the city-centre Hyde Park flats complex as an athletes' village. The cost of such facilities would hamstring the city with a debt that would likely take 30 years to pay off. Graffiti was painted on city-centre walls claiming: 'Three weeks of games, 30 years of debt'. Posters appeared from sources unknown demanding the arrest of Council leader Clive Betts. The Council was accused of neglecting the city's homeless in favour of the 'World Stupid Games'. The City Council could have had a suitable stadium at hand and at little cost to them, built using private money, had they come down on Brealey's side in 1983.

There was further bad news for Brealey around the same time as the rejection of the planning appeal when South Yorkshire County Council began High Court action to recover an alleged unpaid bill of £54,145, which the Council claimed was owed by United for the provision of police personnel outside the

Bramall Lane ground on matchdays. Brealey was the first man in English football to challenge the policing arrangements around the professional game. Brealey's argument was that matchday police officers had been provided by the Police Authority; United had not requested them. Therefore, why should he have to pay for something he had not asked for? He elaborated on his standpoint in *Blades News*: 'There are two types of football grounds - designated and non-designated. First and Second Division grounds are always designated. Under the Safety of Sports Grounds Act 1975, designated grounds are obliged to have a police presence inside the ground. A contribution towards the costs of such a presence is a sum agreed between the club and the Police Authority. The number of police in the ground can be based on a criteria guideline, laid down by the Football League. Bramall Lane is a non-designated ground [United were in the Third Division at the time] and does not come within the 1975 Act in connection with the police presence. They are there by invitation. The South Yorkshire Police Authority invoice a sum without any consultation.'

Brealey had disturbed a hornets' nest of issues. According to law, the Chief Constable of any police force had a right to station police inside the ground, if he considered it 'in the interests of law and order'. No football club would ever refuse police entry and thus be accused of preventing them carrying out their duty. If they did, the Chief Constable could apply to the courts to have the match cancelled. The dispute went on for three years before being settled, on appeal, in the local authority's favour. The judge stated that police duty at the match constituted 'special police services' within the meaning of the 1964 Police Act. According to Brealey, Peter Wright, the then Chief Constable of South Yorkshire, had stated to him: 'I can't allow you to play football matches without policing the ground,' but as Brealey argued, 'Yet the law stated that the police were only in the ground at my invitation. I told him, "I don't want your police in the ground!"' Another thorn in Brealey's side was the issue of the business rates Sheffield United were forced to pay. The Inland Revenue re-rated the Bramall Lane site and came up with an annual figure of £63,140, which was almost double what United had been expecting. Part of the increase was for new car-parking facilities behind the south stand, which angered Brealey. Why, he asked, should the club be penalised for taking cars off the streets? By comparison, Sheffield Wednesday were to pay £29,646 per annum. Brealey called this situation 'very unfair' and successfully sought a reduction at a local rating court. At last Brealey was the victor; the bill was reduced by some £20,000.

Sheffield United was proving an expensive hobby for Brealey. In March 1984 he revealed that since he joined the board he had invested £1.25 million into the club and promised £1 million more to save potential interest charges of £150,000 per year. Despite a reported bank overdraft of £1,222,236 at the end of the financial year (June 30, 1983), Brealey told the delayed Annual General Meeting that he believed the club had 'turned the corner'. There had been a profit of £208,771 in the preceding six months but this had to be offset against a big loss for the whole year. The accounts showed an annual loss of £691,000, including outgoing transfer fees of £300,000 and interest charges of £142,000. Brealey told shareholders; 'This is the third year running that the club has suffered what can only be described as catastrophic losses but the year has seen the end of long-term contracts which had to be honoured. By reducing the number of people employed by the club, I am pleased to say that in the six-month period to 31st December 1983 the club has broken even on its trading account including bank interest and when taking transfer fees into account is showing a profit of approximately £200,000.' He added that it was his intention to relieve the club of all its bank debt. By the end of 1984 Brealey was circumspect in his forecast of future prospects. He said, 'It has taken a lot of doing to get the club to break even and if things go wrong on the field of play we could slip financially. I do not think you must panic and risk getting the club into the terrible financial trading mess again.' He pleaded for supporters to be patient, saying that he club was not in a position to pay a transfer fee of £150,000 and then pay the player £700 per week, which at the time was the level of investment required to acquire the quality of player demanded by supporters.[2]

Brealey came to Sheffield United confident he would be able to turn around the fortunes of an historic but ailing football club. To a great extent he did but the rejection of the planned sporting complex, the police bill controversy, the dispute over the rates and United's continuing financial troubles weighed on his mind. Because of the slow take-up of the share issues Brealey had assumed overall control of the club; all the problems were his to solve. When the 'socialist' Council refused the club's planning application his heart was no longer really in the job. Over the next few years he tried on and off, unsuccessfully, to find buyers for his shares. The monies enjoyed by Ian Porterfield in the early 1980s were no longer available to Porterfield and his successors. On one occasion Porterfield accused Brealey of meddling in team affairs when the chairman apparently put a £400,000 price tag on winger Terry Curran, who at the time was on loan at Everton. Porterfield wanted to sell Curran so that he could use the money to strengthen his squad elsewhere but feared that £400,000 was too high a valuation. He demanded to know who was in charge of the team – the manager or the chairman? Curran was eventually sold to Everton several months later for a fee of just £90,000.

On another occasion, in October 1984, Porterfield selected a strange-looking line-up for the visit to Oxford United, leaving out experienced first-team regulars Colin Morris, Joe Bolton and Ray McHale. United were well beaten, 5-1. It was rumoured at the time, though the notion was never confirmed by the manager, that Porterfield had deliberately picked a weakened line-up to demonstrate to Brealey just how thin his first-team squad was, showing starkly that the chairman needed to release the purse strings to allow him to strengthen. Porterfield's apparent protest didn't work as he was subsequently forced to recruit - on free transfers - former top-

---

[2] United may not have been able to pay £700 per week at this time, but in 1986 Peter Withe was reputed to be the club's first-ever four-figure weekly earner.

class players moving towards the end of their careers, such as Mel Eves from Wolves, Phil Thompson from Liverpool and Peter Withe, John Burridge, Ken McNaught and Denis Mortimer, all from Aston Villa. Four of these players were European Cup winners but the Second Division was alien to them. It was a policy that led directly to Porterfield's departure in March 1986, when supporters finally became fed up of this team they had christened 'Dads' Army', playing dull, uninspiring football. Ironically, he left with United in their highest league position for a decade. Brealey took notice of the supporters' car-park demonstrations against Porterfield and removed him from his position after a 5-2 home defeat to leaders Norwich City, despite the team being ninth in the table at the time and the manager having five years of his ten-year contract remaining. Porterfield insisted he was not sacked – and that he walked out. He was still being paid by the club almost a decade afterwards – he was thus neither sacked nor resigned; there was some form of agreed departure, reported to involve a payment of £40,000. However, as late as 1996 Porterfield was threatening the club with court action in his attempts to secure compensation. With the completion of the boardroom offices and players' facilities in the south stand coming only four years earlier, this car-park protest was the first of what would become many at Bramall Lane in subsequent years.

Porterfield did well after leaving United. He was appointed manager of Aberdeen, thereby succeeding Alex Ferguson, who was on his way to Old Trafford having over his eight years in charge at Pittodrie won three league championships, four Scottish cups and the 1983 Cup Winners' Cup, beating Real Madrid in the final. In later years Porterfield managed Reading (1989-91) and then became manager of Chelsea in 1992, before becoming the Premier League's first managerial sacking in 1993. In the same year Porterfield became head coach of Zambia and took the national side to within a goal of qualifying for the 1994 World Cup finals. A series of overseas coaching positions followed, ending in Armenia in 2006. Porterfield died of cancer of the colon in 2007.

Brealey remained in charge of the boardroom as United's on-field fortunes momentarily improved under Porterfield's successor, former youth team coach Billy McEwan, whose appointment was seen by supporters as a money-saving exercise. Outgoings were further reduced as McEwan was told by Brealey to purge Porterfield's ageing former stars to reduce wages. They were replaced by younger players from McEwan's 1986 Northern Intermediate League-winning team, such as Chris Marsden and Clive Mendonca. After showing some promise in McEwan's first season, the youngsters and low-cost signings found the going hard in 1987/88 and a 5-0 home defeat to Oldham in January 1988 provoked McEwan's resignation. McEwan later recalled, '[Brealey] said to me, "It's not working out; [the fans] want you to go. I don't want you to go, but I can't back you." Then he broke down and cried.' Brealey told McEwan that he wanted to sell the club to fellow director Paul Woolhouse, at which point the manager informed the chairman of his resignation. A month earlier Brealey had made public his intention to sell his shareholding. The *Sheffield Star's* front-page headline read: 'BLADES FOR SALE' and Brealey said that although he had personally invested £2.5 million in the club, debts had increased to £3 million. His shares were now available – the only problem was there were no buyers.

Brealey then made the inspirational choice of former Wimbledon and Watford manager Dave Bassett as manager. On Bassett's appointment, managing director Derek Dooley enthused, 'He's more than a breath of fresh air – he's more like a hurricane.' This was true – but it took a while to get blowing. After failing to keep United in the Second Division in his first few months in charge, Bassett offered to resign but was told by Dooley, 'We hired you to do a job for us. I suggest that you go back to your office and get on with it.' Bassett was one of the best managers of his generation. Possessed of infectious enthusiasm and great motivational skills, he oversaw an immediate promotion to Division Two, fuelled by characteristically shrewd signings of unknowns from football's bargain basement, such as strikers Brian Deane for a paltry sum of £30,000 from Doncaster Rovers, Tony Agana on a free transfer from Watford, unheralded Scottish winger Ian Bryson from Kilmarnock and veteran Bob Booker from Brentford, all of whom later went on to play for United in the top division.

United were prominently placed halfway through the following season when Brealey was quoted in monthly magazine *Football Today* as saying; 'Last year could be one of our best financially; things are not as bleak as they seem. We actually owe only £850,000 to the banks. Our problems really came from when Ian Porterfield spent a lot of money on players and got us into the Second Division but we didn't have the team to sustain it.' He also defended his own record at the club. 'Whatever my own future at this club may be, there are one or two things that I would like you always to remember. Firstly that I never brought anyone on the board of this club who was not a Sheffield person. I never once used my voting power to secure any advantage, or majority decision. I never sold one square inch of your Bramall Lane assets. Far from it, we even re-purchased part of Shoreham Street which had been sold many years ago, thus re-establishing the complete island site.' Brealey's comment about appointing Sheffield-based directors was true – in his time as chairman, sports-shop owner Tony Barrington, snooker promoter Mike Watterson, Michael Wragg, a director of Alco Builders' Merchants, metals trader Paul Woolhouse and football icon Derek Dooley - all local-born men - were appointed to the board. All were wealthier than the average working man, but none possessed the means to materially affect the affairs of the club. Watterson's directorship was short-lived and Barrington lasted a couple of years. Wragg, Woolhouse and Dooley would go on to play important roles in the club's future travails.

At the end of the 1980s Brealey had the team to not only sustain the club's position but to push on further, mainly thanks to the motivational brilliance of Bassett. Promotion to the top division, for the first time since 1976, was secured with an emotional 5-2 victory at Leicester in May 1990, backed by an estimated 10,000 Blades followers. The team's chances of promotion had been somewhat dented only a couple of months earlier by the appearance of a mysterious man from the east.

This man a few years later was no longer a man, but would become a man again shortly after.

Chapter 3

Samantha of Arabia
Sam Hashimi

Reg Brealey's shareholding had been on the market for over two years, but attracted no serious offers. Then in early 1990, Brealey found his man – or so it seemed. The club was to make national news over this issue as it concomitantly made national viewing. In a hitherto never before evident open-door policy the club allowed into its decision making a *BBC TV* documentary crew. Titled *United*, the six-part series provided in mid 1990 at times a remarkable insight into the workings of an English football club. The programme makers wished to get a 'fly on the wall' view of a reasonably sized football club outside of the top echelon. They couldn't have wished for better subject matter as United were doing well on the pitch whilst in tumult off it. The camera crews followed the later stages of United's 1989/90 promotion campaign and in doing so revealed so much about how a football club succeeds despite the people trusted to run it. The documentary filmed news of a buyer for Brealey's shares. During a January 23 board meeting Brealey revealed to the other directors; 'I do have a bit of information I must bring forward to the board today. I do have now a decision to make.' He then read out a letter that confirmed an offer for his entire shareholding, inclusive of all the outstanding loans and liabilities. According to Brealey, this offer would wipe out all the club's debts and all the loans of directors. He then added, 'It may well be that the time is right for a change at the helm.'

Director Alan Laver broke the silence that followed, stating, 'I think it wants a lot of serious thought and I would also like to know who the people are.' Brealey responded, 'Now I have to say either get lost or I will present it to the board. The club wants to go in the First Division and David [Bassett] wants a clear run, it all adds up.'

After the board meeting Brealey spoke to the documentary camera alone. He was to partly reveal the identity of the bidder and explained his strategy: 'I don't think you can play about with this, you either knock it on the head and forget about it or pursue it with vigour and I intend to pursue it with vigour. You've got to have a wide horizon, you've got to be able to envisage a wider spectrum of the game of football than just as it has been for the past hundred years, which is purely the local town, the local city, if you want to survive in the big time. It's a foreign involvement from the Middle East. They don't want to step in and organise the club or run the club, they want participation of this club in the Middle East. The ground has got to be improved, we've got to have development. We've got to rebuild John Street, we've got to rebuild the kop. It can't be done unless we have commercial activity with it as well, as the Council have made it clear that they're not going to do anything to help this club as long as I'm chairman. I may as well accept the fact.'

It took another six weeks before more announcements regarding the share sale were made. It was March 5, the day of United's second FA Cup fifth round replay against Barnsley. The draw had already given the winners a home quarter-final tie against Manchester United. With United second in the league entering the season's home straight, it was a momentous time. Promotion to the top division for the first time in 14 years and a massive FA Cup match beckoned. Brealey chose this day to reveal his intentions to the world and in the process stirred up a storm, which had repercussions for the next four years. Brealey opened the press conference he had called on the morning of the Barnsley game, stating, 'We've just completed our board meeting upstairs and subject to one or two items that protect the club, I'm very delighted that they have consented to go along with it and I think that we keep that same cohesion that we've had in the past. I am pleased to welcome a new member - on my left is Sam Hashimi, he is a businessman in this country. He has Middle East connections and from the club's point of view as I see it we have a tremendous opportunity to launch ourselves into the international arena.' This was the first time most people had seen or heard of Hashimi. The more observant, however, had spotted his presence alongside Brealey in the directors' box at the home game against Newcastle United in late February. Regardless, Brealey handed over the floor to the newcomer. With hair as thick as his accented English, and sporting a large moustache and spectacles that almost hid his face, Hashimi hesitantly declared; 'I love to be the chairman of this football club and I have great plans to turn the Bramall Lane into an international arena where we can be very proud to invite overseas visitors and overseas teams. I am delighted for the board support as well and I wish them all success and I wish Mr David Bassett, our manager, continuous success and a new challenge introducing the Middle East angle. I love the football and I love the city.' Hashimi came across as a shy, gentle soul who might just have some good ideas.

The fans seemed in love as well, chanting, 'We're so rich it's unbelievable!' as United won the cup replay. Days later the United manager was photographed with Hashimi on the Bramall Lane pitch, both covered in United apparel. However, the United director Paul Woolhouse was unconvinced by the man from the Middle East. He shared his feelings with the BBC documentary camera; 'If everything is right that Sam's said then I suppose I should feel happy but at the moment, no, I've got a wary feeling. I have a marvellous intuition; my intuition tells me things aren't right. He isn't a Unitedite, he isn't a Sheffield person, he isn't British, and the board are very, very wary of the shareholding going out of the UK.' Woolhouse was a Sheffield-born Unitedite. His intuition would see him leave Sheffield and travel east as quickly as he could a few years later. Perhaps he knew intuitively that a prison cell awaited him. But more about that later.

The day following the announcement, BBC's *Breakfast TV* programme presenter Bob Wilson told Blades fans a bit more by way of Hashimi's biography: 'Sam Hashimi is an Iraqi businessman with the backing, apparently, of four Arab sheikhs and a prince, with high hopes for the future. His plans include redevelopment of their Bramall Lane stadium up to international standards.' Hashimi, captioned as 'Owner, Sheffield United FC', was interviewed, saying, 'I think it's a great club, I really do, because I looked at other English clubs and given the history of Sheffield United and the success they had lately, coming back from the Fourth Division to the Second Division and look like going to the First Division now, I have considered it to be the pick of all the English football clubs.' Brealey was allowed his say, speaking ambitiously of the great commercial avenues for football available in the Middle East. These could be facilitated by live satellite broadcasts from Bramall Lane and sales of videos. The two men told of plans to take five fans from the kop, of all places, to Saudi Arabia on a marketing exercise. Brealey said of Hashimi, 'I like him very much, he likes football, he wants to learn, he's going to link us with the Middle East in a very big way.' Part of Brealey's desire to sell was that he was fully aware that Bramall Lane had to be developed to bring it up to date with modern requirements, an imperative made more urgent following the deaths on overcrowded terraces of 96 Liverpool fans at the Hillsborough stadium, home of Sheffield Wednesday FC, less than a year earlier. But in Brealey's words; 'There is no chance of development at Bramall Lane; not with the present Council. Although they have given outline planning permission for some developments, they are all in the wrong place and have effectively killed off our plans.'

Hashimi and his Middle Eastern contacts seemed too good to be true. To complicate matters, Brealey's own business and personal problems were coming to light. Brealey's jute producing company in India was experiencing employee unrest over pension rights. He was also in the midst of investigations by the Stock Exchange regarding accusations of illegal 'Insider Trading'. This provoked his fellow director Paul Woolhouse to comment, '[Reg has] certainly brought a lot of bad publicity and embarrassment to the club. It may have been better if he had decided to stand aside and appoint somebody else as chairman during these times. I feel sorry for him, he's got problems, but I feel that his problems should not be brought to the club. Reg has made no secret of the fact that he wanted to sell his shareholding. This has been the case in '86, '87, '88. Nothing happened in '89 so it was an odds-on certainty that in 1990 something had to happen. But I think he could have been a lot more faithful to the board by actually putting the package on the table without advising any of this to the press. Then if the board couldn't have competed then by all means he could have opened it to the press and off we go. It's Reg who didn't want to invest in players, he wanted to keep the same side. A defeatist attitude… three or four members of the board wanted to go out and buy two new players for the final push, hopefully [to] the First Division.'

Within 48 hours of the announcement of Hashimi's planned purchase of the club, Else (1982) Ltd, the company that owned the shares on behalf of Brealey, invited Woolhouse to make a counter offer to that of Hashimi. Hashimi meanwhile wished to send in accountants to examine the club's books but was denied access by Woolhouse. He was also denied access to Bramall Lane for the FA Cup tie against Manchester United - which disappointed the waiting television camera crews. Not long after Derek Dooley evicted him from Bramall Lane when he found him taking down measurements on the kop. Things moved fast. Woolhouse was suspicious about Hashimi and his 'four sheikhs and a prince'. A Sunday national newspaper claimed that Hashimi lived with his wife and two children in a modest terraced house in West London and therefore could not conceivably possess the money and contacts he claimed. For his part, Hashimi said he had financial backers who 'like their privacy protected'. Brealey later said that Hashimi's backer was the Mayor of Jeddah, Saudi Arabia, who 'at that time was investing in England in a big way'. Woolhouse and his fellow directors had their suspicions confirmed and Woolhouse issued a statement via *BBC Radio Sheffield,* stating: 'The other directors of Sheffield United Football Club wish to express their great concern relating to the chairman's announcement and a press conference has been called on Monday in respect of the future ownership of the club.'

By this time United had played Manchester United in the FA Cup quarter-final, losing 1-0. Brealey meanwhile was away in India trying to ease his troubles. Manager Dave Bassett was caught in the middle, not knowing whom his boss would be as United entered the closing stages of their promotion race. Exasperated by the lack of information, Bassett held a news conference at which he complained of being 'a pawn in a power game' and of being used just to give Hashimi publicity pictures for his campaign. He now realised he had no money available for transfers. He also suggested (ahead of its time) that ownership of football clubs should be subject to scrutiny by the Football Association and the Football League. Bassett stopped short of endorsing Woolhouse ahead of Brealey or Hashimi but stressed that Woolhouse had during the current season personally provided the cash to buy him two players, Carl Bradshaw and Mike Lake, at a total cost of £160,000. Bassett later wrote in his 1997 autobiography *Harry's Game*: 'Ali Baba had nothing on this pantomime. It was said that Hashimi had offered £6.25 million for control of the club using Middle East funds transferred through Barnacle Holdings, a Jersey-based company. Barnacle Holdings? Shellfish Sureties might have been a better title - get someone to swallow it and the world's your oyster. The photographs that appeared in the national press have been a constant source of embarrassment ever since. I felt a complete mug. I felt that I had been used to give credence to something which had more to do with 1,001 Arabian Nights than 1,001 Arabian Banks.' Richard Caborn, then just a Sheffield MP but later to hold the office of Minister of Sport, supported Bassett's call for a Government review of the ownership of British football clubs. When in power, Caborn put his words into practice by being instrumental, along with the Football Association and the FA Premier League, in the formulation of the 'Fit and Proper Person Test' to vet the potential owners of football clubs. Before he did this Caborn was to sit on the United board at the invite of people whose activities might have tested the very concept he promoted.

It all came to a head towards the end of March. Shortly after Woolhouse had revealed his intention to lodge a rival bid for Brealey's shares to try to keep Hashimi out, an emergency board meeting was called. The press prowled and cameras clicked as the directors arrived at Bramall Lane, in Woolhouse's case in his Rolls Royce. Managing director Derek Dooley told the press that he hoped 'first of all to get the situation cleared about the ownership of the club and really for Mr Brealey to let us know what's happening'. The outcome of the meeting was that Brealey was to withdraw his shareholding from the market; none of the bids from Hashimi, Woolhouse or a third party (named in the Sheffield weekly sports paper the *Green 'Un* as Keith Haslam, son of former United manager Harry, who would later take over Mansfield Town FC) would be pursued. Brealey emerged from the board meeting to make a statement to the gathered press: 'Albeit that the board of directors gave their qualified blessing to the involvement of Mr Hashimi in the club earlier this month, recent publicity now leads them to believe that his involvement would not be in the best interests of Sheffield United and wish all negotiations to cease.' BBC *Look North's* Simon Schofield reported; 'Two main bids were on the table for chairman Reg Brealey's £6 million controlling interest, one from Iraqi-born businessman Sam Hashimi, the other from Paul Woolhouse. If Mr Hashimi had taken control, the club's other five directors would almost certainly have resigned or been sacked.'

Interviewed, Paul Woolhouse explained, 'When Mr Hashimi came on the scene it happened very, very quickly and we didn't know anything about him and after doing some homework the board agreed that certainly he wasn't the man that we thought should be taking over the football club. As a move to keep Hashimi away from the club I decided to put an offer in and that offer was accepted along with Hashimi's and another from a third party as well and that's when Reg decided to calm it all down and take the shares off the market. The board were unhappy about Hashimi coming, Dave Bassett was unhappy about Hashimi coming and certainly if certain members of the board had left probably David might have left and certain players would also have left and so that could have wrecked the whole club at a very important time.' The *Green 'Un* reported days later that Brealey had paid Hashimi damages under the terms of a 'get-out clause'. Hashimi appeared shocked at this development when interviewed by Harry Gration live on BBC's *Look North* regional news programme:

Harry Gration: 'Mr Hashimi, how do you react to today's news?'

Sam Hashimi: 'Well, first of all it's a shock because I didn't know that from Mr Brealey. I just read it in the paper in my arrival to Sheffield this evening. I really think that I like to buy Sheffield United, I like the club, and I'm still going ahead to force Mr Brealey to sell me his shares.'

HG: 'The question is, have you got a watertight agreement? He obviously says it's not watertight, it's merely an understanding.'

SH: 'Well I think it has to be to the lawyers to interpret that but it is a watertight agreement, otherwise I wouldn't be here, we wouldn't have progressed the matter this far unless we had the agreement signed.'

HG: 'So what you're saying is that it's not over as far as you're concerned. You're going to press ahead and presumably that means you've got one or two plans in that respect as well?'

SH: 'My plans is always been simple. I picked Sheffield United as the English club who has the most potential, or one of the clubs who has the most potential, and to market the club and to establish the trade links with the Middle East. Now I had backing from the Middle East from all levels and everybody in the Middle East are so excited for this takeover.'

HG: 'So why have they changed their minds? Has Mr Brealey been forced to change his mind?'

SH: 'Well he's talking about some publicity which is harmful to the club. I agree with him, but that was not any of my doing. I didn't make any publicity or anything, I've been away from the publicity since the day of the announcement.'

HG: 'And yet when you arrived there was a great deal of razzamattaz, champagne corks were popping and so forth. We all thought that you'd bought the club. Clearly that wasn't the case and isn't the case?'

SH: 'Well it is, you know I have indeed exchanged heads of agreements, which has bound Mr Brealey to sell his shares to me.'

HG: 'So what are you going to do now?'

SH: 'I'm going to proceed on my agreement with Mr Brealey and purchase the club.'

You could not make it up. Despite Hashimi's apparent strenuous defence his words turned out to be hot air. He disappeared as quickly as he had arrived and nothing was heard of him again until 1998, by which time United's boardroom had been occupied by numerous chairman, directors and regimes. In the spring of 1998 when United's then chief executive Ian Townsend announced his intention to leave, Hashimi reappeared. Or rather, it was the same individual but it wasn't Sam Hashimi any longer. In the meantime he had undergone hormone treatment and a sex-change operation; Sam Hashimi was now the voluptuous siren known as Samantha Kane. After his failed takeover attempt in 1990 Hashimi's business affairs collapsed and his wife and children left him. Over the next few years he decided he wanted to be a woman. Following hormone injections and surgery she returned to Sheffield in 1998 chasing the vacant chief executive job at Bramall Lane. Pictured in the *Sheffield Star* wearing a short, leopard-skin dress, in the accompanying interview Samantha stated how much good she could do for the Blades: 'Football is becoming attractive to women and I'm ideally placed to capitalise on this. I just don't think my sex is an issue.' Others, however, did. Ms Kane was granted an audience by the United directors but probably had little chance of being given the role. She told the directors of her plans to invest half a million of her own money and several million from Middle-East businessmen to build a leisure complex and set up an Arabic-speaking satellite channel dedicated to

Sheffield United. She told of her footballing pedigree, 'I used to play [football]. And when I lived in Baghdad, my parents always insisted on football. I was captain of the college team. I was a forward - I have lovely long legs, so I ran fast. My parents encouraged me because they were trying to make a man of me. However, they didn't succeed.' Then, just to confuse matters further, she blamed the 1990/91 Gulf War for her failure - when Sam Hashimi - to take over Sheffield United.

Ms Kane was - according to her own publicity - a successful interior designer who enjoyed mixing with the jet set, with whom she sipped champagne in the best hotels and bars in Cannes and Monte Carlo. In 1998 she released an autobiography, *A Two-Tiered Existence,* in which she described why, as a Muslim father of two, university-educated engineer and close friend of the Saudi royal family, all those privileges were left behind to become a Kensington-based party girl. The issue was gender problems experienced in childhood years in a life that was never straightforward. Teenage crushes on boys led to attending gay and transvestite clubs, and what was a wild phase of experimentation. Admitting to 'fluid sexuality', transsexuals had told him how fantastic it was to be a woman. The sex was great, apparently, and they were happy. Admitting he was not really transsexual, he explained: 'A true transsexual is someone who is so determined to be a woman that they don't care if they look like an 18-stone trucker in drag'. The pursuit of being the 'perfect woman' was a fantasy.

He came through this phase and married, having two children. He arrived in Britain in the late 1970s, built up a property empire of wealth and then went broke because of a series of bad investments during the early 1990s recession. His marriage ended in acrimonious fashion in 1995 when he found himself in prison for breaching an injunction preventing him from approaching his ex-wife Trudi's home. He also failed in a bid to obtain custody of his children. He then suffered a breakdown and was in a mental hospital, unable to work, having slid from affluence to impecuniousness. Admitting to sexual confusion, he was then diagnosed as suffering from gender dysphoria and given female hormones. Trusting doctors, he accepted the diagnosis without question and underwent sex-change surgery. He became Samantha Kane, and was now confident enough to approach Sheffield United about the post of chief executive. However, just like eight years earlier, Ms Kane's plans for United were never realised and she disappeared – only to reappear as a different person.

The character that was Hashimi/Kane could only be out of the headlines for so long. Early in 2004 he (yes, he) made the news again. By this juncture he had come to the conclusion that the sex change had been a mistake. The catalyst for her decision to revert was a broken engagement to a wealthy man aware of the sex change. Wanting to be a man again he had undergone reconstructive surgery in an attempt to reproduce that which he had lost. Furthermore, he was now living by the name of Charles Kane and was suing consultant psychiatrist Russell Reid, the UK's best-known transsexualism specialist. Holding the title of 'expert' in gender identity disorder (GID), Reid had referred Kane (then Hashimi) for gender reassignment surgery when he had lived as a woman for just a month, apparently in breach of international standards of care. A sex change was performed just four months later.

The General Medical Council (GMC) investigated Dr Reid's conduct. The case was initiated by three senior consultant psychiatrists, Donald Montgomery, Richard Green and James Barratt, from the NHS Charing Cross Gender Identity Clinic in West London. They submitted the cases of 12 of Dr Reid's patients, including Hashimi/Kane, to the GMC for examination, claiming that some of his clients regretted changing sex. The Charing Cross psychiatrists alleged that Dr Reid repeatedly breached internationally recognised guidelines laying down 'flexible directions' for the treatment of people with GID. They also claimed that Reid had not adhered to the guidelines' minimum eligibility requirements for the prescription of hormones and referrals for genital surgery. Reid, a member of the Royal College of Psychiatrists' Gender Identity Working Party, had the support of other experts in the field and more than 150 patients. The international guidance stated that patients should have been living in their desired gender role for at least three months before being prescribed hormones, or have had at least three months of psychotherapy. Patients should also have had at least 12 months of hormone therapy and have lived as their desired gender for the same period before referral for surgery.

In May 2007 the GMC found Reid guilty of serious professional misconduct for rushing five patients into sex-change treatments (Charles Kane was not one of them) but he was not struck off: there was apparently 'insufficient cogent and credible *prima facie* evidence' to suspend him or impose restrictions on his practice. The GMC ruled that he could continue to work but only under strict supervision for the next year. Reid was admonished for his 'lack of caution in initiating hormonal and surgical gender reassessment treatment in patients without more careful and thorough investigation and assessment'. He was instructed to provide the GMC with three-monthly records of his treatments of any patients with gender identity disorders. On hearing of this outcome Kane said, 'I am happy with the verdict because with these conditions he cannot really treat anybody else the way he treated me. I really believe that Dr Reid and the general public should view gender reassignment and sex change very seriously and this is a warning to doctors and patients not to rush into it. I think generally he is a kind-hearted doctor and he didn't really mean to be malicious. He is a caring, almost father-figure.'

Kane was the subject of an autumn 2004 BBC TV documentary titled *One Life: Make Me a Man Again*. During this broadcast he was filmed outside Bramall Lane blaming his failed 1990 ownership bid on his subsequent mental breakdown and sex change. The Gulf War was not mentioned. The holder of what was described as a law degree and the owner of a £2 million property in Holland Park, West London, Kane was apparently a 'wealthy property tycoon'. He, however, was not happy with his lot. He told the viewers that what he really desired was a lasting relationship but every date he went on was short-lived as women would tell him they wanted 'a real man'. Such rejection hurt Kane, who remonstrated, 'I am a real man. I feel 100 per cent a man, but

I am a sensitive, modern man. People can be so narrow-minded. All I want is to be accepted and loved for who I am.' His still-feminine nose, smooth skin and lack of stubble suggested he was not quite the man he wished to be. Kane described, from first-hand knowledge, the differences between being a man and a woman. 'At first it was very enjoyable being a woman, especially being a beautiful woman in business. People notice you and it is much easier to make your presence felt at a meeting. I was flattered by the attention. I became much more creative as a person, and less aggressive. People completely underestimate the effect of male and female hormones. They affect every part of your life, physically and emotionally. And then there is the sex. As a man, sex was a very physical and more enjoyable experience, but as a woman it was much more dependent on my mood and emotions. As a man, I thought about sex every day, but as a woman if I hadn't had sex for a couple of months I wasn't really bothered. Sex as a woman isn't as good anyway. It is not as intense.' Having undergone surgery to reconstruct his penis using tissue from his stomach, he described in graphic detail the mechanics of his subsequent air-pump-generated erections. Having difficulty in getting things to stand up, he was also experiencing trouble getting hold of the ownership documents for a yacht he had bought in Newcastle Marina. Sam did have an inordinate amount of trouble obtaining ownership documents.

But just who was Sam Hashimi? What was his 'real' business? And how did Reg Brealey come across him? Hashimi really was a mystery man, then woman, then man again. Other than being a 'businessman who made his money in property', the details of Hashimi's business dealings and connections remain sketchy. It was known that he studied engineering after he left school. He got a job heading the investment arm of a Saudi-owned company and, it was reported, made millions. But nothing more reached the public domain. Perhaps Paul Woolhouse's investigations discovered that there was nothing of any substance and that the 'four sheikhs and a prince' were myths. But if this was the case surely Brealey wasn't gullible enough to have been taken in. He may have been naïve when it came to football, but in the world of business Brealey was no fool. Brealey was either conned by Hashimi, which is hard to believe, or he was part of the con. The only conceivable reasons why Brealey should be party to a deliberately misleading and false takeover bid was that he wanted to use Hashimi's supposed offer to: (1) find out once and for all who were his friends and who were his enemies on the United board and (2) entice a counter-offer from someone else for his shareholding, as it was common knowledge that he wanted out. Interviewed in 1999 Brealey gave a clue as to the scenario when he explained; 'He [Woolhouse] was talking about "no way we are having the club owned by an Arab". But I knew nothing would come of the Hashimi offer. Then it was up to Paul to make his offer.' Brealey's objectives succeeded. When it came to the crunch he discovered that the other directors were against him and he forced Woolhouse into a making a bid. But where and how did Brealey and Hashimi meet and plot this cunning plan? That is a mystery that remains unresolved, one on which Brealey shed little light - and was positively evasive - when probed on this issue by Gary Armstrong in 1999. He said, '[Hashimi] just appeared via my broker and said he wanted to buy a big club.' Another possible reason to explain the farce was that it was deliberately contrived by Brealey to liven up the BBC documentary series, which Brealey denied. 'I can assure you there was no acting,' he later said.

Whatever the motives of Brealey and Hashimi, it was both annoying and sad to see a football club used as the plaything of rich men claiming to want the best for the club but more motivated by personal gain and status. They possibly dreamt of rubbing shoulders with minor royals at Wembley or of development opportunities that could fill their own pockets but the uncertainty they created most keenly affected the manager and, beyond him, showed contempt for the fans. Hashimi had said he had chosen United as a club of great commercial potential in the Middle East (and indubitably for the development potential available at Bramall Lane). He barely mentioned Sheffield United as a football club. The ineluctable conclusion is that had Hashimi taken over, United were to be used for other, wider purposes.

Chapter 4

The Fugitive
Paul Woolhouse

Under pressure from the other directors, Reg Brealey agreed to take his Sheffield United shares off the market rather than sell to Sam Hashimi. He was, however, still looking to dispose of his shareholding. Several months after the Hashimi affair, Paul Woolhouse, on Brealey's invitation, negotiated a deal with Brealey to buy him out. Woolhouse was to explain, 'I received a phone call informing me that the trustees of Else (1982) Ltd [the company that owned the shares on behalf of Brealey] would be selling their shareholding unless I could come up with a better offer within seven days.' After lengthy negotiations Woolhouse acquired the controlling interest in the club. What he did not realise was the full extent of the problems he was inheriting: the club was saddled with long-term debt and urgently needed to improve stadium facilities following the 1990 Taylor Report into the Hillsborough Disaster. Woolhouse, born in Sheffield in 1949 and a former pupil of King Ecgbert School in Sheffield's affluent West End, was a metals trader who started life as a scrap metal merchant but developed his business into selling specialist metals for industry and technology. He paid himself a salary of £242,000 in 1989 – a very impressive wage for Sheffield. He lived with his wife Margaret and son Giles in an extensive property with stables and grazing land in the Mayfield Valley on the edge of the Peak District National Park. In 1986 he purchased £105,000-worth of United shares, a 12.5 per cent holding, thereby buying himself a place on United's board. Despite this he remained in the background as the Blades recovered from their mid 1980s slump to challenge for promotion to the First Division under the guidance of Dave Bassett, Reg Brealey and Derek Dooley.

Woolhouse came to prominence during the Hashimi affair and from then on he remained in the limelight, which he seemed to enjoy. Shortly after his purchase of Brealey's shares Woolhouse claimed he had preserved the very existence of Sheffield United Football Club by saving Bramall Lane from the property developers that would inevitably have followed the mysterious Arab. He argued, 'If I had not been successful then I have no doubt that Bramall Lane would have ceased to be a football ground and become a development site. The club would probably be playing its matches at somewhere like the Don Valley Stadium and what would have happened to the club and the team just doesn't bear thinking about.'

At this point Woolhouse owned 75 per cent of the club's shares and despite continued stories of United's financial troubles he argued otherwise: 'We definitely have the lowest bank borrowings of any club in the First Division. If we were under so much pressure we would have accepted an offer of £2.5 million for [top scorer] Brian Deane recently and solved all our problems at a stroke, leaving us with money in the bank. What we do have are long-term debts of around £2 million in the form of loans, which have to be serviced and eventually repaid. My aim is to provide United with a strong financial base but this will obviously take time. Unfortunately there isn't a queue of people wanting to plough money into football and it would be pointless appointing someone to the board who was not prepared to invest a seven-figure sum.'

The deal to buy Brealey's shares was concluded in December 1990. However, Woolhouse's elevation into the chair had to be ratified by the shareholders at the Annual General Meeting at the end of the month. Shortly before contracts were signed, Brealey wistfully looked back on his decade in charge: 'Sheffield United has certainly changed my life. I entered as just A.N.Other, a member of the board simply to do a job, i.e.

finance director. No loyalty or love, simply a cold, clean, clinical job – but I ended up falling in love like the rest of you – which became the most expensive love-life man can imagine.'

Brealey knew that his personal circumstances would prevent him from devoting all his time and efforts to Sheffield United and was glad to have agreed the sale of his United shares. He said of his problems; 'I was warned ten years ago that I had bitten off more than I could chew [when I became chairman of Sheffield United] but that has turned out to be minimal in relation to what I have bitten off by becoming chairman of the Titaghur jute company in Calcutta [now Kolkata].' Money brought him love; lack of money brought him heartache. Brealey needed money to fund a legal defence as he was facing charges, brought by the Stock Exchange and the Crown Prosecution Service, of 'Insider Dealing' in the shares of Titaghur. The charges were subsequently dropped when the trial judge described the case against Brealey as 'lamentable' and criticised the prosecution's 'appalling catalogue of omissions'. However, Titaghur was de-listed from the stock market in December 1990 when the Stock Exchange decided that the company's heavily qualified accounts provided insufficient financial information. On top of these difficulties, employees of Titaghur were angry at what they alleged was Brealey's use of their pension fund monies to keep the company afloat.

At United's 1990 AGM Brealey duly resigned the chair (unusually, by means of a fax read out by stand-in chairman Alan Laver - Brealey was in India) and Woolhouse officially took over as both chairman and majority owner. It was reported that he had agreed to pay £2,750,000 to Else (1982) Ltd for control of Brealey's shares, via scheduled payments. The figure was well below the price of £6.25 million that Sam Hashimi was said to have agreed nine months previously. Was Brealey so desperate to sell? Or perhaps the debt of £3 million, which was reported in the company accounts at the AGM, influenced the price paid by Woolhouse. Asked if there was any money available for the manager (United had just won their first game of the season after 16 unsuccessful attempts and were stranded at the bottom of the First Division), Woolhouse gave a rather ludicrous response, stating; 'If we need a player for survival, who knows?' Woolhouse's first months in charge went better than even the most optimistic Blades fan could have hoped. In remarkable fashion United escaped the bottom position they had occupied when the new chairman took over. Thanks to an astonishing series of victories in February and March United retained their Division One status with much to spare. United defeated Derby County, Southampton, Everton, Manchester United, Aston Villa, Sunderland and Chelsea in consecutive matches. Everything seemed to be running smoothly in the boardroom, with no arguments or disputes making headlines.

This was to change early in the 1991/92 season. Dave Bassett had signed for £650,000 notorious self-proclaimed 'footballing hard-man' Vinnie Jones from Leeds United early in the previous season to provide on-pitch leadership. Justifying the purchase Bassett said of Jones' reputation; 'When you're building a team you're looking for good players, not blokes to marry your daughter'. Having kept United up, Bassett decided a year later that Jones's job was done and sold him to Chelsea for £575,000 but he needed another player of similar qualities to take his place. After Vinnieless United lost to two late goals at Crystal Palace on the last day of August, Bassett, thinking he had over half a million burning a hole in his pocket, said he was looking at 'two or three positions'. Asked when he'd be able to spend the money, Bassett added somewhat ominously, 'As soon as we get it in the bank....'

As luck would have it, Jones was back at the Lane with Chelsea the following Tuesday and was taunted by Blades chants of 'What a waste of money!' but had the last laugh as his new club won 1-0. United now had just two points from the first six matches of the season and the following night's *Sheffield Star* claimed that the Blades were on the brink of breaking their transfer record to sign centre half Brian Gayle from Second Division Ipswich Town. Bassett knew Gayle well from their time together at Wimbledon in the mid 1980s. Gayle's signing was officially announced by United and the new man commented; 'Once I knew Dave Bassett was in for me it didn't take long to make up my mind. Bassett was a big influence on my decision. He signed me as an apprentice at Wimbledon and we were together for six or seven years. He has the ability to get the best out of players and make them believe they can achieve things they never thought they could.' Bassett, by way of response, said, 'I have felt that central defence was a priority position for us for some time. I asked about Brian in June but when [Ipswich manager] John Lyall told me he wanted £700,000 I told him to forget it. But he has stuck to the price and now the sale of Vinnie has given us a bit of money to play with and I have signed a very good centre half.'

Despite Gayle's appearance in front of the press, the first signs that things were not quite right came prior to the game at Oldham the following Saturday. When the team line-ups were read out Gayle's name was not included. United reporter Tony Pritchett's *Green 'Un* report stated that his absence was because of 'a hitch in the registration of his move at League headquarters'. Pritchett followed this up on Monday by writing in the *Sheffield Star*; 'I understand that United missed the 5pm Thursday deadline by a matter of minutes but that the Gayle move will be finalised today.' However, it wasn't finalised and no explanation was given. Embarrassingly, the programme for the following Saturday's game against Everton featured Gayle on the front cover in typical new-signing pose, holding up a Blades scarf. But he still wasn't cleared to play and Brian Deane's unexpected absence from the team further stirred up the angry crowd. Unbeknown to anyone, Deane was suffering from the first symptoms of glandular fever but rumours abounded that he wasn't playing because he had been sold. A story went round the ground that Bassett was going to resign after the game. Chants of 'Where's the money gone?' and 'Sack the board!' reverberated around the Lane but the team responded brilliantly in adversity, gaining their first win of the season.

Days later the board of directors released a mysterious statement that posed more questions than it answered: 'In anticipation of funds being available the board sanctioned the purchase of Brian Gayle. The board regrets those funds are now unavailable and have taken urgent action to ensure alternative funds are obtained.' The Football League confirmed that it was not satisfied that the transaction had been properly completed and that the required 50 per cent deposit had not been lodged. It later emerged that United hoped to use the money from the Jones sale to go towards the purchase of Gayle but instead it had been seized by the club's bank to defray debts.

Bassett bit his tongue and restricted himself to saying, in public anyway; 'Obviously I'm disappointed and disappointed for the player. We wanted him today. We still want him and hopefully he will be available on Tuesday.' He admitted that the week had been 'difficult' and he was even summoned by South Yorkshire police to quell fan unrest manifest in a car-park demonstration after the Everton match. Bassett used a police loud-hailer to declare to the 200 or so protestors; 'I'm staying here. Deano's going nowhere.' Having pacified the crowd he proceeded to enthuse about his hoped-for signing; 'Through all of this Gayle has been tremendous. I have known him since he was 14. Now he is a man, a real man. He understands the situation is out of his hands and mine. He has behaved very well.' Of the car park demonstration he told reporters; 'The fans get involved because this is their club. They don't always know the facts and sometimes they can't be told all the facts. But hopefully we shall resolve the situation and get Brian Gayle playing. I do not think there is any doubt that Gayle is our player. If you sign the papers and exchange you have got to find the money. It will cost us a lot of money plus interest but it has to be done.'

Finally, on Tuesday September 17, almost two weeks after his signing was first announced, funds were found and Gayle's transfer formalities were completed. Not surprisingly, given the traumas Gayle had gone through and his lack of match practice, he looked uncomfortable on his debut at home to Notts County as United were beaten 3-1. He admitted afterwards, 'I know I can be sharper and have to do some more work. What is disappointing is that we have lost to a team which will not be the best side we shall play this season.' Bassett's confidence in what Gayle would bring to the team was not immediately apparent as United continued to stumble but it all came together one November Sunday morning when high-flying Sheffield Wednesday visited Bramall Lane to play the lowly Blades and were sent packing 2-0. Gayle's influence increased by the game and he proved to be exactly what Bassett wanted - a leader on the pitch - and United improved to the extent that they rose to a ninth-place finish.

It was another few years before the truth came out about what happened with Gayle's transfer. Bassett's autobiography *Harry's Game* recounted how a fee of £700,000 was agreed, which was a record for Sheffield United, and Gayle signed a contract. But Ipswich revealed that they had not actually received the money and were therefore legally within their rights to recall the player. To help clinch the transfer Bassett personally loaned the club £100,000. Bassett was on record as stating that he liked Paul Woolhouse because 'he had taken the club on for the right reasons' but this was one of many situations during Bassett's time at Bramall Lane that the manager's efforts were frustrated by boardroom disarray.

Only two months after the Gayle fiasco, Paul Woolhouse appeared to have forgotten about it and claimed he had virtually wiped out United's debts despite further rumours about a financial crisis at Bramall Lane. The dissent amongst the supporters that had been triggered by the delayed Gayle transfer escalated at that year's Annual General Meeting when it came to light that Woolhouse's shareholding was lodged in the British Virgin Islands and questions were asked about his motives and future plans. Woolhouse answered equivocally, stating that the shares were held offshore because that was what suited him personally. He told shareholders that the club's borrowing had been reduced, extra funds had been put into the club, its borrowing rate was one of the lowest in the Football League and the financial base was becoming stronger. Then in February 1992 it emerged that there were problems regarding the very ownership of the club. Else (1982) Ltd, the company fronted by Reg Brealey's brother Len and registered in Gibraltar, started proceedings against Parkland Holdings, the British Virgin Islands-based company owned by Woolhouse that held his shares, alleging breach of contract over the purchase of 2,096 shares in Sheffield United Football Club. Len Brealey, like his brother, was a self-made man. He began his working life as a farmhand but was to make his money in property. His hobbies were opera, horse racing, cricket and, in his words, 'keeping Reg out of trouble'. Woolhouse came out fighting, saying he was to take on a 'bigger role' at the club, adding, 'I have never had any intention of leaving United – I have a job to do.'

Any potential heat from supporters was taken off Woolhouse by United's strong finish to the season, including a league double over Sheffield Wednesday, and the publicity surrounding the inauguration of the Premier League, which commenced operation in August 1992. United were founder members of the new league and scored its first goal, a header by Brian Deane in the 2-1 win over Manchester United on August 15, 1992. Despite this fine result, United had their now customary difficult first half of the season, but attention turned to boardroom affairs once more when in October 1992 the *Sheffield Star* announced; 'BLADES FOR SALE - Woolhouse may go in shares riddle.' Len Brealey was quoted as saying, 'The plain facts are that Mr Woolhouse failed to meet payments in an original contract so we set up a new agreement. Again he has not honoured his pledges. A deadline of the close of banking hours on September 30 was set and we spoke to his legal advisor last Thursday about the situation. But the deadline has come and gone and we now have no alternative but to reclaim the shares and place them back on the market. If my brother Reg, the former chairman of the club, wishes to buy them then he must come up with the money but there are a number of interested parties, individuals and consortiums who have expressed a desire to take over the club. In the meantime we cannot have a vacuum at Bramall Lane so, on behalf of the holding company, I have today invited Derek Dooley to return as chairman as a temporary measure. He is the one man who commands enough respect to hold things together at this time.'

Matters got worse for Woolhouse and very embarrassing for the club. Parkland Holdings was due to pay Else (1982) Ltd £860,000 by September 30. This sum was not paid by the deadline so a clause in the contract kicked in: on payment of £875,000 from Else to Parkland the shares would revert to Else and Woolhouse would resign as chairman. It got worse for Woolhouse with the news that four companies (one of which was formerly owned by him) were to take out a High Court injunction to freeze his assets.   In mid October Woolhouse was served with a second injunction to freeze his assets by Belgian firm Almetal Holding NV, which by now owned his former company Wolmet.   Almetal directors claimed Woolhouse had used their company's money to pay for his share purchase.   Former Blades director and current shareholder Tony Barrington went public, demanding 'some answers' from Woolhouse.   Across the city Wednesdayites were enjoying their team's success – they were towards the top of the league, won the 1991 League Cup and played in European competition.   It didn't help the fans' sense of embarrassment or Woolhouse's position when United were placed under a Football League transfer embargo for the first time in the club's history for failing to pay £25,000 still owed to Leeds United for the Vinnie Jones transfer.

On October 16 Woolhouse finally acquiesced to the pressure of his business affairs by stepping down as United's chairman. The following day Else (1982) Ltd served a writ on Woolhouse in the Elland Road car park before United's game against Leeds. It wanted to know why Woolhouse had not resigned from the board in defiance of a deed of agreement dated August 29, 1992 that required him to step down if he did not pay the remaining £860,000 owed to Else. The issue of the share ownership was scheduled to be heard in the High Court in London in December but the hearing was adjourned until January 18, when it was revealed that Woolhouse had paid £1.5m of the £2.75m price that had originally been agreed. A Guernsey-based millionaire named Ray Brehaut was reported to be interested in taking the shares off Woolhouse's hands. Len Brealey stated, however, he had 'no chance'. Brealey wanted to have his day in court. In the meantime Woolhouse carried on as if nothing was amiss. Continuing in his role as chief executive he announced that United were planning to rebuild the John Street side of the ground to comply with the requirements of the Taylor Report.

On February 15, 1993, the day after the Blades had beaten Manchester United in the FA Cup fifth round, a High Court judge began his deliberations as to who would end up in control of Sheffield United. The hearing was held at the Royal Courts of Justice in the Strand. Charles Falconer QC, barrister for Else (1982) Ltd (later to become a member of Tony Blair's Cabinet as Lord Chancellor and Secretary of State for Justice), told the court that if payments fell more than £300,000 in arrears Else had the right to stop the sale of the shares by repaying to Parkland half the instalments already paid. Between January 1991 and July 1992 there was what the prosecuting QC termed a 'persistent history of default' by Parkland. On August 29, 1992 Woolhouse signed a second agreement to pay £860,000 by September 30 in a 'full and final settlement'; this was never paid. It was also detailed in court that Parkland Holdings Ltd was based in Tortola, British Virgin Islands, apparently because lodging the shares 'offshore' would prevent Woolhouse's ex-wife Margaret's lawyers from freezing them during their somewhat acrimonious divorce settlement.

The £300,000 default figure was reached in August 1992. Close to the date fellow United director Stephen Hinchliffe tried to negotiate a compromise with Len Brealey but to no avail – he had run out of patience. The judge, Justice Kay, reached a final decision in early March, when the *Sheffield Star's* front-page headline read; 'LIES DISGRACE OF BLADES CHIEF: New board in waiting after Woolhouse loses shares battle.' The report told of Justice Kay's ruling, which read: 'I am satisfied that he [Woolhouse] ventured over the bounds of over-optimism and was at times positively dishonest. Even in evidence Woolhouse had misrepresented the position. Woolhouse tried to smear Reg Brealey with allegations he was a homosexual to sow seeds of doubt in Len Brealey's mind about bad publicity for the family.' He added that Woolhouse had not anticipated the economic difficulties that lay ahead when he agreed to take over the club. Woolhouse was reported to have a personal debt of £646,000. The recession of the early 1990s, which lasted longer than any economic downturn since the 1930s, badly affected the cash-flow situation of Woolhouse's companies. His company

Wolmet Ltd lost orders from British Steel when the scrap metal market slumped. The judge said, 'An attitude of living for today is reflected throughout his dealings...... he simply couldn't be trusted.' Outside court Len Brealey remarked that as the judge had branded Woolhouse a liar, he should do the honourable thing and resign, along with Michael Wragg and Stephen Hinchliffe. This way Brealey believed a new board, new money and new players would see the club at Wembley in the FA Cup and off the bottom of the Premier League. According to Brealey, people were waiting to invest in the club but first needed to know its true financial position.

Woolhouse, who had been granted a 'stay of execution' by the judge to consider an appeal, said only: 'I am appealing against the judgement and will carry on business as normal. I shall definitely be at the match tonight.' That night United thrashed Spurs 6-0. Director Michael Wragg, whom Len Brealey wanted to resign, said, 'I am considering my position and will make it in the best interests of the club. But I do not see how wholesale changes at this stage is the way to see Sheffield United prosper.' Reg Brealey, married with children, was reported to be 'dismayed, distressed and anguished' at the homosexual smear, adding that he had accepted the offer of £2.75m from Woolhouse despite getting a better offer of £6.25m from a company called Albany Development and Construction because he thought the former was the best for the club. A few days later the *Sheffield Star* announced, 'It's One Out, All Out', claiming that Stephen Hinchliffe would leave the United board 'in a few days'. In a further twist, director Alan Laver was now demanding repayment of his £750,000 loan and would resign if a meeting were called to oust the other directors. Woolhouse remained silent but Hinchliffe issued a statement saying that he personally put in money for the Brian Gayle transfer, adding: 'United is not in a strong financial position and does not have access to the wealth which other Premier League clubs benefit from.' This contradicted what he had said when he joined the board but was backed up by persistent stories of unpaid bills, transfer bans, a winding-up order and late payment of staff and player wages. The club even cancelled the delivery of newspapers to the ground to save £3 per week. The company accounts published (late) in May 1993 showed a loss for the year of £128,394.

The vanquished Woolhouse, still clinging on to his chief executive role, kept out of the public eye for the next few weeks. But United's progression to the all-Sheffield FA Cup semi-final in April presented him with an opportunity to raise his head above the parapet. The two semi-final ties would be local derbies – Sheffield United v Sheffield Wednesday and Arsenal v Tottenham Hotspur. The London tie was immediately scheduled for Wembley Stadium. The much smaller capacity Elland Road, Leeds, was selected for the Sheffield game. Officials and fans of the two clubs joined forces in a bid to have the match moved to Wembley. Their arguments were threefold:

1) Tickets would be much harder to come by if the game was played in Leeds, as it had a capacity of only around 35,000 compared to Wembley's 80,000.
2) The winners of the Arsenal/Tottenham game would have an advantage over whichever Sheffield team got through as they would have already experienced the atmosphere of Wembley.
3) The pitch at Leeds was in poor condition as the ground was shared with Bramley Rugby League Club.

The downside, as the Football Association's chief executive Graham Kelly emphasised, was the problem of transporting 80,000 people from Sheffield to London on the same day. However, Blades and Owls fans were prepared to overcome any logistical difficulties for the chance to have a 'day out' at Wembley. Eventually the Football Association relented and fixed the tie for Wembley on Saturday April 3, a day prior to the Arsenal/Tottenham fixture.

Woolhouse and Wednesday chairman Dave Richards were interviewed live on the BBC's *Look North* regional evening news programme, giving their views on the decision. Even Len Brealey, still in the midst of the battle to eject Woolhouse from the club, issued some conciliatory remarks, saying, 'Get your money on [United] being in the final and so long as the team is playing I don't care who is representing the club at director level on that day.' It was Woolhouse who represented the club at the semi-final but Len Brealey would have lost his money as Wednesday won 2-1 after extra time to reach their second cup final of the season.

In early May 1993 attention now returned to Woolhouse's appeal to the High Court. It predictably failed. The failure was followed by an Extraordinary General Meeting, held on May 21 at the Moat House Hotel in Sheffield, called by Else (1982) Ltd with two resolutions: for the removal of Woolhouse and Michael Wragg as directors and the appointment to the board of Bernard Procter, a North-East Derbyshire businessman who owned a car dealership, Kevin McCabe, a Sheffield-born, Scarborough-based property developer, Derek Dooley and Len Brealey. Woolhouse was finally supplanted. Newly appointed director Dooley was re-installed in his old office that had been taken over by Woolhouse. Upon his return Dooley described, with understated distaste, discovering chintzy drapes, black uplifters, neo-Georgian pink and cream stripes and a huge marble fireplace. Woolhouse had spent considerable amounts of the club's monies on soft furnishings, albeit in the club colours.

Company accounts published in December 1993 contained a detail about a 'service contract' between Woolhouse and the club dated March 19, 1993. A claim, plus expenses, with no figure mentioned, had been made by Woolhouse for damages for alleged breach of this contract. United refuted it. A second claim had been made in the name of Woolhouse's former company Wolmet in respect of an alleged loan of £150,000 to the club. United were disputing this too. Stephen Hinchliffe's name was mentioned regarding the ownership of a plot of land on Shoreham Street. The plot was now owned by Propland Investment Ltd, a company once owned by Woolhouse but now controlled by Hinchliffe on behalf of one of his companies, Chase Montague Ltd. Hinchliffe informed the club that his company had acquired an option to purchase the leasehold but United maintained that the club had rights over this land. Who actually owned the plot was obviously contentious; more pertinently if it had passed outside the control of the club, how had that happened?

Three months later, in March 1994, Woolhouse disappeared from his Mayfield Chase home in the midst of a police investigation into his business affairs. His solicitor was taken into custody 'helping the police with their inquiries' and was subsequently released, but the whereabouts of Woolhouse was unknown. Owning a Bentley and a Range Rover and paid a salary reported to be £100,000 per annum, commensurate with the role of a chief executive of a Premier League club, Woolhouse had a lot to lose by disappearing. Meanwhile, the club's cash-flow problems were problematical - a hotel sued the club for an unpaid bill of £1,400, a coach company refused to carry the team to an away game because of money owed, then £6,400 ticket money, in cash, went missing from Woolhouse's office. Woolhouse had told the Official Receiver's office that he was going abroad. Furniture had been removed from his house, in his words, for 'security reasons'. A week after his disappearance Woolhouse contacted the *Sheffield Star* by letter. 'I Am Innocent,' proclaimed the newspaper's front-page headline, followed by the sub-heading; 'Missing tycoon breaks his silence over "trip".' Woolhouse had broken cover to deny that the reported £1 million owed to creditors was the reason he vanished. He was on 'an overseas trip' planned weeks earlier. The letter gave no clue of his location and was franked with an advertisement for a cross-channel ferry service. As for the missing ticket monies Woolhouse said somebody must have stolen it when he left it there overnight.

A warrant was then issued by South Yorkshire police for his 'arrest on sight'. Woolhouse made allegations in the letter to the Sheffield Star against three men in the Sheffield business community whom he claimed wanted 'to destroy any proposal that I have put forward to fulfill my alleged debts'. These men may have been Richard Ibbotson, Michael Beahan and Kevin Jones, all formerly directors of Woolhouse's Propland group of companies. On March 17, 1994 the Sheffield Star reported that Woolhouse had been traced to Miami but quoted Detective Chief Inspector Alan Timms, head of South

Yorkshire's Fraud Squad, as saying that he suspected Woolhouse was no longer there. Woolhouse had been declared bankrupt in December 1993 and a Department of Trade spokesman commented, 'People who are bankrupt can go abroad but they must fulfill their obligations and attend meetings with the Official Receiver.' This was not going to happen.

The trail of the fugitive went cold as Woolhouse simply vanished. Just over two years later, in June 1996, the *Sheffield Star* front-page splash told: 'We Find Blades Tycoon - Exclusive: Fugitive Businessman Finds a New Life and New Love Down Under.' Journalist Mark Hanna reported in his 'Special Investigation' that he had unearthed the ex-Sheffield United chairman in a bungalow in Queensland, Australia, where he denied accusations of 'multi-million pound swindles' but said that he would not return to Britain 'to face the music'. The apparently bankrupt Woolhouse had given investigators the slip by flying around the world before settling, for the time being at least, in Brisbane. The *Sheffield Star* reported they were 'surprise visitors at his hideaway' where he was living with a woman friend, by the name of Eli Blondiau. Woolhouse greeted the pressmen wearing a white bathrobe. The newspaper told police of his whereabouts but international red tape slowed down their pursuit of him. Seemingly unperturbed, Woolhouse told his inquisitors, 'I'm not worried about police - I've done nothing wrong. I can sleep at night. I have nothing on my conscience. All I want to do is make a fresh start. If it was not for the football aspect, all this would not have been blown out of all proportion.'

Woolhouse's stated reasons for leaving Sheffield were rather mundane – if not quite believable. He told the *Sheffield Star* the reason he left Britain was because he had not had a holiday for over two years and so visited friends in Europe, the USA and Canada. These friends had paid for his air tickets, hotel accommodation and other expenses. He had then earned money as a consultant for a Brisbane engineering company. He continued, 'All I have are my clothes, pictures of my son and a few personal belongings. I have not got any sum of money hidden away. The only thing I have got left is a good brain. I have got to put that to good use now. If I had a nest-egg hidden away I would not be here now. I would definitely be somewhere more exciting than Brisbane.' The Inala area of Brisbane in which he now lived was not a salubrious district and the house he rented was small, with a broken window and walls bearing graffiti. On hearing of Woolhouse's new life, Detective Chief Inspector Timms said, 'We are obviously keen to be able to speak to Mr Woolhouse at the earliest opportunity.' They never did. Meanwhile, back in the UK, Ibbotson, Beahan and Jones appeared in Sheffield Magistrates Court accused of conspiring with Woolhouse to defraud creditors between 1990 and 1993. Ibbotson was also charged with dishonestly obtaining £6.5 million from Propland's Belgian partner company.

After this everything went strangely quiet for a few years. There were fanciful stories in the late 1990s that Woolhouse was an occasional visitor to Bramall Lane wearing a wig, false beard and glasses. An away game at Millwall saw plain-clothes Sheffield police seeking his rumoured appearance. He was also said to have been spotted in various countries. Then in October 2002 the search for Woolhouse was resurrected on BBC television's *Crimewatch*, no less. Detectives hunting for him were to make a national appeal to the public. Now aged 54 and on the run some eight years, Woolhouse was still wanted by South Yorkshire Police on allegations of serious fraud. In February 2002 detectives investigated claims that Woolhouse may have made a new life in Turkey, with a German girlfriend, and started a metals business. A police spokesman told the *Crimewatch* viewers; 'We are appealing to people who might have spotted him on holiday abroad. Mr Woolhouse failed to turn up to court to explain the alleged disappearance of millions of pounds belonging to other people and his businesses. Anyone with information should ring South Yorkshire Police.' Nothing came of the *Crimewatch* appeal and Woolhouse remains a fugitive. The most recent rumours were that he may be in either Cyprus or Russia but in reality the trail has gone cold. Woolhouse proved to be the best proponent in Sheffield United's history of being able to lose his man.

Chapter 5

Stephen Hinchliffe
The Grounded High Flier

Stephen Hinchliffe, a Sheffield-born businessman, was invited in August 1992 to join Sheffield United's board of directors by the then new chairman Paul Woolhouse at the outset of the FA Premier League. He replaced Derek Dooley after a fall-out that might best be described as a clash of cultures. Dooley was asked by Woolhouse to take early retirement and banned from his decades-long duty of travelling on the team coach to away matches. Commenting on the ban, an angry and dismayed Dooley said, 'From what Stephen Hinchliffe says it would seem that I am regarded as part of some sort of rival consortium aimed at removing the board and that is absolutely untrue. To hint I am part of organised opposition to the board is out of order.' As well as becoming chairman, Woolhouse took over Dooley's old position of managing director - he renamed it chief executive - so that he could pay himself a salary. Interestingly, on his appointment Hinchliffe publicly stated that he had not been brought on board to put money into the club. He was of the opinion that the club was well financed and solidly structured. As a qualified accountant with experience in business finance and administration he felt he could make a contribution in balancing the books, stating: 'The same level of professional management and control is needed at a major club that is found in running any other sort of company. The days when being a director of a club was a rich man's hobby are gone.' He was wrong about this and a few other matters as well.

Hinchliffe was a name well known in Sheffield business circles as both Stephen and his brother David owned several companies in the city. A former pupil of Herdings Junior School and Gleadless Valley Secondary Modern School in the south of the city, Hinchliffe's modest upbringing did not hinder his education, which led to his attending New College, Oxford and a subsequent qualification in accountancy. A contemporary of his at school, Ken Cotterill, now an Australian citizen, described what Hinchliffe was like as a youngster: 'He was the gangling giant in the next class up, the one who looked odd in short trousers. Always popular, Steve made his first killing on our school trip to London airport in 1961 by buying souvenirs and selling them to his friends back in Sheffield. While we were gawping at the aircraft Steve's mind was already programmed into the adult world. He was quite clearly a millionaire in the making.' In later life Hinchliffe described how his mind worked: 'I've got a talent for numbers. It was the only thing I was good at. I wasn't ever so good at studying but once you've got a formula in your head you've got the message.'

From selling Heathrow Airport souvenirs Hinchliffe moved on to bigger things. He began working in Sheffield's Crookes district from a wooden hut, in a solo business venture selling computers. Bored with bits and bytes, Hinchliffe accelerated into the used car business by acquiring Abbey Motors and later Highfield Motors, the latter located in a showroom near Bramall Lane, but by 1982 his car empire had collapsed. On December 1, 1982 the *Sheffield Star* reported; 'TYCOON CALLS IN RECEIVER' and described how six of Hinchliffe's companies were put into receivership, including three car sales outlets. A Rotherham-based dealership was reported as having lost almost £1 million in one year. The motor businesses were sold as going concerns but the others were liquidated. Hinchliffe explained that his financial problems were a product of a difficult market in a city suffering badly in the economic recession. This was true and the good-with-numbers dealer explained how: 'When 1,700 people lose their jobs at British Steel, 1,700 people are not buying new cars.' In November 1982 there were 40,085 people on the dole in Sheffield, and 3,063,026 out of work throughout the UK. Many large manufacturing companies in South Yorkshire were on short-time working or were laying people off, including 1,500 at steel company Firth Brown, 470 at River Don Stampings, 180 at BSC Orgreave and 130 at Fullerton Machine Shops in Rotherham. Some 350 white-collar jobs disappeared due to the merger of Firth Brown with BSC River Don. In December the steelworkers voted to strike, while National Union of Mineworkers leader Arthur Scargill threatened that nationally coal miners would involve themselves in 'wild cat' strikes to support the Welsh miners if they voted to strike. To make matters worse for the consumer, inflation was running at 6.3 per cent.

Undeterred by failure and economic uncertainty, Hinchliffe bounced back by acquiring a couple of restaurants but he proved as successful at selling meals as he had been selling cars. He then left used cars and dinner plates and returned again - as only failed businessmen can - by leading a consortium that bought out Derbyshire-based Wade's Furniture Group from parent company ASDA. He turned the ailing Wade's round in two years before selling it off to Waring and Gillow for a cool £7.3 million profit. As Hinchliffe held a 40 per cent shareholding in Wade's he personally made around £3 million. He thus moved with new-found confidence into his next deal. This was to be James Wilkes, a Banbury-based company with interests in welding, beer mat printing and packaging. Hinchliffe bought the company and relocated it to Sheffield, to a new headquarters at a large old 'country' house, Beauchief Hall, just off Abbey Lane in an affluent south-west Sheffield suburb. The hall had once belonged to the De La Salle Catholic religious order and had served as an exclusive boys' school. Surrounded by a golf course, it boasted bar and leisure facilities. He was able to dazzle clients and investors from the City by helicoptering himself to his new workplace. His landed chopper was often in danger from big hitters playing cricket in the grounds of the house. Also in six-hitters' range were the resident deer, peacocks and four full-time gardeners. Hinchliffe rejuvenated Wilkes so decisively that it won the Small Company of the Year Award from US merchant bankers, Warburgs. As well as being chairman of Wilkes, Hinchliffe controlled Allied Industrial Estates, a holding company that specialised in buying 'name' companies such as food producers Batchelor's. He also bought Sheffield toolmaking firm Spear and Jackson.

Then entered Graham Avery, the chairman of WB Industries, a West Midlands steel spring group. Avery was moving into property development under his company's subsidiary WB Estates. In 1989, under Avery's guidance, WB Estates agreed to buy an office block from Batchelor's, located in the Wadsley Bridge area of Sheffield, for £1.7 million. By February 1990 £1.4 million had been paid to the vendors, Allied Industrial Estates. However, by April of the same year WB Industries ousted Avery in a boardroom revolt due to what they thought were ill-judged purchases. WB Industries then withheld the remaining £300,000 owed to Allied pending a police investigation into the deal. WB Industries believed that the Wadsley Bridge property was overpriced, implying that Avery and Hinchliffe had conspired to defraud WB Industries. A court ruling cleared Hinchliffe of wrong-doing and decided in Allied's favour. The WB Industries deal, the helicopters, the use of the luxurious Beauchief Hall, a (ultimately failed) takeover bid by rivals Petrocon and the economic recession were too much for James Wilkes shareholders: Hinchliffe had to go. He resigned his position in February 1992, but left with a pay-off of £533,000. Petrocon's advisors had warned Wilkes shareholders that Hinchliffe's extravagant lifestyle appeared to have been funded at their company's expense. Within weeks Hinchliffe was forced out of another publicly quoted company, computer services group Lynx Holdings, after a boardroom coup. Once more he received a handy compensation package. Keith Butterick, editor of business magazine *Finance North*, opined that in the course of his dealings Hinchliffe had 'stepped on a lot of people's toes'.

But Hinchliffe wasn't away from the public eye for long. Soon afterwards he reappeared as chairman and chief shareholder of En-Tout-Cas, a Leicestershire-based company that supplied all-weather sports surfaces – tennis courts, athletics tracks, horse race courses and football, cricket and hockey pitches – and which later bought Stockport-based sportswear firm Bukta. Hinchliffe won for En-Tout-Cas the contract to resurface the prestigious Shatin racetrack in Hong Kong. Over the next few years Hinchliffe's fortunes typically swayed. He resigned from Sheffield United's board, then rejoined and resigned again, citing 'intense business pressures' for his change of heart. He then left En-Tout-Cas, by now renamed Boxgrey PLC, and in 1998 was barred by a judge at a hearing at Newcastle District Registry from being a company director for seven years following lengthy legal proceedings into that company's affairs: En-Tout-Cas collapsed in 1994 with debts of £5.2 million. Hinchliffe was alleged in court to have taken money out of the company for his own benefit, syphoned through his private investment company Chase Investments. In court, Jonathan Holmes, for the Department of Trade and Industry, which had brought the case, said Hinchliffe and finance director Christopher Harrison had transferred money from En-Tout-Cas to other organisations in which they had interests, then failed to repay the cash when the firm started to struggle. Hinchliffe had offloaded En-Tout-Cas, claiming he needed to prepare the ground for his proposed purchase and development of a string of High Street retailers, including jewellers Torq, cigarette lighter manufacturers Colibri, lingerie specialist Contessa, menswear group Oakland, shoe chain Freeman Hardy Willis, Sock Shop, luggage stores Salisbury's and fashion designers Red or Dead, under his umbrella group Facia. His idea was to bring the diverse individual retail businesses together under the same management and warehousing systems, cutting overheads in the process.

Soon after Hinchliffe's founding of Facia, the *Independent on Sunday* told of the bewilderment of the City of London as a Sheffield mystery man, i.e. Hinchliffe, bought up high-street chain-store failures. All had made spectacular recent losses. But Hinchliffe had come from nowhere to become Britain's second largest private retailer after the Littlewoods department store chain. Such purchases mystified the City and the retail trade. The paper stated: 'It is a puzzle that the colourful Mr Hinchliffe has done little to clarify: Facia has yet to file its first report and accounts.' The article then quoted Manchester businessman Mike McDonald, who at the time was chairman of Sheffield United and who had fended off a counter offer from Hinchliffe to take control of the club. He was to say: 'I've been trying to find out about him myself. He's a bit flamboyant and likes to be the person in the limelight but when you go to check him out on the business side you hit brick walls. You can't even draw the accounts. I understand he is buying businesses that are thought to be old dinosaurs. If the big boys can't make it pay, how can he?' The only conclusion McDonald could draw about Hinchliffe was that 'you don't need money to buy lame ducks'.

The *Independent on Sunday* tried, but failed, to find out more about Hinchliffe. Their request for an interview was rejected with the question 'what do you want to interview me for?' Whilst nobody could discover quite how much Hinchliffe had spent developing Facia's spectacular growth, the *Independent on Sunday* could report that: 'Mr Hinchliffe has indicated the string of deals were financed from a mixture of the company's resources and short-term loans from unnamed backers. But the almost total absence of any published information makes these claims impossible to verify. City analysts and business rivals alike are perplexed as to why Mr Hinchliffe is so keen to expand on the high street when trading conditions are so tough and the clear trend is towards out-of-town shopping centres. The main concern centres on Facia's ambitious strategy of expanding aggressively through buying loss-making and largely unrelated businesses, while keeping a grip on financial controls. Critics remain unclear exactly what Facia is bringing to the party and Mr Hinchliffe faces an uphill task convincing the many doubters.' Some financial experts believed that Hinchliffe's objective was more personal than business-based – he wanted to prove himself to the City. John Richards, retail analyst at NatWest Securities, was one who expressed reservations. 'There is a high degree of scepticism among other retailers about who he is and what he is trying to do. The businesses acquired were not making money, the trading environment has remained difficult and it is not quite clear what has been done to improve their performance. There is a feeling it will all end in tears. There is no history of other retailers achieving what Facia is trying to do. It's not a compulsive story.' Such concerns proved well founded. Hinchliffe was very much a mystery man, for reasons that would become clear later. His proved to be a compulsive story and, one suspects, tears were shed.

For a while it seemed that Hinchliffe had the midas touch. On the surface, his chain of stores was doing well, but in reality all except Red or Dead were losing money. Hinchliffe was then fined £1,000 for failing to file accounts for Sock Shop. Facia's financial difficulties then became acute, forcing his resignation from the Sheffield United FC board and provoking a police investigation into Facia's business affairs. This began with a police raid of Facia's headquarters at Parkhead Hall, a large house in Sheffield's wealthy Ecclesall district. A story then broke on May 11, 1996 that Hinchliffe was the subject of a second investigation. The *Sheffield Star* reported, 'The probe is believed to centre on allegations that millions of pounds of pensions and other money was not available to employees when companies he had previously owned collapsed.' Hinchliffe denied the claims, stating he would challenge them in the courts. He also began legal proceedings against the *Daily Express* for an article Hinchliffe regarded as 'highly defamatory'. He insisted that any problems arose after he had sold the companies involved. One of them, Boxgrey, went into liquidation in 1994 with liabilities of £5 million. The liquidators, Sheffield firm Poppleton and Appleby, passed documents concerning the case to the Department of Trade and Industry's insolvency branch. These enquiries passed without any charges being brought but Hinchliffe was not to be so fortunate when the investigation into Facia's ill-fated operations got underway.

Facia's failure was brought about when the London branch of Israeli-based United Mizrahi Bank (UMB) called in its loans to Facia; the bank recovered its money but other Facia creditors lost theirs, to the tune of £30 million. About eight thousand jobs were also lost from the Facia Group when some 850 stores were closed. The four-year long ensuing criminal inquiry into Facia resulted in criminal charges of corruption being brought against Hinchliffe. In the meantime he returned to football, even though his disbarment prevented him from being a director of any club. In the mid 1990s Hull City FC, then owned by tennis and fitness centre magnate David Lloyd, was in danger of going out of business as it plummeted down the leagues. At one time its playing squad was so small that reserve goalkeeper Alan Fettis had to play in attack to make up the numbers. He scored winning goals in two games!

In November 1998, along with Nick Buchanan, Tom Belton and David Bennett, Hinchliffe paid £100,000 for the Hull club but could not afford to buy its Boothferry Park ground from Lloyd. Lloyd agreed to pay off the club debts of £975,000 but kept Boothferry Park, charging the new owners £150,000 a year in rent and giving them a four-year option to buy the ground for £1.35 million. During Hinchliffe's tenure the club was subject to a winding-up order in the High Court for money owed to the Inland Revenue, placed in administration and its officials and players locked out of Boothferry Park by Lloyd, who sent in bailiffs to reclaim unpaid rent. Yet there were evidently some monies available. In April 1999 Hull City purchased a 12-year-old luxury coach for £82,250 from another of Hinchliffe's companies, D'Elegance Travel. Buchanan described it as a 'brilliant deal' for Hull. The bus was bought on the same day that the Professional Footballers' Association loaned the club £50,000 because it could not afford to pay its players' wages. There was also an unpaid bill running into the thousands owed to a Chinese restaurant in Hull.

Suspicions as to who was to blame for all this fell on Hinchliffe. For a man who ostensibly did not own the club, Hinchliffe had some inordinate influence. At times he left his seat in the directors' box and in the players' tunnel instructed joint managers John McGovern and Warren Joyce to change tactics or substitute players. At away games he was received by other chairmen as their Hull City equivalent. He was also accused of negotiating transfer deals. In March 2001 the *Independent* newspaper claimed that it had evidence in its possession, in the form of a letter signed by Hull City FC director Richard Ibbotson, that proved that Hinchliffe and his colleagues indulged in unscrupulous transfer activity. It was alleged that Hull offered to pay £40,000 direct to the chairman of non-league Winsford United and £10,000 to the club to forego the sell-on clause attached to the transfer of goalkeeper Andy Oakes, whom Hull had bought from Winsford. Winsford's chairman Terry Savage did not accept the offer. In June 1999 Hull sold Oakes to Derby County for £460,000 and were therefore required to pay nearly £120,000 to Winsford. Savage suggested that he negotiated this offer almost entirely with Hinchliffe.

One fellow director, Ibbotson, who had been on the boards of at least seven of Hinchliffe's companies and was a former associate of Paul Woolhouse, revealed that Hinchliffe continued to advise and attend board meetings but that, because of his disbarment, stopped (somehow) short of acting as a 'director'. However, Tom Belton (another Hull City director) wrote to Hinchliffe, Buchanan, Ibbotson and two other directors in May 1999 stating his concerns that Hinchliffe had become involved in the day-to-day running of the company, entered into financial commitments on behalf of the club and had negotiated new contracts for Joyce and McGovern, thereby *de facto* continuing to run a company whilst disqualified. And, in defiance of a two-year prison sentence if found guilty of such activities, the *Independent* claimed that it was Hinchliffe who then removed Belton from the Hull City chairmanship. Hinchliffe meanwhile was rumoured to chair unofficial Hull City FC 'board meetings' in a public house in the Nether Edge area of Sheffield, over jolly evenings of sausages, brown sauce and beer.

Not all onlookers were passive. The Football Association's compliance officer, former South Yorkshire Constabulary detective Graham Bean, mounted an investigation into the alleged transfer irregularities but his enquiries hit a dead end. But Hinchliffe's touch failed him again, and Hull fell into administration once more early in 2001, before being bought by Adam Pearson, who set the club on the road to recovery and eventual attainment of Premier League status in 2008. Hinchliffe's affairs at Hull had consequences for other employees. In March 2002 Sheffield United's commercial manager (recently returned from a similar position at Hull

City) Andy Daykin and former United club secretary (and late Hull City club secretary) David Capper were arrested and questioned by Humberside Police in relation to possible fraud at the Hull club. Two years later they learned that no charges would be brought against them after Football Association and police investigations could not find evidence of fraud or malpractice.

Evidence was, however, found elsewhere to convict Hinchliffe. The Facia case was heard at the Old Bailey, London, in 2000. In February 2001, after seven months of evidence and 70 hours of the jury considering its verdicts, Hinchliffe was convicted of ten charges of bribery and one of conspiracy to defraud the United Mizrahi Bank. Hinchliffe was jailed for five years, guilty of handing bribes disguised as legitimate fees totalling £800,000 to a UMB bank manager, John Doherty, so he could gain the £10 million in loans he required to buy the Facia Group. The prosecution said Hinchliffe was prepared to pay 'bribes, back-handers and corrupt payments' to get what he wanted. UMB had an upper limit of £2 million for commercial loans; the fact that Hinchliffe was allowed to borrow five times this amount was hidden from senior management. Hinchliffe's barrister, Ken McDonald, claimed that the UMB staff had not been corrupted by his client and that the underhand deals could only have been done because the bank employees were already corrupt. Doherty and a compliant businessman, Robert Leckie, set up several overseas companies and Swiss bank accounts to accept Hinchliffe's 'sweeteners'. Doherty's colleague Paul Brady also took money and tried to cover up the fraud when auditors discovered false invoices in Facia's accounts. Hinchliffe insisted to the Serious Fraud Office that he was innocent and that the £800,000 fees were legal 'loan arrangers' to help set up the loans, and that he was an unsuspecting victim of a scam by perfidious bank employees. Prior to Hinchliffe's trial, Doherty, Leckie and former UMB finance manager Paul Brady were found guilty at a separate hearing of various fraud and conspiracy offences and received sentences ranging from two to five years. Doherty then appeared as a prosecution witness in Hinchliffe's trial. Sentencing Hinchliffe, Judge Graham Boal told him: 'Corruption involving a powerful and high-profile businessman and a senior bank official strikes at the very root of commercial integrity. Your motive was greed and self-aggrandisement. You stood to gain a great deal and must lose a great deal.'

Well before his conviction Hinchliffe was widely mistrusted by many amongst the Sheffield business community. Some questioned whether his schemes were as grand as he made them out to be. The chief executive of Sheffield's Chamber of Trade, John Taylor, said that there were always rumours about Hinchliffe's credentials: 'Too many things were said in too many places over too many drinks.' An unnamed former associate of Hinchliffe said that the millionaire believed he was 'invincible' and 'untouchable' but accused him of treating small businesses with disdain by not settling their invoices. There were also allegations that he did not always pay his employees' wages; on one occasion his excuse was that the employee had broken company equipment; on another a former chauffeur, Rob Griffiths, had to go to County Court to recover £1,900 in unpaid salary. Griffiths described what it was like working for Hinchliffe: 'It would be the same every day. I would drive him from his house between 11 o'clock and noon to [Facia HQ] Parkhead Hall. He would be there for half an hour and then without exception it would be into Sheffield, somewhere like Champs [a sports bar] on Ecclesall Road or a pizza restaurant. We would go back to Parkhead between 4pm and 6pm until about 8pm and then without exception I would take him to the Rising Sun round the corner until closing time and then take him home.' The chauffeur was well aware of Hinchliffe's fleet of vintage and high-performance cars. Logically he pointed out that Hinchliffe could have sold one to pay his wages.

Hinchliffe's collection of over 90 classic cars was on top of the Porsche, Aston Martin and Bentley he regularly drove. He lived in a huge walled mansion in the up-market south-western Sheffield suburb of Dore. A tractor was needed to tend his landscaped garden. The house had a helipad and a swimming pool with an underwater sound system. There was also a football pitch in the grounds. His headquarters, Parkhead Hall, was embellished with expensive artwork and Georgian furniture. He favoured fine restaurants, such as Hanrahan's in the Broomhill area of Sheffield, which was the haunt of Sheffield footballers and professional socialites. He was so well liked there that a dish - 'Hinch's Chicken'- was named in his honour. When he celebrated his 40th birthday he instructed his guests to bring their passports as he was flying them to Cairo. In the mid 1990s his personal fortune was estimated at £60 million. An unnamed friend, quoted in the *Sheffield Star*, said of him; 'He was an immaculate dresser, he always wore a smart suit with a white shirt and polished shoes and his hair was always perfectly combed. He had a very high opinion of himself.' Another anonymous associate described him as 'a very amusing man, very charismatic and full of humorous anecdotes, especially across a dinner table. He was good company. He loved entertaining and socialising, getting a crowd of people for a meal out and a laugh. He had pretty simple eating habits but he loved champagne and Chablis.' He enjoyed a practical joke, but sometimes it went too far. He was once banned from a game shoot for offending his fellow shooters, aiming at their birds rather than his own.

But there were signs that all wasn't going well for Hinchliffe behind the scenes. One restaurant owner told how he had to accept goods in place of money to settle a bill. Hinchliffe had apparently offered to pay for a meal partly with cash, but also with a watch, a pen and some Colibri cigarette lighters. The restaurateur said, 'I had to take them otherwise I would have lost his business.' Another former friend told of his meanness: 'He would always try to wriggle out of buying a round, wriggle out of paying for a luncheon. When it came to business you didn't ever let him owe you money because you would not get it back.' Another former acquaintance who had fallen out with Hinchliffe, who also wished to remain anonymous, added, 'He took the mickey out of people financially, never reciprocated. I don't think he had any true friends quite frankly.' Yet another disillusioned one-time associate remarked, 'He could be flamboyant for sure but he was stingy too. It was always very futile and always to do with business. It came down to being motivated by greed. He was ruthless and wanted as much money out of every deal as he could possibly make. He always wanted that bit more, he was never satisfied.' Amidst such tirades Hinchliffe's barrister said the conviction was his client's 'obituary', describing him as a ruined man, adding, 'If he was greedy it wasn't for wealth so much as success.' Prison, he added, would be 'shocking and unpleasant' for Hinchliffe. Following the conviction, detectives who had worked on the case revealed that Hinchliffe thought he was too clever to get caught. 'He assumed police were stupid,' said Detective Inspector Clive Barnes.

It wasn't over yet. Hinchliffe appealed against the verdict and was partially successful; his sentence was commuted to four years, of which he served just under two. In the meantime, Hinchliffe's creditors started a 'paper chase' to track down his assets, which were to be scrutinised by PriceWaterhouseCoopers' insolvency experts in order to discover exactly how much Hinchliffe was worth. It was also reported that they would look at Hinchliffe's former links to Sheffield United and Hull City. But it seemed his guile had not deserted him. When his fleet of cars came up for auction at the bankruptcy court they were bought *en masse* by one buyer, alleged by some to be a close associate of Hinchliffe

Twenty-four hours after his release from prison in 2002 Hinchliffe reverted to habit, quaffing champagne in a Sheffield wine bar. He was also seen outside a former Mercedes dealership near Sheffield city centre, apparently discussing the future of the building with a surveyor. Virtually as soon as he was released, however, he was facing yet more criminal proceedings relating to nine transactions with the Facia Group, the allegation being that he had drawn off company assets for his own personal use. An out-of-court deal was struck whereby if he pleaded guilty to just one count of conspiracy to defraud he would escape a jail term. If he had been found guilty of all charges, Old Bailey Judge Jeremy Roberts said that he could have expected a two-year sentence. The unusual offer meant that the other charges would not be pursued and the judge intimated he would pass a suspended sentence of about 15 months. Facia's former financial director Christopher Harrison admitted the same offence. Judge Roberts was happy to accept the guilty pleas to the lesser offence because he said a new trial would be held at 'enormous expense', which, as both defendants were bankrupt, would fall on the public purse. In his argument the estimated £10 million expense of the trial would be disproportionate to the benefit gained by the public if Hinchliffe and Harrison were convicted on all counts. In court, prosecuting barrister Timothy Langdale QC claimed that Hinchliffe 'filched large amounts of money to line his own pockets' during the 22 months Facia was in business; Hinchliffe was reported to have personally made £1.75 million. Hinchliffe and Harrison admitted issuing false invoices that overcharged Facia for business services. On April 24, 2003 they each received the expected 15-month suspended sentences. The Serious Fraud Office, however, having deliberated as to whether to refer the sentence to the Attorney General on the grounds that it was 'unduly lenient', went through with its threat. The Attorney General, Lord Goldsmith QC, referred the case to the Court of Appeal, where a panel of three senior judges had the power to either increase or decrease the sentence. The appeal was heard in July 2003 and the panel declared that the 15-month suspended sentence was indeed too light and instead sent Hinchliffe to jail for 18 months.

Hinchliffe served less than a year in custody and as soon as he was out was back in the news. This time he was angering local people near where he lived in Dore, when planning to sell part of his land for a housing development, to which a local residents' group was opposed. Their research as they prepared their case discovered that Hinchliffe had erected large security gates across a public highway that fell within his boundary. They demanded the City Council order Hinchliffe to take down the gates. Hinchliffe retorted that the road was never a public highway, adding, 'If anybody wants to go to court and say otherwise, let them.' A Council spokesman confirmed that the gates were indeed erected across a public highway but added that the situation was not uncommon. In the Council's opinion the road was not needed as a public highway as it only led to the property – Hinchliffe's – at the end. The Council then proposed that it no longer be classed as a public highway. Hinchliffe had at last won a legal contest. The gates were finally closed.

But Hinchliffe, by now a resident of High Peak Hall in the Derbyshire village of Hope, returned to the front page in March 2010, as the *Sheffield Star* reported: 'Tycoon Faces Paying Millions'. The 'exclusive' story told of how Hinchliffe and his wife were being sued for damages by Sheffield brothers Shaun and Alex Smith. Introduced to them by a mutual friend, the brothers engaged Hinchliffe to act as an agent in their 2007 purchase of umbrella manufacturers Hoyland Fox, a deal that was to cost £1.4 million. Hinchliffe's wife's company Mozaic contributed £1 million to complete the purchase. Unusually, the £1 million was loaned to Mozaic by Hoyland Fox to fund its own takeover, a procedure known as 'whitewashing'. Despite his background, the brothers were happy to work with Hinchliffe as they considered him 'a reformed character'. They believed he had 'a good business brain and a lot to offer'. According to the Smiths, the arrangement was that ownership of Hoyland Fox would immediately be transferred to them by Mozaic. This version of events was denied in court by the Hinchliffes. They claimed that the company was to be owned 50 per cent each by Mozaic and the Smith brothers. By early 2008 the Hinchliffes expressed concern over the way Hoyland Fox was being run by the Smiths, so Mrs Hinchliffe appointed as directors of Mozaic three of her associates, giving them a boardroom majority. At this point the brothers withdrew money from Hoyland Fox and moved it into another of their companies, forcing the umbrella-making company into administration. They then instigated legal action against the Hinchliffes, claiming their boardroom manoeuvrings were unlawful.

After a hearing at the High Court, Judge Hazel Marshall QC ruled in favour of the Smith brothers but deferred a decision on the amount of damages the Hinchliffes would have to pay. In the meantime their assets were frozen. Judge Marshall stated that the Hinchliffes' actions were 'unlawful' and described Stephen Hinchliffe as 'manipulative, calculating, ruthless and utterly self-interested'. Hinchliffe's motive was 'revenge', she said, for the Smiths' delay of payment of consultancy fees. After the ruling Shaun Smith said. 'We are delighted with the judge's findings. We are seeking damages of several million pounds.' Hinchliffe called the judgement 'ridiculous' and 'unbelievable', adding that he was considering an appeal. The case was ongoing in the middle of 2010.

It seemed that whatever business or enterprise he undertook, Stephen Hinchliffe could not stay out of the headlines for long.

Chapter 6

Back To Basics
Brealey Returns

Sheffield United had finished the 1992/93 season comfortably clear of relegation and with an appearance in the FA Cup semi-final for the first time in 32 years. Reg Brealey had just regained control of the club from Paul Woolhouse, at the same time forcing out directors Stephen Hinchliffe and Michael Wragg. The departure of the former was no bad thing considering what he would get up in the future, but Wragg was from a Sheffield family that had been involved with the club for years – his father Dick joined the board in 1960 and was once chairman of the Football Association's International Committee. Another director, Alan Laver, whose family had been on the United board for decades, had initially threatened to immediately call in a loan to the club of £750,000 if Hinchliffe and Wragg were forced out. He then had second thoughts, probably believing he could exert some influence if he remained.

Surprisingly, Brealey made what would turn out in later years to be inspired appointments - he brought in two Sheffield-born men and Blades fans in Kevin McCabe and Bernard Procter. However, McCabe soon departed when let down by an unnamed financial backer, whose promised £5 million to back his bid to buy out Brealey failed to materialise. Procter took his seat on the board and proved a steady if somewhat conservative influence. To replace McCabe Brealey brought in another local in the shape of fruit and vegetable merchant John Plant. Brealey sold ten per cent of his reclaimed shares to Procter claiming he wanted to return the club to local hands. He also stated he wished to remain on the board for just one month so that a full audit of the club's books could be undertaken. The news that previous directors (by which he possibly meant Woolhouse, Hinchliffe and Wragg, albeit he did not name them) had charged full bank overdraft rates for their loans to the club did not go down well with supporters, who believed that if the directors were true fans they would lend the club money without demanding interest. Brealey was clearly trying to curry favour by pointing out the faults of the previous regime. However, despite Brealey's apparent attempts at reconciliation it became clear that the boardroom was split; in one corner sat the Brealeys and John Plant; in the other were Bernard Procter, Alan Laver and Derek Dooley.

It was at times easy to forget that Sheffield United had a football team. Those involved on the playing side were worried about the boardroom dramas. Manager Dave Bassett feared the worst after the Brealeys' High Court victory. He believed it was a backward step for the club and deliberated over his future. The primary reason he decided to stay was the backing he received from supporters, to whom he felt more loyalty than he did to his directors. His fears proved well founded. Len Brealey had told Bassett that £1 million transfer money would be made available to him. It wasn't. Then, just after the season ended, Brian Deane, scorer of over one hundred goals for United since his arrival in 1988, shocked the club by handing in a transfer request, claiming that he needed a move in order to further his England international ambitions - he had just been awarded his first caps. It was hoped by everybody, not least Bassett, that his wish to leave would be denied as he still had a year remaining on his contract. A year previously Deane, then out of contract (this was long before the Bosman ruling allowed out-of-contract players to leave for no fee[3]), had reportedly been offered three renewal choices; one year, two years or four years. He opted for the two-year contract, so Bassett was of the opinion that if Deane now wanted to leave why had he not gone for the one-year deal? When interviewed in October 1993 for United fanzine *Flashing Blade*, Deane denied he had been offered a one-year deal, stating: 'What would have been the point of me signing for one year? And don't you think it would have been foolish on the club's part to offer me a one-year contract because I would have been a free agent [at its conclusion] and I may have gone for peanuts then. I didn't intend staying at United for nine years [he had been at the club for five years at this time] so that's why I signed a two-year deal.' He also confirmed that Paul Woolhouse informed him he would be able to leave if he wished after one year: 'I was told at the time they would only be able to keep me for another year anyway because of the [financial] state of the club.'

Leeds United, in the market for a big centre forward having just sold Lee Chapman, were perceived to be in pole position to sign Deane. The fact that Deane came from Leeds only added weight to this rumour. However, Leeds were also openly chasing Dundee United's Duncan Ferguson. Others, notably Everton, Aston Villa, Crystal Palace, Chelsea and even Sheffield Wednesday were said to be interested in signing Deane. Deane told the *Sheffield Star* of his desire to leave: 'After five years I think it is time for me to go. I have had five tremendous years in Sheffield and I feel I owe it to the fans to explain why I want to leave. The time has come for me to ask questions of myself and it is not a decision I have taken

---

[3] The 'Bosman ruling' was a 1995 European Court of Justice decision concerning freedom of movement for workers within the European Union (EU), allowing professional footballers to move freely to another club within the EU at the end of their contract. Jean-Marc Bosman was a Belgian player whose contract had expired in 1990. He wanted to move to FC Dunkerque in France. Dunkerque did not offer his Belgian club RFC Liège a high enough transfer fee, so Liège refused to let him go. Bosman took his case to the European Court of Justice in Luxembourg and successfully sued Liège for restraint of trade. Subsequently, all such out-of-contract free transfers became known as 'Bosmans'.

quickly or lightly or because some club has got to me. I have been thinking about this since the end of last season and I need to get my career sorted out and see how good I am. I have been on the fringe of the England side for a year or two without establishing myself and this is something I desperately want to do. I have no idea if anyone really wants me and I have certainly not done it because I have one particular club in mind that I want to play for. I do not even know if United will accept my request. I hope they do and that the fee they will get for me will stabilise the club. But if they keep me to their contract, which is their right, I shall continue to be the same player I have always been. Ever since I came I have had a special relationship with the crowd and I shall never be as popular as I am at Bramall Lane. But I hope they will understand my thinking. I have to admit that the continuing struggle to stay in the top division has got to me a bit. But that is not to say that I think I am too good for Sheffield United; I am not. It is just that every player in the country wants to play at the top and win honours and I am no different.' These were well-considered and articulate words from a genuinely modest and decent young man, aware that he could make a lot more money out of the game away from Bramall Lane.

Not all appreciated his sentiment. Manager Bassett responded, 'I have not been shown any letter from Deane but if he says he has submitted one he must have. He certainly didn't give any letter to me. I shall recommend to the board that they take this decision [to deny his request]. I certainly don't want him to go.' The interest in Deane began to gain momentum and although the United board had made no official statement most Blades fans expected him to leave. If he were to leave, there were two clubs to which no United supporter wanted Deane to go. One was Sheffield Wednesday (this was never really an option, as Deane said later, 'It would have been easy to go to Wednesday, but Blades [fans] would have hated me'); the other was Leeds United. For a while it appeared that Leeds were favourites to land their number-one target Duncan Ferguson, and radio sports bulletins were listened to with rare interest in Sheffield, hoping that the news would come through that Leeds had signed the Scot as that would mean they would lose interest in Deane. However, Ferguson decided to sign for

Glasgow Rangers. It was obvious what the next development would be. Shortly afterwards Leeds made an official approach for Deane and their chairman, Leslie Silver, even announced that he had signed for them. Two days later Reg Brealey said Silver had 'jumped the gun', adding that he had only told Silver that he would recommend to the board that the offer be accepted but the move had to approved by the other directors. Sheffield Wednesday then came in with a late £3.2 million bid but the opposition of some of the United directors meant that this offer was not seriously considered. Said Brealey, 'Some of the board were hostile to this move to our neighbours, and Deane indicated that he didn't fancy it. No player can be forced to accept a transfer. The offer from Leeds was the only one that could be processed.'

Some were to argue for brinkmanship. Fellow director Derek Dooley was of the opinion that United should wait a little longer for better offers closer to the £3.5 million valuation United had placed on Deane's head. Brealey did not concur, despite an informal enquiry from Chelsea intimating that they might be willing to pay £3 million. Brealey got his way and Leeds' offer was accepted by United's board. Blades fans were livid; so was Dave Bassett, who learned of the sale while on holiday. He wrote in his 1997 autobiography *Harry's Game* that: 'On 14 July 1993 it was announced that Brian Deane was joining Leeds for £2.9 million. I did not want to lose Brian - which is why the deal was done in my absence. The directors were split on the decision but Reg Brealey used his casting vote to push the deal through. The directors who voted against threatened to resign and when I heard about it I hit the roof. I told Reg Brealey that he had taken a decision which would get the club relegated. I meant it too.'

The board had been divided. On one side, wanting to keep Deane, were Laver, Procter and Dooley, on the other were the returning chairman Brealey, his brother Len and John Plant, the man Reg had brought in for precisely such scenarios. Split at three-three, Brealey used his chairman's casting vote to decide that Deane should be sold, after which Dooley walked out of the meeting at a Wakefield hotel, saying, 'If that's it Reg, I've resigned.' Procter threatened resignation too, while

120

Laver said he was 'greatly disturbed' by the transfer. Unperturbed, Brealey remarked, 'If any directors wish to resign over this issue, so be it.' Speaking to Gary Armstrong in 1999, Brealey defended his stance, blaming the position Woolhouse had left the club in: 'The club were pariahs in the hotel industry – unpaid bills. No coach company wanted to take us – unpaid bills. There were no postage stamps. The only way out was to sell Brian Deane. He was the only goalscorer at the club and we shouldn't have sold him, but unless we did we were bust. Deane had been promised his release by Paul Woolhouse – ask him. I honoured that promise and it suited me to do so.' After the sale he described the consequences – the short term ones anyway. 'We paid all the bills and reduced our number of creditors from 400 to 50. Ninety per cent of the phone calls to Bramall Lane stopped; the morale of the office staff trebled.'

That may have been so, but the morale of the supporters halved. The supporters also wondered what had happened to the club's financial status so soon after Woolhouse had said how much better the situation was, since when there had been a lucrative FA Cup run to the semi-final, £300,000 in Premier League prize money, £1 million in season ticket sales and several matches live on *Sky TV* at £100,000 a time. Ingoing and outgoing transfers balanced out. But there had been the fiasco of the Brian Gayle transfer, the High Court battle over Woolhouse's shares and it was now necessary for financial reasons to sell Brian Deane. Just what was going on? It was hard not to consider the possibility that Woolhouse might have been using the club's money to try to bale out his own ailing businesses. Meanwhile the belief would not go away that Brealey was only intent on getting his money back for the shares he had retaken control of by default.

It was from this moment onwards that Brealey lost the confidence and support of the majority of Sheffield United fans - all believed that in selling Deane Brealey had sold their club down the river. The relationship between chairman and team manager rapidly declined. Bassett said, 'It was increasingly difficult to talk to Brealey [after the sale of Deane] – mostly because I didn't want to. The boardroom infighting and broken promises were something in which I didn't want to be embroiled.' He likened the boardroom squabbling to being a passenger on a Jumbo jet and hearing the pilot and co-pilot arguing about how to fly the plane. Dooley, Laver and Procter were considering their positions. Dooley, whom Bassett said was 'a big help…. a person that I could talk to' during these turbulent times, was persuaded by the manager to stay. The futures of Laver and Procter remained uncertain as both failed to attend a board meeting the day after Deane was sold. Brealey assumed that their absence confirmed their threats to resign but the *Green 'Un* reported on July 17 that both wished to attend a full board meeting.

Into this swamp waded the irrepressible Stephen Hinchliffe. No longer a United director but still a major shareholder, Hinchliffe decided to get involved in the Blades' boardroom dramas once again. Mindful that he had been forced to resign ahead of an Extraordinary General Meeting called by Else (1982) Ltd when it regained control from Woolhouse, Hinchliffe reckoned on getting his own back by putting the Brealeys' dealings into the public spotlight. His 419 shares and his associate Barrie Lake's four shares were enough to force another EGM, to be held on August 27, with the meeting being asked to consider and, if thought fit, pass seven resolutions regarding the sale of Brian Deane and the financial state of the club.

But it was the rebellion that never was. If Brealey was expecting a hard time he was in for a nice surprise. For some reason Hinchliffe seemed to get cold feet and instead of attending he sent his solicitor Michael Block to speak on his behalf. This was a bad move as it immediately dissipated some of the support he might otherwise have won from waverers. An air of expectancy was evident amongst shareholders, many believing they were to be privy to the innermost secrets of the Brian Deane transfer and the finances of the club. Instead Reg Brealey took the microphone and made it clear that the meeting could go on for over five hours if shareholders insisted on poll votes rather than a show of hands. He then emphasised that Else (1982) Ltd would vote against all the resolutions and because they owned 52 per cent of the shares how other shareholders voted would make no difference. He did, though, say that the board had nothing to hide and that full, open discussions of the resolutions would be allowed. Brealey knew how to conduct a meeting correctly and to his advantage and followed both procedure and convention to the letter, unlike his brother Len who continually interjected in debate, with no attempt to put his points through the chair. His lack of decorum brought Len Brealey a rebuke from a female shareholder and thereafter he adhered to procedure.

The discussions brought up some discrepancies with figures published in the media. Brealey told the meeting that Leeds actually paid £2.7 million for Deane (it was reported as £2.9 million) and that Sheffield Wednesday had verbally offered £2.9 million (reported as £3.2 million). He also said that the financial accounts presented to the Annual General Meeting in May included player valuations and Deane was valued there at £2.5 million (Derek Dooley had reportedly claimed that a valuation of £3.5 million had been put on Deane). By making the point of Deane's valuation in the accounts Brealey was attempting to claim that he had been sold for more than he was worth. However, a valuation in the accounts is not necessarily the same as the price one would accept for that asset. Brealey said he personally believed Deane was worth more than £2.7 million but that his price was fixed by market forces. Leeds' offer was the only one in writing and there appeared to be no more forthcoming. Nobody, he said, was prepared to pay more than £2.7 million for a player with three England caps. This statement was baffling, considering that three players, Paul Warhurst, Stan Collymore and Julian Dicks, all with no England caps, had been recently sold by other clubs for more than £2.7 million. Crucially, Brealey made it clear that there had been a 'grave financial necessity' to sell.

Len Brealey then commented that during the course of the legal proceedings with Paul Woolhouse various parties within the Sheffield business community had made promises that they would provide money for new players should Else (1982) Ltd regain control of the majority shareholding. Subsequently those promises had not been kept. Later Bernard Procter spoke to inform the meeting that it was he who advised Kevin McCabe not to inject money into the club in early summer as United 'would not receive maximum benefit from this investment at this time', i.e. that it would be immediately swallowed up by interest payments and to appease creditors chasing their money. When questioned about how much of the Deane monies manager Dave Bassett would be able to spend, Reg Brealey told the meeting that Bassett had received just over £1 million, with which he had purchased Norwegian international striker Jostein Flo for £475,000 from Sogndal, midfielder Willie Falconer for £300,000 from Middlesbrough and defender David Tuttle for £300,000 from Tottenham Hotspur.

Reg Brealey continued by saying that he inherited a mess when he resumed control of the club but now felt that the situation was in hand. Dave Bassett had a budget to work within, which he was very clear about. Brealey told shareholders that if they were given copies of the unedited version of the accountants' report then litigation could follow because of the sensitive nature of such information. The directors believed that it was not in the interests of the club to enter into another period of legal wrangling. Brealey announced that the Annual General Meeting would be held in October, when an up-to-date balance sheet would be presented, adding he was confident that shareholders would be 'pleasantly surprised' by the good news contained therein. One resolution concerned the directors' loans to the club, and was passed over rather quickly as Brealey maintained that individuals' financial interests in the club should remain confidential. He did confirm, though, that apart from one outstanding figure, the club's debts and overdraft were paid off. Finally, Brealey commented that there were now three priorities: (i) that the club would enter a period of peace following the legal battles of the recent past; (ii) that the John Street side of the ground would be redeveloped, hopefully for the start of the 1994/95 season (draft plans were available for shareholders to view at the end of the meeting), using monies allocated by the board and grants from the Football Trust[4]; (iii) that the club would regain control of land behind the kop, ownership of which was in Paul Woolhouse's name due to an 'administrative error'. Brealey concluded by informing all gathered that he was in the process of transferring the 52 per cent shareholding from Else (1982) Ltd to himself, as this would make it easier to sell.

The meeting was over inside an hour. All seven resolutions were rejected without a poll. In effect, Brealey had received a vote of confidence from the shareholders. The much-anticipated showdown with Hinchliffe never materialised, while another potential adversary for Brealey, local engineering entrepreneur Martyn Burke, who earlier had reportedly led a consortium that wanted to take over the club, was the first person to leave the room. Members of the media were not permitted entry. Brealey told them afterwards that the days of unpaid bills were over and he insisted that the club was now on a much firmer foundation: 'The staff are now under a lot less pressure; no one is ringing us up asking for money any more, which is a wonderful tonic to the people who work here. We are back on a solid footing and I hope and plan that it will stay that way.' Two years later, when quoted in the *Sheffield Star*, Brealey said of the situation he found when he returned to the club: 'Remember, this should not be my problem. I thought I had finished with it when we did a deal with Paul Woolhouse. But I had to come in and find a situation that horrified me. I could have sold out for peanuts, walked away and let someone else carry the can, but if you take peanuts you get monkeys and the club deserves better than that. I had the ridiculous situation that although, legally, I still owned the club I was not welcome, not allowed in the boardroom. Paul Woolhouse left instructions with the commissionaire to keep me away and he hadn't even paid for them [the shares] although he told everybody else he had.'

---

[4] Set up by the Labour Government in 1975, the Football Trust (originally the Football Grounds Improvement Trust) was a Government funded body to improve the safety of sports stadiums in the United Kingdom. It was replaced in 2000 by the Football Foundation.

Having shaken off Hinchliffe's attempted derailment, Brealey took total command of the boardroom. There was no more internal dissent, or if there was it was not made public.

Plans for the demolition and rebuilding of the John Street stand were then revealed. In December the club's best balance sheet for years was published in the annual accounts. The *Green 'Un* wrote of the expectation that the directors would get 'a quiet and comfortable ride' from shareholders at the AGM. However, ordinary supporters were not happy as United struggled near the bottom of the table. Furthermore Brealey received criticism for not letting Dave Bassett buy a striker early enough to save the team from relegation. Without Brian Deane United found it hard to score and whilst Nathan Blake was signed from Cardiff City for £300,000 in February 1994 and scored a few goals, it was too little, too late. United were relegated in heartbreaking fashion, losing 3-2 with virtually the last kick of the season against Chelsea at Stamford Bridge. Dave Bassett's prediction that by selling Deane Brealey had taken a decision that would see United relegated had come to pass.

Meanwhile people in India, who probably knew nothing about Premier League football and even if they had done would not have concerned themselves with Sheffield United's fortunes, were now attacking Brealey. Workers at Brealey's Indian company Titaghur were in rebellion against him and once they realised that the firm's owner was also chairman of an English football club became determined to bring their grievances to a wider audience. In the spring of 1994 leaflets appeared around Sheffield, pasted to subway walls and bus shelters and handed out in the street. Produced by an organisation calling itself the South Asia Support Group, the leaflet alleged: 'BLOOD ON HIS HANDS? Sheffield United FC Boss Steals Indian Workers Pension Fund. In January this year an Indian Jute Mill worker died of starvation in the line rooms of the Victoria Jute Mill in Calcutta. His family hold the mill owner Reginald Brealey (who is also the owner of Sheffield United Football Club) responsible for his death. Brealey also stands accused of syphoning off £2.5 million in pensions and statutory benefits and more than six months' unpaid wages from the workforce who are living on the edge of starvation in Telenipara in the outskirts of Calcutta.'

Being held responsible for the demise of a football club was one thing but being blamed for the death of an employee was another. Over the next few months the same man would find himself under ever-increasing pressure from both football fans and Indian workers living at subsistence levels.

Chapter 7

Rebels With A Cause
Brealey Under Attack

The late 1980s and the early 1990s were a period of intense football fan activism in the UK, the like of which had never been witnessed before. There were several reasons for this, the major ones connected with tragedies and hooliganism. The Heysel Stadium disaster at the European Cup final between Liverpool and Juventus in Brussels in May 1985 saw 39 (mainly Italian) supporters killed in a crush as Juventus fans tried to flee from fights on the crumbling terracing after Liverpool supporters breached a flimsy dividing fence. A few weeks earlier 56 spectators died in a fire that destroyed Bradford City's Valley Parade wooden main stand during a match with Lincoln City. On the same day, a 15-year-old boy was killed by a collapsed wall outside Birmingham City's ground during fighting between home fans and Leeds United supporters. There were riots and violent pitch invasions in March 1985 at Luton Town's Kenilworth Road and Chelsea's Stamford Bridge. After the latter Chelsea chairman Ken Bates threatened to erect electric fences in front of the terraces. Then in April 1989 came the worst incident of the lot, when 96 spectators were crushed to death at Sheffield Wednesday's Hillsborough Stadium before the FA Cup semi-final between Liverpool and Nottingham Forest. The football authorities in general, the police and the Conservative Government, which, led by Margaret Thatcher, had never liked football or its supporters, laid most of the blame at the door of hooligans and football fans in general. Football, in this era, was shabby indeed. Clubs existed in a constant state of disrepair and make-do-and-mend. The men who ran the game at club level and at national level were largely clueless and pompous to boot. The English game was sleeping and the wake-up call was one that cost lives. The resulting political outcry meant that English football would never be the same again.

The predominantly working-class male fan was the target for reformers. Prime Minister Thatcher's response was to propose the introduction of football identity cards, with Sports Minister Colin Moynihan the man charged with expediting it. Under his proposal every fan seeking to enter a football stadium in England would have to carry an ID card and to obtain one would have to register all their personal details with the appointed authority, which was to be led, appropriately enough, by the former head of prisons. Doubts about the workability of such a system were many; football supporters were not the only ones to express those doubts. Even Tory backer Reg Brealey disagreed strongly with the plans: 'The Government are completely out of touch. I can't understand their thinking on the matter. As a Conservative supporter I did not think Mrs Thatcher would make this decision. I thought the Tories had more intelligence than to plough on with this infringement of civil liberties.' Unhappy with such a course of events, English football supporters for the first time got themselves organised into campaigning groups that came together under the banner of the newly formed Football Supporters' Association (FSA).

The FSA was begun by a group of Liverpool supporters in a Merseyside pub in 1985. A 30-year-old Liverpool University lecturer by the name of Rogan Taylor was the instigator; the catalyst was the fatal events at Heysel. Taylor, today senior lecturer at the University of Liverpool Management School, described the anger that provoked him into taking action: 'The feeling was that UEFA had stuck us in a stadium which was falling down, they hadn't given us enough tickets, many had been sold on the black market, there were no police inside the stadium, there was blue murder in Turin four months earlier, there was even worse blue murder in Rome twelve months previously: and we all knew. Except them.' The FSA soon developed into a democratic, national organisation that lobbied on behalf of fans, represented them in the press - which saw 'fan' and 'hooligan' as one and the same - and sought to influence the Government and the game's authorities. Independent football-themed publications started to spring up around the country, inspired by the punk music 'fanzines' of the mid-late 1970s. This was agitprop of a demographic more accustomed to chanting its message. The photocopier and desktop publisher were changing the relationship between fan and club for ever.

The first great victory for ordinary football supporters was the abandonment of the identity card scheme, but shamefully it took the Hillsborough Disaster to bring it about. The Rt. Hon. Lord Justice Taylor's report into the incident, presented to Parliament in January 1990, poured scorn on the Government's proposal and catalogued a series of arguments against its implementation. These included the reliability and efficacy of the technology available, the folly of the requirement of turning away from the turnstile those in possession of an invalid card if there was a 'phalanx' of supporters behind, and doubts about the scheme's effectiveness in reducing hooliganism. Most tellingly, Taylor expressed 'serious misgivings about its likely impact on safety. I also have grave doubts about the chances of its achieving its purposes and am very anxious about its potential impact on police commitments and control of spectators.'

Fans continued to pursue the common aims of making the voice of the ordinary punter heard, to better the conditions in which they could watch their football and to campaign against what they saw as unnecessary Government interference. Sheffield United's first fanzine, *Flashing Blade*, was founded in September 1988 by three Blades fans, Jamie Pigott, Jon Middleton and Brian Exford, who first met at meetings of the South Yorkshire branch of the FSA. The editorial of the first issue included the statement of intent: 'We cannot leave the future of our beloved game in the grabbing hands of the property developers and the fists of the hooligans, nor can we sit idly by and do nothing as the directors, the Football League and the gutter press act with mind-blowing stupidity over matters as important to us as life itself. Football is as much ours as theirs.' Fans - including those of Sheffield United - began to realise that if they pooled their resources they could influence virtually any campaign or cause.

In 1993 Sheffield Council youth worker Howard Holmes, dissatisfied at the way Sheffield United Football Club was being run and having seen what could be achieved at a national level and at other clubs, considered setting up a local pressure group for Sheffield United fans but felt, at the time, that the necessary support and enthusiasm might not be present. A collective sense of dissatisfaction would not unite United fans into an organised group. A singular, definite campaigning subject was required and May 7, 1994 provided it – relegation from the Premier League. Holmes was now determined to bring his idea to fruition and spent the next few days planning his course of action. He realised that there was already an organ in existence that provided a platform for fans' opinions – the fanzine *Flashing Blade* – and knew that his idea would not get off the ground without the backing of the two-thousand circulation publication that was probably read by twice as many. His first telephone call was to Matthew Bell, the editor of *Flashing Blade*. The response was positive. He then spoke to two of his long-time friends, Jon Duckham and Pete Bright, and a meeting was arranged to discuss the formation of an independent Sheffield United supporters' association. On May 13, 1994 Holmes, Bell, Duckham and Bright met in the Red Lion public house, previously an old 'Little Mesters' workshop, on Charles Street in the cutlery industries quarter in the centre of Sheffield, a venue chosen for its renowned beer as much as any other consideration. Discussion centred on an interview given by Reg Brealey to BBC TV's *Look North*, in which he suggested that the Premier League may not be an appropriate place for Sheffield United if the money the club had spent on players - about £2 million - was insufficient to safeguard Premier League status. It was decided that the first step for the fledgling organisation should be to write a letter to the 28,000-circulation *Green 'Un* Saturday evening sports paper in which the objectives and desires of the new association would be outlined and further backing sought. A name for the group had to be decided upon; after discussion of various possibilities incorporating 'United' and 'Blades', the quartet eventually settled on the epithet 'Blades Independent Fans' Association'; BIFA for short. It was important that to be a creditable campaigning organisation, such a body should have no official connection with the club, hence the inclusion of the word 'independent'. The Supporters' Club had been quickly rejected as a vehicle for promoting the agreed course of action as it was perceived to be too 'close' to the club in its organisation of travel to away matches, its arranging of social events using club facilities and its sponsorship of the 'Player of the Season' award.

A letter was compiled and a few more supportive signatures obtained before it was dispatched to the *Green 'Un* in early June. The letter was not printed in either of the next two issues, which was surprising considering the newspaper normally jumped on anything remotely concerned with football in the barren close season. It required a telephone call from Holmes to the newspaper's Paul Thompson, ironically the paper's Sheffield Wednesday correspondent, to discover that the letter was lying in United reporter Tony Pritchett's in-tray (he was on holiday). Holmes convinced Thompson that it was in the interests of both the newspaper and Sheffield United supporters for it to be published. If nothing else it would provoke letters of response that the *Green 'Un* would be only too happy to use to fill its pages. Thompson agreed and on July 2 the letter was included, unedited. Under the headline 'REVOLUTION – Loyal Blades followers in plea for fan power at the Lane', it read:

Sheffield United chairman Reg Brealey said on television on Monday, May 9 this year: 'Funds have been provided...... I think approximately £2 million, and if that's not enough then we're a club that's not capable of being in the Premier League.' Due to this continuing lack of ambition by the Bramall Lane board and having once again failed to consolidate and progress from a position of strength (15 changes of division in the last 45 years tells the story), now is the time to provide a voice for the fans' frustration and disappointment, a chance for all true Blades to show their commitment to their club. Letters to the Green 'Un *and grumbles on radio phone-ins might help let off steam but we believe the lack of an organised movement to speak up for the fans' interests has cost us dearly in recent years. Fans at other clubs have shown the way. Independent supporters' pressure groups have had real success.*

We Blades have accepted second-best long enough. The club is fortunate to have a first-class manager with ambition to match his ability but he must have more financial support. We must get organised and ensure that we never again have to suffer the shock, anger and sheer frustration we all felt at 4.45pm on May 7, 1994. The first step therefore is to form an Action Group that will plan the formation of our own Supporters' Organisation. We are not seeking to be simply a protest movement with purely negative and confrontational aims. A number of clubs, for example Bristol City, have created a place on the board for a representative of a supporters' organisation, whilst a fans' shareholding co-operative could provide a long-term stake in the club's future. We therefore ask any like-minded Blades to contact us at the Blades Independent Fans' Association if they are willing to help in any way. In particular we are looking for skills and experience to assist us in the struggle ahead. A 'legal eagle' might be useful for starters! Letters of support will also be very welcome. They will stiffen our resolve and encourage us to fight on! Blades – the fightback has begun. We want our club to realise its full potential. We need your help to put Sheffield United back where it belongs and then keep it there! (signed)

Howard Holmes, Matthew Bell, Jon Duckham, Pete Bright, Ray Kinsey, Kevin Titterton, Ian Cumming, Geoff Podmore, Dave Burkinshaw, Ian Blakemore.

The first four signatories were the men who attended the meeting at which BIFA was formed; the remaining six were like-minded Blades-supporting friends.

Crucially there was no mention in the communication of BIFA's objective to unseat Reg Brealey from office. That ambition became public later. Meanwhile a Post Office Box was set up and letters of support started to arrive. Each correspondent received a standard reply, thanking them for their interest, asking what were their particular skills and requesting them to enrol as a BIFA member. A series of further meetings was held, each better attended than the previous one, a room having to be hired at the Earl of Arundel and Surrey pub on Queen's Road, close to Bramall Lane, such was the increasing interest. Then in August a provisional Steering Committee of twelve was chosen from the regular attendees. The intention was that committee elections would take place at an open meeting to be held later in the year. A logo in United's colours of red, white and black was designed by founder member and graphic artist Pete Bright. When one of the new members, Nick Davies, a qualified accountant, presented a paper with his recommendations for the structure of the organisation, it was decided that BIFA should be set up as a company limited by guarantee, with a democratically agreed Memorandum and Articles of Association.

During the summer the ancient and wooden John Street stand, which no longer met stricter safety standards introduced following the production of the 1990 Taylor Report into the Hillsborough Disaster, was demolished. However there were no signs from the club of any coherent plans or timescale to construct a new one. In fairness the club was in an impossible situation. The 90-year-old John Street stand belonged to another era and the Hillsborough Disaster was changing the face of football stadia in Britain forever. The stand had to go, despite there being no finance in place to replace it. To his credit Brealey was in negotiations with banks in Switzerland and the Middle East to find such funding, but to no avail. Before the Hillsborough tragedy there were no specific safety rules for football stands in operation; an annual Council-accredited safety inspection was usually carried out, and the crush barriers were tested for durability and that was about it – till the next year. After Hillsborough, club secretary David Capper met with the City Council's safety representatives, sometimes four times a week. The Council's licensing officer, John Derricott, laid down the law, at times to the chagrin of managing director Derek Dooley. Sensing a battle of egos,

Capper trod the middle ground, and became the United representative in the face of Council and national government bureaucrats, who were, to be blunt, closing the stable door after the horse had bolted. The negotiations over ground safety were to take months, the ability of those in power to find fault unbelievable. A Boxing Day fixture in 1993 against Liverpool required a new exit route to be highlighted on the Shoreham End kop. This was duly done, but at the Christmas Eve inspection, the eight men from the Council found that the exit was one centimetre short of requirements. As a consequence, the repairs had to be made and Capper, along with Dooley, had to meet with the Council on Christmas Day to have the work approved. Arising out of Hillsborough, the kop's capacity was reduced from 18,000 to 11,000, with a threat of it being lowered to 5,000 if changes were not made. As a consequence, United faced having the ground capacity reduced from 30,000 to 15,000 and therefore had to act fast to rebuild the kop. Such re-building cost £1.6m, 75 per cent of which was paid for by the Football Trust, but this still left United with a £400,000 bill. The Football Trust was stringent and procedural and required that any work it funded had three competitive quotations. It would then grant to clubs the value of the lowest quote. It also paid retrospectively after the work had been done and paid for by the club. Rebuilding the John Street stand would prove to be an even more difficult task. It would also cost a lot more than the new kop.

In a promotional leaflet posted to 250,000 Sheffield homes in a bid to rally support for the newly-relegated club, Brealey wrote; 'We may have been relegated but not as a Premiership club in status terms. The challenge now is to return next season. When the John Street development is completed Bramall Lane will be among the finest grounds in the country. From then on, monies received from whatever source will be totally allocated to the playing side of the club.' Around the same time - early June - there came reports of a 'mystery multi-millionaire' who wanted to buy out Brealey's 52 per cent shareholding. The *Sheffield Star* believed that the bid 'could be made before the start of the new season'. The identity of the 'mystery' man remained unknown and nothing came of his reported bid. On June 6 the board met to talk about the

135

development of the John Street side of the ground but no word of their discussions escaped Bramall Lane. However, at the end of the month United revealed that a grant of £200,000 had been agreed with the Football Trust to go towards the construction of the new stand.

At the start of the new season BIFA cranked up its efforts to gain members and support. Thousands of leaflets were handed out by BIFA members to Blades fans outside Bramall Lane before the new season's first home game against Watford, expounding BIFA's ideas and objectives and including a membership enrolment form. The leaflet informed readers that BIFA's main aim was: 'To help Sheffield United Football Club realise its full potential' and listed methods that were to be employed to achieve that objective. The leaflet drop and *Flashing Blade* publicity was enough for 300 fans to sign up within a couple of weeks. Members and prospective members were then invited to an open meeting held in mid September at the Trades and Labour Club on Duke Street, half a mile from Sheffield city centre. Just under 200 people braved atrocious weather to attend, many of them non-members who wished to hear what BIFA was all about. Howard Holmes told the meeting how a bud of an idea had grown from four people meeting in a pub at the end of May, to a current membership of 451. Membership was open to anybody and the organisation would be democratic – one member, one vote. The meeting ratified the appointment of the Steering Committee officers: Chair – Paul Blomfield; Vice Chair – Tim Surr; Secretary – Anne Surr; Treasurer – Nick Davies; Publicity – Howard Holmes; Membership – Matthew Bell. Aside from the officers, membership of the Steering Committee was fluid. A recent addition to the Steering Committee, solicitor Jon Stittle, stated that in the 1992/93 season Sheffield United was the 11th-best supported club in the country and had the 10th-best operating profit. By these figures alone, he said, United should be an established Premier League club capable of occasionally challenging for a European place or a cup win. The Articles of Association were agreed with a few minor amendments. Then the meeting was thrown open to the floor, from where questions and complaints ensued. What were Reg Brealey's future plans? Did the club have a business plan? How much did the club owe and to whom? Why weren't fans kept informed about the commencement of building work on the John Street stand? Why had no drawings of the John Street stand been published in the press? Why didn't the club consider lower admission charges for early-round cup ties against lower division opposition? Who actually owned the land behind the kop? Why did certain directors charge bank interest rates on their loans to the club? Why didn't supporters get a say in the choice of kit designs? The meeting closed with a call for everyone to recruit as many members as possible and the disclosure that Derek Dooley had already been contacted with a view to arranging a meeting with him and/or other members of the board.

Five members met with Dooley in early October. Whilst nothing remarkable or particularly revelatory came out of the meeting it was seen as a first step on the path of setting up a process by which club and fans could meet and discuss. In mid October it appeared that this first step had become a second when a telephone call to Jon Stittle from Reg Brealey's secretary confirmed that Brealey had agreed to meet members of BIFA in the Memorial Hall of Sheffield City Hall on November 26, 1994. This information was conveyed to BIFA members in the first edition of its newsletter *Communiqué*, under the headline: 'The man from Lincoln he say "Yes".' The *Green 'Un* reported: 'Reg Brealey has agreed to meet the newly-formed Blades Independent Fans' Association, an organisation which claims to have a membership of 800 "from millionaires to the unemployed".'

When the rich and poor fans collected in the Cherry Street car park after a home defeat to Luton Town, chanting 'Sack the board!' beneath the boardroom windows, BIFA was blamed by some callers to *Radio Sheffield's* Saturday evening post-match *Praise or Grumble* phone-in for organising the demonstration. This was nowhere near the truth. BIFA members may have been there, but it was a spontaneous gathering prompted by a poor team performance. Even so, it made Brealey wary of the motives and intentions of the association. Brealey became even more concerned in early November when BIFA printed

137

and distributed 10,000 A5-size red cards to fans before a home match. The cards carried the words 'Spend Or Go!' on one side, a demand aimed at Brealey, and instructions on the other to hold them up in protest as the captains shook hands just before kick off, as no disruption was wanted during the match. A BIFA spokesman told the *Sheffield Star*; 'We want to bring home to the board how strongly supporters feel about the need for an urgent major investment in new players. We are sure there are candidates around who would welcome the chance to stop the slide. Only a massive investment in players can turn the club round.' BIFA had learned at their meeting with Dooley that Dave Bassett had £600,000 to spend, since which time he had sold Franz Carr to Leicester City for £100,000 and Jamie Hoyland to Burnley for £130,000. He had spent only £158,000 on bringing Phil Starbuck from Huddersfield Town. Why wasn't he allowed to use what had been promised to him? Bassett privately confirmed that he had been told he had no more money but that no one on the board would tell him why the situation had changed.

On the day of the red-card protest BIFA announced that it had recruited its 1,000th member. She was 16-year-old Tapton School pupil Claire Furbey, carefully selected to portray BIFA in a positive light. She was one of a number of people who joined at around the same time, taking the membership into four figures, but was deliberately given the number 1,000. Who could possibly believe that a 16-year-old schoolgirl from an attractive Sheffield suburb would become a member of what was termed in the media as a 'militant' organisation? BIFA was gaining members at a rate of 100 per week; membership would peak during the 1994/95 season at 1732, making it at the time the largest independent supporters' association in Britain. The membership included three former United players (Bob Booker, Carl Bradshaw and Paddy McGeeney), a Sheffield-based millionaire food magnate (Lawrence Wosskow), relatives of a former United director (Richard and James Wragg), a former European champion boxer (Herol Graham), a top boxing trainer (Howard Rainey), two local newspaper journalists (Rob Waugh and Ian Waugh), a former Olympic athlete (Joslyn Hoyte-Smith), a *Sky Sports* presenter (Sheffield-born Anna Walker), a well-known local artist (Terry Gorman), the head of Sheffield's largest independent estate agents (Mike Blundell), a Sheffield City councillor (Jean Cromar), the wife of a Sheffield Labour MP (Judith Michie) and someone who in later years would become a Sheffield United club director (Simon McCabe) and whose father would one day be United chairman.

Not all involved with the club saw value in fan activism. Following the red-card protest game, which United won easily 3-0, Dave Bassett complained, 'I would rather not have these demos. In an ideal world we would have 15,000 inside the ground, getting behind the team, not 12,000 with some of them having a go at the directors.' With typical bluntness Bassett described the atmosphere inside the ground as 'poxy'. In the *Sheffield Star* United reporter Tony Pritchett wrote that Brealey was 'under pressure' (from where was not stated) to cancel his proposed meeting with what Pritchett called the 'militant' BIFA.

A couple of weeks later it looked as though the man both Brealey and BIFA were looking for might have arrived. BIFA wanted somebody with lots of money to make a major investment in the club; Brealey still wanted to sell his shareholding. Or did he? Blades fan and millionaire engineering boss Martyn Burke, a Caribbean-based tax exile, offered to put an immediate £250,000 into the club for a seat on the board as a first step towards making a move to buy out Brealey. 'I have spoken to all the board members about this with the exception of Bernard Procter, who is in Australia. My last session was with the chairman himself and I am disappointed he has not come back to me. I felt that if I became a board member, for which I am prepared to make a £250,000 gesture, I could then look at the situation and consider whether I could put together an offer to Mr Brealey. I would say that whoever has control, either individually or in a consortium, is looking to an £8 million to £10 million investment. I went to Bramall Lane at the end of the board meeting on Tuesday, at their invitation, and had a long session with the chairman. But with no response I am left wondering if Mr Brealey does not want to sell to me. I feel Mr Brealey, as controller of the majority shareholding, is holding back the club.' Burke was founder of South Yorkshire-based company M.P.Burke, whose vans and lorries were often seen in the local area, accompanied by teams of workers digging up roads to lay cables and pipes for the water, gas and electricity utilities. In 1993 he sold 70 per cent of the company to Southern Electric for £11 million and two years later he sold the remaining 30 per cent, again to Southern. He had money and was a long-time Blades fan.

There was also a reported interest from a Manchester-based businessman by the name of Mike McDonald, who claimed that negotiations with Brealey were taking place. Brealey kept his cards close to his chest, until he revealed them in his inimitable style. During the half-time interval of the home game against Derby County on November 12 the electronic scoreboard at the Bramall Lane end of the ground was put to a use quite different from its normal operations of displaying advertisements and football scores. Instead, Brealey decided to use it to issue a statement informing Blades supporters that he had officially put the club up for sale. If a fan had gone for a pie or a pee they missed the news, but there were more people talking about this in the second half than there were chatting about the (rather dull) match. The statement read:

'I have decided that the time is right to make available the majority shareholding to a buyer who must be a man of substance and able to inject funds into the club, if necessary, to strengthen the playing staff. It is not the intention to dispose of the majority shareholding to someone who either has sufficient monies just to buy the shares or to sell on any delayed payment basis. We have been down this route before to the detriment of both my family and the club. The building of the new John Street stand will not be jeopardised in any way. The development will proceed according to plan. The financial state of the club is stronger than at any time in its history, despite having spent £2 million of its own resources (excluding loans) on ground safety and eliminating £2 million of internal loans. Accounts, to be published shortly, will show substantial reductions in trading liabilities. It is expected that an appropriate agency will be appointed to handle any inquiries in due course but genuine supporters should note

that many wild and exaggerated offers are usually made for publicity reasons. I will ensure that the supporters are kept fully informed if and when an inquiry of a serious nature is made.'

Brealey had at last stated his intentions, but he had not named his price. If fans were expecting a quick transfer of power they were to be disappointed. Brealey said that family concerns were behind his decision to get out; 'I can stand the flak but my family are fed up with all the pressure and the publicity.' He went on, 'If the people want a change, and it appears that they do, I am willing to sell, but only to people who are committed to the club.' The last part of this statement could be interpreted in a number of ways. Some thought it demonstrated that he did, after all, have the best interests of the club close to his heart. Others believed it a lie and that he would sell to whomever came up with the cash. Some believed he would use it as a delaying tactic; that he would never consider any potential buyer as suitable, because he didn't really want to sell. Yet more reckoned it was a purely selfish motive: Brealey didn't care to whom he sold providing he could avoid another Hashimi or Woolhouse fiasco. Two days later the *Sheffield Star* reported that Mike McDonald was the leader of a three-man consortium wishing to buy out Brealey. McDonald said that the other two members of his team wished to remain anonymous but he confirmed that one was a Blades supporter; 'I suppose if the deal is done I should think that it will be a guy who is quite well accepted. An offer has been made that matches the price that he [Brealey] has asked for.' The asking price was not publicised but McDonald added that his consortium if successful, would be able to invest £10 million in the club, over and above the purchase cost. However, after previously denying he had received a bid, Brealey now admitted that he had, but that it was 'peanuts'. He also said that it was from a company whose name he did not 'associate with McDonald'. He added, 'I have had dozens of offers for the club. None of them stand up. As soon as we talk figures, they melt away.'

Brealey did not officially inform BIFA that he would no longer be attending its meeting at the City Hall on the morning of the

Southend home game at the end of November but it had been quite obvious for a while to those involved that he would not. The meeting went ahead anyway in front of around 200 members and a moment of humour arose when Paul Blomfield, from the chair, announced that now, at last, we would hear from Reg. The audience, wondering if Brealey was really about to enter the auditorium after all, went silent and fell into laughter when the next speaker revealed that he was indeed Reg, but that his name was Reg Hobson, a member of the BIFA Steering Committee. Now that Brealey had made clear his plans to sell, BIFA wanted to turn up the heat on him. The dates of the regular Steering Committee meetings, which now had a permanent venue in the Railway pub literally across the road from the United ground, were publicised in the press so that any BIFA members could attend. Over the next few years the monthly meetings saw attendances fluctuate between half a dozen and a maximum 20.

As various schemes were thrown around, BIFA maintained its insistence on peaceful, non-violent and non-criminal protest. There were however sometimes more reactionary views put forward at meetings, which always received short shrift. One member, a matchday regular at the Railway, suggested turning over Brealey's car in the club car park and then setting it on fire. His proposal was speedily rejected, as was another to push dog faeces through Brealey's letterbox, in favour of another pre-match card demonstration. The composition of BIFA's Steering Committee heavily influenced the methods of protest employed and actions undertaken, largely because it comprised mainly educated – even respectable – professionals, such as Paul Blomfield, then a high-ranking member of the local Labour party and since May 2010 Labour MP for the Sheffield Central constituency, Howard Holmes, a well-known and respected local youth worker, Dave Webster, a barrister, and Jon Stittle, a solicitor. The committee believed that 'direct', even violent, action would be counter-productive in that it would alienate many of its members and provide ammunition for an already unsupportive local press. BIFA did not have a 'provisional wing' – it hoped to rely on dialogue and the ballot box, rather than angry mobs with sticks and stones, to achieve its aims. Despite setbacks, this policy ultimately proved successful.

The red card 'send him off' protest had been popular: another, however - 'Green for Go' - was to follow three weeks later. Thousands of cards were once more distributed outside the ground by BIFA members for the crowd to hold above their heads just before kick off. This time the cards were green and displayed a simple statement to Brealey: 'Go!'. Also printed and distributed by BIFA were bright yellow stickers showing a cartoon face of Brealey, drawn by local artist Phil Maynard, and various slogans, such as 'Nightmare on John Street', 'Fairweather Fan', 'The Chairman From Hell' and the more to-the-point 'Brealey Out'. BIFA spokesman Alex Waugh insisted to local press: 'People say we are emotional, militant and fickle, but we have been very patient. Our main complaint has been that he [Brealey] has not been prepared to invest in players. We feel if he is not prepared to put money into the club he should sell to someone who is.' In the meantime the average home gate had gone down from 20,000 to 11,500. The team was also drifting towards the foot of the table.

Brealey's reaction to the latest demonstration was dismissive: 'They may want a change but I will not be rushed into a quick sell. If I can find someone to take over from me, I will. Maybe my presence is a starting point for the aggro. If so I will remove it on matchdays but come to the club in midweek and do my work. Without me maybe the fans will revert to being genuine supporters again as they were when I came to Sheffield 15 years ago. I was drawn to United by the fervour of their fans at Grimsby when they were solidly behind a team losing 5-1 [it was actually 4-0]. I contrast this with what happened on Saturday when we won 2-0 and wonder if they can possibly be the same people. Just suppose there had been a potential buyer at Bramall Lane on Saturday, a buyer with money and ambition. He would have run a mile at what he saw and heard. It hurts when one has done so much and it is now of so little value.' Brealey also said that all he wanted for his shares was his 'capital and nothing more' and for the first time he mentioned a price: £3.5 million would 'sort it out'.

Meanwhile, Dave Bassett was trying his best to distance himself from the squabbling between Brealey and the fans and protect his players from events. United had won the two 'protest' games 3-0 and 2-0 but Bassett could contain his feelings no longer. Speaking to the *Sheffield Star*, he lamented how the atmosphere at the club on matchdays was 'terrible'. He continued, 'It is created by the fans because of their frustration. The players feel that the fans are waiting for them to lose so they can beat up the stadium and smash it. To be quiet, wait until we go 2-0 up and then chant "sack the board" is not helping the team. The players are sensitive like anyone else. They can sense that some of the fans are not happy.' Bassett's comments summed up BIFA's problem of getting its message across. The organisation was fully behind Bassett and the team and didn't want to take any actions that might be perceived to affect the players' performance, which is why any organised protests or demonstrations were designed to take place moments before kick off. Any collective chanting inside the ground during the game was not orchestrated by BIFA – how could it be when its members were spread out all over the stadium? But any dissent was ascribed to BIFA, either mistakenly or deliberately. And now the manager, whom BIFA went out of its way to support, was wondering if they might start ripping seats out of the kop. He seemingly did not understand BIFA's intentions. However, there was a postscript to this incident as it appeared that Bassett was more upset at the manner in which his words had been reported in the *Sheffield Star* and spent much of his column in the following home match programme restating what he actually meant and not how the *Sheffield Star* interpreted his words.

The normally stoic Derek Dooley was also unhappy at events. He too was under a misapprehension. Speaking in the *Sheffield Star* after a match, he said, 'The atmosphere out there was terrible,' adding, 'The board runs the club and as such we are there to be shot at if the fans feel that way. But the way they are going about it is destroying everything. I can't believe the treatment to Jostein Flo; he comes on as sub for the last five minutes and gets the bird immediately. If the fans want to demonstrate against the directors we have to take it. But they should still help the team better than this.' BIFA was facing a dilemma; as an organisation, it never directed vitriol at any player or the manager, yet it was being accused of doing so. Now, despite ever rising membership there was also a similar increase in people opposed to BIFA's cause, blaming the organisation for the 'terrible atmosphere' at matches and the abuse aimed at players from the stands. Detractors then used the *Green 'Un* letters page to accuse BIFA of accepting payment from a possible buyer of Brealey's shares in exchange for promoting and supporting that bidder's proposal. This was not true.

One letter writer to the *Green 'Un*, Elaine Williamson, exhorted the official Supporters' Club branches to rally to 'boot out the BIFA bullies' and accused the BIFA Steering Committee of feeding 'lies and propaganda' to the organisation's members. BIFA, in her eyes, was guilty of 'dirty tricks and troublemaking'. She called BIFA spokesman Howard Holmes 'the Fuhrer' and accused him of encouraging BIFA members to 'harass [the directors'] old grannies'. She claimed an unknown person was 'pulling [BIFA's] strings' and alleged that BIFA was taking bribes; '30 pieces of silver' were the words she used. BIFA members were aghast and disappointed that such a deliberately inflammatory letter should be given such prominence and a one-inch headline by a publication recently voted Britain's best weekly sports paper, especially when letters from BIFA supporters were either heavily edited or not printed at all. Ms Williamson's letter was conveniently followed by a request from the editor that the BIFA/Brealey debate should now end, thus denying any reply to her preposterous claims. In his weekly column on the Sheffield United page in the *Green 'Un, Flashing Blade* editor Matthew Bell attempted to respond to some of Ms Williamson's points but was informed by *Sheffield Star* reporter Tony Pritchett that this wouldn't be permitted as it might be perceived to be the official stance of the newspaper, even though the column was publicised as an independent fan's view. No letters renouncing Ms Williamson were printed and when one individual contacted the newspaper to ask if he could write to her directly he was told by the editor that 'we've lost her address'. Who Ms Williamson is or was remains in the realm of conjecture. Such a provocative letter would not normally see the author's details carelessly 'lost'. The whys and wherefores of provincial journalism contain multiple layers of back-scratching and 'accommodation'. In the long history of the *Green 'Un* this incident was not its finest hour.

BIFA tried to lighten the mood before the next home game by displaying helium-filled balloons and large inflatable champagne bottles at its recruitment stalls on the four corners of the ground. Furthermore, it paid for and handed out thousands of red and white balloons to fans for them to release as the teams came out on to the pitch. Whether these ideas improved the atmosphere at the match or the performance of the team was inconclusive. Four musical members of BIFA reckoned a good way to show the organisation's support of Dave Bassett was to set up a group in his name. Calling themselves 'Hanging On To Harry' ('Harry' was Bassett's nickname since his teens), they played their own brand of blues and rock music in pubs and clubs throughout the city. Bassett wrote in his autobiography that this ensemble 'amused me' – albeit he never attended any of the band's dozens of gigs – considering it 'a great gesture and provided some light moments at a tense time'.

BIFA initiated positive ideas, such as sponsoring a United player. Interestingly, whilst the club disowned BIFA it was happy to take its money for sponsorship. BIFA also agitated for naming the new stand (if it were ever built) after the club's former goalkeeper Mel Rees, who died of cancer in May 1993. It actively encouraged the involvement and support for United from minority groups in the city. These and other objectives were consolidated by the introduction of a 'Fans' Charter', formulated by BIFA member Tim Pinto. BIFA was conscious that it was increasingly being seen as a single-issue organisation and sought to concentrate on wider concerns to run alongside the core campaign of deposing Brealey. The Fans' Charter was a 'mission statement' detailing the ambitions of BIFA for the development of the club. Its aims were worthy, but the Charter received negligible publicity and minimal response - good or bad - from the club. In fact it faded into obscurity. This declaration was where, in the eyes of some, BIFA went wrong. From being a single-issue pressure group it went too 'right-on' and tried to become everything to everybody. Had it stuck to its original task it might not have lost the support of a large chunk of Blades fans. In going all 'New Labour' with its vision of inclusion and gesture politics, it was losing both focus and the support of the more working class and, indeed elderly, of United followers.

The Fans' Charter, however, must have been read by one person at Bramall Lane as just days after its publication one BIFA member was invited by Promotions Office manager Mick Rooker to study the accounts of the Blades Revival lottery scheme. At the time the fund stood at £28,828 – it was lower than normal as instalments had just been paid out of the fund to Millwall, for the purchase of Mark Beard, and to Mansfield Town for Paul Holland. A desire for more open and frequent communication between the club and the fans was one of the points of the Charter. The invitation to see the Blades Revival accounts was an example of this, which BIFA believed would not have occurred without its pressure. BIFA also canvassed its members by post to ascertain their opinions on the effectiveness of BIFA's campaigns. From 30 returns, the comments included: 'We should try to get at Brealey personally'; 'We should stop the anti-Brealey abuse'; 'Protests should be more aggressive'; 'Hit Brealey in the pocket'; 'Don't do anything to affect the income of the club'; 'Add more humour to BIFA'; 'Just keep up the pressure' and 'Brealey campaign is out of order'. The wide variation of responses was not surprising given the size of the association; the Steering Committee's task was to filter the various suggestions to formulate a legitimate and expedient plan that would satisfy the majority. This was not an easy task.

A deliberately restrained demonstration against Brealey was held outside the Annual General Meeting at Bramall Lane on a freezing morning in late December 1994, as some 25 BIFA members held placards stating, 'Where's Our Stand Reg?', 'Brealey - Set a Fair Price!', 'BIFA Backs Dave Bassett' and 'Three and a Half Million? Do you really want to go Reg?' Members of the press were refused entry by Brealey to the

AGM for the first time in living memory. Some received sympathy, and hot coffee, from the BIFA assembly. Even the *Sheffield Star's* Tony Pritchett, whom BIFA claimed was biased against its objectives and in their opinion was Brealey's puppet, was the beneficiary of BIFA hospitality. *BBC Look North's* Damien Johnson and freelance radio reporter Alan Biggs were particularly pleased to be able to warm themselves. Brealey thought it necessary to employ 'heavies' on the door, in the shape of a couple of burly men, no doubt fearing an attempt at forced entry from BIFA. Shareholder Robert Jackson, a one-time presenter on *BBC Radio Sheffield*, asked that the press be allowed entry but his request was declined. Brealey informed the meeting that the reason the press was barred was because an item in the accounts was *sub-judice*, with a court hearing due to be held early in 1995, over an issue 'not connected with Sheffield United'. Reacting to the news that he wouldn't be allowed in, Pritchett was overheard complaining about 'having been coming to these things for 20-odd years' and 'not having been given any forewarning'. Someone commented, deliberately within his earshot, that if his years of attendance counted for nothing and if communication had been non-existent and if he'd been left to wait in adverse weather and if he felt he'd been dumped on, he now knew just what it was like to be treated like a regular (and loyal) Blades supporter.

Inside the meeting Brealey told shareholders that contracts for the new John Street stand would be signed in January and the stand would be open for the start of the following season. If the deal were not finalised by the end of January the price would go up; he assured the AGM that he expected to 'press the button' before then. Director John Plant had announced live on television before a home game against Barnsley in October that a start on the stand would soon be made and Brealey's comments at the AGM backed up the belief that the commencement of construction work was imminent. An artist's impression of the proposed stand had already been presented, when a few weeks earlier Brealey had re-introduced his early-1980s idea of the *Blades News* newspaper. The first issue for 11 years (it now cost 30p, formerly it was free) focussed on the stand. Brealey wrote in an article entitled

'The Way Ahead': 'Building a new stand on the John Street side of the ground and providing Sheffield United with a stadium fit for Premiership football is, in my view, an absolute priority. Its completion will start an exciting new chapter in the history of the club and it has to be ready for next season. This is not just a dream, it is a commitment to which, as chairman, I am dedicated. Once that is complete, the three corners of the ground have to be tackled but that can be reserved; the implementation of our resolve to replace the old John Street structure with a stand worthy of the next century is something that cannot be reserved. If we miss this window of opportunity and the construction industry moves further out of recession then we will move into an area of financial commitment which we cannot afford. If I had sat here alone with total responsibility I would have pressed the button before now and found the money afterwards but because I have a cautious board around me I had to get the money right first. We are within striking distance of starting. Our bank have been very supportive and understanding, full credit to Barclay's. But there is a shortfall between what they are prepared to do and what the stand will cost. This balance is called "mezzanine" finance; that is unsecured finance and that is what we have investigated. I have spent days here and in the City attempting to get the finance together because I am determined to go ahead. We have a fixed maximum of £4 million. We think it [could be] contained at under this but £4 million would give us the superb stand I want. Many people might be puzzled that the club can afford this but is apparently unable to invest large sums in buying new players.'

He went on to describe the reasons why money could be borrowed for construction projects but not for purchasing footballers and concluded, 'Some of the supporters might want to say "chairman out" and I accept the criticism; it goes with the job. If they want change I do not mind changing. But I have never flinched from taking a decision, however unpopular, that I felt to be in the interest of Sheffield United, and I never will. Those who have responsibility for control must never forget that the club belongs to the supporters. The shares might belong to individuals. But the ground is the home of the supporters and if I protect their "home", I protect their club.' These were fine words, informative and, in truth, probably spoken from the heart. The supporters were in part placated.

Because members of the press were not permitted entry to the AGM they had to rely on comments from shareholders to report what had happened. One stated on the *ITV Calendar* local news programme: '[It was] very disappointing really, much as we thought it would be. The chairman has no intentions of investing any money in players at all, so he's relying on Dave Bassett to keep the team afloat on a shoestring budget.' Another was less analytical stating: 'We don't know what's going on behind the scenes but we just wish he'd hurry up and go.' Brealey was portrayed as 'evasive' and 'inconclusive' by one shareholder and another demanded of Brealey, 'In God's name, go!' Tony Pritchett wrote in his *Green 'Un* column the following Saturday: 'I had expected to tell you tonight all about Sheffield United's annual meeting; what BIFA said to Reg Brealey, what Reg Brealey said to BIFA and who won the argument. Individual shareholders say Brealey won the day but, if he did, he lost the public relations battle. Shareholders who insisted they were neutral gave game, set and match to Brealey when BIFA representatives questioned him.' *Green 'Un* letter writer L.Smythe did not concur, writing the following week: 'I was at the shareholders' meeting and disagree with Tony Pritchett's tennis-loving friend. I have never seen Reg Brealey under so much pressure and so shaken at a meeting. BIFA members, inside and out, were well behaved and dignified.' Pritchett concluded his report, 'BIFA, naturally, offer contrasting reports and insist they gave the chairman a hard time. What a pity, for supporters' point of view, there will be no independent reports of what took place.' Independence wasn't the issue, competing truths were.

Chapter 8

Christmas Cards,
India and Scotland
Brealey Feels The Heat

That any report in the *Sheffield Star* or *Green 'Un* written by
Tony Pritchett would have been 'independent' of Sheffield
United's influence was very much doubted by BIFA members.
Their caricature of him on a Christmas card circulated to all
members and sympathisers provided the backdrop to the next
big fall-out between BIFA and Brealey. BIFA had printed a
couple of thousand Christmas cards, for the purpose of raising
funds through their sale and for campaign publicity purposes.
On the cards was depicted a cartoon, drawn by local cartoonist
and BIFA member Phil Maynard, showing Pritchett as a
ventriloquist's dummy sitting on Brealey's knee, the
implication being, of course, that the journalist only said what
Brealey wanted him to say. Predictably it didn't go down too
well with Pritchett, but it was the alleged words in the
messages inside the cards that provoked Brealey's anger.
Seasonal 'greetings' to Brealey were written by BIFA
members and associates and on the morning of Christmas Eve
a small group of BIFA members and their families set off from
Sheffield for Brealey's home in Lincolnshire, in the hope of
delivering the cards to him personally so they could prove to
him that BIFA members were not 'militants' but ordinary,
committed, supporters of all generations.

One of their number, Tim Surr, a member of the BIFA Steering Committee, takes up the story: 'Six adults (one dressed as Santa Claus) and two children made the journey. The number of cards we were to deliver was 1,700, each having been individually vetted [by the BIFA Steering Committee] to remove obscenities. We pulled in to Reg's village and approached Reg's house. The delegation drew up outside the walled garden of Reg's mansion, to be met by a reporter and photographer from the *Lincolnshire Echo*. We posed for photos and gave a classic quote of "Ho ho" in reply to a request for a comment from Father Christmas. We peered through the iron gates, pushed open the gate and entered. To our great surprise, who walked round the corner from the front door but Reg, resplendent in his SUFC tracksuit. He greeted us warmly, shook Santa by the hand and looked at one or two cards we gave him. Then, to our absolute amazement, he invited us in. He took us into his sitting room. At this point he stopped the reporter taking notes, saying some things might be *sub-judice*. He then waffled his way through the questions asked about his future plans and the stand and he blamed BIFA and the publicity we generated for a bank withdrawing funds (he couldn't remember which bank). He also said that all the talk of Dave Bassett not having any money was a game the two of them played. He added that Bassett was a good manager who did a good job. He then told us there was a difference between fans and supporters. We didn't ask him to expand. He couldn't remember why he didn't attend the BIFA meeting at the City Hall but stated that if BIFA were under the umbrella of the Supporters' Club he would visit us any time, any place, anywhere. We listened to what Reg had to say, but the thing that shone through was the insistence that he would sell when and to whom he pleased.'

At this stage there was no indication of any controversy around the visit to Brealey's house. It was only a couple of weeks into the New Year that stories began to appear in the Sheffield press that some of the Christmas cards given to Brealey contained obscene messages. BIFA vehemently denied this and whilst admitting that some of the cards had included 'unacceptable' language, stressed that all the offensive ones had been removed before the remainder were given to the chairman. Someone was not telling the whole truth. Brealey told *Blades News*; 'I acknowledged your 1346 Christmas cards and received your postmen in the true Christmas spirit, but I feel you could have still made the point by delivering half the number and burning the other half which contained vulgarity that was not befitting genuine Blades supporters. I read every one and retained a handful for posterity. I suppose the appalling spelling says something. It's amazing how many people do not realise that off has two fs. One card wished me away in eight words of which only two were spelt correctly, "Reg" and a four-letter word beginning with "f". It was quite an eye opener, and I suppose some consolation for my efforts at your club.' Brealey's horror at the language was somewhat rich, considering that he once told a local journalist that his own definition of the acronym 'BIFA' was 'Bunch of Interfering Fucking Arseholes'.

The chairman continued his tirade in the next edition of *Blades News*: 'I am still mystified as to what BIFA wish to achieve. If it is to remove me, I have already indicated my intention, and have the patience to wait for the right person. The club cannot afford to be sold to someone who says he has the wherewithal to support it when he hasn't. We could never recover from a second mistake. There are, however, limits to everyone's tolerance and the anti-Blades behaviour of BIFA may well be the ruin of the club. I repeat again what I said some months ago, if you are genuine supporters of the Blades then join the genuine Supporters' Club – do something useful for a change – quit being a critic.' This was the same man who a few weeks earlier had said that 'the club belongs to the supporters.' Then *Sheffield Star* columnist Paul Licence jumped on the bandwagon. Mr Licence had never been noted for his views on football before, yet now he felt fit to comment on 'the sending of obscene cards', when he had no actual knowledge of what had happened and based his story totally on second-hand evidence. One *Green 'Un* letter writer, whose correspondence was given leader status despite its being semi-literate and poorly constructed, complained about BIFA members not revealing their names and addresses at the foot of letters but then his own letter ended 'name and address supplied'.

Meanwhile, claims made by BIFA supporters that the cards had not contained obscene messages were given scant attention. The allegations made by Brealey and reported by the *Sheffield Star* seemed to be part of a campaign to smear BIFA. What was actually going on in the editorial office will never be fully known, but it looked as if such publicity was designed to give the organisation a hit from which it would never be able to regain its credibility. Such publicity did affect BIFA's reputation amongst Blades fans, often articulated in the form of verbal abuse from passing fellow Blades at home matches, directed at the BIFA campaign tables near the ground. In the meantime, BIFA made a big play of stating what it had and had not done. In its members' newsletter and in a press release it explained that it had:

1) Become a nationally recognised organisation that represented the views of ordinary supporters, winning the support of the Football Supporters' Association and *When Saturday Comes* (the independent football magazine. In truth, the 'recognition' was really not much more than an acknowledgement of BIFA's existence).
2) After BIFA representatives met Derek Dooley, United released various financial details in the *Sheffield Star*. Would this have happened otherwise?
3) Even though Reg Brealey refused to meet BIFA, he agreed to meet the Executive Committee of the Official Supporters' Club. Would this have happened without the presence of BIFA?
4) BIFA members were able to put more pressure on Brealey at the AGM than he had ever faced before. He was evasive, but flustered.
5) 788 BIFA members were also members of the Blades Revival, the lottery begun in 1986 designed specifically to raise money for purchasing new players. At the subscription rate of £2 per week this meant they were paying almost £41,000 per year into the club. 924 BIFA members were season ticket holders, so based on an average price of £200 this was another £185,000 per year paid to club by BIFA

members.   Sixty members of BIFA were also shareholders who paid £500 per share in 1981.   All in all, not a bad investment from people whom Brealey branded 'fairweather fans' and 'not genuine supporters'.

BIFA had not:

1) Sent obscene cards to Reg Brealey.
2) Spread rumours that Dave Bassett would resign after the Southend game.
3) Called supporters with opposing views 'fairweather fans' or questioned their intelligence.
4) Taken, or even been offered, any money from prospective buyers of the club.
5) Backed any prospective bidders.
6) Harassed directors' grannies.

Early in 1995 news came from the North East that Brealey was planning a takeover of Fourth Division club Darlington but Football League rules prevented him doing so while he was still connected with Sheffield United. Did this mean that he had a buyer for the Blades? In a bid to try and smoke out whoever Brealey's potential purchaser might be, BIFA decided to involve itself in an act of subterfuge. In mid February the *Green 'Un* reported that Mike Blundell, owner of the Sheffield estate agents of the same name, was trying to raise funds to buy out Brealey. Blundell was a BIFA member and attended several Steering Committee meetings. At one meeting he agreed to front a drive to get together a consortium to raise enough money to make an offer to Brealey, deliberately avoiding any mention of his BIFA connections.   An advertisement was placed in local newspapers, which produced a potential backer of £500,000, but Blundell announced that he himself would not be a substantial investor. Blundell's was never intended to be a serious bid as it was highly unlikely that he would be able to raise the required £3.5 million, but it kept the campaign to force out Brealey in the public eye and gave Blundell and his business good publicity in the process. If it provoked Brealey to act more quickly, or forced any other prospective buyers to show their hand, it would have been doubly useful.   Blundell informed a BIFA

Steering Committee meeting in March that he had been pledged around £800,000 but that the bogus consortium idea appeared to have 'died a death'. The episode was quietly put to bed.

Meanwhile, Brealey's self-imposed deadline for signing contracts for the new John Street stand of January 31 passed without any agreement. Brealey, however, insisted that the stand would be built in time for the start of the 1995/96 season. He also believed that the price would go up by £500,000 on February 1, which was the deadline of the validity of the tender of the contractors, Mowlems of Leeds. Tony Pritchett then reported in the *Green 'Un* that Mowlems had not imposed such a penalty - the agreed price stood. But for how long? It was also reported that for the stand to be completed by early August the structural steelwork would have to be delivered to the site by the end of March. It was now mid February. Pritchett ended his article by saying, 'If the club cannot find the money they should say so. It will be a bad day for United if it comes to that but better, surely, than leaving the fans in the dark as they troop to Bramall Lane, match after match, and see no sign of activity.' For once, BIFA agreed with everything Pritchett wrote.

In an attempt to counteract bad publicity BIFA introduced a new campaigning fanzine called *The Red and White Wizaaard*, designed to keep members (and non-members - it was on sale to everyone outside the ground on matchdays) more up to date with news than was possible with its quarterly newsletter *Communiqué*. Selling for 50p, the fanzine would also be a modest source of income for BIFA. In the first issue contributor Ray Kinsey, a member of the BIFA Steering Committee, related a comical story of how he and a group of fellow BIFA members attempted to employ some light-hearted tactics to keep the lack of progress on the new stand in the forefront of supporters' minds. They decided to make a large banner, fashioned from white bed sheets and red paint, on which was daubed 'The Reg Brealey Stand'. It was their intention to hang the banner over the red perimeter fence surrounding the area where the old John Street stand had stood during the early stages of the home game against Stoke City in

February. However, they had miscalculated the height of the fence and faced a problem of how to get the banner up and over so that it would be visible to everybody inside the ground. They told a couple of policemen what they were planning, stressing phrases like 'peaceful protest', 'no harm intended' and 'law-abiding citizens'. The good officers strategically turned their backs. Despite a group of latecomers who had just left the Cricketers pub offering assistance to the farcical attempt to place the banner in the ideal location, the two policemen - laughing so much they could hardly speak – returned to explain to the protagonists: 'We've just had a call from our boss. He's told us to confiscate the banner. We gave you as long as we could, sorry.' It turned out that whole episode had been watched by a number of policemen stationed in a nearby building, on standby to deal with any potential crowd disorder!

Brealey put forward his reasons for the delay in the commencement of construction of the stand in *Blades News*: 'What the supporter wants to know is when does the John Street Stand commence? The answer is as soon as the final financial aspects are complete, as explained some time ago. Monies borrowed have to be repaid and profit records, forecasts and repayment projections have to be written up and approved. It is a fact that one setback for me occurred following the first BIFA demonstration which called for a new board. This type of hassle worries lenders who are lending to a club on the merits of its board and, when the board looks as if it could change then people obviously worry (another reason why BIFA should shut up). We have had our final plans approved with amendments made. The builders are ready to start and upon laying the first brick will declare a completion and opening date. I am as committed as ever to its building and to see its completion. I am working as fast as I can to get the balance in hand and ask for no more than to be supported and left in peace to complete the job free from the snide, cynical comments that do nothing other than spread despondency and despair. The role of chairman has been much more difficult this time around. I still feel aggrieved at having to pick up the pieces of a diabolical mess, and being criticised for doing it, having left it so sound financially.' The

157

delay in building the new stand was, in the eyes and words of Brealey, BIFA's fault.

Unperturbed by such comments, BIFA staged a march from Sheffield Town Hall to Bramall Lane prior to a Saturday home match, carrying a plywood 'coffin' draped in a United flag and a wreath, to signify 'the death of the club'. Four BIFA members carried the coffin, with a further dozen following. The procession received a small amount of coverage in the *Sheffield Star* and kept BIFA's campaign in the public eye. BIFA's next plan to up the pressure on Brealey was to hold a poll, asking Blades fans to express their 'confidence' or 'no confidence' in the chairman. Ten thousand 'voting slips' were handed out to fans at the turnstiles before a home match and, when completed, were collected inside and outside the ground. Although the poll would never receive the approval of the Electoral Reform Society, its results were conclusive. From some 3,700 returns, 3,593 expressed 'No Confidence' in Brealey, with only 54 giving him their full backing. If Brealey ever learned of the overwhelming vote against him, he considered it meaningless and ignored it completely.

What Brealey couldn't ignore, however, was the headline of the *Sheffield Star* on March 3, 1995: 'INTERPOL SEEK BLADES CHIEF: World warrant out for Brealey.' A global warrant had been issued by Indian courts for Brealey's arrest in connection with allegations that he had defaulted on payments into the workers' savings fund at Titaghur, his Indian company. The courts wanted him extradited to face 16 cases of alleged payment default recorded by West Bengal authorities, the maximum sentence for which would be 15 years in prison should he be found guilty. Under Indian law, employers had to match payments made by workers into long-term savings funds. The courts claimed that Brealey had failed to fulfil these obligations and owed millions of pounds to the Provident Fund. The European-based international police intelligence sharing agency Interpol had been contacted by the Indian authorities and its spokesman was quoted as saying, 'An arrest warrant has been issued by a judicial court for an R.J. Brealey. We have yet to receive full extradition papers.' United director Derek Dooley defended his chairman, saying, 'It seems there's some sort of witch-hunt. Reg is easy to pick up because he's at home. He came to the club yesterday. He's not hiding.' Brealey was used to the Indian legal processes; in 1990 he had been held in police custody to 'help with inquiries' over allegations that he breached foreign currency exchange controls. No charges ever resulted.

One Titaghur employee, an engineer and shop steward, claimed he hadn't been paid for five months. He was lucky. According to him, 'Some workers have started begging on the streets. The children go out in the evenings begging for food for their families. We won't be able to survive like this for long.' The Commissioner of the West Bengal Provident Fund, which was responsible for workers' pensions, said: 'It is a very major problem and it is a huge amount which the Brealey group has not paid.' According to the Commissioner, Titaghur owed some £8 million in outstanding pension contributions, which included money deducted from workers' pay but subsequently not handed over. The Provident Fund seized Titaghur's head office in Calcutta, which it intended to sell to defray the debts. Interpol confirmed that its help had been sought in the requested extradition of Brealey but it was unable to act because the documentation provided by officers in New Delhi was 'unsatisfactory'.

In January 1995 the *Mail on Sunday* reported that it wasn't only the Titaghur workers who were unhappy at Brealey's running of the company. So were its shareholders. The paper reported that: 'Investors in jute company Titaghur are calling on the police, the Stock Exchange and the Department of Trade and Industry to investigate the company's failure to honour promises. Investors who bought shares on the back of [plans to re-float the company on the American Nasdaq market] are angry that these and other initiatives have come to nothing. Reg Brealey's brother Len is one of a dozen shareholders demanding an investigation. They claim that Titaghur's directors procured investment in the company "by false representation", thus artificially inflating its share price.' Now, even Reg's brother was after him, and Len described Reg as 'not a man to do business with' (Reg admitted in 1999 he no longer talked to Len). What angered some shareholders

159

was what they said was a list of promises made by the chairman that had not been fulfilled, such as listing the company on Nasdaq, raising $50 million there for investment in Titaghur, developing its western market with bio-technical products and making plans to pay off its outstanding Indian provident fund dues.

Brealey seemed unconcerned, claiming in *Blades News*; 'When I agreed to take the chairmanship of this Indian jute company I looked upon it as just another chairmanship and as at one time I held 18 chairmanships, thought it an easy role. I knew it was the world's biggest jute company with 18,000 workers, six villages plus dependants, but still I thought it a standard task. How wrong I was. Operating in a communist state with very strong union control it became increasingly difficult as we tidied up, bringing the company up to date. I will not bore you with details but as sportsmen imagine this – Wembley Stadium on FA Cup final day, packed to capacity, 85,000 people. Close your eyes for a moment, visualise it, and then imagine having a responsibility for feeding that number every day. That's what this company has to do; workers and dependants total that number. No work, no food, no social security out there.' His figures were probably accurate, as over four million families survive on growing and processing jute in West Bengal.

Brealey continued: 'I must state no one has taken one rupee of workers' pensions or any statutory dues. Any deficiency has been provided for in the balance sheet. Paucity of funds arises when the finished goods sales value falls below production costs. Mill managers have to take decisions – close factories and starve workers or work on and temporarily default statutory dues. For many years the latter has been the rule of the day in the jute industry with union support – default creates problems and warrants are issued ten-a-penny and can be cancelled overnight. India is a litigant's paradise and a legal nightmare. One quickly learns the rules by which to stay alive. I remember being told never to drive in India, always be a passenger, and if someone steps in front of your car and you knock him over don't get out of your car. If you must get out then run like hell to stay alive. I will solve my jute problems the same way as I will solve football problems, and very soon, but one's enemies use character assassination as a weapon and, of course, to identify the character in media terms is ideal. Mike McCarthy of *BBC Look North* said he would not have been interested in the company had its chairman not been SUFC chairman. It's so easy to be a critic.' It was thus all the fault of the Communists, the Indian social structure, and the Western media. Brealey's apparent lack of compassion for injured pedestrians was controvertible and hardly compatible with his Christian beliefs.

Brealey then quoted Theodore Roosevelt, the former President of the USA: 'The credit belongs to the man who is actually in the arena, whose face is marred by dust and sweat and blood; who strives valiantly, who errs and often comes up short again and again, who knows the great enthusiasms, the great devotions and spends himself unto a worthy cause, who at best knows in the end the triumph of high achievement, and who at worst if he fails, at least fails while daring greatly, so that his place shall never be with those cold and timid souls who know neither victory or defeat.' The relevance of such heroic rhetoric with ownership of a football club was tenuous, but what Blades fans were absolutely sure of was that hundreds of them had shown 'enthusiasms' and 'great devotions', spending themselves 'unto a worthy cause' by making long treks on consecutive Saturdays to opposite ends of the country at this time (to Sunderland and Portsmouth) to watch their team surrender meekly to two pitiful 1-0 defeats at the hands of relegation-threatened clubs. On another occasion – soon after relegation from the Premier League in 1994 - Brealey mystifyingly wrote, 'Teams wax and wane, they die and come alive again, but if a supporter dies through club negligence such as a collapsed stand, weak barriers, or even fire, and we have seen them all, he cannot be brought back alive.' And this was in a leaflet distributed to supporters urging them to buy season tickets! Brealey at times considered himself as a bit of a philosopher - he did after all sit on the General Synod of the Church of England - but by quoting the Roosevelt passage he perhaps stretched his sagacity too far. He was not averse to using quotations of the famous to stress a point. Several years earlier he had asked fans to be patient by urging them, in the

161

words of Rudyard Kipling, to keep their heads when all about them were losing theirs.

In mentioning Mike McCarthy, Brealey was referring to the reporter's BBC television documentary programme about Brealey's involvement with Titaghur. According to McCarthy, when Brealey bought Titaghur he was considered by the locals as 'a man with vision'. Fellow Titaghur director Ronald Kumar described how Brealey, 'a sincere man', wished to completely update the company with new machinery (much of the existing equipment was imported from Scotland almost a century before), providing the place with a general facelift and instigating discussions with the factories' notoriously militant trade unionists. When news of Brealey's takeover reached the London Stock Exchange (LSE) shares in Titaghur shot up from £1.30 to £2.15 in one day and rose to £5.10 by the end of the year. In 1988 Titaghur was the LSE's top performing share, peaking at more than £18. Former Titaghur employee and shareholder Wayne Lumsden told the programme that it was expected that Brealey would re-finance the company and diversify its interests, while at the same time rejuvenating the chronic state of the jute industry. But, as McCarthy reported, it soon became clear that there would not be an upturn in Titaghur's fortunes as the company continued to suffer heavy losses and long periods of closure of its four mills. When the mills were closed, workers did not get paid – some it seemed barely ate. One mill worker was quoted, saying; 'They don't give us any kind of money, nor do they pay us on time. I don't have enough money to feed myself. You can ask in every house – they cook once and miss the next two meals.'

The jute industry in India had been long renowned for its union-inspired industrial militancy. Some of this was praiseworthy as it had made it an employer's legal duty to provide funds for special hospitals to treat workers who could not afford regular health care. West Bengal was a state run on Marxist lines. Workers claimed that in the six years since Brealey took over their rights had been undermined. Many said they were unable to retire because of Brealey's alleged non-payment of provident fund dues, though McCarthy added that Titaghur was not the only jute company to default on such payments. The mills were dirty, dusty, noisy and hot – illnesses of various types were an occupational hazard. It was alleged that Titaghur had deducted dues from workers' pay but not passed them on to the hospitals that treated sick workers. One Titaghur director, a Mr Srivastava, angry that he was the only one arrested and imprisoned because of the default, argued publicly that as chairman Brealey was the man ultimately responsible. 'He's the head of the actual management, so ultimate responsibility lies on the chairman,' he opined. At Titaghur's Victoria Mill one employee said, 'When Brealey came here we greeted him with garlands. We shouted, "Long live Brealey!" After he came here our condition deteriorated.' Debgopal Chakrobarti, leader of the local Bhadresbwar Council, said that Titaghur had not been paying its dues for five years.

McCarthy displayed copies of documents that proved that Brealey was aware of the shortfalls. McCarthy was also in possession of a letter in which Brealey had promised to settle the provident fund monies by March 1994. This promise, according to the documentary programme, was not kept. One mill was at the time in the hands of a receiver. Brealey refused to be interviewed for McCarthy's documentary but through a letter from his solicitor stated that there had been 'no misappropriation of provident fund payments' and that 'the jute industry has been notorious for the past 20 years for defaulting on statutory dues in order to keep workers employed during lean periods. The company for many years kept on staff at times when the cost of jute was more than the sale price. In doing this the company supported its workers. Provident fund monies were used [in this way], the workers always knew. Any default of statutory payments in India results in arrest warrants but that does not stop Mr Brealey from travelling within West Bengal.'

Brealey was then under fire from another corner of the globe – this time in the shape of the residents of an isolated peninsular on the west coast of Scotland. This was known as the Knoydart Estate, a piece of land that had no proper roads and could only be reached by boat from Mallaig on the Scottish mainland. In October 1995 the *BBC Radio Four* programme

163

Face the Facts, presented by John Waite, investigated how Brealey became involved in such an obscure part of the world and why the people who lived there couldn't wait to see the back of him. The story began when Brealey tried to cultivate interest in the shares of his company Titaghur by producing a lavishly-illustrated brochure advertising what he called the company's 'Back to Basics' international 'boot camps' for disadvantaged youngsters. This mantra adopted by the Tories in the early 1990s as an election-winning call to restore Britain to some never-defined previous era of milk and honey (or warm beer and maidens cycling to evensong) was, according to Brealey, his idea. The glossy brochure used the language of austerity Britain in the late 1940s to claim that the camps - for errant boys - would help them to develop 'self control, self discipline, self reliance'. It also stated; 'Basics currently operates from five international locations - Scotland, Malaysia, Thailand, India and Nepal.' The brochure went on to describe each individual boot-camp location. At Knoydart [Scotland] there was apparently 'comfortable, permanent accommodation'. In Malaysia 'trainees refine their outdoor skills and are introduced to jungle survival techniques'. In India they could participate in 'a three-week trek into Nepal', while in Thailand the youngsters could 'trek in the jungle and take a train journey on the famous Burma Railway to visit the notorious Bridge on the River Kwai'. The idea of forcing young men, potentially against their will, to re-trace the ordeal of the Allied soldiers who built the Burma road and lost their lives by the thousands might be considered by some people as beyond irony.

However, there was just one problem: the camps were not in operation. They were just ideas. All the same, several businessmen were taken in by the pitch and invested in Titaghur. One suitably impressed person was an associate of Brealey, fellow Lincolnshire businessman Frank Jennings, who paid £10,000 for 100,000 Titaghur shares. Others saw the brochure and invested, believing that Brealey's 'Back to Basics' scheme was up and running. Another Lincolnshire businessman, John Hodgson, said, 'As he explained it to me there was a set-up of discipline camps.' In that year's annual report of Titaghur PLC, Brealey boasted, 'The project has taken three years to get off the ground - time enough to see its motto "Back to Basics" recently adopted by the Government.' However, although Jennings and Hodgson didn't know it, Brealey's plans existed entirely on paper. According to the man he hired to get it started, ex-soldier Colonel Mike Reynolds, there were no boot camps in faraway places. Colonel Reynolds admitted that the brochure's exciting pictures of trainees in the jungle actually came from projects he had been involved with in the past. At the time that Brealey was handing out his glossy brochures he had not even won planning permission for the Knoydart camp. When he applied, permission was refused. Brealey had legitimately purchased the Knoydart peninsular and effectively became the new 'Laird' of the estate, but disgruntled workers, like their counterparts in India, complained they hadn't been paid. Estate employee Grant Holroyd said, 'I'm two months in arrears. Two of the staff had to leave quite recently because they couldn't afford to be behind with their pay.'

Other parties also said that Brealey's involvement in the Highlands had cost them money. Philip Rhodes, who sold the Knoydart Estate to Titaghur, claimed he was still owed £40,000 from the sale and was suing for recovery of such monies. An entrepreneur named Chris Gardner entered the picture, along with his scheme to grow protein-rich algae for the health food and animal feed industry. In spring 1994 Brealey offered Gardner £100,000 to build a commercial production plant for the product on behalf of Titaghur. Gardner said, 'At every meeting we had he said, "Don't you worry about selling it - you make the stuff at the right price and right quantity and I'll get on with selling it." He mentioned several times that he was hoping to involve Glaxo.' The much-discussed interest from the pharmaceutical giants didn't materialise, nor did much of the financial backing Brealey had promised. 'From July onwards it became much more difficult both to get payment and even to get hold of Mr Brealey to discuss payment. The next time we were paid was in October 1994, we were then paid again in November. Since then we haven't been paid,' lamented Gardner. As a result, Gardner and his team called it a day and set about chasing Titaghur for the thousands of pounds they claimed they were

165

owed. In the meantime, some 2,000 shareholders in Titaghur were counting the cost of their involvement with the one-time darling of the Stock Exchange. Pensioner Len Bayless and his family invested £200,000 in Titaghur and said, 'He [Brealey] persuaded me that he had the way to turn this company into a good affair and I felt it was such a good affair that I persuaded my family to become involved.' Now, said *Face the Facts* presenter Waite, their shares were worth pennies and their wealth had vanished, gobbled up by the failed schemes and mountainous debts of Brealey's Indian disaster.

Brealey agreed to respond to the various claims and allegations in an interview for *Face the Facts*. He admitted that Titaghur's mills owed millions to workers and the West Bengal Provident Fund. The fault, however, in his opinion, lay with local jute suppliers to whom he leased the mill and who had reneged on contracts under which they had promised to pay the workers and their pension fund contributions. Brealey accepted responsibility, but not blame. 'I'm admitting that the company running the mill at that particular time has defaulted. I haven't defaulted - I don't pay the wages and deduct the provident fund. I'm just a non-executive chairman 7,000 miles away doing a grotty job quite frankly but if the people who had the licence at the time defaulted on the provident fund, they've run away and we have litigation against them in the courts, but it does not alter the fact that the company has accepted the liability of that default and has included it in its liabilities audited, and have to be paid. It could well be that they are £7 million in default. It has not "gone missing", it is calculated, identified and accepted as a liability and will have to be paid but we have now licensed agreements with reputable companies to take the full responsibility of these mills off our shoulders and I think, at long last, that we've got a safeguard for the mill workers. From now on I hope that there will be no further defaults at all.'

Presenter John Waite then enquired why the West Bengal Provident Fund had seized Titaghur's offices in Calcutta. Brealey responded, 'I've been trying to close the head office for six years. If there's anything that can be sold in West

Bengal it will go to our statutory dues and obligations and I would welcome that. In fact we've already offered surplus properties to the provident fund to join in on the sale to take the benefit to the provident fund.' When asked about the Interpol warrant he replied, 'I don't know about that. Warrants in India happen to all personnel in the mills and, being the chairman, I've got added to every single one that's ever issued there. Over the past two years I think that it's been that they've added the directors, and all the directors have got these warrants, but I did check when this thing was stated, I checked with Interpol, and they said we don't have it recorded. I'm quite prepared to walk into India. I have no fear of being arrested for misappropriation. If I'm responsible as a chairman for the problem I'm responsible and I can't escape from that.'

Waite then asked Brealey about the 'Back to Basics' scheme and for his reaction to complaints that he had misled people into investing in it on the basis that it was a reality when in fact it was no more than a dream. 'It wasn't a dream, it was a reality. It's running at this particular time but it's not running in the magnitude at which it was designed to do. It was going to be quite a large scheme but we were restricted from numbers on the [Knoydart] peninsular and in the end we just decided to scrub the whole thing.' When Waite reminded Brealey that the brochure he showed to investors claimed that 'Basics currently operates from five international locations', Brealey replied, 'Well, we had the locations established. It was operating at the base, it was operating at the first one. The scheme had not gone to the other venues with the youngsters but it had operated at the first one. It was operating on one because that was the beginning of the scheme. This was down in Borneo, this was Sarawak. I think [those who invested] knew at the time that it was a new project.'

The interviewer turned to the subject of Knoydart and the people there who said Brealey owed them money. Brealey responded, 'You say they weren't paid but I rang and checked and they had been paid. I think there was a hiccup there by the company. I'm not even a director of that company - it's just a subsidiary. They had a hiccup on their cash flow and they recovered and paid.' When Waite told Brealey that the man who sold the Knoydart Estate to Titaghur, Philip Rhodes, claimed that Brealey still owed him £40,000, Brealey replied, 'If we owe Philip Rhodes any money and he can substantiate it he will be paid, as he has been paid in the past.' Rhodes said he had been promised the money in January, then March, then April, then May, then June, when 'most of' it was paid. Rhodes, who had creditors and employees of his own to pay, claimed that the late payments nearly bankrupted him. The man with the protein-rich algae, Chris Gardner, also claimed that Brealey owed him £7,000. Said Brealey, 'No, I understand that is paid. I cleared it before I came down here with my office, [I said] give me a list of the accounts that are outstanding and I saw that particular name. It is no longer there.' When informed by Waite that Gardner said he had not received payment and asked whether the cheque 'could be in the post', Brealey replied, 'It could be, yes. I asked the question of the accounts department before I came down here because I thought this would be one of the things that would come up.'

By now Brealey was becoming agitated by the course the questioning was taking and turned on his interrogator: 'You take great delight in having this scurrilous programme, but you don't come down here and face you without checking your facts. You have a good go at everybody anyway.' Unprovoked by Brealey's attack, Waite asked Brealey what a Titaghur share was worth at the time. 'No idea. Pence. Two, three, four, I've no idea. Yes, it's been a big tumble, but I've taken the tumble as well.' Waite concluded the programme by saying, 'Like Mr Brealey we check our facts. Interpol confirmed it has been approached for help in extradition proceedings but neither we nor the Gurkha experts we spoke to could trace the "Back to Basics" camp in Sarawak that Mr Brealey mentioned. The man in charge of the "Back to Basics" scheme, Colonel Mike Reynolds, did, however, mention that he hasn't been paid for a year. As for the cheque that was "in the post" to Chris Gardner, it duly arrived and has now been cleared.'

Other people also claimed Brealey owed them money. The local residents' association at Knoydart condemned Brealey as 'an Englishman without honour who has failed to discharge his obligations and should stand aside in favour of new owners'. Nine workers who maintained the estate's deer herd, felled timber and looked after the main estate house were not paid for two consecutive months. In August 1995 Brealey appeared in court when Titaghur was accused of failing to pay a £92,000 debt. In the Dundee Sheriff's Court (Titaghur's registered office was in Dundee), Philip Rhodes, former owner of Knoydart and manager of a Surrey firm called Eastern Way Trading, claimed he was owed this amount by Titaghur for producing a report on a possible takeover of former nationalised factories in Ukraine to make jute and hessian sacks. Payment was to be 400,000 Titaghur shares at 23p each, said Rhodes. Brealey reckoned the report 'had nothing to do with jute. I read it in detail and realised it was the wrong report.' He also denied there had been any agreement to give shares to Mr Rhodes, arguing that: 'Mr Rhodes ceased all contact with us in the middle of 1993. I took it that the whole matter was dead and buried.' Rhodes disagreed: 'If I have to wind up KPL [Knoydart Peninsula Ltd], Titaghur, Brealey or anybody else, I will get my money. It is owed to me. It would have been very simple to have avoided the situation.'

Local postmaster and chairman of the Knoydart community association, Bernie Evemy, then told the *Yorkshire Post* that the estate workers had not received payment for two months, and that Brealey's employees made up about 25 per cent of the population, thus non-payment of wages had a knock-on effect for everyone on the peninsula. Evemy added: 'Quite frankly most people would be glad to see the back of him. He appears to have no real interest in the place apart from its commercial value. He can only be described as an absentee landlord.' Brealey's explanation was that the workers had not been paid because Titaghur was facing a takeover bid, which would be 'resolved in the next few weeks', after which all monies owed would be settled.

Brealey was evidently having trouble aplenty in Scotland. There was no prospect of 'Back to Basics' ever getting underway at Knoydart as planning permission had been denied by Lochaber District Council, which felt it would have a 'devastating effect on the character of the estate'. Brealey wanted to bring up to 50 deprived youngsters to Knoydart but there were only just over 50 residents living there in all. Virtually everyone in the community was against such a plan. The residents held a poll, which resulted in four in favour, 50 against. The vision of Brealey was an apocalyptic one for local residents. Bernie Evemy explained; 'We often have ceilidhs in the winter. What do you do if these 48 young men storm the village hall, bearing in mind there's likely to be only 30 locals there? It's unthinkable.' Knoydart Peninsula Ltd lost £345,000 in its first year of operation and the losses mounted so much that receivers were appointed in 1998, at which time the estate's debts were believed to be about £1.4 million. Soon afterwards ownership of the estate passed into the hands of one of Brealey's old Bramall Lane adversaries, Stephen Hinchliffe.

The Knoydart problem was discussed in the House of Commons in June 1998. David Stewart, MP for Inverness East, Nairn and Lochaber, told the House that the debate was about not just a 16,500-acre estate on a West Highland peninsula, but the very future of a community. There were also important wider questions about land management, ownership and control. He described the 'chequered history' of Knoydart. 'Following the Highland Clearances,' he said, 'more than 500 people were forcibly evicted from the estate and were shipped to America and Australia. Sixteen brave families stayed on, fleeing to the hills until they were tracked down by the Factor and removed to America. In those days, economics dictated that sheep were more important than people. In 1948, seven men from Knoydart staked out 65 acres of arable land, in defiance of the hated landlord, a millionaire brewer named Lord Brocket. He was a Nazi sympathiser who had met Hitler, and who hosted dinners at Knoydart for senior Nazis, including von Ribbentrop. The land raid was unsuccessful, but the incident has been immortalised in song and verse, and it has become a symbol of the Highland land question.' The MP explained how in 1985 Surrey property dealer Philip Rhodes bought the original

58,000-acre estate for £1.2 million and in 1993 sold the last 16,500 acres to Titaghur.

Stewart then informed the House that he had contacted new owner Stephen Hinchliffe, who made it clear that he wanted to develop the estate. However, if the community were not behind him, he would consider selling it. Hinchliffe assented to meet representatives of the local residents' association to discuss their fears about the peninsula's history of failed directorships and to explain his long-term commitment to maintain and improve the estate. Stewart continued, 'I believe that the community can control its own future by purchasing the estate. Mr Hinchliffe has agreed to negotiate the sale if all else fails. My vision for the estate is not as a sterile zone but as a thriving, dynamic, innovative community that keeps its isolated charm and protects its natural assets. Finally, simply and passionately, I make a plea for the owner to sell, for the Royal Bank of Scotland, the main creditor, to sell and for the Government to support the community in any and every way that they can for good community land management practice. By working together, we can create new opportunities for the dream of the Knoydart community to be realised.' The Minister for Education and Industry, Scottish Office, Mr Brian Wilson added, 'The matters that [my colleagues] have raised are crucial to the community of Knoydart but they also have a resonance that stretches further afield. Knoydart's fate has acquired symbolic importance as well as immediate relevance to the future of the people who live there. Formally, that part of Knoydart on which today's debate is centred is no longer on the market.'

In September 1998 Knoydart residents became even more upset with the owners of their land when they discovered that one of its directors was being held in a German prison. This was Hinchliffe's friend and associate Christopher Harrison, who would, along with Hinchliffe, be convicted of fraud by the High Court, following his extradition from Germany. Harrison was being held in Frankfurt, awaiting trial on suspicion of misappropriating funds from a German company. Councillor Charlie King, chairman of the community-led Knoydart Foundation, said, 'It is an appalling situation and quite unbelievable. How can a company operate when one of its directors is sitting in jail, its estate boat has been arrested three times and its managing director is nowhere to be seen?' A month later, the Highland Council gave the owners ten days to settle a £27,000 unpaid bill, otherwise the authority would call in receivers. At the same time a court order granted to Knoydart's former manager blocked any sale of the estate until he had been paid £12,500 in backdated wages. At this point multi-millionaire theatre impresario Sir Cameron Mackintosh decided to get involved. He wanted to buy the estate and, if successful, lease it to the community for 25 years. Then at the end of October, Knoydart's biggest creditor, the Royal Bank of Scotland, which was owed more than £1 million, confirmed it had called in the receivers. The bank was expected to accept a bid of around £900,000 from Mackintosh.

However, only two months later the *Herald* reported that Mackintosh had pulled out of the deal. According to *Herald* sources, Mackintosh had become frustrated at the other members of the Knoydart Foundation such as the local community, the John Muir Trust, and the Chris Brasher Trust, who were insisting that he write into the lease an option for them to buy Knoydart. Mackintosh had already made it clear that, if the Foundation proved a good steward of the estate, he would be willing to grant another 25-year lease at a peppercorn rent, thereby securing the estate for two generations at least. Finally, in March 1999, the Knoydart Estate was bought by a community trust for £750,000 after Mackintosh decided to rejoin the bid. After years of being messed about, trodden on and disregarded by two former directors of Sheffield United Football Club, the good people of a remote part of Britain that was as far removed from Sheffield as could be, could at last attain the only things they had always desired – peace, quiet, stability and to be masters of their own futures.

For the employees of Titaghur there was a similarly satisfactory closing to the tribulations of the Brealey years. In the late 1990s Brealey handed over the chairmanship of the company to Graham Avery, who oversaw a recovery that eventually led to Titaghur's re-entry on to the Stock Market in

2000 under the new name of Azmara (shares in Titaghur had been suspended after their collapse in the early 1990s). Graham Avery? This was the same Graham Avery that in 1989 had been accused, along with Stephen Hinchliffe, of conspiring to defraud one of Avery's companies. Avery was thus another strand of the tangled web that seemed to inexorably link the complex business affairs of Hinchliffe and Reg Brealey.

Chapter 9

Big Mac And Lies
Football Franchise

Facing simultaneous protests against him from Sheffield, Scotland and India, early May 1995 brought some cheer for Brealey. First, United and Sheffield City Council signed a £3.5 million partnership agreement to build a regional football centre at Abbeydale Grange school, some two miles from Bramall Lane. Then, in the half-time interval of the last match of the season at home to Grimsby Town, Brealey sat at a desk on the pitch and signed a contract with civil engineering company Mowlems of Leeds for the building of the new John Street stand, witnessed by Supporters' Club representative Pete Whitney and United director John Plant. The other directors refused to join Brealey in the pitch spectacle, knowing that the full financial package required was still not in place and Brealey's signing was only a show for the public. According to Brealey, short-term and long-term loans had been agreed, along with a grant from the Football Trust. The first day of the contract was fixed for June 6. The work was to last 32 weeks and would be finished by January 16, 1996. A relieved Brealey commented, 'The repayments should have no effect on the club's ability to buy and sell players.' Brealey had pulled off a minor coup by publicising his signing of the contract in the build-up to the final game, but there was always the feeling that he had timed it to try to quell any possible BIFA-orchestrated demonstrations, a notion backed up by the uncommonly high number of police and stewards that surrounded the pitch at both half time and full time. In fact no protests had been planned by BIFA; a black-card protest to demonstrate the fans' mourning the 'death of the club', to follow the earlier 'coffin march', had been discussed but was called off in deference to the club's own VE Day parade of services veterans to commemorate the 50th anniversary of the end of the Second World War. BIFA showed a sensitivity that many of its critics thought it incapable.

Once the season was over, with the new stand apparently on its way, BIFA sought to maintain its profile. Moves had been made by BIFA Steering Committee members Paul Blomfield and Howard Holmes in conjunction with the City Council, the Rotary Club, Destination Sheffield (part of the tourist office), the local Labour party and the owners and tenants of a particular building in the centre of Sheffield. BIFA was well connected in all these areas, boasting a local councillor and prominent members of the local Labour party in its ranks, as well as one member of the Steering Committee who worked for Taylor and Emmet, the firm of solicitors now resident in the premises in question. This building was No.10 Norfolk Row, the very place where Sheffield United Football Club was founded in March 1889, and BIFA had commissioned a City of Sheffield Heritage Plaque, at a cost of several hundred pounds, to mark this date as a permanent reminder of the origins of the club.

The money to pay for the plaque had been raised when a group of some 20 BIFA members staged a sponsored walk from Sheffield to the Blades' match at Barnsley the previous April. The plaque was unveiled by Sheffield-born actor and Blades fan Sean Bean on June 30, 1995. Bean was accompanied by Labour MP and fellow Blades fan Richard Caborn. Also present were representatives of the organisations involved with the commissioning of the plaque, a dozen or so reporters and photographers and about 100 members of the public. Despite the backing of a Hollywood actor, a Member of Parliament and various respected local bodies, BIFA experienced difficulty publicising the event because of its strained relations with United and the local press. Unfortunately the most important party involved was not represented at the event –

Sheffield United Football Club. The club was invited by Destination Sheffield, who initially were told that one director and one player from the club would attend, but when they found out that BIFA was the instigator nobody came, at the behest of Brealey, who sent out word banning any club employee from attending.

The wording on the plaque was:

'In this building on the evening of Friday 22 March 1889 the Committee of Sheffield United Cricket Club met with senior officials from the Sheffield Football Association in the office of Club Secretary Mr Joseph Wostinholm and decided to form a new football club for the 1889-90 season. The Club would play on the Bramall Lane ground. The next day an advertisement in the Sheffield morning newspapers invited professional players to send their testimonials and particulars to Mr Wostinholm by 30 March 1889. Sheffield United Football Club was born. This plaque has been sponsored by the Blades Independent Fans' Association.'

The club issued no statement explaining why it had accepted the verbal invitation but then declined the official one. United finally recognised the existence of the plaque – 14 years later. In April 2009 chairman Kevin McCabe, former player Len Badger and Pete Whitney from the Supporters' Club were photographed beneath the plaque to mark the 120th anniversary of United's formation. McCabe said, 'I wonder whether those who were at that very first meeting were aware of what they had ultimately created, the magnitude of their efforts.' One wonders if McCabe was aware of the efforts and tribulations that were behind the purchase and erection of the plaque.

If Brealey had scored an own goal by ignoring something as important as recognising the birthplace of the club, the next blow hit supporters like a last-minute winner – for the opposition. On July 7, 1995 the *Sheffield Telegraph* reported that work on the new stand had not started on the scheduled date of June 6 because Mowlems had not yet received any down-payment on the £3.8 million it would cost and would not begin work until they did so.   BIFA had despatched a delegation to the ground on June 6 to witness the commencement of work but found no men in hard hats, no machinery, no surveyors.   Following the passing of this date and the *Sheffield Telegraph* report BIFA decided to call an Extraordinary General Meeting of Sheffield United Football Club to query the delay.   There were enough shareholders enrolled as members to be able to do so.   BIFA spokesman Howard Holmes commented, 'We are obviously very concerned about the lack of progress on the stand and are calling on Reg Brealey to make a clear statement about what is happening because the people at the club don't seem to know. In order to force a full debate on the stand and why it has been delayed, 30 BIFA shareholders are writing collectively to the board to ask for an EGM.   Many people are waiting for some movement on the stand before buying their season tickets [season ticket sales had dropped 20 per cent from the previous season to around 6,000] and it's beginning to look as if the announcement at half time of the last match of the season that work would begin on June 6 was a PR exercise by Brealey to stifle criticism.'   However, Brealey denied that June 6 was indeed the definite start date, arguing that: 'The 6th of June seemed synonymous enough – D-Day – to have a starting date and that's what the date was.   But whether they start on the 13th, the 20th, the 27th or when is up to Mowlems.   They will start whenever it suits them to start and finish within the framework of the timescale, which I'm hopeful will be the case.'   He added that he was within a 'hair's breadth' of completing the necessary financial arrangements and concluded, 'I cannot ask my board to guarantee half a million each for 15 years.   Some of us might not be here.'

To clarify events thus far, in August 1995 (Issue No.43), *Flashing Blade* listed a litany of lapsed deadlines regarding the area of the ground that manager Dave Bassett had with characteristic aplomb christened 'Fred West's Garden', in reference to the Gloucester builder who buried his 13 known murder victims in his garden and cellar between 1967 and 1987.   The first official reference to the new stand came when United wrote to [old] John Street stand and terrace season ticket holders midway through the 1993/94 season.   The fans were informed that if they bought season tickets for the new Bramall Lane end seats they would be able to move to the new John Street stand, for no extra charge, when it was completed during the 1994/95 season. When it became obvious that the stand was nowhere near starting, never mind being completed, concerned fans began to contact the club and the local press, asking what was going on, citing the following:

October 1, 1994: club secretary David Capper said, 'It is the intention of the board that supporters will see preliminary work on the stand this winter. And unless there are unforeseen problems of foundations or materials we would hope to open the stand at the start of next season.'

October 16, 1994: director John Plant stated live on television that work on the new stand would begin 'in a matter of weeks'.

November 28, 1994: Reg Brealey said, 'We are in striking distance of starting.'

December 29, 1994: Reg Brealey: 'I do believe we will press the button in January and will still be on course for completion next season.'

December 31, 1994: United reporter Tony Pritchett wrote in the *Green 'Un*: 'Brealey said he had told the shareholders that the contracts would be signed in January and that he believed that the stand would be open for business at the start of the season.'

January 28, 1995: Reg Brealey said, 'I am spending a lot of time on this project and I expect to have good news for our supporters quite soon.'

February 4, 1995: Tony Pritchett wrote in the *Green 'Un*: 'Sheffield United still make no bones about it – the new John Street stand WILL be up, open and functioning at the start of the season. This was the official line yesterday, some days after a January 31 deadline, which chairman Reg Brealey has highlighted twice.'

March 18, 1995: Tony Pritchett in the *Green 'Un*: 'Any day now – surely the situation will be resolved soon – Sheffield United will make another announcement about the future of the John Street side of the ground.'

March 20, 1995: Reg Brealey: 'What the supporter wants to know is when does the John Street stand commence? The answer is as soon as the financial aspects are complete.'

May 6, 1995: Tony Pritchett in the *Green 'Un*: 'Sheffield United today pressed the button on the new £4 million John Street stand project. The official first day of the contract has been fixed for D-Day, June 6.'

June 6, 1995: Mowlems spokesman: 'No one from our company will be on site at Bramall Lane today.'

July 7, 1995: Mowlems spokesman: 'We are concerned about the situation. We have a contract in place that quotes the commencement date as June 6. We are in a position to start right away and wish to do so as soon as possible.'

July 12, 1995: Tony Pritchett in the *Sheffield Star*: 'In private briefings I have been assured that the problem was under control and that the money was in place. Why won't the banks support [United] in the way that they have supported other building projects up and down the country?'

July 13, 1995: Reg Brealey told the *Sheffield Star*: 'Despite what some of our critics say, the commitment to build is made; the contract is signed, the finance available but we have one problem. We have to provide individual guarantees. I am not in a position myself to do it any more. But it is imminent, all of it is imminent. It is not easy but we have to overcome it by insurance bank instrument and new directors coming in. Then we go and we go fast.'

July 14, 1995: Tony Pritchett in the *Sheffield Star*: 'It was clearly unwise of Brealey to trumpet that D-Day, June 6, was the starting day and he could not resist the gesture. But it only stored up more resentment when the day came and went. An

179

assurance that building would begin in the close season would have been sufficient.'

What supporters could not understand was why were promises made when it appeared obvious they would not be kept? There were two possible answers. First, fans were being deliberately misled and misinformed by club officials in an attempt to appease them. The second possibility was that the statements were made in the genuine belief that, at the time, they were true. If this was the case, it was hard to believe that a businessman of Brealey's experience and acumen could be so naïve. Surely it would have been better to keep quiet until a deal was signed, sealed and delivered? Eventually Brealey did come up with some sort of comprehensible explanation for the delays. He claimed that much of the finance had been in place for some time, using the Bramall Lane ground as security. However, there was a shortfall that could only be covered by individual directors giving personal financial guarantees. With none of the existing directors in a position to be able to do this, Brealey was forced to look for new board members who could. If he could find them, he said, his 'waving goodbye would not be a problem'. Alternatively he needed new finance, which he was unable to find. But surely he knew ever since the major loan was agreed that this would be the case?

United were soon to embark on their second season after relegation from the Premier League with the whole club in a state of what could only be described as apathetic resignation. The supporters, the manager and, very probably, the players were all aware that the 1995/96 season might well be one of struggle unless there was drastic change evidenced at the head of the club. The malaise could be traced back to the April 1993 FA Cup semi-final against Sheffield Wednesday at Wembley. That was United's highest point since the sixth-place finish in the top flight in 1974/75. United finished the 1992/93 season strongly and the fans and club staff were buoyant and confident. The 1993 summer was the moment that United needed to bring in a record signing (maybe even two) and the likelihood of continued Premier League status was strong under the guidance of Dave Bassett. Instead, Brealey regained control of the club from Woolhouse when he didn't really want it back and the first thing he did was sell the team's talisman, Brian Deane. The only solution for the club's financial crisis, according to Brealey, was to sell his prime asset just to keep United afloat. This may indeed have been his genuine appreciation of the state of the club, but three of his directors at the time were discordant. Had United kept Deane, they would have had a good chance of staying up and reaping the ever-increasing benefits of Premier League football. The day that Deane signed for Leeds United was the day that Sheffield United tipped over the edge; it was Brealey who administered the final push.

His subsequent lack of interest, his preoccupation with the problems of his various businesses, his far-from-concerted efforts to sell the club, his persistent evasion of giving out authentic information regarding the new stand, and his continued reneging on promises made to Dave Bassett about the funds available for squad strengthening, all made Brealey unfit to be chairman of Sheffield United. The reason for the delay in building a new stand, 15 months after the old one was demolished, was because Brealey was chairman. No bank or financial institution would loan sufficient money to Sheffield United as long as Brealey was at the helm, no matter how much he tried to claim that the impasse was attributable to BIFA. In the early and mid 1990s, countless other clubs had been able to redevelop their grounds because they had chairmen to whom banks were prepared to lend.

The shameful void on John Street had now come to symbolise the downward spiral of Sheffield United. It was embarrassing for the supporters to look upon it every home match; it must have been demoralising for the players to run out of the tunnel and see opposite nothing but a high, red, wooden fence. In addition, the confusion over the ownership pervaded the club, however often Dave Bassett stated that it didn't affect the players. Brealey was responsible for the two main things that were wrong with Sheffield United in the middle of 1995 – relegation from the Premier League and a three-sided ground. All the supporters could hope for at this time was that he would quickly sell his shareholding and allow someone else to come in and get some bricks laid and concrete poured; a move that would give a huge boost to the whole club. If there was to be a successor to Brealey, in the long run he might prove to be just as bad, but the fans desperately wanted to find out if that would be the case. Surely it couldn't be worse?

Dave Bassett was desperate for some positive news regarding the ownership of the club and the building of the stand. His strained relationship with Brealey meant that the pair rarely spoke and Bassett had to seek advice, encouragement and, no doubt, solace from Stephen Hinchliffe, Bernard Procter and Derek Dooley. All three, said Bassett, were 'honourable men.' In the summer of 1995 Bassett was entering the final year of his contract and was torn between merely seeing it out or trying to negotiate a new one. Only Procter seemed keen for him to stay longer; Brealey was cold and non-committal. Bassett wanted assurances about the future of the club – he had been told frequently by Brealey that money would be available to buy players, but it never arrived. The only assurance Bassett got was that he could only spend what he generated from the sales of players, which didn't exactly make him happy but now at least he knew where he stood. Knowing he had the backing of Procter, Bassett signed a contract extension to the end of the 1996/97 season.

Then in an 'exclusive' on July 17 the *Sheffield Star* reported: 'BREALEY FINDS A BUYER FOR THE BLADES: Millionaire Mike is poised to take over before new season'. The buyer was revealed as Mike McDonald, who had been connected to a possible deal with Brealey for several months. McDonald, according to the *Sunday Times* 'Rich List' was the 731st-richest man in the country. The report said McDonald could be in charge as early as the following week. A week earlier Brealey had revealed he was in talks with potential new directors and said, 'One must strengthen the board so that people of substance can guarantee, if not inject, large sums.' He added that he wanted to hand over to a successor who could 'take the club to greater heights than I can. I will only sell for the right reasons.' But only a week later there was deadlock as McDonald would not agree to buy Brealey's shareholding until he had had time to pore over the design of the stand and determine what his financial commitment should be. Understandably he wanted to see exactly what he was committing himself to before signing contracts. Said McDonald in the *Sheffield Star*, 'I'm sure the purchase of the club will happen. I've looked at the accounts and they are fine. But I want to be sure the stand is right. People are reluctant to give me information about it. At the moment it is the only stumbling block.' Contractors Mowlems would not comment.

Mike McDonald was chairman of Texas Group PLC, a 60-year-old company based in Eccles, Manchester. In 1993 Texas, which had interests in commercial property, metal recycling, environmental protection, demolition, hotels and leisure and automotive engineering, purchased diesel engine manufacturers L.Gardner, a 125-year-old company, from tractor maker Massey Ferguson. McDonald floated Gardner on the Alternative Investment Market (AIM[5]) in 1995 and its share price immediately jumped 20 per cent, valuing the company at £16 million. McDonald, who boasted of his 'Romany origins', had a background in the scrap metal and machine tools trades. He transformed Gardner's six-figure annual losses into profits of £1.8 million in two years by selling his engines to bus companies all over the world. It was estimated that 90 per cent of Hong Kong's buses ran on Gardner diesel engines.

McDonald made a shrewd move by contacting BIFA as soon as his bid became public knowledge. He discerned the strength and influence of the fans' organisation and knew what effect its pressure was having on Brealey. He wanted that force on his side and reckoned, correctly, that the best way to achieve that would be to open a dialogue. Although BIFA didn't back any one prospective bidder over another, they were

---

[5] Founded in 1995, the Alternative Investment Market (AIM) is a sub-market of the London Stock Exchange, allowing smaller companies to float shares with a more flexible regulatory system than is applicable to the main market. Flexibility is provided by less regulation and no requirements for capitalisation or number of shares issued. The AIM has significant tax advantages for investors, as well as being a less regulatory burden for the companies.

more than happy to talk to McDonald, if only to find out more about him. McDonald's conduit to BIFA was Howard Holmes, and the pair spoke on the telephone several times. McDonald told Holmes that the deal to buy out Brealey was still going through, if slowly, and repeated that the design of the stand was the main sticking point. United had cut facilities to a minimum: for example, the 32 proposed 'executive boxes' had had their individual en-suite toilets removed. McDonald wanted them put back in. He also wanted the specification improved to allow for the Bramall Lane and Shoreham Street corners to be infilled in the future. McDonald also informed Holmes that he had attended a meeting with both Brealey and Barclay's Bank. He said that he did not mind taking responsibility for the stand but he added that Brealey's asking price 'has to come down'. And even when the deal went through the decision on the stand wouldn't solely be McDonald's – full board approval was required before it could go ahead. McDonald had also met directors Bernard Procter and Alan Laver and, having got to know Brealey well, intimated that he didn't really trust him. He believed that Brealey was desperate to sell and that he needed money fast.

In early August at last McDonald was to go public, declaring his satisfaction with events, saying, 'I have today had a meeting with the contractors for the new stand and I am now satisfied with what we are getting for the money. I wasn't when we started but we are now happy with the costing and the facilities. I shall now try to organise a meeting with the other directors and I see no insurmountable problems left. There is no reason why we cannot go forward. But I have been in this position before and the goalposts have been moved.' Brealey's view of the delay was slightly different. When questioned in 1999 Brealey recalled a contrasting scenario: 'The fans were calling for my name and telling me to get my act together, but the negotiations with Mike took over a year. He had to do two flotations to raise the money.'

Running in parallel to McDonald's talks with Brealey and Mowlems, BIFA continued with its strategy to force an Extraordinary General Meeting to try to discover the real reasons for the delay in the commencement of the building of the stand. They also proposed to nominate BIFA Steering Committee member Reg Hobson to stand for a place on the board. Hobson, in his sixties and retired, was chosen for this position as he was one of the few members of the BIFA Steering Committee who owned a Sheffield United Original Share. It is required by law that a company director be a shareholder of the company. BIFA wished to get a supporter on the board but acknowledged that the representative should not necessarily come from its own organisation. If the Supporters' Club, Executive Club or Senior Blades could suggest a better candidate than Hobson from within their ranks, then they had to declare that person. BIFA therefore proposed that different fans' groups should run their own elimination contests to produce a shortlist from which the board would make a selection. It was important that the board had the final say on the person chosen, otherwise there was little likelihood of success. The successful candidate would not be a 'Trojan Horse' who would circulate confidential information around supporters – he or she would have a clear mandate from the board about what information was to remain inside the boardroom and what could be disseminated. The 'fan on the board' would be a 'two-way conduit' between the directors and the supporters. Hobson stressed that he would be willing to perform the 'dirty duties', such as accompanying the reserve team to Hartlepool on a wet and windy February Tuesday night. The proposed selection process didn't progress beyond general ideas and was never discussed with Mike McDonald or the United board.

The signatures of the required 30 shareholders for the EGM were obtained - a relatively simple task as the majority were sympathetic BIFA members - and the formal request submitted to the club's registrars. However, United's first tactic was a delaying one as they rejected the EGM call; it was the view of the directors that BIFA's requisition of the EGM was improper. The club tried to claim that two of the signatures submitted were invalid. After Hobson made enquiries it transpired that one signature was quite valid, but that the proposer should also have indicated that he was signing on behalf of a company share. Of the other one, the club had completely misread the name 'Taylor' (even though it was also printed), for something dissimilar. It also came to light that Brealey had telephoned this particular shareholder, for what purpose remained unclear. The outcome was that the shareholder now claimed he was unsure of what he was signing!

By September, Taylor and Emmet, solicitors acting for BIFA, said the club was badly advised about their rejection of the signatures on BIFA's petition for the EGM. They argued that there was no basis in law for the given objections and wrote to the club giving them notice to convene the meeting in seven days. At BIFA's Annual General Meeting at the Trades and Labour Club, attended by just under 200 members, the meeting was asked whether the committee should proceed with its request for the EGM and, following the generous offer of Kassim Ahmed, a well-known Blades fan and publican of the Railway Hotel on Bramall Lane, to pay half of any legal fees BIFA might incur, there came a unanimous vote to call an EGM. However, soon afterwards the Steering Committee agreed that, thanks to McDonald's intervention, events had moved on so as to make the calling of the EGM irrelevant, therefore it was decided not to pursue it further. It was also felt that this decision would prevent some of the shareholders who had signed the petition from being placed in the position of being forced to make a personal choice about whether or not to continue, as it had come to light that Brealey had put considerable pressure on them, by means of telephone calls, to withdraw their names.

As observers were wondering where Mike McDonald's offer was heading, an old protagonist re-entered the fray. In mid August Stephen Hinchliffe, the club's second-biggest individual shareholder with a 15 per cent holding, said he was going to mount a bid to rival McDonald's. A 'source' close to Hinchliffe was quoted in the *Sheffield Star* as saying; 'Mr Brealey wishes to hand over control to someone who could help the club go forward and there is no more committed Unitedite in the frame than Mr Hinchliffe. Supporters will remember that he spent time on the board of directors and it coincided with the club's most successful and prosperous season, showing a profit of around £1 million.' Hinchliffe's commitment to United once saw him pay £2,500 for an original Sheffield Wednesday share. Hinchliffe could not resist a dig at McDonald, at the same time emphasising his own local background, stating, 'My belief is that Sheffield United should be owned by Blades fans. I don't see the point in some outsider who in one breath wants to buy Manchester City and in the next breath Sheffield United.' He had a point. According to the *Sheffield Star*, a 'put up or shut up' ultimatum followed, whereby McDonald insisted he had paid a deposit and was close to finalising an agreement, adding, 'I am prepared to take a back seat in all of this if Mr Hinchliffe can put together a deal that is acceptable to the club. But I have to have a decision within seven days.' Hinchliffe responded: 'I cannot be influenced by any timescale Mr McDonald wishes to impose. At the end of the day the best deal will win. If Mr McDonald can make an offer better than mine then presumably it will be accepted by Mr Brealey and that will be the end of it.' McDonald spoke of 'problems with Barclay's Bank over the release of a charge' by way of explaining the delay. He then added that he had put up a lot of money already and the deal 'was on again'. Attempting to woo Blades fans, he also said that that very day he had personally prevented the sale of United's Irish international goalkeeper Alan Kelly to an unnamed club.

There was much speculation amongst supporters and in the press about who was doing what to whom in the boardroom. One rumour suggested that the liquidators of Paul Woolhouse's estate would shortly require Brealey to pay around £1 million to obtain full control of the shares he had taken back from Woolhouse and that demand could possibly bankrupt him. At least this rumour backed up McDonald's theory that Brealey was 'desperate to sell'. For his part, Brealey told *Sheffield Star* reporter Tony Pritchett that 'neither Mike McDonald nor Stephen Hinchliffe [are] realistic bidders. They were dismissed [by Brealey] as not having the money to tackle the job.' McDonald and Hinchliffe both claimed otherwise. Not long afterwards, Pritchett, now seemingly as exasperated as the fans, wrote, 'It is time, surely, for the chairman to make a statement of intent. The present situation is embarrassing.' Equally frustrated were directors Bernard

Procter and Alan Laver. In September they broke ranks. Procter stated, 'There is as much concern within the directors as there is in the press. We are absolutely fed up with the publicity regarding buying the club, selling the club and if it is going to be sold. Brealey perhaps doesn't want to sell it. We don't know do we?' Procter wanted Brealey to promise that the club would be either sold or pulled off the market on terms that satisfied everybody connected with the club. Directors such as Procter and Laver were seemingly as helpless as the fans. They began their own protest, which took the form of a refusal to give the bank permission to pay the club staff's wages by automatic transfer. Instead, the £150,000 per month that was paid in wages was to be given via cheques, signed by the two protesting directors. This move was designed to embarrass Brealey into some form of action without unduly inconveniencing the players and staff. Procter said, 'People have been paid. There is no problem with the bank. The only problem United has got is regarding where it is going and its ownership. Until that is resolved we shall flutter from crisis to crisis. It was a question of trying to bring the subject to a boil. It is humiliating for us that the club's future has not been resolved.'

The publicity and the obvious pique of these two respected co-directors had the desired effect - Brealey agreed to meet them. Meanwhile, United's goalkeeper Alan Kelly admitted that he and his playing colleagues were anxious about the cash flow: 'We didn't know why the money didn't go in [our accounts]. We normally get it through the bank's automatic system.' An increasingly frustrated Dave Bassett, who up to now had generally displayed a calm exterior, could remain quiet no longer. 'There has been no leadership from the top and the club must now make decisions,' he fumed. 'The club must decide if it is to go forward or if it is to settle for second best. I'm expected to do everything without money [to strengthen his playing squad].' He added that since relegation the club had 'gone backwards' by not investing in players and not building the new stand. Privately he confessed that Brealey's tenure since 1993 had been 'a disaster' and said that Brealey, to borrow from a London entrepreneurial expression, had 'tucked me up' (i.e. to be stranded on account of deceit).

On September 21 an end appeared in sight. Following talks that continued past 11pm Brealey and McDonald agreed a deal and all that remained was for McDonald to sign the papers. The next day McDonald confirmed the agreement, adding the populist adage, 'I have not bought the club to see it live in the shadow of Sheffield Wednesday.' Then came the rallying cry that drew on metaphors of war and Christendom: 'Today is the start of a new era for the Blades. I want the troops on the march, I want everyone behind me as we strive to put the club where it belongs. We must see supporters return to the fold and join me in what lies ahead. This is not a job for a new chairman alone; it is a crusade in which everyone with the future of the Blades at heart can play a part. We want a winning team and a new stand but we cannot build the stand and see it stand empty. That is why we need to see a positive reaction from everyone to what has taken place today. I started out on this takeover when the team was in the Premiership with gates approaching 20,000. Now it is in the bottom half of the First Division with crowds half that number. The task, therefore, is much bigger. That is why everyone must pull together. The first thing we want is a good result from Huddersfield on Sunday. There has been too much drama and politics; let us get back to playing football, winning matches and cheering crowds.' McDonald could not attend the next few games as he was abroad on business but left Roger Newton, a director of the Texas group of companies, to prepare the financial plans in conjunction with Dave Bassett and the directors. There was now movement on the John Street stand as a spokesman for Mowlems announced that McDonald had asked them to submit proposals to enhance the original design.

United won the game at Huddersfield with a rare good performance, after which Bassett commented, 'There has been upheaval and change and it has affected everyone. The players could feel the apathy in the club and my mind has not been 100 per cent on the game because of what has been going on but hopefully that is over. More [fans] turned up at Huddersfield because, all of a sudden, they see their club coming out of the mortuary where they think it has been for so long. We have definitely been resuscitated.' Bassett then spoke to McDonald to discover what the future might hold for him. Questioned afterwards Bassett revealed, 'He didn't want to make any immediate decisions or promises other than that he is getting the deal finalised and then he wants to come in, look around, get on with the stand and take it from there.' He added, somewhat cryptically, 'He is a businessman and when he makes an acquisition of a company there is usually more than meets the eye. Or perhaps less.' Meanwhile, McDonald's opinion of Dave Bassett was hardly a vote of confidence: 'Dave is a character and a good manager but he could be getting despondent. He has my backing in the short term.' BIFA celebrated the news of McDonald's impending takeover by arranging with the vicar of St Mary's church, adjacent to the Bramall Lane ground, for the church bells to be rung immediately prior to the next home game against Ipswich Town. This was how it was publicised anyway – in reality the church bells were not operational and their 'ringing' was produced by a sound system belonging to the church. Several BIFA members had to carry – with difficulty – a tape deck, an amplifier, cables and a couple of large speakers up a narrow spiral staircase to the top of the church tower.

The feeling of optimism generated by McDonald's apparent takeover and the Huddersfield victory evaporated rapidly. United reverted to type, losing five consecutive matches in October, one of them to Fourth Division Bury in the League Cup. A 2-1 defeat at Southend saw chants of 'Bassett Out!' as pro- and anti-Bassett factions amongst the Blades fans almost came to blows and had to be calmed by police and stewards. Amidst this McDonald now faced a problem – cash flow. With the ownership of the club still in limbo the payment of the October wage bill was placed in jeopardy. McDonald was still away on business in South Africa but his spokesman explained, 'We always knew this would not be a quick fix and a decision by Reg Brealey to change his solicitors has not helped.   But the facts are that we have paid a substantial deposit for the shares and have a binding contract with Brealey. There is no way Brealey can ever return to Sheffield United. Nor is there any chance of Mr McDonald losing his patience and pulling out.' A portion of the shares (some four per cent) was still held by solicitors appointed by the High

Court after Brealey won back control from Paul Woolhouse. Ownership of them was preventing final completion. Meanwhile, the team was stuck at the bottom of the league. The fans were becoming more and more disgruntled with what they were watching on the pitch and more and more frustrated that Brealey, albeit no longer in charge, was still around. The players were badly affected too; their inept performances showed it.

The finalisation of the takeover was being obstructed, some said deliberately, by Brealey changing his solicitors almost as often as he changed his socks. Various legal undertakings were not being allowed to proceed until the necessary professional fees were paid, in advance, from Brealey because, it was alleged, he wasn't trusted to settle after the fact. Even though the handover had not gone through, Brealey resigned as chairman at a board meeting on October 19, with director Alan Laver taking over in an acting capacity. The board was to be re-constituted and McDonald invited to become chairman. However, McDonald said he had no wish to be chairman at this stage: 'I am involved in the Stock Exchange flotation of my company and I could not give the chairmanship of the club my best shot at the moment. It suits me to have Mr Laver assuming the responsibilities for the time being. I will accept control of the club but there will be others here to take charge. I am talking about a chief executive who I will appoint.' Although given scant attention at the time, the final part of this statement would prove to have a pivotal bearing on the club's fluctuating fortunes over the next three years. Brealey expressed a sense of 'relief' at finally handing over responsibility. 'It will make a change not to be on call 24 hours a day, anywhere in the world, when there is a football problem.'

Still it dragged on. At the start of November the club released a statement: 'Acting chairman A.H. Laver confirmed today that, at a recent board meeting, Mr Brealey and Mr McDonald informed the directors that that the question of the ownership of the club is not expected to be resolved until 30 November 1995. The directors feel, therefore, that no decision can be made with regard to the purchase of players until that time.'

Bassett, informed of the situation, was nearing the end of his tether: 'It is one more twist in the sorry tale that continues to run. I had players lined up, now I have had to withdraw [the *Sheffield Star* claimed the players were striker Phil Masinga from Leeds United and full back Rob Ullathorne from Norwich City]. It began last week when we lost out on [defender] Carl Tiler who went from Forest to Villa after I had been trying to bring him to Bramall Lane.' As well as missing out on Tiler, Bassett also had a young Australian defender over on trial and wanted to sign him, but was not given the clearance to be able to do so. This was Kevin Muscat, who went on to have a long and successful (if somewhat controversial) career in England and at international level. Muscat was as frustrated as Bassett. As his trial period came to an end Muscat explained privately that he wanted to sign for United and knew the manager wanted to sign him but the absence of anyone with authority to sanction the move prevented him from doing so. The angry Bassett, outspoken as usual, continued, 'I have been here nearly eight years. What has been achieved in that time has been achieved by me, and it has been done in spite of the board. If we are ever going to start talking seriously of promotion there is no other way than spending real money on the side.'

At regular intervals after this Bassett vented his feelings in the press. Acknowledging the poor displays of his team, he remarked, 'We have got to win games and get our confidence back but at the same time I have to see if there is any money available for players because we need to inject money or players into the team. I am in limbo, the club is in limbo.' A few days later he said, 'We need to bring some fresh faces in but with the state of the club as it is, not knowing who the owner is and not even knowing if the takeover deal has been done, all this is hanging over us'. Bassett wouldn't let it drop. He wanted the supporters to know that he was banging his head against the proverbial brick wall: 'Technically, I have got around £200,000 to £250,000 to spend. That's because at the start of the season the board promised me that any money I raised I could spend and Mike McDonald confirmed that, but it appears I haven't even got that now. Nobody is in actual authority so, really, I'm in a state where I can't even get a decision on purchasing players even though I've got a few bob. Typical Sheffield United.' Still later he lamented, 'There is apathy written all over the club. The situation is ridiculous. I have never been in a position like this. This is the most remarkable situation of my life in football, by far.'

The local press got off the fence and Paul License, the *Sheffield Star* columnist who not so long before castigated BIFA for trying to oust Brealey, now changed his tune: 'It is time for Reg Brealey to pull out of the club for good. Let those who can do something about Sheffield United get on with the job!' Elasticity of principle sat well with Mr License. Another *Sheffield Star* writer, Martin Smith agreed: 'No one, not Dave Bassett, Johan Cruyff or Santa Claus can achieve anything at United until the absurd boardroom drama is sorted out. The club, its fans, players and manager speak as one: "Get lost Reg, give United a chance."' Dave Bassett remained encumbered by his frustrations and, despite the boost of a rare victory at Port Vale, bemoaned, 'One win does not hide the fact that we are going nowhere at present. All we have to do now is get the people upstairs sorting themselves out and that will help us. It's nice to be talking about football but that is just for now. The politics are still far from finished.'

Alan Laver explained that the boardroom stance on player signings was necessary not because the club was insolvent but because the bank had set a limit on the overdraft and until the ownership was decided the club would have to live within its means. McDonald was adamant that the takeover would go through and he tried to ease the fans' worries by insisting the deal would be done in the next couple of weeks. He had, he said, enjoined his lawyers to ensure a speedy completion. 'I'm sick and tired of it going to be this week, then next week, so I've given them a month to do it. We could have taken over ICI in less time than we have spent on Sheffield United,' he said. 'There are days when I ask myself, "Is it all worth it?" but I feel Sheffield United have a lot to offer and should be in the big time. I've told Dave Bassett to get on with the football and I'll look after the finances.' Then, in his typically bluff and abrupt manner, he added, 'And if he [Bassett] needs any money for players he has a squad of about 40 and should get rid of some. We don't need so many.' Bassett had heard a similar sentiment before: a few years previously Reg Brealey had said publicly in response to Bassett's plea for transfer money; 'He's got 39 players. How much choice does he need?'

Bassett was furious at McDonald's comments and demanded, in the *Sheffield Star's* terminology, a 'showdown'. He told the press; 'McDonald made a statement that we had a big squad, I should sell some of those and I could have the money for them. We need to find out where we stand. We need clarification on the ownership and on the transfer policy, which seems to have changed since the start of the season.' To compound matters, the Football League imposed a transfer ban on United because a loan of £50,000, made earlier in 1995 by the Professional Footballers' Association to help pay players' wages, had not been refunded. Meanwhile, former England winger David White arrived from Leeds United to sign on loan but was immediately informed the deal was off. Bassett seethed, 'To say I am disappointed is putting it mildly. We have been told that the [transfer] ban applies to loan deals as well. I have had the difficult task of telling David White that there is a hold on his move.' Another player who became unavailable for selection was Norwegian striker Jostein Flo, who for the first four months of the season was a first choice, missing only a handful of games. He was then omitted from the line-up, with no reports of an injury and no explanation from the club. It transpired that he had started 79 league and cup matches for United and one more would have triggered a further contractual payment to his former club Sogndal. Flo never played for United again, returning to Norway.

Surely it couldn't get worse? Could it? On November 24 the front-page headline of the *Sheffield Star* splashed; 'I want my £300,000', and informed readers of acting chairman Alan Laver's writ to Reg Brealey demanding repayment of a loan made to Else (1982) Ltd in 1993. Laughably, the writ also included an additional sum of just £10 lent by Laver to Brealey in December 1994! Laver apparently had applied to the courts for repayment of the loans and the judge ruled in his favour, telling Brealey that he would have to repay the

£300,010, plus £41,303 interest. Two months later Brealey had not paid up; a second writ now demanded immediate reimbursement. Before it got to court the pair came to an agreement. Said Laver, 'I am not saying whether he has paid up. We have come to a satisfactory arrangement. I have arranged for the proceedings to be withdrawn.' The details of the 'satisfactory arrangement' were never made public.

Amidst this chaos McDonald agreed to meet a delegation of half a dozen BIFA Steering Committee members in early November as a way of introducing himself. Also present at the meeting at the Novotel on Sheffield's Arundel Gate was the man who over the next couple of years would become as powerful an individual as McDonald at Bramall Lane. This was South Yorkshire-born Charles Green, who sat, minder-like, at McDonald's side. McDonald introduced Green as his 'advisor'; he would later be appointed as the chief executive McDonald spoke of earlier. The first impression of McDonald was of a big and forceful man used to getting what he wanted and not afraid to speak his mind. Green was a brooding presence who considered every word before speaking and only spoke if he thought he had something useful to say. It was an informal meeting where everything was discussed openly and, apparently, honestly. McDonald reckoned he had a watertight agreement with Brealey to purchase his 52 per cent shareholding, plus he was to purchase the ten per cent of shares owned by Bernard Procter. He had quickly learned that nothing was straightforward where Brealey was concerned. He confirmed that the hold-up was due to the Stock Exchange withholding some shares that had been transferred from Woolhouse to Brealey, with the possibility of 'fines being imposed'. In layman's terms, according to McDonald, the shares were 'mortgaged up to the hilt'.

McDonald also said he had 'two wealthy backers' who did not want any of the limelight. One of them was a Unitedite [this may have been Martyn Burke, but McDonald later named Burke as someone he had 'spoken to', as he had also done with Kevin McCabe and Sean Bean]. When asked about the progress of the John Street stand, Green stated emphatically that it would be built, as failure to do so would result in

Mowlems suing the club, a situation that could endanger the very existence of Sheffield United. Another obstacle, said McDonald, was the fact that Stephen Hinchliffe still owned a piece of land to the rear of the Shoreham Street kop and was using this as leverage to try to influence proceedings. Potential backers were also wary because of the uncertainty over this parcel of land, which, until it was resolved, would affect further ground development - McDonald wanted to infill the corners to bring the stadium capacity up to 41,000. His enthusiasm about the stand and future ground developments dispelled any doubts the fans present may have had about his rumoured intentions to move the club to the Don Valley Stadium in the east of the city and his selling off Bramall Lane, which was, in estate agent parlance, a prime site close to the city centre and the railway station.

Finances dominated McDonald's concerns. During the Novotel meeting he stated that 'vast amounts of money' were being wasted at the club and he had already taken steps to cut costs, the major one being the amount being paid for police cover on matchdays. Under the guidance of club secretary David Capper, United were one of the first clubs to recruit and train professional (i.e. private) stewards to be employed inside the ground in place of police officers. Appointed in January 1989 after a spell as assistant secretary at Stoke City, Capper's duties included ensuring ground regulations were adhered to, a task that included stewarding of Bramall Lane. In the period immediately following the 1990 Taylor Report, the club was told to train stewards. Capper had no idea where training could be found, but had no choice but to implement the demand. The professionals in this duty were not available in Sheffield. In the end, such advice had to be sought from Fulham, Luton and Manchester United, and a specialist organisation, paid by the hour, was brought in to steward the crowd and train local people. The consequence was the cost of stewarding went up by £2,000 per game. Eventually, the local police worked with the stewarding company and were able to reduce their personnel deployment. United eventually bought in a retired police Chief Superintendent, who was able to do in-house training of stewards, and formed a company whose personnel could be hired out for stewarding other events, such as concerts, awards ceremonies and political rallies.

Another expense incurred by United was an architect's fee of £375,000 for the plans for the new stand that had been drawn up but not used due to McDonald's desire to modify the design. Despite all the difficulties McDonald was confident that the club could be, in his words, 'sorted out'. He intended to run the club 'strictly as a business' with a plan of achieving promotion to the Premier League in three years and entering European competition in five. However, his benchmark for success would not necessarily be measured by achievements on the pitch – what he wanted most of all was to see average crowds of over 20,000. With an obvious lack of conviction, he stated at the Novotel meeting that he had no plans to replace Dave Bassett as team manager. McDonald was adamant he would put none of his own or his businesses' money into the club until he had ownership of the shares. As soon as he had such ownership Brealey would be on his way. His most revelatory answer came when he was asked why he wanted to take over Sheffield United when his first love was Manchester City. He stated he had looked closely at other clubs (he mentioned Stoke City, Luton Town and Leicester City) but believed that Sheffield United was the one that could best fulfill his ambitions, on and off the pitch. He had taken over Sheffield United, he said, because, 'I can make money out of it.'

On November 25, 1995 the *Sheffield Star* reported: 'McDonald in control at last.' McDonald was finally in charge and Brealey was going. Or so it seemed. McDonald was reported to have parted with £3.5 million in cash and signed over a hotel property to Brealey to bring to a close his two-year struggle to take control of United. A somewhat ominous club statement read: 'The obstacles surrounding the acquisition have been overcome. The challenges facing the club are daunting but will be overcome.' McDonald told the *Financial Times*: 'The negotiations were horrendous. Getting the shareholders to agree was bloody difficult.' The *Financial Times* report continued, 'Mr McDonald's credentials for reviving [Sheffield United's] fortunes seem as good as any.

Unlike many football club owners, his connections with Pele's "beautiful game" are anything but tenuous' because in McDonald's words: 'I've played amateur football at a decent level. I am a roots-football person.'

Then, in stark contradiction to what he told BIFA members during their meeting at the Novotel, McDonald was quoted as saying: 'You've got to be very realistic. You don't make money out of football, it's not like a business. You do it for the enjoyment and seeing it grow.' McDonald's continued preoccupation with Manchester City, something that would remain with him all the time he was at Sheffield United, then surfaced. 'Gates are the problem [at United],' he said. 'Being a Lancashire person, I don't really understand the Yorkshire people. I don't see the logic of staying away. Take Manchester City. They had a disastrous start to the season but their support remained very strong, averaging 28,000. But at Sheffield United it has halved in two years and we need 14,000 just to break even. That's a major, major concern because nobody can build success in any walk of life without having support.' Perhaps McDonald's main problem was not understanding Sheffield and its demographics. Supporters, on both sides of the city, won't turn up in greater numbers on the mere promise that if they do they'll be given, at some unknown future date, a better team to watch. He also seemed unaware that Greater Manchester has a population twice that of South Yorkshire.

McDonald immediately set to work trying to find new blood to bring on to the board. He also resolved to break up the shareholding so that no individual would have overall control: 'I do not want to own the club,' he said, adding: 'and no one man should be in that position.' Why this should be so he never articulated. The method he would employ to bring about the fragmentation of the shareholding was made evident a year later, and was something that not many shareholders would have envisaged. The possible new directors were not new to Blades followers – they were said by the *Green 'Un* to be Stephen Hinchliffe and Martyn Burke. The prospect of two wealthy Sheffield-born men joining up with McDonald seemed to be confirmed two days later with the *Sheffield Star's* front-page headline: 'Millionaires United'. The accompanying report claimed that Burke was to buy half of McDonald's newly acquired shareholding and that a third man, Kevin McCabe, who had flirted with joining the board a couple of years earlier, was also to be recruited.

McDonald and Burke promptly arranged an open question-and-answer session at Bramall Lane, at which they told the supporters packed into the Executive Suite that McDonald would be the new chairman, Burke the vice chairman and that McDonald's 52 per cent shareholding would be split down the middle. Reg Brealey, the meeting heard, had officially resigned, while talks were continuing with Hinchliffe and McCabe. Derek Dooley, meanwhile, was to step down from the board and be offered the role of vice president, with some director's duties. Dooley was apparently happy with the change, stating: 'I am content that at last things are being put on a more businesslike level.' McDonald also said, 'We want to support Dave Bassett and build the stand and we need the support of the fans. We can do nothing without that. On 10,000 gates we are struggling. We have a strong board put together and there will be no more false promises.' Burke said that he had only become involved 'nine or ten days ago' and estimated that around £1.5 million would be made available to Bassett 'from directors' pockets' for team strengthening.

Less than a week after outlining his plans, Burke did an about turn. He explained why: 'My investigations during the course of this week have shown to me that the club's financial affairs are worse than previously disclosed. Mr McDonald disagreed with my request that all directors dig deep not only to buy players but also to address what I believe to be a short-term funding requirement. My fear in the short term is that the £1.5 million being talked about for team strengthening will not find itself being used by Dave Bassett. Two and a half years ago we were in the Premiership and the turnover was about £5.3 million. My own assessment is that the turnover this season will be around £3.75 million. But conversely the running costs have not had a commensurate drop in salaries. Two years ago they were £3.15 million and they still are. It does not take a genius, a mathematician or a qualified accountant to see that the club is now running at fairly horrendous losses.

That is why the board that is about to take over has a tremendous responsibility.' Burke had sent in his accountants weeks earlier and had been given full access to the books; one has to assume he found some skeletons in the Bramall Lane cupboards between Tuesday and Thursday.

McDonald remained unperturbed, reiterating his commitment: 'Many people have tried previously to buy the club and have foundered in the morass of legal complications. I have had a difficult time and it was not made easier by the pressure of the poor performances on the field. Clearly the players and manager also found the uncertainty difficult. The constant quest by the media for information, and a lot of misinformation being thrust in front of the fans, did nothing but hinder progress and I feel sorry for the fans and all the staff at the club who have had to endure this difficult time. That is all in the past now and I can get on with the job in hand, which is to return the club to its former glory and give back the pride that everyone associated with the club craves for. I will lay the foundations to ensure that never again will Sheffield United be controlled other than by a balanced board of directors who have the financial strength to ensure that the club and its manager has the facilities it needs to deliver up a winning team on the field.' Fine words, but not prophetic.

With Burke now out of the picture attention turned to the two other prospective directors, Hinchliffe and McCabe. McDonald's scheduled meeting with Hinchliffe had been cancelled and McCabe was away on business. However, director John Plant offered his support to McDonald. Eventually, on December 7 United announced that Hinchliffe and McCabe would be joining the board and that McDonald had been elected chairman, with Hinchliffe, still the second-biggest shareholder, with some 14 per cent, as vice chairman. Both the new men had been asked to commit £1 million each to the club. Said Hinchliffe, 'I am delighted to be joining at what I hope will be a new era for the club.'

Now that the make-up of the boardroom was ostensibly settled, McDonald could concentrate on the playing side. The following Saturday United lost at home again, to Huddersfield

Town, and were precariously placed second from bottom of the division. The regular 12,000 supporters booed the players off the pitch. McDonald acted. He knew that only drastic surgery could revive the team's fortunes. Dave Bassett, after almost eight years in charge in which he had taken United back to the top division for the first time in 14 years, had been worn down by all the boardroom uncertainty and could no longer raise the enthusiasm necessary to drag himself and his players back from the low point at which they now found themselves. He had known for some time that McDonald wanted to bring in a new manager. It was time for him to go. On December 12, 1995 United announced that Bassett was leaving 'by mutual consent'.

The official statement was read by Hinchliffe: 'Both the manager and the board now feel that it is an appropriate moment for the club to make a fresh start. With the establishment of a new board, both parties feel that events have run their natural course and that the circumstances are such that now is the right time for the manager to seek fresh challenges and for Sheffield United to go forward under new managerial direction. Both parties wish to stress that this separation is entirely amicable.' Surrounded by tearful supporters outside the players' entrance at Bramall Lane, an emotional Bassett read out his own statement to the press: 'I now feel that it would be best if I parted company with the club. I leave reluctantly with my head held high, knowing that I have done my best with the limited resources available to me. There was no money for players and despite promises that work would begin, no progress on the new stand. I was disappointed because I made a substantial profit dealing in the transfer market during my time at the club and I firmly believe that money had to be spent to improve the team. I was fighting with one arm tied behind my back. Time ran out a little bit for Dave Bassett and professionally it's correct for me and it's correct for the club.' He knew this day had been coming, as he wrote in *Harry's Game* that after the Huddersfield game 'we opened a bottle of champagne in the physio's room and everyone knew it was the end. I wasn't sacked. I didn't resign. We just drifted apart. I had become a kamikaze pilot. I had taken out Brealey, but taken out myself as well.' In truth, the parting was not amicable, despite the content of the official statement. Bassett later claimed that his pay-off wasn't the full amount owed to him and that an argument ensued with Charles Green. The club's management style of the time decreed that Green offered to settle the dispute by physical means in the car park; it wasn't the first time he had employed this unique style of 'diplomacy'. But Bassett called his bluff and Green backed down. Four years afterwards Bassett said, 'I would have loved to have had the chance to take negotiations further in the car park. He didn't want to.'

The prickly situation died down enough for a farewell dinner to be held in the Bramall Lane social club, at which two of Bassett's players, possibly having learned from Charles Green, fell out and began fighting. The altercation was broken up by colleagues. Bassett stormed out, furious at the turn of events, loudly berating the 'poxy family club'. He was to return in a better mood six years later for a dinner in his honour. Some 500 Blades, including dozens of former players from his time at Bramall Lane, gathered to pay tribute to him. The night was probably the most scurrilous and slanderous - and hilarious - evening ever witnessed at Bramall Lane as Bassett recounted tales of hitherto private incidents that took place during his time as manager. It was a fitting close to a period in the club's history that was never dull.

Chapter 10

Howard's Sway
Floating Balls

Before Dave Bassett's departure was made public, talks had been held with his successor, Howard Kendall. This was good business practice, claimed a spokesman for McDonald: 'We are bringing business standards to football. In business you have to be one jump ahead and we foresaw the day we might need another manager.' To the supporters, this statement meant that McDonald intended all along to replace Bassett. Kendall, the former Everton, Manchester City and Notts County manager, was appointed the day after Bassett fell. The change in the team's playing style under Kendall was immediately apparent, as was the improvement in results. There was fun to be had in the moment. Kendall's first game in charge, away to Ipswich Town, some 48 hours after his appointment, saw a newly revealed passing game that merited mock chants amongst the Blades following of 'Kendall out!' The match ended 1-1. Bassett was renowned for playing the 'long-ball' game but it was said that on his first day in charge Kendall strung up a rope on sticks across the middle of the training pitch a couple of feet off the ground and fined anybody who kicked the ball over it. United drew six and won one of Kendall's first seven games in charge and by the end of the season were the form team of the division and comfortably avoided relegation. McDonald certainly stood by his word and provided funds to Kendall that were never available to Bassett, so much so that former Liverpool and West Ham

United midfielder Don Hutchison became United's first-ever £1 million-plus signing.

McDonald was clearly ambitious. Although he had recently experienced a barren spell in terms of trophies, at Everton Kendall had won the League twice, the FA Cup and European Cup Winners' Cup. United were also thinking big in playing personnel. On January 31, 1996 United were 'linked' with a big-name international footballer, reported by the *Sheffield Star* to be Danish international Michael Laudrup, currently with Spanish giants Real Madrid, and previously at Juventus, Lazio and Barcelona. A 'Bramall Lane spokesman' was quoted in the *Sheffield Star* as saying, 'We have been alerted to his availability and are pursuing it. This is a serious issue for us and should show our fans that we mean business in trying to attract the best players we can afford to Sheffield United.' This was the first of what was to become a lengthy list of several world-class players – England international John Barnes and Brazilian World Cup winner Bebeto were others - whom United were supposed to be trying to sign over the next three years. The cynical - and realistic - Blades fans maintained their 'believe it when we see it' attitude, which proved in the long run to be the correct one. Laudrup never signed for the Blades, nor did any other of the 'superstars'. Several months later the *News of the World* reported that United had made an 'audacious £4.2 million bid' for England star Paul Gascoigne, then at Glasgow Rangers (offers for well-known international players were always 'audacious'). Howard Kendall was quoted as saying, 'I can confirm I have spoken to Walter [Smith, the Rangers manager] about Gascoigne, but what was discussed must remain private.' The most astonishing thing was that none of the reports expressed any surprise whatsoever that Sheffield United should be in a position to contemplate paying £4.2 million for any player, never mind 'Gazza', considering the position the club was in a few months earlier - in Brealey's last weeks United couldn't even afford to pay the staff's wages. After the Gascoigne revelations, Kendall said he was looking to land an undisclosed big-name player to help 'put bums on seats'. At the AGM at the end of December, Kendall was asked by a shareholder about the seriousness of the Gascoigne story.

Kendall responded that United made an enquiry but not a bid, concluding; 'It was no publicity stunt.'

The influence of new chief executive Charles Green, appointed by McDonald to replace Derek Dooley, began to increase. Kendall was an experienced manager but, strangely, was happy to let Green, a man with no previous experience in such a role, negotiate players' contracts. The players couldn't believe their luck. Dave Bassett had been known as being 'tight' with the club's money when it came to wages and contracts. He wouldn't recommend to the board one penny more than he thought the player was worth. Then along came Green, who started handing out contracts the players did not warrant and that the club not afford. If Kendall wanted a player, Green would do his utmost to try and get him, whatever the cost, hence the regular links with 'big name' players'. Initially this arrangement worked, as Kendall led United to comfortable safety. Green, a qualified engineer, was a loyal servant of McDonald, having joined the Texas Group in 1983, working his way up to become its business development director. He was South Yorkshire born and bred, so was returning to an area he knew well, and he was also not ignorant of football matters. He had been a regular player and goalscorer for a number of semi-professional clubs in the 1970s and early 1980s, he was on Sheffield United's books as a schoolboy and was later offered a full-time professional contract at Barnsley but turned it down, stating years later, 'I was never really interested in a pro career because in those days the money wasn't good enough. I got £3 [per week] in my first engineering job and a fiver a match to play [part time] for Mexborough. Looking back I know I was a lazy player but I never scored less than 30 goals a season.' As well as being a player of talent, Green revealed himself to be a bit of a character. A former playing colleague recalled that on coach journeys to away games he would sit on the back seat with all the 'Jack the Lads', cracking jokes and generally entertaining everyone. During his time as chief executive at Bramall Lane, Green proved to be a self-confident, some might say arrogant, man who had the 'gift of the gab' but only when he considered it necessary: he wasn't someone who spoke for the enjoyment of hearing his own voice. Indeed, when Welsh international striker Dean Saunders, formerly of Liverpool and Aston Villa, signed for United several months later he said that after only a few minutes in Green's company he thought he was signing for Real Madrid.

As events on the pitch were improving, a series of simultaneous off-the-field 'own goals' showed that McDonald, although an improvement over Brealey, maintained some of the outgoing chairman's bad habits: namely unfulfilled promises and a lack of information being released to the supporters. Despite fielding questions from Blades fans and answering them frankly at an open meeting arranged by BIFA on January 20, 1996 at Sheffield City Hall, another embarrassing delay occurred in the start of work on the John Street stand. After several large holes were dug, everything mysteriously came to a halt. The biggest disappointment, though, was not the fact that work had stopped, but that the new regime at the Lane did not see fit to say anything about it in public. It took several pressing questions from one persistent shareholder after the club's AGM for the Mowlems representative to disclose that the reason for the delay was due to a change in the methods of stage payments by United. There was nothing unusual about that - major projects of this nature are often subject to delicate negotiations over how the contract price will be paid - but something else that was not unusual was that the fans were still being kept in the dark. During the home match against Barnsley, which United edged 1-0 to maintain their climb away from the relegation zone, referee Eddie Lomas allowed several additional minutes of play as United wasted time, hoofing the ball into the John Street building site so that it took a while for it to be returned from the mud and rubble.

When the possibility of relegation was eventually over, McDonald said, 'Howard's [Kendall] first priority was to steady the ship, stop the leak of goals and then build a side to make sure we would still be in the First Division next season. Our next goals are to build the new John Street stand, get in the Premiership – and stay there.' New director Kevin McCabe told the club's Annual General Meeting, 'By August 1996 you will be able to sit in the John Street Stand, if you wish. We shall have a super stand, which will make Bramall Lane one of the best stadiums in the country.' McCabe's and McDonald's words were not empty. The first concrete evidence that serious work on the John Street stand would eventually get underway came with letters to season ticket holders of the old John Street terrace and stand, offering them season tickets in the new stand at the same price as 1996/97 kop season tickets. By the Saturday of the Sunderland home fixture in April, 75 people had bought seats in the as yet non-existent stand. Then, on Wednesday April 17, a huge pile-driver, a concrete mixer and men with hard hats were spotted in the vicinity. The new Sheffield United board had commendably stood by a commitment made by the previous regime in offering seats in the new stand at a reduced rate to those who were forcibly moved to other parts of the ground two years previously. When someone raised this question at the BIFA-organised meeting with the board at the City Hall in January, McDonald confessed he knew nothing of such a commitment being made, but if it had been, he promised to fulfil it. To his credit he did just that, even offering 'match credits' to people who booked seats in the new stand, should any building delays occur that put back its opening.

There was more news to come regarding the future development of the ground when it was announced that United had plans to convert spare land around Bramall Lane into a giant leisure, retail and hotel complex. The *Sheffield Star* reported on July 11, 1996 that the club hoped to make use of their 20-acre Bramall Lane site as well as two pockets of land across Cherry Street, which were owned by Arnold Laver timber merchants and Sheffield City Council. The Council land was the site of the former Sheffield Works Department joinery shop. United apparently owned more adjacent land than any other club in the country. Six months later United issued plans for the proposed leisure park. Unlike Reg Brealey's plans 14 years earlier, this scheme received more support from the local residents following extensive consultation - the club had been quietly, and deliberately, meeting regularly with the City Council to obtain outline planning permission and to this end canvassed local residents prior to the formal application for planning permission. 'If people thought we were in the business of compulsory purchase and knocking down houses, they have been reassured,' said McCabe. 'We want to take them with us and when our planning is approved I shall call more meetings.' The cost of the project was a reported £25 million but most of the facilities – a hotel, a theme pub, a multiplex cinema, sports shops, retail and fast-food outlets – would be self-financing. There was also to be a nursing home, for, as Charles Green joked, the more senior members of the United board!

On Valentine's Day 1997 'Application for Planning Permission' notices were posted on lampposts and telegraph poles on Cherry Street. Later in the year further details of the leisure complex plans were revealed, along with a promise from United that the complex would create 200 new jobs. Peter Cromar, of local action group the Sheffield Community Forum, welcomed the proposed development, praising the club's months of consultation and agreed that it would upgrade and bring benefits to the Sharrow area, which had one of the highest unemployment rates in the city. Outline planning permission for the second part of the development, on the adjoining Arnold Laver and Sheffield Works Department land, would be decided in subsequent weeks. City Council solicitors advised that no councillors with involvement with the club, such as season ticket holders, shareholders or beneficiaries of free hospitality, should take part in the planning decision. Accordingly, one member of the planning committee, Blades season ticket holder Richard Eastman, stood down. However, this policy did not affect Cromar, another Sheffield United season ticket holder, who publicly sang the praises of the proposals.

The same *Sheffield Star* report made first mention of United's plans to float on the Stock Exchange; financial advisors English Trust Ltd had been commissioned to examine the prospect. Two days later the *Sheffield Star* published a back-page photograph of a large mobile crane erecting steel girders on the John Street side of the ground. The stand was going up at a cost of £6m, £1.5m up on the contractors' original tender. A total of £600,000 was spent on demolition and site preparation, £300,000 on professional fees, and the remainder of the increase on closed-circuit television facilities, fixtures and fittings and car parking. When it was opened, just two weeks later than scheduled, on October 12, 1996, BIFA once more arranged for the (artificial) bells of St Mary's church to be rung to celebrate its completion. It was 30 months since the John Street side of the ground was last used. The stand, which could hold 6,700 spectators, was nearly full for the opening game against Tranmere Rovers, while 27 of the 31 executive boxes had been sold for the season. The ground capacity was now 30,500. Nobody could determine exactly how much of the £6 million Mike McDonald had personally put in. All he would let on was that his contribution was 'serious money'.

However, there were still some unfortunate stories coming out of Bramall Lane. For example, one regular figure on the sidelines at both home and away matches would be seen no longer. He was club photographer Martyn Harrison, who had been covering United matches, players and events for many years. He had supported the Blades for nearly 30 years and originally treated his photography as a hobby, following United all over the country in the process, his bald head becoming a familiar sight behind the goal United were attacking. When he decided to set himself up in the sports photography business, financial arrangements for his services were agreed with the club. A few months after McDonald's takeover and Green's appointment as chief executive, Harrison claimed he was owed nearly £2,000 by the club, and refused to hand over photographs from one home match until he was paid. According to Harrison, Charles Green declared that he 'didn't like anyone holding a gun to his head' and immediately terminated Harrison's employment. He did eventually get paid, but only after taking the club to the Small Claims Court. The club therefore became dependent on agencies to provide its images. A subsequent distinct decline in quality of match-action pictures in the club programme followed. Further stories of Green's 'ruthlessness' would arise. In January 1996 United were to play Aston Villa at home in the fourth round of the FA Cup but a heavy snowfall the previous day threatened the game, which was to be broadcast live by BBC television. Groundsman Glenn Nortcliffe and two assistants worked late into the night and from early the next morning to clear snow from the pitch and even from the streets surrounding Bramall Lane, in order that the tie could go ahead. The match was played and United got their television money. The reward for Nortcliffe and his men? They were called in by Green and McDonald, who, rather than thank them for their hard work, informed them that had the snow not been shifted and the pitch had been unplayable they would have been sacked. One former club employee privately claimed that the McDonald/ Green regime was built on 'fear and harassment'. He said that new ideas and suggestions were stifled and staff morale was low. No appreciation was shown and no incentives given by those in authority. Staff believed that 'moles' had been placed in each department, with the result that people were afraid to speak their minds as they did not know whom they could trust.

Another departure from United came at the end of August in the sizeable form of Stephen Hinchliffe, who had been on the board only since the previous December but who now resigned because of the police investigation into his outside business dealings. McDonald was not leaving though, despite finding himself forever linked in the media with any consortium that expressed interest in buying Manchester City. A few years earlier, when Manchester City fans were campaigning to remove chairman Peter Swales, McDonald was reported to be interested in taking over the club but withdrew when he realised former City and England striker Francis Lee was the fans' preferred option. Now Lee was under pressure himself. In late August McDonald confirmed he had been approached by an unnamed group to gauge his interest in joining them. His answer was: 'Find someone else; I've got a big club to run here.' It wasn't the last time he would deny or reject the idea that he would be departing Bramall Lane for Maine Road. A few months later he reportedly repelled further approaches from City, saying, 'Four years ago I was committed to going in [to City]; now the timing has changed. I have a job here and I will do it. I am being talked to all the time but as far as I am concerned it is in an advisory capacity; people seem to think that after what I have done at Sheffield I can come up with another winning formula.' He joked, in reference to Manchester City, that he 'would have to be a crackpot to want to sort that lot out'.

McDonald was not the only person at Sheffield United wanted by Manchester City. City had just sacked manager Alan Ball and, having been turned down by former United boss Dave Bassett, switched their attentions to Howard Kendall. City's approach was firmly rebuffed by an angry McDonald, twice, the second time in his usual abrupt style: 'I am well aware of what I consider to be an illegal approach for our manager. I am brassed off with all this publicity and I am preparing an official complaint from my club to the football authorities. I assure our fans that Howard Kendall is not leaving Bramall Lane.' If McDonald and Kendall were not leaving the Lane, joining Stephen Hinchliffe out of the boardroom exit door was John Plant, Reg Brealey's last ally amongst the directors, who cited 'pressures from an expanding business and a growing family' as reasons for his resignation. To reinforce the now depleted board McDonald looked to two men he knew well from Manchester; one, long-time friend Freddie Pye; the second, scrap metal merchant Stewart White, who was the father of United and ex-England player David, also formerly of Manchester City. Pye was well known in footballing circles thanks to a playing career that took in several low-ranking north-west clubs and subsequent football directorships at Altrincham, Stockport County and Manchester City. Pye expressed his admiration for McDonald: 'I am chairman of a £50 million group of companies and I'm doing very nicely but this fellow has left me in the slow lane. I have watched him operate and he never ceases to amaze me. [He] is a very talented and ambitious man. Underestimate him at your peril.'

McDonald's comments regarding Manchester City's approach for Kendall were typical of the way he went about things. There would be many instances of his brusqueness and two examples of his 'brutal honesty' were evidenced early in the 1995/96 season. Whilst it is not common for a chairman to comment directly on the performance of the team, especially a bad one – such criticism is usually left to the manager – McDonald was to let the United players know in no uncertain terms that he was dissatisfied with one particular defeat and ordered them to watch a video of the match the following day, saying, 'I had to suffer through 90 minutes and the players must be expected to do the same.' He then got into a slanging match with Crystal Palace chairman Ron Noades over the late postponement of a game between the two sides due to international call-ups in the Palace squad (this was before the weekends of international matches were left blank in the league, as they are now). Afterwards he stormed, 'It is right to assume I said my piece on behalf of the club. No one was left in any doubt about United's case.' Another time he went public to put in words what the fans were thinking after one particularly bad League Cup defeat at Preston, then a division below United. He reckoned United's performance was 'disgusting', adding, 'I think they should be giving their wages to charity this week.' When United lost at Huddersfield he was confronted outside the McAlpine Stadium by supporters angry at the team's recent displays, after which he publicly issued his own outburst: 'Some of the players should be disgusted by their recent performances. We have a problem and something has got to be done about it. We have signed a lot of quality players and it is not gelling at the moment. The fans are frustrated at the results but no one is more frustrated than I am. It is disappointing when you look at the amount of money that has been spent.'

On the face of it, such words were a dig at Howard Kendall, but McDonald continued, 'He [Kendall] has a proven track record and is the man to sort things out.' In late October, for the second time in a matter of weeks, McDonald was unimpressed with more 'Kendall will leave' speculation, this time regarding Blackburn Rovers. 'Howard is going nowhere,' he stated. 'He supported me [during the Manchester City rumours] and said that he loved United and was happy with his job. That still goes. I want to assure our fans that as far as I am concerned the issue is stone dead. I am flattered that every time a big club wants a manager they turn to our man. But this is a big club and it is going to get bigger. If a major, major club comes for Howard that would be a different matter. But Blackburn? No way.' Soon after this he attempted to scotch rumours claiming that Kendall had a contractual agreement enabling him to talk to Premier League clubs. Kendall was said to be 'astounded' to hear that he was supposed to have had a 'bust up' with McDonald over this supposed agreement. Kendall later played down media stories linking him with other clubs, stating; 'I owe something to the chairman here. I owe him loyalty. This is a big club and together we can make it bigger.' The manager's attitude was to change.

McDonald had by now hit a snag concerning the club's plans to develop a new training complex at the Council-owned Abbeydale Grange school grounds. There had been numerous objections to the proposed scheme from the local middle-class residents, who complained that it would bring unacceptable additional noise and traffic to the area and that their access to the land would be restricted. After being told that there would be further delays in the planning process, McDonald complained, 'We've been messed around enough. We need to know now so that we can begin laying pitches to use next year. The deadline for doing that is this week. If that is delayed it's another year lost. We need these facilities; the city needs these facilities. A lot of money has already been spent drawing up all of this and we had a lease all prepared.' The delay was caused by the Council's calling of a meeting between United and the protesting residents. Councillor Viv Nicholson, chair of the leisure committee, said she would make no rushed decisions: 'We have a responsibility to listen to the residents, who have come forward with their own scheme, which appears perfectly viable.' United had erected a high metal fence around the site, which upset the residents as it prevented them from gaining access to the sports fields. United hit back with a statement that claimed the fence had been put up because the area was a danger to children, citing 'a dangerous and unsatisfactory environment' because of the indiscriminate dropping of waste materials, which included used hypodermic needles, dog faeces, used condoms and broken bottles. Furthermore, the area fenced was being rotovated, fertilised and re-seeded to provide new football pitches and needed to be left undisturbed.

One local resident, BIFA member Reg Hobson, who lived directly opposite the school grounds, was 100 per cent in favour of United's proposals and carried out his own personal research to refute many of the protestors' claims:

Claim 1: The school was not in favour. Hobson said it was – he had asked Jan Woodhead, the headteacher.

Claim 2: The school would not have as much use of the playing fields. Hobson argued that the school would have exclusive use of all but two of the pitches. This was confirmed by the headteacher.

Claim 3: The teams that currently used the football pitches had not been consulted. In fact, said Hobson, they had been consulted and would enjoy both continued use and improved changing facilities, albeit at a higher rent.

Claim 4: There was insufficient public transport on the adjoining Carterknowle Road. Hobson counted nine buses every hour during the daytime.

Claim 5: There would little or no way across the playing fields. According to Hobson, a regular walker, there were two wide designated paths, easily sufficient to traverse the site.

Claim 6: Dogs would be banned from the playing fields. Hobson's response was 'about time too!' From his living room he had carried out a survey of dog walking on the fields and counted 80 dogs in an eight-hour period. Assuming every dog 'did its business', this amounted to over 29,000 piles of dog excrement a year (not including the other 16 hours every day), a real health hazard to anybody using the facilities in the way they were intended. Hobson possibly had too much time on his hands.

Hobson accused the protesting residents of a 'Nimby' ('not in my back yard') attitude and believed that the project would benefit the school, Sheffield United, the local area, the city, indeed the whole region. Kevin McCabe told *The Red and White Wizaaard* fanzine soon after that United had negotiated a 135-year lease at Abbeydale Grange and had submitted a £3.25 million bid for National Lottery assistance for its development by designating it as a 'Community Sports Centre'. It appeared that there might be a compromise solution with the hostile residents, who titled themselves the

'Carterknowle and Millhouses Action Group', by re-designating one of the full-size pitches as available for community use. The National Lottery application, McCabe pronounced, was valid because it was a project 'which provides comprehensive amenities for the use of school children and the community at large, as well as giving the club excellent training facilities.' However, the bid for Lottery funding was turned down in May 1998, putting the future of the project in jeopardy. United were told that aid to professional football clubs did not have a high priority rating in Lottery funding.

Another blow came when it was revealed that the club's new replica kit would not be ready in time for the start of the 1996/97 season. The delay would cost the club £250,000 in lost sales from its souvenir shop and other outlets. Indeed, only one set of first-team strip had been delivered; the reserves and juniors had to use last season's out-of-date kit. A set of training kit, ordered by the club in February, was still to arrive. The club was considering taking legal action against Claremont Garments, the company that manufactured the kit under the trade name Avec. When it did arrive, the Avec kit and replica shirts were memorable for having two neck labels. For those that could be bothered to look closely, the surface label informed the wearer that the shirt was 'Sheffield United', but when removed it revealed that the original label specified 'Sunderland'.

In August 1996 the details of the flotation were promulgated. The club intended to float the club on the Stock Exchange, raising £5 million in the process. Fans would be able to buy shares in the new company. 'A team has been put together to handle the flotation and the new rights issue,' Charles Green was to declare. 'There are now a number of institutions getting involved in football and a lot of fans out there for whom owning shares in a football club has become fashionable. And of course there are our own fans who we would expect to be keen to be involved.' United were embarking on what was called a 'reverse takeover', which was a method of taking a short cut to the Stock Exchange by means of a smaller company effectively taking the place of a company already publicly quoted. Manchester-based sports and leisure company Conrad PLC, which marketed the Le Coq Sportif brand of sportswear and owned the rights to use the name 'Bobby Charlton' in the endorsement of products, was to make an offer for 2,633 Ordinary Shares of Sheffield United, representing 91.33 per cent of the shareholding, and eight Original Shares, which made up another 1.68 per cent. The offer valued the club at £9.9 million and, if successful, a further 20,840,000 shares would be issued to raise approximately £12.5 million. Conrad PLC would then change its name to Sheffield United PLC. This 'back door' method of entering the Stock Exchange was quicker than a full application. There would henceforth be two boards (one for the PLC and one for its subsidiary, the football club), with McDonald heading both. Directors of Conrad would be expected to join the new PLC board. Conrad wanted to become involved in football as it was now an attractive proposition following increasing attendances and major television deals negotiated between *Sky TV* and the Premier League and the Football League. After failing to buy out Leeds United, Conrad had been reported to be initially interested in taking over Sheffield Wednesday.

However, as always with Sheffield United, a potential problem raised its head. According to Conrad, the deal could be 'complicated' unless some shares previously held by Stephen Hinchliffe were placed in what they defined as 'friendly hands'. McDonald and Green assured United's merger partners that the shares were back in the control of the club. Said Green, 'We have a signed agreement with Mr Hinchliffe, endorsed by his legal advisors and ours, to release the stock transfer forms. Where the original share certificates are is not a relevant issue. This is not an insurmountable problem, the takeover will go ahead. Guaranteed.' The shares in question, 417 in number, were registered in the name of one of Hinchliffe's companies, Chase Montague. Hinchliffe was understood to have made extra demands over the transfer of the shares, to which McDonald refused to commit. It was later revealed that McDonald had paid Hinchliffe £953,644 for these shares. The club's accounts were published in early December and showed that a loss of £850,000 had been accrued in the previous year. Continued losses, said McDonald, were the catalyst for Stock Exchange listing.

After the flotation Sheffield United PLC would be valued at over £20 million. McDonald enthused, 'My ambition and my dream is to make United financially strong enough to stand alongside any club in the Premiership. One of the biggest names in the City of London is involved. Down the line it will result in new investment in the club, allowing us to complete the stadium, finance the development of the land around the stadium and, of course, provide money for Howard Kendall to make sure that when we reach the Premiership we are strong enough to stay there. Bringing the club to the stock market will provide access funding at a higher level.' Charles Green followed suit: 'We are on the brink of a great new era for Sheffield United. This is the ideal way to give the fans a chance to buy into their club.' United's *Green 'Un* reporter Tony Pritchett was similarly enthused, writing: '[United are] perhaps the richest club outside the Premiership and comfortably better off than some that are in it.' He added, somewhat melodramatically; 'If there is a Man of the Year at Bramall Lane, it has to be McDonald.'

Ironically, former chairman Reg Brealey now revealed that he was once on the verge of a similar takeover deal for United 15 years earlier: 'I had reached what I thought was an agreement to take over a company called Sheffield Assessment Houses, then a PLC with a Stock Exchange listing,' he said, 'but overnight the giant brewery conglomerate Vaux stepped in to top the bid and the deal fell through. But for Vaux, United would have been the first football club to be quoted on the Stock Exchange.' Brealey added that he had tried to find another suitable merger target but was never able to do so. Brealey planned to make the club a publicly quoted company because he believed that major companies could be interested in taking shares. A financial broker was quoted in the *Sheffield Star*, saying, '...several major companies [were] prepared to take a 50 per cent interest in clubs with which they have some geographical link. The rest of the shares would go to supporters, giving them an added interest in their club.' The scheme had come to nothing a year later; no one had made an offer. Interviewed by Tony Pritchett, Brealey explained: 'The situation is that those people who did show an interest wanted to know all about planning permission and development. Football and the progress of the club seemed a secondary consideration and so the talks stopped.' In his early days at least, Brealey always put the welfare of the club above short-term personal goals.

The timetable for the flotation was extensive and had to follow strict Stock Exchange procedures. Underwriting would be on November 13 and formal application for Stock Exchange listing would be heard by the Stock Exchange Council a week later. The process of flotation was completed in mid December, with the Stock Exchange listing due in January, when, somewhat predictably, the front page of the *Sheffield Star* prominently featured a photograph of the United team posing in football kit and bowler hats. Manager Howard Kendall was sitting in the middle of the front row, wearing a suit, reading the *Financial Times*, with a briefcase by his feet. The accompanying headline read: 'WE'RE IN THE MONEY'. To add to the hyperbole Charles Green was quoted, citing the Stock Exchange listing as 'the most significant move in the club's history'. Sheffield-based stockbrokers Nicholson Barber were handling the sale of shares, priced at 60p, to the general public. 'We have been swamped with interest', said their spokesman Jon Dunn, 'but we have only a specific number of shares to sell. We asked for a minimum investment of £300 but it seems that a lot of people won't get the shares that they wanted.' But while most of the talk was of shares, McDonald still had his mind on the fortunes of the team, saying, 'If serious, quality players come on the market we shall be competing for them.' Green refused to put any figures on manager Kendall's flotation-boosted transfer kitty, arguing sensibly that: 'If we start shouting about millions of pounds, the first time we make a bid the price is quadrupled.'

The terms of the deal for current shareholders were that ten new shares would replace every one existing share. This applied to both Ordinary and Original shares. There were 477 of the latter, issued in the 1890s, which had recently been selling at auction for approximately £4,500 each. The

Ordinary shares, by contrast, cost only £500 when issued in 1982 and were changing hands for just £200. The two types of shares were now classed as being the same, at a stroke drastically reducing the value of the Original shares. Coincidentally or not, Mike McDonald owned around 1,500 Ordinary shares and no Original shares. This anomaly would come back to haunt McDonald over the next few months.

The first sign of trouble from the holders of Original shares came at the Annual General Meeting at the end of December. As well as the value of the Original shares having dropped alarmingly, they also previously held the privilege of permitting free entry to Bramall Lane for life. This perk had now been taken away. At the meeting, described in the *Sheffield Star* as 'stormy', the holders of the Original shares complained of 'shabby treatment' during the flotation. McDonald, typically, did not hold back in his defence. 'I have put a lot of money into this club,' he fumed. 'When I came in you could not pay the tea ladies. Now you have a brilliant new stand, a new manager and a team that is near the top of the league. Financially this is the worst deal I have ever done in my life. I am trying to bring £12.5 million into Sheffield United and get it into the Premiership. Frankly I am a bit naffed off with all of this!' One shareholder angrily complained, 'I cannot believe how I have been treated. I shall withdraw my support.' He was shouted down by the majority present. McDonald tried to reassure the dissenters that their free entry to games would continue – but with a rider attached: 'While I am in this chair Original shareholders will be allowed to retain their privilege, if they wish. But I cannot guarantee what the next chairman or the next board will do.'

There was more than a hint of irony about the Original shareholders' dissent. When Reg Brealey was grilled by BIFA supporters at the 1994 AGM they were heckled by some of the very same people, who at that time were content with their rather cushy arrangement. Now the boot was on the other foot. The club was also criticised at the AGM by some shareholders who had not received their prospectus outlining the details of the flotation. Charles Green defended himself and the club: 'The document was not prepared by us, not printed by us and not posted by us. [Its] distribution is out of our control.' Explaining the reasoning behind the flotation, Green added, 'The heart of the plan is to dilute the shareholding so that no individual can control the club again and fulfill a promise made by Mike McDonald when he came in, and also to provide access to cash from the City and financial institutions. The days of wealthy backers underwriting clubs are over. We could have sold the shares three times over to the City but the board insisted that the fans should have an opportunity to buy. We are raising £12.5 million for Sheffield United. This deal is right for Sheffield United. Your board members are not becoming millionaires with this deal. They were millionaires before and they put their money at the club's disposal to allow it to pay its way.'

The potential benefits of the flotation were emphasised above all else. There was little mention of the fact that share prices could fall as well as rise. Typical was a report by Tony Pritchett in the *Sheffield Star*: 'The shares have been placed at 60p but sources in the City of London today tipped the United issue to follow the boom trend of football clubs and they are forecast to end the first day priced at between £1 and £1.20. And if the club reaches the Premiership this season they could soar to around £4 each.' However, United's directors would not be able to make a quick killing as the terms of the deal forbade them from selling any of their shareholding for two years. The financial predictions proved correct – Charles Green was present in the Square Mile to see the name 'Sheffield United PLC' light up on the traders' screens for the first time. The market opened at 8.30am and shares were being traded for around £1.45. Around £1.5 million-worth was traded in the first 15 minutes before the share price levelled at between £1.18 and £1.20. The demand from 'ordinary' fans was great but small investors were not allocated the number of shares they had requested; there was insufficient stock to meet the local demand. A week later the share price had fallen to £1.05, still a healthy margin above the 60p flotation value. The share price had shot up by well over 50 per cent in its first few days, but reality set in. By the end of March the price had dropped to 70p, a trend that replicated the fortunes of other publicly quoted football clubs. To celebrate the successful Stock Exchange listing, United threw a party for HSBC, Commercial Union, Newton Investment Management, Singer Friedlander, Gartmore Investment and Grant Thornton executives, all companies that assisted with the flotation process. The Bramall Lane car park was full of expensive cars belonging not to footballers but to bankers, investment consultants, accountants and financial advisors, as they enjoyed a tour of the ground and a kickabout on the pitch.

At the time of United's flotation there were 11 other football clubs listed on the Stock Exchange, with five more preparing to float. Manchester United, Tottenham Hotspur and Millwall had been listed for several years, though Millwall's share price had fallen so much that soon after United's flotation trading in them was suspended. The desire to float was based on the prospect of an 'instant payday' as it was anticipated that shares bought at 60p could be sold soon afterwards for a much higher price. But many City analysts and advisors believed that football clubs shares were generally around one-third overpriced. The average fall in football club shares during 1996 was 28 per cent, which tended to support this argument. John Barnwell, chairman of the League Managers' Association, put it this way: 'I don't think the trend to be floated on the Stock Exchange will slow down. The City is all about short-term gain, and that is not conducive to the long-term good of football.' Tony Fraher, chief executive of Singer Friedlander Investment Funds Ltd, observed the situation differently. He said, 'We look at this thing as impassively as possible. If it stacks up as a business then we'll back it. If it doesn't, we won't. Daft we're not, and we can see football has a great future.' He also thought that being publicly quoted would increase democracy at clubs. 'Where you had the all-embracing chairman – Peter Swales at Man City springs to mind – you had the supporters baying for him to go. Now you will see the business people running the clubs because the City will insist on it. And because players' transfers hit the profit and loss accounts you'll see clubs being encouraged to invest in youth policies.' These final statements proved that Mr Fraher knew a lot more about investments than he did about football as over the next few years clubs spent more and more millions on ready-made foreign international players rather than concentrating on home-grown talent. There was also little sign of the predicted outbreaks of democracy at the top level of British football. What fan representation there is is nominal and cosmetic. Buying shares in a football club notionally gives supporters a say in how their club is run but in reality their influence is negligible. They can attend the AGM and vote, but their vote is usually irrelevant in comparison to the huge blocks of shares held by the directors and other organisations. Except at the lower levels of the game, the utopian ideal of one-man-one-vote, fan-owned football clubs such as Barcelona is not close to arriving in Britain.

Meanwhile, a couple of weeks after the AGM the disaffected holders of Original shares entered discussions with the club regarding an improved offer. Charles Green claimed that one unnamed Original shareholder, unhappy with his part of the deal, made a last-minute appeal to the Stock Exchange Takeover Panel to stop the flotation on the grounds that it was prejudicial to a minority interest. Green added, 'I am willing to talk to a delegation [of Original shareholders]. The [flotation] offer must stand but the club is willing to see if we can smooth out the situation.' The Original shareholders' appointed spokesman was local businessman William Beckett, who admitted to seeking advice from lawyers and financial advisors. Former *BBC Radio Sheffield* presenter Robert Jackson was a holder of three Original shares, one obtained by inheritance and two at auction in the 1960s, for which he paid a combined cost of £2,000. Jackson claimed the three shares should now be worth £12,000 and was very unhappy with the proposed new arrangement. He said, '[These shares] have been held in families. Sheffield people who have been loyal to the club all this time are being kicked in the teeth. There is a strong feeling of injustice amongst us.' Charles Green claimed to understand why people were unhappy but touchingly could not believe that any one person should hold themselves higher than Sheffield United Football Club.

It was reported that only 169 of the 477 Original shareholders had accepted the club's offer. Beckett then arranged a meeting, attended by 224 shareholders, to discuss the group's legal options. The outcome was their asking United for 'eleventh-hour peace talks'. All but one of those present voted to 'pursue all means of achieving justice and obtaining a revised offer that is acceptable'. The shareholders felt it was essential to stay united in their opposition to the offer. After lengthy discussion, which included comments by Sheffield United director Bernard Procter, also an Original shareholder, in favour of accepting the club's offer, a vote of confidence was called for over the chair of the meeting and ended with a directive that before seeking recourse to legal action Conrad PLC should have the opportunity to amend its offer. The dispute continued into the summer. In June 1997 the shareholders made a request to be given a free season ticket for 30 years or for a sliding scale of payments to sell their shares back to the club over the next 25 years. Beckett said that no further offer had been made by the club after almost four months of discussion, adding: 'United stated that before any additional offer could be made we would have to accept the original offer and then trust them. That was a situation we did not think acceptable.'

McDonald was becoming increasingly frustrated and agitated by the ongoing dispute. Privately, Charles Green told one BIFA member, 'He'll walk away you know', if the Original shareholders didn't 'back off'. McDonald more or less confirmed Green's insight when he was quoted in the *Sheffield Star*, saying, 'I am trying to resolve the situation and am getting tired of it. I have tried to do my best for the club and there are some shareholders who feel they have not got enough out of the deal. If there are people out there who can run the club better than me I am ready to go now.' United had offered the protestors reduced season ticket prices for 20 years; some accepted, but others were holding out for free entry to Bramall Lane for life. It was ironic that, at a time when the club was in its best position for years, both on and off the field, the intransigence of a handful of shareholder 'rebels' - a term that not too long before was being applied to BIFA - was threatening to hold it back. Was it all about personal benefit holding the club to ransom? If it was then the shareholders were not the only ones at Bramall Lane manifesting such selfishness.

The dispute came to the boil just before Christmas 1997 at the football club (as opposed to the PLC) Annual General Meeting, where, as a protest against the share offer, a show of hands rejected the adoption of the company accounts and similarly voted against the re-election of chairman McDonald and vice chairman Freddie Pye. McDonald had to hide his anger as Kevin McCabe chaired the meeting during the voting process. Forty-five of the 64 original shareholders present voted against McDonald, 52 against Pye. However, all three resolutions were passed by large majorities when the poll votes were added up. Afterwards McDonald said, 'Some people think they have a grievance, but they are few. There are 20,000 fans out there and that is where I am coming from.'

The club then made a further offer to those Original shareholders who still refused to sell. The compromise suggested by McDonald was 1108 new PLC shares, the prospect of future shares and a free season ticket for ten years. This was accepted by 204 of the 477 original shareholders. Another deal put on the table was a free season ticket until season 2021/22 but the holder would no longer be able to vote at the Annual General Meeting. The argument rumbled on into 1998. In early January the *Sheffield Star's* back-page story, headlined 'Peace bid in Blades share row', reported that Mike McDonald was planning a 'peace move' to end the feud. His compromise was to offer the shareholders £3,000 each to purchase their shares, with which they seemed happy, but the sticking point was for how long a free seat would be theirs by right. McDonald was willing to offer ten years' free admission but this was deemed to be unacceptable by the 'rebels' – they wanted 30 years. McDonald made the wise move of letting the less volatile Bernard Procter handle further negotiations.

Apart from buying shares, a different way for the fans to become involved with the club was with the setting up of what became known as the Consultative Committee. The brainchild of BIFA, the committee was to be a formal method by which supporters could raise questions and complaints with the club, and for the club to disseminate information through channels different from the more usual channels of press and matchday programme. The very fact that the United board of directors had agreed to even discuss the possibility of regular meetings with the 'militant' BIFA emphasised the relative openness of the new regime and its willingness to ensure that it remained as - superficially maybe - transparent as possible. It was a long way removed from the days of Brealey. However, because BIFA knew that its proposals would only be accepted by the club if all existing supporters' organisations were involved, the official Supporters' Club and the Senior Blades were invited on board. The Consultative Committee would be chaired by Blades fan and Labour Member of Parliament, Richard Caborn, whose constituency included Bramall Lane. BIFA chairman Paul Blomfield described the ideas behind the Consultative Committee in *The Red and White Wizaaard* fanzine: 'The idea that football clubs should listen to the views of their supporters doesn't seem particularly radical, but it clearly hasn't struck those in charge at many clubs around the country. The need to augment communications between the club and its fans was one of the main objectives when BIFA was founded. Clearly there wasn't a lot of scope to move forward when Reg Brealey was in charge at the Lane, but Mike McDonald has offered a new approach.'

The dispute between the Original shareholders and the board appeared to affect the team's performances. Despite a stuttering end to the 1996/97 season, including no away wins after Boxing Day, United finished in the top six and qualified for the promotion play-offs, where they would meet Ipswich Town in the two-legged semi-final. This tie was won by United on the away goals rule after two draws, 1-1 at Bramall Lane and 2-2 at Portman Road; United were bound for Wembley to play Crystal Palace in the play-off final, the winners to take their place in the Premier League. Charles Green was, as usual, bullish: 'We have considerable sums left over from the flotation and these will be more than doubled if we win promotion.' However, it all went wrong. Palace clinched a dour encounter in strength-sapping heat with a goal out of keeping with the rest of the match, a spectacular curler from David Hopkin as injury time approached. Howard Kendall made an intriguing statement at the post-match press conference, saying, 'What happened was a real stunner to everyone connected with the club, from top to bottom. Basically it will be my job, if I am still manager of Sheffield United next season, to lift the players, start again and hope we can be more successful.' When questioned on what he meant by 'if I am still manager' Kendall answered even more cryptically: 'That's not my decision is it? You people write about the rumours, I only respond to them.'

The play-off final took place on Bank Holiday Monday at the end of May. The following day, when the Stock Exchange re-opened, United's share price immediately fell from 65p to 40p, meaning that around £11 million was suddenly wiped off the valuation of the club. It then transpired that Kendall's future as manager of Sheffield United was actually his own decision as a few weeks later, when what he called his 'first love', Everton, came calling, he resigned to take the manager's job there. Everton had approached United about taking Kendall a week earlier but he had turned it down. When he changed his mind McDonald was furious. 'I feel I have been kicked in the teeth,' he said. 'Last week when the first approach came I gave Howard 48 hours to sort it out. He wanted an extra day but I told him I had to have an answer by ten o'clock that night and, on the dot, he called me to say he was staying. I brought him back into football when no one would give him a job. Now he has let me down. Basically he told me then what he told the papers; that I would have to kick him out of Bramall Lane to be rid of him.'

Everton made a compensation offer to United, which was rejected, but did not come back with an improved package. Charles Green accused Everton of trying to 'wriggle out' of their responsibilities and being greeted by 'deafening silence' when he tried to contact them. McDonald termed Everton's offer 'a pittance' and angrily demanded, 'Unless they come up with a decent amount acceptable to my club, they can send him back to work for Sheffield United.' Everton did finally offer an acceptable compensation package - £200,000 and a promise of a pre-season friendly game against United at Bramall Lane. After being on the brink of promotion to the Premier League, a new man was needed to take United to the next level.

Chapter 11

Deano Returns
It Ends In Tears

Kendall was replaced, at first temporarily, as manager of Sheffield United by one of the players he had brought in the previous season. This was Nigel Spackman, the former Chelsea, Liverpool and Glasgow Rangers midfielder. When United decided to make his appointment permanent, Charles Green explained that after receiving over 100 applications for the vacancy, Spackman, as opposed to a manager with a proven record, was considered the right man: 'We feel that the successes in English football latterly have come from people who had little or no experience, the outstanding examples being Danny Wilson, Ruud Gullitt and Glenn Hoddle. If Nigel achieves half of what they have done it will be a major success for Sheffield United. [Spackman] has a three-year contract but we hope to be together for a long, long time.' Mike McDonald added, 'He [Spackman] has conducted himself impeccably through a difficult period and committed himself 100 per cent to the club. His attitude embodies that which we would wish and demand of any manager.' Their opinion of Spackman was soon to change.

Despite Spackman's managerial inexperience United were amongst the favourites for promotion after their play-off final defeat, especially as the club had splashed out to bring former star Brian Deane back to Bramall Lane from Leeds, handing him a big signing-on fee and the then best contract ever offered to a Sheffield United player, rumoured to be £10,000 per week. Crucially, the contract included a clause that would allow Deane to leave should a Premier League or top European club come in for him, a fact not made public at the time of his signing. Along with the purchases the previous season of Norwegian international striker Jan Åge Fjørtoft from Middlesbrough for £650,000 and experienced central defenders Carl Tiler (£650,00 from Aston Villa) and David Holdsworth (£500,000 from Watford), and the summer recruitment of Greek international right back Vassilis Borbokis from AEK Athens for £750,00 and former Manchester United and Ireland captain Paul McGrath on a free transfer from Derby County, Spackman had a strong squad. The signing of Deane was seen as the keystone, the final piece that held everything together. Apparently McDonald had been told by those supposedly in the know that signing Deane would instantly add 5,000 to the gate. One might therefore imagine his despair at the 17,324 attendance for the first home game of the season against fellow promotion favourites Sunderland, particularly when 2,500 were visiting supporters. It was far short of what McDonald expected, but the fact that the match was shown live on *Sky TV* provided some mitigating circumstance.

The level of support was one of McDonald's pet hates. He simply could not understand why lapsed supporters were not returning to Bramall Lane. He was showing the ambition that previous regimes had lacked, he insisted, so where were the missing fans? He had been particularly distressed at an attendance the previous season of only 12,301 for the visit of Swindon Town. He appealed for more support: 'We appreciate everybody who does come but we really want to see more people here.' McDonald consequently initiated all sorts of wacky ideas to improve attendances. At the time Sheffield Wednesday had a band that played various brass and percussion instruments on their kop during home games (the band was later adopted by the England national team). McDonald wanted something similar: 'Are we going to let Sheffield Wednesday get away with having what is called the best supporters' band in the country?' he asked via the local media. 'Surely we have far more talented musical Blades out there who are willing to put us in top spot and help the team at the same time.' His plea fell on possibly tone-deaf ears: Blades fans reckoned they didn't need artificial aids to create a 'good atmosphere', and if Sheffield Wednesday had a band, that was reason enough for the Blades not to have one. To be seen to be copying the Owls was an anathema to the red and white half of the city. Most Blades fans had been contemptuous of the Owls' efforts, dismissing the cacophony and the tedious chants they engendered as faux-naff and even kitsch – a feeling encapsulated by the dismissive term 'Euro-Wednesday'. Other United officials clearly felt the same as Blades fans. A few years later United banned the Wednesday band from bringing their instruments to a Bramall Lane derby match for, according to United's safety officer Rob McRobbie, 'safety reasons'.

When he wasn't complaining about the level of support, McDonald was crowing about United's unbeaten start to the 1997/98 season. As well as Deane, big money - £1.5 million - had been paid out for Borbokis and fellow Greek Traianos Dellas. McDonald said more money was available if the manager wanted it. Not only was McDonald confident, so was the City, as the share price climbed back to its original level of 60p for the first time since before the unsuccessful play-off final. However, despite Charles Green's assertion that Spackman had agreed a three-year contract on his appointment, rumours persisted that he had not actually signed it. He was still registered as a United player, even though he had not appeared on the pitch since he took over as manager. The reason he had not put his name to the managerial contract was simple - his playing terms were financially more advantageous! Spackman eventually confirmed that he had not signed a managerial contract but denied it was a problem. However, reports of unrest in the camp began to leak out of Bramall Lane when the team's good start (unbeaten in the first 12 games) was damaged by subsequent poor results. Blamed for the downturn were Spackman's contract wrangling, injuries to two influential players - Paul McGrath and Dane Whitehouse - and the sales of Mitch Ward and Carl Tiler to Everton in a player-exchange deal that saw midfielder Graham Stuart and £600,000 arrive at Bramall Lane. Spackman insisted that Stuart was a player he had been chasing for a long time, but fans saw the sales as a sign that United needed money. The team never really recovered from the loss of McGrath and especially Whitehouse and performances began to suffer.

Both McGrath and Whitehouse were hit by career-threatening knee injuries and in fact neither ever played first-team football again. Fans believed that the board should have been decisive and acted quickly to replace them. After Spackman had attended a board meeting at the end of November, he told the *Sheffield Star*; 'I made my point that although we are in a good position in the league our performances lately have reached a plateau and that, in my opinion, we needed freshening.' The first accounts of the new Sheffield United PLC, published in October, showed that the club lost £5.9 million in the year ending June 30, 1997. The major part of the loss was due to spending £3 million on player transfer fees and a 'one-off' charge of £2.4 million from the disposal of sportswear company Le Coq Sportif, which was previously owned by Conrad PLC. This figure was explained in the 1997 *Report and Accounts* as being accrued due to the closure of two existing Conrad offices and the consequent redundancy payments to former employees. Charles Green said that the club had plans to sell £2.5 million-worth of players but unconvincingly insisted this would not damage the team's promotion prospects. The players to be sold were reported to be Irish international goalkeeper Alan Kelly, Norwegian international left-back Roger Nilsen and defender Lee Sandford.

The subjects of Spackman's contract and his freedom to do his job were issues that would not go away. Spackman confessed he was 'getting irritated' by continued questions on the topic. On December 2, McDonald attempted to put an end to the persistent accusations from fans that Charles Green was 'running the team' instead of the ostensible team manager Spackman. McDonald revealed: 'We got everyone together on Tuesday and thrashed it out for three hours. That was the quietest meeting Charles Green has ever been at. Spackman said he wanted certain things doing and we told him to get on with it. It was not Charles Green making suggestions. There are a lot of rumours around. I assure you Nigel Spackman is manager.' To which Green intriguingly added, 'We have the situation of Nigel Spackman and his contract which people keep dragging up. Nigel, if he was on a contract, would have the same opportunity to leave as Kendall so being on a contract does not bind anyone here.' At the PLC Annual General Meeting, when questioned about his role in team affairs and the sale of players, Green responded, 'The players [Mitch Ward and Carl Tiler] signed for Everton for three times the wages they were receiving here. And Ward, out of contract in the summer, could have gone without a fee. As for Tiler our view is if people do not want to stay and back Sheffield United they should be allowed to seek a career elsewhere.' Green also said, 'Brian Deane feels he has come home and should we get to the Premiership I am confident he will sign up with us again. If we don't, then we will still do our best but the decision will be his.' This was an ominous statement.

In early December physiotherapist Denis Circuit decided to leave Bramall Lane for a new job with German club Werder Bremen. The reason he gave was that at Bremen it would be 'a five-day career, not a seven-day commitment as it is [at United]'. Spackman appeared surprised at the decision, commenting that it left the club with a problem that needed to be rectified quickly. United were to advertise for two new physios to replace the overworked Circuit. The physio was quickly followed out of the club by kitman John Greaves, who announced that he was to leave United for a coaching position in the USA. However, rumours circulated that he had resigned without another job to move to. Both men left without replacements being appointed, suggesting sudden departures. Spackman had lost two of his valuable backroom staff in the space of a couple of weeks and although the posts of physiotherapist and kitman are not high-profile, they are crucial in their differing ways to the smooth running of a professional football club, especially one with aspirations of playing in the Premier League. Both were to later reveal that they didn't know who their boss was and Circuit, in particular, told friends how he was unable to perform his job the way he wanted to and therefore found his position untenable. He was once ordered in to work at short notice on a Sunday to treat the injured Brian Deane, having to cancel a previously arranged family outing. Meanwhile, the first team had to make do with the junior squad's physiotherapist.

Some of the players were also grumbling. Jan Åge Fjørtoft said he was unhappy to be left out of the team but added that he had not asked for a transfer: 'I have to watch what I say because I do not want to be fined. But maybe sometimes people look at qualities players do not have rather than qualities they do have. Mine are finishing and getting goals. I always score goals and everyone knows that, apart from perhaps a couple of people.' Just who can he have meant? Was he hinting that the manager was under pressure from higher up not to pick him? Midfielder Mark Patterson, just after he was sold to Bury, was scathing of his former employers: 'The players are just pawns now; we are tools to be used. I leave Bramall Lane with mixed feelings. I shall miss so many things, but not the way the club is being run. There is a massive gulf between directors and players. Once upon a time directors got involved, now they are business people and it's sad. I suppose it's this PLC thing that has changed the game. At Sheffield some players didn't know if they were coming or going; there is transfer talk and then nothing happens. There is unrest with some individuals and it's a great pity because it's a great club with a great opportunity this season, if they get their act together and sort things out.'

One of the 'pawn' players Patterson was referring to was striker Gareth Taylor. In December Charles Green told the press that Dutch club FC Utrecht had enquired about Taylor. The player went public, claiming he hadn't been informed about it. 'I am in the dark,' he said, 'I don't know what is happening.' A couple of days later Taylor, who was previously in good form, was surprisingly omitted from the team to play at Charlton Athletic. The next day he explained why: he wasn't in the right frame of mind. 'I wasn't involved because I talked to the manager and told him I was totally confused and felt I couldn't concentrate. Nigel [Spackman] understood and told me to come home. I have to know am I staying or do they want me out the door? I just want someone to tell me what role I have at the club.' When Taylor was restored to the team and scored against Stoke away and Charlton at home, the threat of an unwanted transfer still hung over him. The reaction of the fans was unambiguous – they wanted him to stay. Taylor gave his shirt to a young supporter at the end of the Charlton game, clearly indicating that he thought he had played for United for the last time. Manager Spackman's reply to the *Sky TV* interviewer after the match was revealing: 'I'm just the manager picking the team. The financial side of the game is not down to me, it's up to the chairman and the board of directors and if they feel they can sell people for good money so it gives me more money to spend on other players then that's down to them but I don't want anybody to leave here. I've said that before but obviously with the pressure from the board you can't keep everyone.'

For his part, Taylor said, 'I played as if it was [my last game] but I just wanted to show my appreciation to the fans; they've been absolutely superb with me. They don't want me to go and I don't really want to leave. But after I turned down [a possible transfer to] Huddersfield I was out in the cold and sent to train with the juniors. But I am back in the side, the manager seems keen to select me and I want to stay here.' A spokesman for FC Utrecht believed that United would change their mind about selling Taylor when he said, 'We were told that there was a possibility that Fjørtoft could move and if that happens the chances of Taylor going are poor.' The Utrecht official's mention of Fjørtoft was unwittingly prescient. It seemed likely that someone would be sold after Mike McDonald said that Taylor might have to go to stave off 'financial suicide' - the wage bill for the 1997/98 season was over £7.5 million. The attendance for the Charlton game was around 19,000 but this wasn't good enough for McDonald. 'To be successful we must have better support than this. We have too many players to hold; we cannot afford the wages bill for all the people we have.'

Taylor's transfer was called off, due, in the words of the *Sheffield Star*, to 'Fan Power'. The displeasure the supporters displayed at the Charlton match was not so much a rebellion at the loss of an individual player (Taylor was a good centre forward and capable of improvement, but he was not a world-beater), but more a demonstration of their unwillingness and inability to accept what was seen as an undermining of the manager's control of team affairs. The supporters' dissent was seen by both reporters and people inside the club as fans expressing their preference for Taylor over Fjørtoft. This was palpably false; the fans wanted to keep both. In their defence, the United board had done well over the previous two years but they were in danger of letting this progress be undermined because of the impression they were 'meddling' with the most important part of the club: the team.

There were probity and truth issues. McDonald denied that FC Utrecht had ever made a realistic bid for Taylor: 'When we brought in Brian Deane and later Dean Saunders we had players available but the plain fact is that we never had an acceptable offer on the table from the Dutch people for Taylor. Taylor was going to Huddersfield some time ago for £750,000 and this price remains – if we decide to sell him. But we are giving no one away and the money we will raise will go towards strengthening our defence after losing so many players with injury.' By the end of 1997 the season was not progressing as promisingly as it had been in August and September. Stories unsettling to both fans and players continued to emerge. McDonald persisted in blaming the sale of players on the supporters not turning up in sufficient numbers. The New Year came and Taylor had still not been sold. Perhaps that should have been a glaring indication that the board was looking to raise money from other sources.

But the events of January 15, 1998 came as a massive shock to Blades followers. It was expected that one striker might be sold and if it wasn't Taylor then it would probably be Fjørtoft. The prospect of Brian Deane leaving never entered anyone's estimation. Deane had sat out the FA Cup replay at Bury in mid January with an ankle injury, but Fjørtoft played in United's win. It was common knowledge that then Premier League Barnsley's manager Danny Wilson was at Gigg Lane to watch Fjørtoft; the eventual departure of the Norwegian was not a surprise. But the reaction when the *Sheffield Star's* front-page headline read, 'Blades Transfer Turmoil – Goal hero

Deane may be off" was astonishing. Deane was free to leave for Portuguese giants Benfica and flew out to Portugal that very morning apparently without the knowledge of manager Spackman. United claimed they then attempted to block Fjørtoft's proposed move to Barnsley but this later proved to be specious. Spackman tried to stop the deal as soon as he found out about Deane but it was too late - Fjørtoft had agreed personal terms - and Spackman had lost his two leading scorers in one go.

There was uproar amongst the fans. Charles Green had to defend the move, stating that the transfer was not money driven and that the balance sheet showed no financial problems. The issue was a moral one, he said. When Deane signed for United, Green gave him his word that if a major club came in for him, from anywhere in the world, he would be informed and left to make up his mind. How else, Green added, would top quality players come to a First Division club? Without that promise, Deane would have taken up one of the two offers he had from Dutch club Feyenoord or the Spanish team Real Zaragoza. Deane had now received an offer from Benfica that United could not possibly match and therefore they could not keep him. Fjørtoft, meanwhile, was desperate to be picked by Norway for the 1998 World Cup and wanted to play in the Premier League to maintain his chances of selection.

In a bid to deflect fans' anger the club let it be known that they were pursuing an immediate replacement and had lodged a £3 million offer for Colombian international striker Hamilton Ricard. McDonald explained the situation: 'We got virtually no money for Deane and £750,000 for Fjørtoft. Yet I am prepared to go and bring a major international player to Sheffield United - and if this does not nail all the rumours that we have financial problems I do not know what will.' There was at least a small amount of substance in McDonald's words. A week before Deane and Fjørtoft were sold, McDonald and Green were seen dining, according to the *Green 'Un*, in 'one of the city's top restaurants', accompanied by a couple of Spanish-speaking men and a translator. It was ascertained that the men were officials of an unnamed

Colombian football club. Various assumptions could be drawn from this not-so-secret rendezvous. One was that McDonald knew they would be spotted, in which case speculation would mount that he was to buy a Colombian player. Second, it could be suggested that he was laying the groundwork for purchasing a replacement for Deane, whom he knew would soon be leaving.

McDonald made out he was helpless when it came to Deane leaving. In his words it was 'three years' work down the drain in one afternoon. This is the lowest point of my time with United. I think I must be cursed. If there is a better man – or luckier man – out there who can do a better job than me, let him come in.' The *Sheffield Star* reported that the club had refused two offers of £3 million for Deane from English clubs - one of them believed to be Middlesbrough - but ended up with a 'nonsense deal' with Benfica, about which McDonald expanded: 'After we have settled with Leeds United we end up with nothing except a return of the money we have paid out in wages and bonuses. The plain facts are that Benfica, one of the biggest clubs in the world, offered Brian Deane around £4 million to play in a country where tax is only 15 per cent. We had promised Brian that we would inform him of any offers and he said he was sick of getting kicked to death in the First Division every week.' It also transpired that Leeds United were due 20 per cent of Deane's reported £1 million transfer fee as part of a contractual 'sell-on clause' inserted when Deane joined the Blades. 'As for Fjørtoft,' continued McDonald, 'we had given him permission to talk with Barnsley before the Deane affair. He wanted to go and the fans had made it plain that they preferred Gareth Taylor. Jan was asking for a guaranteed first-team place, the manager couldn't give it to him so he insisted on taking his chance with Barnsley.' Spackman confirmed the situation regarding Fjørtoft, saying, 'In view of this [the crowd's reaction to the Gareth Taylor transfer speculation and Fjørtoft's desire to play in the World Cup] I promised him he could have his chance if a Premiership club wanted him, so when Barnsley came in we allowed the talks.'

The two men who rubber-stamped the moves were still in the firing line so they sought to explain further. Green said, 'On the afternoon of the talks [with Benfica] we were called by an English club who had no idea that we would part with Brian. We were told that whatever transfer fee we were receiving they would double and whatever wages Brian was offered they would be doubled also. The reply we got back [from Deane] was that unless the club was Sheffield United or Manchester United he was not interested.' The decision to sell Deane and Fjørtoft was based on continuing criticism from some directors - mainly Kevin McCabe - about player dealings, in particular the lack of information Green had provided to the board with regard to players' contracts. McCabe demanded to know every aspect of all contracts Green had negotiated. It was a courageous move as McCabe knew open criticism of McDonald's loyal servant would set him against the chairman. In a short space of time Green appeared to have gone from wanting to buy every player in the world to wanting to sell every player United had. When Green and McDonald were informed by other directors that they would be lynched if Deane and Fjørtoft were sold at the same time, Green replied that he didn't give a damn and would try to sell Taylor as well.

McDonald once more shifted the blame to the supporters for not attending matches in sufficient numbers, stating; 'I told [Deane] it was impossible, that on gates of 19,000 it was a battle to pay our present wages. Unfortunately there is not the support here to keep him. Had he been playing for Middlesbrough, Manchester City or Wolves, with the backing they get, he might not have moved on.' McDonald managed to express himself in a more cold, calculated fashion in his chairman's statement in the company's 1997/98 *Interim Report*, wherein he wrote; 'The [financial] position since December is much improved, and the easing of the injury situation has enabled the football club to reduce the playing squad numbers to more normal levels. The sale of Brian Deane, Jan Åge Fjørtoft and Don Hutchison means that the net [negative] transfer fees reported in these figures will be substantially reduced in the second half [of the financial year].' Now, far from nobody wanting Deane to go, McDonald was telling the shareholders that his sale had been both planned and a success. Nothing ever seemed to make sense at Bramall Lane. A few days after the sales Fjørtoft broke his hitherto dignified silence, saying, 'Nigel [Spackman] is one of my neighbours and somehow I feel a bit sorry for him. I left because United told me they had agreed a fee with Barnsley, which meant that they wanted to sell me and that I was not part of the plans at United. People ask me if I was taken by surprise by that and, well, if you look at my scoring record, I left with the best record ever at Bramall Lane, which I am very proud of.' Fjørtoft had scored 23 goals in 42 league and cup appearances.

McDonald and Green then tried to justify Fjørtoft's sale by publicly criticising him, accusing him of being 'lazy'. Fjørtoft in response threatened court action, though it never came to that. He was furious: 'I can't have people slagging me off. It is out of order. This time something has to be said. I have nothing against Sheffield United and the fans - it is against Mr Green and Mr McDonald. It is totally untrue I went to the manager's office every day for eight days. I can't believe how silly that is. I have witnesses saying that after the Bury game, when [Barnsley manager] Danny Wilson was watching me, Charles Green told me that as I had been loyal to the club I would be allowed to talk to a Premier League club. There was also a story in the papers saying that United tried to stop the transfer. That is not true at all. They wanted to delay it until after the weekend so I could play against Wolves to take the pressure off them for selling Brian Deane.' Spackman, in his weekly column in the *Sheffield Star*, wrote, 'The story of this week's turmoil began for me on Wednesday morning when I was asked to a meeting in Manchester when the chairman told [head coach] Willie Donachie and me about the Benfica offer to Brian Deane, which had apparently come out of the blue. He also informed us of Barnsley's interest in Jan Fjørtoft. When the Deane business emerged on Thursday I wanted to pull the plug on Jan's deal but it had gone too far. He had agreed money with them and he was not in the mood to change his mind. It has just been an unfortunate clash of timing that proved beyond our control.'

This version of events (that he first heard about Deane's possible transfer the day before it happened) conflicted with other accounts. In his 2005 book *Kicked Into Touch*, Fred Eyre, head of scouting at United at the time, recalled the following scenario: '"Brian Deane's a bit late," said Nigel, rubbing his hands together at the prospect of fining our most prized asset a few bob. We all had a good chuckle, because we knew how painful it was for Brian whenever he was called upon to part with his cash. It was not like him to be late and as 11 o'clock approached our mood changed and we began to wonder if he was all right. I rang his mobile and found it to be switched off. It illustrated the seriousness of the situation because Brian's mobile phone appeared to be permanently welded to his ear. Half an hour later he made contact with us. "Where are you Brian?" "Just outside Lisbon." "What are you doing in Gisburne?" "No, Lisbon, Portugal." "Oh, right. I didn't know they had given you a few days off." "I'm signing for Benfica."' Eyre's account of events gave no mention of a Wednesday meeting in Manchester.

A source inside the club told a similar tale. Deane, according to him, had phoned Spackman from Heathrow airport to inform him that he was flying to Lisbon for talks with Benfica. This was the first Spackman knew about it. A few days later Spackman was more forthright: 'I have heard a great deal about our fans being angry and devastated at the events at Bramall Lane this week. I can tell you nobody is angrier than me. Far from being on a high after the Bury result I was on a down with the prospect of losing two of my better players. My plans were scuppered.' The manager was dealt another two blows a month later when midfielder Don Hutchison was sold to Everton for £1 million and assistant manager Willie Donachie left to join Joe Royle at Manchester City. Royle and Donachie were long-standing associates, having played together at Manchester City in the 1970s and coached together at Oldham in the early 1990s. Spackman was losing his most important colleagues in quick succession but he put a brave face on it: 'I do not believe he [Donachie] would have gone to any other club but City. His loss is a massive blow to myself and the team.' PLC director Ian Townsend attempted to put a positive spin on affairs: 'The supporters of this club had to

239

swallow the bad news when Deane and Fjørtoft left. They don't know the good news that is coming. We shall definitely be bringing in new people if that is what Nigel Spackman wants.'

In the meantime, McDonald insisted he was still chasing Hamilton Ricard, and claimed he had reached an agreement with Ricard's club, America de Cali, who had accepted a £3 million package. McDonald said, 'As I see it, Sheffield United have first refusal on this player and he has promised to sign for us when the work permit problems have been solved. We have been treading carefully and working behind the scenes with the Department of Employment about the work permit'. McDonald must have learned soon afterwards that Ricard had been speaking to Middlesbrough too, as he then lamented, 'It strikes me that [Ricard and his agent] are trying to play Middlesbrough and us off against each other and I am having none of that'. Ricard signed for Middlesbrough. Whether United ever actually had a chance of signing him or it was merely that McDonald was using him as a smokescreen to take attention away from the Deane and Fjørtoft affair is a matter of conjecture. Several months later, when Ricard was scoring goals in the Premier League for Middlesbrough, McDonald came out in 'I told you so' mood: 'I had contacts in South Africa raising the money from my interests there and I was prepared to pay the £3 million fee. But then things went wrong and I pulled out. He wouldn't have been a bad investment would he? And remember this, I was going to find the money, not the club.'

McDonald stressed that despite the furore over the departures of Deane and Fjørtoft his own future lay at Bramall Lane: 'I was approached to lead a takeover of Manchester City by a very wealthy group of people. I am flattered by this. They are a big club and I have supported them since I was five years old but I turned down the offer because I still have a job to do at Sheffield United and I intend to complete it. When I took over here I had six targets in mind for the club. I have achieved four of them in stabilising the club, stopping the slide of the team, building the John Street stand and removing control of the club from the hands of one man. I still have two targets to reach; getting promotion and winning a trophy.' But McDonald's dream would have to be pursued without manager Nigel Spackman, who resigned a few days later. The exit of Donachie was probably the last straw. After trying and failing to get an immediate meeting with Charles Green, who was in Birmingham, Spackman handed in his resignation letter to club secretary David Capper. News of the resignation provoked an incredible outburst from McDonald: 'Spackman was never the same man after Willie Donachie left. When the pressure came he couldn't cope with it. I was persuaded to give him his chance when we lost Howard Kendall to Everton. I had an experienced manager up my sleeve then and I do now. But Nigel got the job although I was never 100 per cent sold on him. And today it looks as if I have been proved right. By going now he has put his own self-interest ahead of the club and no one can forgive that. We spoke last night and I asked him about his problems. It turned out to be all hot air. At the end of the day, on his own, he was not experienced enough to handle it. We have spent millions on players and changed the scene and people talk about a lack of ambition and blather on about a shortage of money and the need to sell players. All I ask is that people look at the mess I inherited and if that isn't progress I do not know what is. At my time of life I don't need any of this hassle. Frankly if there is a concerted movement against me or the board I may well leave someone else to it.'

United were playing Ipswich Town at home that night. On entering the ground McDonald had to contend with a congregation of a couple of hundred angry fans in the south stand car park. An interview with *BBC Radio Sheffield* was cut short when someone shouted, 'Fuck off back to Manchester!' In the absence of Spackman, assistant and reserve team coaches Steve Thompson and Russell Slade were handed control of the team but, somewhat inevitably, United lost their 24-match unbeaten home record. At the final whistle, the chants of 'Charles Green, he sells the team!' were interrupted only when the fans applauded the players off the field. The traditional killing fields of the car park witnessed a post-match demonstration. Some 500 fans now gathered below the boardroom windows to shout for the reinstatement of Spackman and the resignation of McDonald and Green.

The protests did not impress the chairman. McDonald's response, given next day to the *Sheffield Star*, was indignant: 'After all I have done for this club I am not taking that [the car park demonstration]. I shall oversee the appointment of a new manager Thursday morning, tidy a few things up and then hand over. I said if ever the day came when the fans turned against me that would be the day I would walk. I am 55. I should be on holiday with my wife in South Africa. At my time of life I don't need any of this hassle. The club is owned by the fans and they don't want me so that is me finished.... after witnessing the mob out there, you won't see me at any match at Bramall Lane again. I will now plan my exit route. We are in the last eight of the cup, fifth in the league and have lost one home game in nearly a year. I wonder what they would do if we were bottom of the league.' But he added that he'd be remaining on the PLC board. Immediately the futures of McDonald's cohorts Freddie Pye (who had stated, 'If McDonald goes, I go.'), Stewart White, Ian Townsend and Charles Green were put into question. If they were to go, United would be left with a two-man board of Kevin McCabe and Bernard Procter. Green seemed unperturbed, claiming defiantly, 'I can take it. I am chief executive. I take the decisions and live by them.'

Supporters believed McDonald's resignation was another example of his impetuosity and insensitivity. He was in fact walking out the first time he was on the receiving end of vocal and collective criticism. Where McDonald – and Green – had fallen down was by not taking heed of the unease all around the club that had been growing since the autumn sales of Mitch Ward and Carl Tiler. They tried to explain their actions but failed to allay the anger generated by their perceived 'meddling' in team matters. Fans were used to the team manager having the biggest say in buying and selling players and Green's role in such dealings came as a culture shock. When the team's declining fortunes coincided with players being sold, Green and McDonald could not dispel fans' disquiet. Spackman found himself in a no-lose situation. If the team was successful he would be praised. If it failed Green and McDonald would take the rap. He also knew that if he resigned over what he saw as a point of principle – not being able to do his job the way he wanted to – he would receive the backing of the supporters.

On Thursday events took another twist as the ten o'clock press conference apparently called to announce the new manager was put off to 2pm, then 3pm. The rumoured reason for the delay was that former Manchester United player and Swindon Town manager Lou Macari had initially agreed to take the job but had a late change of heart. When the press conference did take place there was no new manager and the only announcements were those of the official resignation of McDonald from the board of Sheffield United FC (he was to remain as chairman of the PLC) and the announcement of the PLC's £3.1 million half-yearly loss. McCabe and Procter, who handled the press conference, stated that four managerial candidates were being considered, one of them being..... Nigel Spackman. McCabe also suggested that 'one or two' of his colleagues had 'spoken out' and may have regretted it, but quickly called McDonald 'an excellent leader and chairman'. 'It's very sad,' continued McCabe, 'that the events of Tuesday evening have emotionally left [McDonald] drained and with no alternative in his own mind than to resign from the football club board.' It was also announced at the press conference that Charles Green's job would be 'redefined' and he would be given 'a slightly different role at the club away from team and management affairs'. Green, one of the major reasons for Spackman's departure, later said. 'I think Nigel was under pressure since his right-hand man Willie Donachie left. He may be repenting that decision. I would be prepared to say; where can we take it from here? We would want to get that show back on the road; we did not want him [Spackman] to go.' But Spackman insisted, 'I have not reconsidered my position. In any event I would want a public apology in the press for the remarks made [by McDonald] and I could not return while McDonald and Mr Green remain at the club. If I was asked to go back I would need certain assurances from the board. If the club want me to continue as a player in the reserves then I will do that. I will not walk out on Sheffield United.'

McCabe, who a few days later took over as temporary football club chairman, told *Calendar* reporter John Shires that 'All board members, Mike [McDonald] included, have realised that we just need to restructure a wee bit, better reorganise ourselves, have better presentation to the media and of late, not just this week but weeks gone by, perhaps we've had too much media presentation that has worked against the better interests.' Taking no heed of McCabe's wish to improve media presentation and not let emotion get the better of him, vice-chairman Freddie Pye followed McDonald by firing a broadside at Spackman, and some of the players. Writing in his column in the *Stockport District Advertiser*, he said: 'Spackman has been screaming about having to sell his best players but the truth is there has been £5 million spent on players and roughly 16 players coming in and about seven going out. And when Spackman moans about his best players being sold – the honest-to-goodness truth of that one is that the gate money was not coming in to support that level of spending. At the end of the day it's the directors who are responsible for balancing the books and if the best players are being sold there is obviously a reason for it. What do you want to do? Close the club down? You don't need a degree in economics to suss out that if the money is not coming in, then you can't pay out. And some of the so-called superstars of Sheffield United were not performing and not earning their money and Spackman can moan till he is blue in the face, but the club comes first and if the gate receipts are not what they should be, well then you have got to trim the wage bill. If you don't, that is the quickest way to bankruptcy that I know, but the like of Nigel Spackman doesn't worry about things like that. I can emphasise that he will not be coming back to Sheffield United.' What Pye failed to clarify was the folly of handing out large contracts to players in the hope that attendances would rise enough to be able to pay them. Once more the predicament the club found itself in was not the board's fault for agreeing contracts they could not afford, it was the supporters' fault for failing to turn up in sufficient numbers.

All this was happening in the week leading up to the FA Cup quarter-final away to Premier League Coventry City. There, inspired by the superb goalkeeping of Alan Kelly and a cracking goal from the Brazilian-born forward Marcelo, United grabbed a tremendous 1-1 draw to bring the Sky Blues back to Bramall Lane. This must have impressed the stand-in board and just as everyone was tipping a quick managerial appointment, United sprung a surprise by giving the job until the end of the season to caretaker boss Steve Thompson. The Sheffield-born Thompson (a footballing journeyman with Leicester City, Lincoln City, Charlton Athletic, Southend United and for a few months in 1989 Sheffield United) seemed unperturbed by his sudden appearance in the spotlight, joking to *BBC Television* before the game at Coventry, 'I'm either famous for a day and the supporters love me or Steve Thompson didn't do a very good job.' The same day, McCabe took over as full-time chairman of the football club, while Pye did an about turn and decided to remain on the board. Unlucky for some, on Friday, March 13 Charles Green's role was indeed 'redefined' as he stood down as United's chief executive, being replaced in an acting capacity by Ian Townsend of the PLC board. Townsend vowed he would stay well clear of team affairs. McCabe later told a BIFA meeting that McDonald's 'faction' on the board made it 'very difficult' to get rid of Green. McCabe didn't elaborate as to who constituted this 'faction'. Thompson got his charges past Coventry in a penalty shoot-out in the replay, but went on to lose 1-0 to Newcastle United in the semi-final at Old Trafford, as he edged them, shakily, to the play-offs. He was to manage United for just 18 matches. Whilst always good value for a quip when interviewed, Thompson was not held in high regard by many of the United players. Despite being promised, and given, a coaching role when United appointed Steve Bruce as manager in the summer of 1998, the following November Bruce fired Thompson, stating; 'A new manager likes to appoint his own team.'

The bust-up between Spackman and his employers had begun one of the most turbulent weeks in the history of the club. Never before had the club's three top men (manager, chairman, chief executive) departed in such a short space of time. At the end of February United's manager was Nigel Spackman, the chairman was Mike McDonald and the chief executive was Charles Green. Just a couple of weeks later the manager was Steve Thompson, the chairman was Kevin McCabe and the chief executive was Ian Townsend. Upheaval, disruption, turmoil - and yet the team continued to hang in the play-off race and performed wonders to reach the FA Cup semi-final. The professionalism and dedication shown by the players in the weeks leading up to, during and immediately succeeding these events was exemplary.

Selling Deane and Fjørtoft cost United promotion. They struggled into the play-offs, having to rely on Birmingham City not winning on the last day to scrape into sixth place. Despite beating Sunderland 2-1 in the home play-off leg and putting up a brave show in 2-0 defeat at the Stadium of Light, United, weakened by the trail of sales, particularly of Deane, were no match for a powerful Sunderland side. The supporters had little hope in the club. For the home fixture the crowd of 23,800 included some 5,000 from Sunderland. For the away leg United's following was under 2,000 and one that did not sell all the tickets allocated to them. Following the defeat, club captain David Holdsworth made an impassioned plea to his board of directors, defending his team-mates and asking for stability and better support from above: 'Whatever has been asked of the boys they have given as much as they can. You cannot say we have failed. We have had three managers and have lost players and the boardroom has moved around like a chess game. The club needs to decide where it is going and I believe we have a great team spirit. It is now down to people in the right places to pull together.' Fine words to end the most disruptive season ever witnessed at the Lane.

At the end of May, continuing the worrying trend of important officials departing, long-time commercial manager Andy Daykin left the club after a 15-year tenure. Months later he joined former United director Stephen Hinchliffe at Hull City in a similar capacity. The official statement that accompanied his departure thanked him for his 'outstanding' work and explained that he was to move into consultancy work. The unofficial word was somewhat different. It was not the mutual parting the club statement suggested. Daykin found out to his cost that one of his line managers was having an affair with another club employee – one he wished to make redundant. Instead of this individual being spoken with or ever disciplined, Daykin instead was sacked. He was replaced by Alf Davies, former fund-raiser at Leeds Rugby League Club. He didn't last long and the position was effectively vacant for almost a year until Sean O'Toole was appointed, having held a similar position at Sheffield Wednesday. It was a strange affair that a football club that had pretensions to be in the Premier League should go so long without anybody ostensibly fulfilling its crucial commercial role. O'Toole lasted only a matter of months before being replaced by Adrian Danes, thus making it three incumbents in just over a year. At a time when the club was in a financial predicament, it was criminally stupid to allow its most successful ever fund-raiser to depart because of an office romance.

The recently appointed chief executive Ian Townsend in an interview in the *Sheffield Star* responded to the depressed mood that permeated the club by explaining the reasons why certain decisions had to be made and detailing what plans were being put in place to try to improve the following season. 'If you compare the wages structure at this club,' he said, 'it comes out extremely favourably with what other major clubs in the First Division are paying. Wages are a big influence on players coming and going and on which teams get promoted. We are most definitely not afraid to pay the sort of wages necessary to bring quality players to Bramall Lane. We have already proved that.' He then added that although they would do all they could to achieve promotion, if they did go up it would be easier to stay there 'if we had the gates of Middlesbrough and Sunderland' - yet another complaint about United's crowds not being high enough. When asked how the money would be raised to pay the required wages, Townsend replied they would come from matchday attendances, season tickets, sponsorship and commercial activities. And, of course, a prudent and wise transfer policy. Townsend acknowledged the failure of the board to get across to the fans the extent of the club's 'genuine promotion ambitions' but then used the convenience of numbers to defend the sale of Deane and Fjørtoft: 'People regard the Deane-Fjørtoft deals as the deciding day of the season but statistics show that in the eight games before they left we won only two, drew three and lost three. And in the eight games immediately afterwards we won five and drew three.' He concluded with a clarion call that would resonate with all Blades fans: 'Wednesday have not always been top dogs and the circle will turn again, but not without ambition and endeavour for us all. Our targets are to win promotion, to overtake Wednesday and then take on the rest of them.' This did not happen in the next few years but Townsend was by then long gone from Bramall Lane.

Chapter 12

Enter The Count
Two Chairs, One Fall-Out

Going into June 1998 without a team manager, United were seemingly in no rush to make an appointment. At the same time, the furore over the resignation of Nigel Spackman remained. Spackman's agent, Dennis Roache, claimed that Spackman chose to leave his post because 'the executive management of the club brought in players he didn't know about'. Predictably United refuted this version of events but publicly said nothing meaningful. Chief executive Ian Townsend stated, 'When Nigel resigned and settlement was agreed there was a confidentiality clause on both sides and we have no intention of breaching it.' Spackman was said to be out of the country and unavailable for comment. The controversy died away, especially when United selected former Manchester United captain Steve Bruce, then playing at Birmingham City, as their new player-manager. Also interviewed for the position were former Arsenal managers Bruce Rioch and Stewart Houston (both ex-United players) and, intriguingly, Jean Petit, who in 1994, had succeeded Arsène Wenger as coach of AS Monaco. The Frenchman's contractual demands probably dissuaded United from deciding to go for a foreign manager – he wanted £60,000 per month, after tax, and £30,000 per month for his assistant! They chose Steve Bruce, who was actually known to McDonald by virtue of their wives being acquaintances. Bruce had an inconsistent start to his reign as United produced some good results, but just as many poor ones. After a 4-1 defeat at West Brom Bruce knew something had to change – he needed to improve his squad, but he soon learned this was not easily done.

As Bruce pursued new players, it was reported that United had not received full payment from Benfica for the sale of Brian Deane. Manchester United similarly had not been paid by the Portuguese club for the transfer of Czech international Karel Poborsky.   United asked for assistance from FIFA, which ordered Benfica to set aside takings from their Champions' League matches to settle these respective debts, reported to amount to £4 million.   Mike McDonald, still chairman of United's PLC, typically fumed, 'We get promises of money in dribs and drabs, to be paid tomorrow, tomorrow, tomorrow. It is just not good enough. If they had wanted a hire purchase deal they should have said so and we maybe could have negotiated something. We cannot go on like this. The bottom line is that we are owed the money and we want it and we expect it. They lured Brian Deane with a package we could not match. I spent days trying to stop it but with those sums on the table for the player, we could not compete.   I got terrible flak for that and I am still getting it because the deal might have cost us millions in promotion. We lost our best player and we haven't been paid yet. I talked before about getting Benfica dismissed from the Champions' League but now it is official. We have gone to the FA and have asked for their help to get satisfaction and made the point that Benfica should not be allowed to use players they haven't paid for. At this rate it will be ten years before we get our money. I just wish we could do as they did: bring in star players, pay a small deposit and win promotion to the Premiership. What a stink that would cause in the game. I demand that FIFA take strong action against Benfica. We will sue Benfica.' Whilst not a man often who provoked sympathy, McDonald was correct in his argument.

Charles Green resigned from the board of Sheffield United PLC in mid July. Andrew Laver, son of recently deceased former director and one-time emergency chairman Alan Laver, and Steve Stothart joined the PLC board, the latter as financial director. Chairman Kevin McCabe and chief executive Ian

Townsend both admitted to buying a large tranche of shares while the price was low. McCabe denied he was about to launch a takeover. There was even talk of a 'power struggle' in the offing between McCabe and McDonald when the latter wanted to sell United's England Under-21 left back Wayne Quinn to Newcastle United but McCabe disagreed. McCabe won this round but sanctioned the sale of Quinn to Newcastle for £800,000 a couple of years later. Off the pitch, McCabe wanted to concentrate on the development of the Blades Leisure Park so that the income it raised could be used to strengthen the playing squad; McDonald was reticent about the idea. The matter went public when McCabe admitted that the football club and PLC boards were 'in conflict' and couldn't agree on a way forward. Townsend then announced that he too was to leave his post to concentrate on his medical instrument company. The turnover of staff at the top of the club in 1998 was quite remarkable. One of Townsend's final tasks was to inform the supporters that Steve Bruce had no money to spend on players. 'We expected to receive £1 million for Deane but the money is coming through in dribs and drabs, although it now totals £500,000. If we had that million and if John Ebbrell and Nicky Henry[6] were able to play, the situation would not have been as it is. Without the Deane payment we found ourselves the better part of £1 million short and, on top of this, our three managers before Steve Bruce spent £5 million net on transfers, over and above any sales. In that period we have bought 18 players and sold eight when the aim of the new management was to reduce the playing staff. We are carrying 35 professionals when we could do with 27. We have to reduce our wages bill and we must either sell or give players free transfers. We can afford the money for a transfer fee but when a Premiership player expects wages that drive a massive hole through our budget, we have to call a halt. Paying Premiership wages on

---

[6] John Ebbrell cost £1 million from Everton in January 1997 and Nicky Henry was signed from Oldham Athletic for £400,000 later the same season. Ebbrell played a total of 45 minutes for the first team before an ankle injury ended his career two years after signing; a cost of over £20,000 per minute. Henry appeared only 21 times in over two seasons at the club.

Nationwide League gates of 18,000 and modest TV money is something that cannot be sustained. It does not mean we have placed a permanent block on major trading, just that we are re-structuring and re-organising and, for the moment, we have to make certain unpleasant decisions about fees and wages. We have a wage bill that is already higher than what we can support through the gate income. Sunderland have double our income so they can move in different circles. As for Carl Tiler [whom Steve Bruce wished to sign] we could not match the wages he was paid at Everton. We are not a Premiership club.'

This plea of poverty contradicted a statement made by Townsend only two weeks earlier. Then he was to say, 'It is pleasing to say that our income levels are ahead of last year and the club is going forward in such a positive way.' No wonder fans were confused. To test Townsend's claim on the amount of money spent on players, the *Sheffield Star's* Tony Pritchett totted up the incomings and outgoings over the period June 1996 to June 1998. His figures were not official but as the journalist who covered the daily goings on at Bramall Lane Pritchett had more idea than the average supporter when it came to transfer fees, which were seldom disclosed by the club when a deal was made. Pritchett's total amounted to £9.995 million paid, £4 million received, a difference of some £1 million above Townsend's quoted £5 million. So, fans asked, where was the missing million?

The news that Bruce could not make any signings shocked Blades fans. Everton quoted a fee of £500,000 to allow former centre half Tiler to return to Bramall Lane. A payment to the player on top would produce a total of £700,000. Bruce complained to the local paper, saying; 'To say I am hugely disappointed [about the failed Tiler offer] is a massive understatement. When I came I said there was money available and there was supposed to be. What has happened in the last few weeks I don't know because I do not control the finances of the club. But the top and bottom of it is that as far as transfers are concerned we do not have any money and it is only right that the fans know this. I hope that will change but in the meantime we have to get on with what we have got. I will not allow our supporters to be fed with hopeful stories day after day if there is no chance of anything happening. I have had two, three, four, five deals lined up but when it was asked can we pay, we can't. When the crunch came we did not have enough money to buy him [Tiler]. End of story.' The fans had seen it all before. The manager was learning slowly. When appointed, Bruce was permitted to state at the press conference that he had been promised money to spend. A month later he was obliged to say otherwise. Soon after these revelations Kevin McCabe attended a BIFA meeting; this situation was one of the main topics of questioning. McCabe disclosed he believed Bruce had been 'lied to' on his appointment and that the manager's futile chase of Carl Tiler had been an 'embarrassing episode' to the club.

The cash problem, he revealed, was three-fold: first, as McDonald and Townsend had already revealed, Benfica had only paid a small proportion of the money they owed for Brian Deane. McCabe admitted that United could not have kept Deane but 'to sell Fjørtoft was crazy'. 'Someone panicked,' he added, 'but it wasn't me.' The second topic of discussion was attendances. Such (poor) numbers – and consequent gate receipts – could not support the wage bill. The club had too many players on expensive contracts; McCabe laid the blame entirely at the door of two men – McDonald and Green, whom he opined had 'wasted money by offering silly wages to players'. Third, United had a lot of money tied up in the salaries of long-term injured players. McCabe was not optimistic about a comeback for Ebbrell but added that United could not claim an insurance payout until surgeons declared he would never play again. Meanwhile, Ebbrell had 21 months left on his contract. Once everybody was fit, Bruce had to sell before he could buy and McCabe admitted that it was likely to be January or February before the manager would be able to strengthen the squad. Club secretary David Capper and club media officer Andy Pack told another BIFA meeting at the Railway Hotel that Bruce was 'staggered' when he discovered the salary levels of his players. They also said that two players, Andy Walker and David White, were 'paid to leave' in order to reduce the wage bill (i.e. they agreed a lump sum in lieu of sitting out their contracts), which had trebled since Dave Bassett left three years earlier. In fact, Capper and Pack claimed, Dean Saunders and Brian Deane together earned more money per annum than the whole of Bassett's 1995 squad combined.

McDonald, meanwhile, still pursued the money owed by Benfica, demanding that FIFA expel them from the Champions' League. When Middlesbrough were reported to be ready to make an offer of £3 million to Benfica for Deane, McDonald was seething and threatened to block the deal unless United were paid in full by Benfica, plus interest. The outstanding balance, around £500,000, was eventually received at the end of October. A few weeks later matters got worse still for Bruce when, instead of merely not being able to buy players, he was instructed he had to sell! Townsend confirmed the position in the *Sheffield Star*, saying, 'It is common knowledge that we have too many players. We need to get some of them out to make way for our juniors or new players. You only need look at the number of senior players in last night's reserve game.' Bruce was able to bring in midfielder Des Hamilton on loan from Newcastle United, and after an impressive debut decided to test the resolve of his board by requesting money to sign him permanently. Soon after, the 18,000 crowds that weren't high enough to support the players' salaries began to slip alarmingly, with a disconcerting 12,000 turning up for the game against Grimsby. United's recent performances saw them striving to merely maintain parity with mediocre teams. The fans were voting with their feet.

As well as trying to improve his squad, Bruce now had the upheaval of a takeover bid for the club. At his meeting with BIFA, McCabe did not hide the fact that he and McDonald had been struggling for control since the spring and although the pair did not often agree, they at least did 'get on'. McCabe revealed he was planning to buy out McDonald but another offer on the table, fronted by an unnamed United fan (but not bankrolled by him), was larger than his own. In his short time on the United board McCabe had made a sound impression with Blades supporters. Born within yards of Bramall Lane, he had followed the club all his life, even though he moved away from the city in 1971, the year of his marriage.

Beginning work in the construction trade at the age of 16, he founded his construction and property company in 1976 in his adopted home town of Scarborough. By 2001 McCabe was annually in the *Sunday Times* list of Britain's 1,000 richest individuals. He was the richest man ever to grace the position of director at Bramall Lane and in contrast to his predecessors a man who, in his own words spoken to Gary Armstrong, would 'disagree with people but not fall out with them.'

McCabe's ambitions were the same as those of the fans. In conversation with Gary Armstrong he spoke of his determination to achieve them, adding touchingly; '….and if we don't, let's have some fun trying.' Much of this, however, depended on the construction and success of the Blades Leisure Park on the football ground land and across Cherry Street on the Arnold Laver's site. McCabe knew that the banks would not loan money to United to buy footballers but they would lend for building and development work. This finance, along with grants from various sources, would allow United to construct the leisure complex, which, when up and running, would bring money into the football side of the PLC in two ways. McCabe explained that having spent, say, £10 million on the complex, the value of the club would increase by £20 million, the share price would improve accordingly and investors would be encouraged. The second income stream from the various retail outlets would come directly to United's coffers.

These ideas had gone beyond the drawing board. Outline planning permission for parts of the leisure complex that lay within the boundaries of the ground had been given a year earlier. In early September 1998 similar planning permission was received for the Laver's and Sheffield Works Department sites. This time the neighbours were on-side. Local community spokesperson Ann Wilson said, 'Sheffield United have shown a tremendous commitment to the local people and the overall opinion is that this can't be anything but a good thing for the area.' There were still hurdles to be jumped, however. City planners declared they were not happy with the proposed matchday safety arrangements. There were also concerns about entry to and egress from the ground for spectators when the new facilities were in place. Planning approval would not be given until these problems were overcome. Almost a year later the *Sheffield Star* reported that United were to join a local business partnership that, with Government and European Union funding, would help create 300 jobs at a business and community centre to be built adjacent to Bramall Lane. Work was due to begin in December. United had to find £1.8 million to build the 25,000-square-feet office building; if they did so they would receive grants matching this amount. The construction, housing 70 offices, was intended to be a long-term source of income for the club, via the renting out of office space. The club considered it a self-financing project. If the bid for funding for the office block was successful the club intended to build a hotel on the corner of Bramall Lane and Cherry Street, for which it had formed a partnership with four companies, including Scottish hotel chain MacDonald's (which - much to the relief of fans - had no connection with Mike McDonald).

In September 1998 United issued a bulletin via the Stock Exchange announcing that McCabe and David Hardisty were to leave the PLC board, the latter after less than a year. McCabe, however, would remain as acting chairman of the football club board. It was now that McCabe announced his intention to buy out McDonald's shareholding. He stated; 'I had hoped my resignation would force the organisational changes that are necessary for stability within the club. Since then, however, I have promoted an offer to take out the shares held by Mr McDonald's company Texas PLC.' News of the potential investment caused the share price to rise from 21p to 34p, and then rise again the following day to 37p. McDonald revealed he had actually been approached by two parties, stating, 'We are looking for around £10 million to invest in players, complete ground developments and get the club's Premiership potential achieved. Companies are looking to invest in football clubs with potential. One [approach] is a Sheffield-based consortium, and one from London. We are not talking about takeovers but we want people to buy shares. Looking at football from a business point of view Sheffield United is potentially in the top 20 in the country. We need fresh cash to come into the club because we can't make any progress on gate money alone. It is difficult to bring in the quality of players we need and pay their wages on 18,000 attendances. Anyone looking to invest in a football club with greater potential should be looking at clubs like Sheffield United. Sheffield has the fourth-biggest population in the country, it has an airport, good motorway links and is in the middle of the country. I believe this club could have a future in Europe but we have to get out of this division first. We also need to expand the commercial side of the club and make better use of our facilities. We will be looking more closely at the bids in the next few days.' Then McCabe claimed his buy-out of McDonald's shares would be concluded within 'the next few days', with McDonald concurring that the deal would be tied up 'within days'. Somewhat surprisingly, it wasn't. Confusingly, though, McDonald also remarked, 'I will not take money from anyone; their commitment to finishing the job and putting United in the Premiership must match my own. Buying me out is not the answer.' Such a statement suggested that McDonald hadn't agreed a deal with McCabe - or anybody else.

The identity of the second possible investor was revealed by the *Sheffield Star* in mid October 1998 under the front-page headline: 'Arrivederci McDonald'. The sub-heading told of how an 'Italian millionaire' was set to take over the Blades. He was London-based lawyer Carlo Colombotti, who had business links with Sheffield in the shape of lifelong United fan Phillip Wood, chief executive of the Peter Wood Group, owners of metals company Resistalloy, based in Sheffield's East End Attercliffe district. Wood was the front man of the consortium and was likely to be appointed as Ian Townsend's successor as chief executive, while Colombotti, who apparently held talks with Reg Brealey some years earlier about buying into United, would be chairman. The company Colombotti and Wood had set up to run Sheffield United was to be named 'Blades Italia Ltd'. Meanwhile, director Freddie Pye said he would be leaving the club along with McDonald if and when Colombotti took over. McCabe's future was now unclear as his bid for McDonald's shares had seemingly failed.

But would Colombotti ever take over? McDonald, who had been on the other end of countless delays when he was trying to buy out Reg Brealey three years earlier, seemed to be running out of patience as negotiations stalled: 'I have taken a back seat but I don't want the thing dragging on. I have said all along that when I see the colour of their money there will be no hold-up from my side.' Colombotti, on the other hand, spoke as though the deal was virtually done. After attending his first match at Bramall Lane – United drew 1-1 with Stockport County - he said, 'I am impressed with everything: the stadium, the history, the fans. This is a great club that can be even greater. We must examine the overall strategy of getting this club into the Premier Division of English football. I want this on track very soon because I am in discussion with Italian clubs. There is a possible involvement with United with one or two clubs and perhaps then the availability of players.' A week later Colombotti insisted he had made a down-payment to buy McDonald's shares after a meeting in Leeds attended by the two men's advisors. However, McDonald disagreed with their version of events, stating, 'My information is that a deal was agreed but sufficient funds were not forthcoming so I am soldiering on. The fans wanted me out and I am willing to go but they are stuck with me until someone takes over. We have called off the proposed share sale. The proposed deal with Mr Colombotti has not been concluded.'

Meanwhile, in October 1998 former United chairman Reg Brealey was declared bankrupt with debts of more than £3 million, mostly to the Inland Revenue. Despite a reported £16 million of assets, bankruptcy was ordered as Brealey could not convert the assets into cash. This meant that he could longer hold a company directorship, although spells in apparent charge at Darlington FC and Grantham Town FC appeared to circumvent the ruling. In 2002 Brealey was fined £2,000 at Blackfriars Crown Court for his 'reckless management of a company while barred after bankruptcy'. The company in question was financial consultants Antrac Investments, which was the majority owner of Grantham Town and under whose control Grantham mounted up considerable debts. It transpired that Antrac's registered address was a house in

Grantham that had lain empty for months. Brealey claimed he merely worked for Antrac as an unpaid consultant. The divided jury was instructed by the judge to continue its deliberations and eventually found by a majority decision that Brealey's involvement in Grantham Town broke the terms of his bankruptcy conditions. Brealey also had to pay £1,500 costs and was banned from being a company director for two years. Timothy Dutton QC told Brealey, 'You were made bankrupt and you were given the plainest of warnings not to become involved in the management of a company. It appears you did become concerned and while you did not deliberately flout the law, what you did was reckless.' Brealey said he accepted the verdict and planned to move to Australia, saying, 'I used to have a sheep farm out there.' This was an appropriate time for Brealey's name to resurface as the club now found itself in a position similar to the one it was in in 1995 when he was in the process of selling up to McDonald. Instead of receiving their monthly salaries through the usual medium of bank transfer, the players were paid by cheque and asked not to deposit them immediately. The club was in such a parlous state that the two or three days it would take for the cheques to clear were consequential.

A week later, on November 7, 1998, the *Sheffield Star* then reported - under the front-page headline 'New era at United' - that a five-man consortium, comprising existing directors Kevin McCabe, Bernard Procter and Andrew Laver, former director John Plant and Carlo Colombotti, had come together to finalise a deal to buy McDonald's 13 per cent shareholding. Colombotti was in the USA and nobody else would comment but that was to be expected as any statement on major share issues would have to be made via the Stock Exchange. But another ten days passed with still no progress; McDonald was losing patience, going public with his belief that Colombotti was 'out of time' and as such he was talking with other interested parties. 'We had an agreement on the table a week last Friday and they have simply not come up with what is required. I feel bitter about it. We have spent huge amounts on legal advice and accountancy bills and there is nothing now to show for it. I gave them a lock-out time during which I would not talk to anyone else. Now I am free to do so and I am involved with two other bidders and putting together a deal which could be even better for the future of Sheffield United.' He then called a board meeting to inform his fellow directors of the situation. However, another version of the truth emerged from McCabe, who was having none of McDonald's posturing. 'I shall not be attending,' he said. 'We have wasted too much time on this already. It is time Mr McDonald made up his mind.'

Then, just a few days after the deal was supposed to be off, it was back on again. Now McDonald was agreeing a compromise with Colombotti, who would become the new PLC chairman, with McDonald remaining as a director. McCabe would be the football club chairman. The full financial details were not revealed but Colombotti had reportedly bought half of McDonald's 13 per cent shareholding, Phillip Wood and another Sheffield businessman, Stuart Johnson, dividing the remaining half between them, albeit the latter was not joining the board. Their company, Blades Italia Ltd, made an immediate £750,000 cash advance to the club, with another £1.25 million guaranteed by four other directors. Blades Italia also planned a new share issue. Colombotti talked big, as all incoming chairman at Bramall Lane do, saying, 'My role in the first few months when we are setting up policies will be an active one, day to day. I am setting up direct contact with Steve Bruce on playing matters. I shall be very much available.' McCabe similarly looked to a better future: 'This is a new beginning for Sheffield United. There is now genuine harmony throughout the club. This is the end of first-stage stability and there are exciting times ahead. This is a big day for Sheffield United. We have great plans. We are up and ready for the future.' Phillip Wood was metaphorically enthusiastic: 'We are in harmony, all singing from the same hymn sheet now. Together there are no stars we cannot reach.' Colombotti then laid out his plans for United, which spoke of the club as an 'investment', and threatened to alter the nationality of the team: 'I am going over [to Italy] to set up co-operation with clubs and a possible two-way movement of players. The ideal outcome is that some interesting and quality Italian players would become available to us. That is what I would like to see. I have contacts right at the top of some major Italian clubs, but it might be premature to mention them. I am honoured to be invited to be chairman of a great club with a great tradition and a great future. We should be in the Premiership and that is priority number one.'

McDonald was stepping into the background after an eventful three years in charge. Could he look back with satisfaction? Upon arrival McDonald announced six objectives: on the field, to save the team from relegation (achieved); to attain promotion to the Premier League (not achieved); and to reach European qualification (not achieved). Off the field, he said he would: build the John Street stand (achieved); break up the shareholding so that no single man controlled the club (achieved); commercially develop Bramall Lane (on the verge of commencement). His decision to buy the club saved it from a lingering death under Reg Brealey. He kick-started the turnaround with the appointment of Howard Kendall, who was held in extremely high regard by supporters at the end of his first half-season in charge. McDonald allowed Kendall to spend money and manage the transformation of the team in such a way that the squad was unrecognisable in terms of personnel and ability from the one that he inherited. Then, despite a couple of hiccups, McDonald achieved something that Brealey was singularly unable to do - he raised the required finance and built the stand. In addition to this he supervised the enhancement of the training facilities at Abbeydale Grange and the planning of the Blades Leisure Complex. He also oversaw - initially anyway - a new openness with supporters, highlighted by the formation of the Consultative Committee and the holding of three 'Fans' Forums'.

His minus points were twofold, but major. He made the mistake of believing United to be a bigger club than it actually was and believed that gates would, with a reasonably successful team, immediately climb to 20-25,000. The term 'successful' is relative. The Sheffield football-watching public, on both sides of the city, is not as volatile in its match-going as in many other places. In this city one will never witness the huge, near instant double increases in attendances seen in the late 1990s at, amongst others, Wolverhampton, Newcastle, Sunderland, Middlesbrough, Chelsea and Barnsley. When Wednesday were in the Premier League, their gates reached 35,000 for the visits of Manchester United, Liverpool and Leeds and otherwise hovered in the mid-20s. Sheffield United's seasons in the Premier League in the early 1990s saw only a few attendances that threatened the ground capacity of around 30,500. McDonald's income through gate receipts was never going to be as large as he hoped or expected.

This had a significant impact on his second error of judgement - ceding too much power in chief executive Charles Green. This ultimately led to their, and the team's, fall from grace. Green was allowed a free hand to influence which players were bought and sold and to negotiate contracts. Whether he held and wielded this authority when Howard Kendall was manager is unclear, but with Nigel Spackman installed Green took centre stage, a role that did not sit easily with the young manager. United needed to attract good players, first to stave off relegation, and second to go for promotion. Relatively low-paid players such as Paul Rogers, Tony Battersby and Paul Holland were discarded, while good experienced players such as Don Hutchison, David White, Mark Patterson, Michael Vonk and Andy Walker were recruited from the English and Scottish Premier Leagues, with wages to match. The players Kendall kept, such as experienced goalkeepers Simon Tracey and Alan Kelly, former youth-team players Mitch Ward and Dane Whitehouse and Norwegian international Roger Nilsen, were awarded new, better, contracts.

This policy initially worked; the blame for United's failure to win promotion in 1996/97 was apportioned mainly to Kendall's negative tactics, which, critics argued, prevented the team turning away draws into wins. To score more goals, McDonald had splashed out on Jan Åge Fjørtoft and, after Kendall's move to Everton, agreed another hefty contract in the shape of centre forward Brian Deane. To stop goals being conceded the club brought in Greek international full back Vassilis Borbokis and former Manchester United and Republic of Ireland international central defender Paul McGrath. At that time no one was finding fault with the ambition and drive of McDonald and Green - it appeared they wanted promotion as much as fans did and were willing to invest to achieve it. For three months, everything ran smoothly. Spackman's team was playing the best football seen at the Lane for years, Deane was the type of centre forward United had been lacking since, well, the departure of Brian Deane, and McGrath was imperious. The first cracks that appeared - the injuries to McGrath and Whitehouse - could not be blamed on anybody but by this time rumours were already spreading that all was not well. As mentioned earlier, the departures of physiotherapist Denis Circuit and kitman John Greaves, with little or no warning, hinted at problems. Soon afterwards Graham Stuart arrived at Bramall Lane in a deal that took Mitch Ward and Carl Tiler in the opposite direction. The latter did not want to go and Spackman did not want to lose him. Mark Patterson departed with his caustic blast and the Gareth Taylor debacle led the supporters' anger to boil over at the Charlton game shortly after Christmas 1997 when supporters came up with a new chant: 'Charles Green, he sells the team....' to the tune of the Pet Shop Boys' 'Go West'. McDonald and Green were getting cold feet. In the words of the former, United were heading down the road of 'financial suicide'. But whose fault was that? The supporters', of course, because the match attendances weren't big enough to pay for the ambitions of McDonald and Green, despite a near ten per cent gate increase on the previous season.

The mismanagement of those in charge of financial matters apparently had nothing to do with it. The sales of Deane and Fjørtoft on the same day signalled the immediate, catastrophic end to one of McDonald's declared objectives - promotion - at least for the foreseeable future. The plug had been pulled on the club's ambition. The wage bill was too big and there was no money for new manager Steve Bruce. Those charged with the responsibility of bringing about these types of deals, the chairman and the chief executive, did so without ensuring that resources or gate and commercial incomes could maintain them. They gambled on winning promotion in 1997/98 but weren't brave or prepared enough to see their venture through.

Their crime was not showing ambition, but cutting it off before it came to fruition.

It was now left to Colombotti to take United to a higher level. Although portrayed as Italian, he was actually born in Tonypandy, Mid Glamorgan, Wales. Despite the ambiguity of origin his employment CV was highly impressive. He obtained a LLB Degree honours at London University in 1961 and qualified as a solicitor in 1965. He later lectured at the prestigious University College, London. Having held a prominent role in London-based law partnership Amhurst Brown Colombotti, he was currently a consultant with a law firm by the name of SJ Berwin and was also a past president of the British-Italian Law Association. He was also legal adviser to the Italian embassy. He was vice president of the Italian Chamber of Commerce and served on the committee of the *Club di Londra*[7]. More interesting than his employment history, however, was some of the company he kept. Colombotti's nickname in the gossip columns was 'The Italian Count' and he was what is known in some circles as a 'socialite'. It was not unusual for him to be seen with a glamorous singer or two on his arm – Shirley Bassey and Sinitta (to whom he was once considering becoming engaged) for example. Sinitta told the *New Statesman* magazine that the glossy weekly *Hello!* wished to do an interview about their engagement and Colombotti was keen to be pictured. Sinitta wanted to tell in the accompanying story-line of her celibacy. Colombotti was not happy. 'He didn't like the truth be known that I was celibate,' said Sinitta. Raine Spencer, the stepmother of Diana, Princess of Wales, was another friend. At a midweek Arsenal v Sheffield United fixture at Highbury he entered the boardroom accompanied by a former Miss South Africa.

Colombotti frequented *Annabel's* nightclub, the ultimate central London members-only club named after Lady Annabel Goldsmith. The venue was alleged to host arms dealers, European monarchy and big-business executives; a location

---

[7] A club that holds luncheons and dinners to debate subjects of British/Italian interest, with high-profile speakers.

where, to its detractors, Euro-trash money spoke louder than breeding. On one occasion when Colombotti was in there, an adjacent table full of raucous City of London types was being rather loud. 'It's not normally like this, I can assure you,' said Colombotti anxiously to his (female) guest. 'Look around,' he continued, 'the groups of people all include wives. But any one-to-one dining is girlfriend only. No man here would spend money just to have dinner with his wife.' Such panache and wisdom was now about to embark as chairman of Sheffield United – 'The Family Club'.

Away from the great and the good of London's High Society, Colombotti had other, not quite so salubrious, connections. In the late 1980s he was a marginal player in what became known as the 'Pamella Affair'. The story, investigated and researched by journalist Christopher Long, was sold to the *Daily Express*, which then appointed its own investigative team to follow up the leads. The 'Pamella Affair' was a major political scandal and threatened to jeopardise the credibility of the Conservative Government. It also revealed that Britain's intelligence and security services were failing to liaise and co-operate to protect national security. The Pamella in question was a very attractive woman aged 27 of dual Anglo-Indian heritage by the name of Pamella Bordes, a research assistant at the House of Commons, who, it was alleged, had links with Libya's Colonel Gadaffi. At the time Gadaffi was one of the most reviled and wanted men in the world having been thought to be behind the bombing of the Pan Am passenger jet over Lockerbie, Scotland, in 1988, which killed all 259 civilian passengers and crew and a further eleven on the ground. Bordes had been spotted socialising with Ahmed Gaddaf Al-Dam, a top-ranking arms buyer in the Libyan security service and a cousin of Gadaffi. Prime Minister Margaret Thatcher was urged to mount an immediate investigation. Labour backbench MP Ted Leadbitter, who previously exposed 1960s traitor Anthony Blunt, said, 'The persistent reports linking Pamella Bordes with people in prominent positions - and more recently actually touching upon areas of possible security risk - suggest, if true, the urgency of the Government undertaking the fullest possible pressing and penetrating inquiry.'

What provoked concerns about national security was that the former beauty queen Bordes had previously dated a Government minister (Colin Moynihan, later Minister for Sport), newspaper editors (broadsheet not tabloid) and MPs. The high-class call girl - which is what she was - was said by a close friend to have made regular trips to Paris where she met Al-Dam. She was also said to have made a number of visits by private jet to the Libyan capital Tripoli. Unfortunately for her and Moynihan, Al-Dam was on the wanted list of several secret service agencies. Reports of Pamella's visits to see him in Paris were given to senior Foreign Office officials in early January 1989. By then Bordes was working as a research assistant for Tory MP David Shaw. Ms Bordes apparently shared many of her secrets with a friend during heart-to-heart conversations at a London health club. Whilst her friend opined that Pamella tended to exaggerate her sexual conquests of the well-known and well-to-do, she was convinced that her relationship with Al-Dam was genuine. Bordes was believed to have been introduced to him by another arms dealer by the name of Adnan Khashoggi, whom she met in America after her failed attempt to win the Miss Universe contest in Peru. Later Bordes moved to France, where she met and married Parisian businessman Henri Bordes but the couple broke up. Carlo Colombotti then entered the story. He shared his £1 million central London house with Bordes on a 'platonic' basis in 1988 and said he was 'staggered' to hear of the revelations. With her friendships with top MPs and senior newspaper figures, like *Sunday Times* editor Andrew Neil, in the headlines, the worry for the Government was what other names might be revealed. A one-time guest of Colin Moynihan at the Tory Winter Ball and with another Cabinet colleague as part of her social set, she was likened to the espionage 'honey-trap'. Colombotti managed to escape any of the fall-out from this affair but links with Libyan arms dealers, if only indirect ones, were nothing compared to what he was to face over the next year or so at Sheffield United Football Club.

Meanwhile, even though the United boardroom personnel changed, the problems for manager Steve Bruce persisted. He still had no money to spend and still his leading players were leaving. And, irony of ironies, the main player involved this time was known as 'Deano' and the club involved was Benfica. Welsh international striker Dean Saunders was one of United's most inspirational and consistent players of the 1997/98 season but he, like Brian Deane before him, had a clause in his contract that allowed him to speak to top British and European clubs if the prospect of a transfer arose. In December 1998 Saunders was withdrawn from the team to play Bristol City as he considered Benfica's interest in him. Bruce, tearing his hair out in frustration, went public with the declaration: 'He either stays or he goes. I will not let this situation drag on and I want the whole business settled by the weekend. Because of a clause in his contract Dean can do whatever he likes. Sooner or later we will lose him if he wants to get away.' Days later Saunders moved to Benfica for £500,000. Whilst Bruce seethed, Colombotti cajoled, saying, 'We have to do something about bringing strikers in if we can. I am in touch with a number of *Serie A* teams of very high level and my talks last week were very encouraging. Action is needed.'

The extent of United's, and Bruce's, financial worries was revealed with the publication of the company accounts for the year ending June 30, 1998. The wage bill had soared to £8.3 million. The overall annual loss was £6.6 million, including a perplexing £107,000 pay-off to former chief executive Charles Green for what was termed 'loss of office'. With a salary approaching £50,000 and other benefits, Green was paid £172,000 in his final year at the club. Gate receipts had climbed from £2.7 million to £3.4 million, with television income up from £1.06 million to £1.2 million. McDonald, still PLC chairman at the time of the formulation of the accounts, commented, 'The disappointment of not reaching the Premiership has left us with some restructuring to do in order to bring our wages in line with the income we can generate.' McDonald came out with a couple of baffling statements in the company's annual report, claiming that '[an] improvement in operating performance….. did not continue mainly due to injuries and the disruption to our fixture schedule due to the success in the FA Cup' and 'new players were brought in to strengthen our chances of qualifying for the FA Cup final.' It was hard to understand how a good cup run, that brought

£800,000 into the club's coffers, contributed to a poorer operating performance. The three players brought to the club in March were all cup-tied and therefore were not eligible to play in the FA Cup, never mind help United qualify for the final. Financial logic was seemingly not available at Bramall Lane.

The Annual General Meeting of Sheffield United PLC, held on December 29, 1998, proved to be a lively affair. But it was conducted with the conspicuous absence of one particular party; McDonald sent his apologies, as he was entitled to do, but no explanation as to his whereabouts. The newly installed PLC chairman Colombotti opined that he may be 'on holiday'. However, McDonald's Texas Group associate Laurie Turnbull, who held no official role at Sheffield United but who often attended board meetings on McDonald's behalf, stood silently at the rear of the hall throughout. After Colombotti's introduction and opening statement, the floor was thrown open for questions. The session was dominated by the recently formed Sheffield United Independent Shareholders' Association (SUISA). Prior to the meeting, SUISA had handed Colombotti a list of 20-plus questions to be directed at McDonald. His absence proved a bit of an obstacle and SUISA tried, unsuccessfully, to get the meeting adjourned until such a time that McDonald could attend. Instead, Colombotti assented to seek written answers to these questions, which would then be made public (a couple of weeks later McDonald met a small group of SUISA members to discuss these questions but his responses were never made public). SUISA's first speaker, local businessman Dave Windle, then pursued a rather dogged line of questioning with little reward, and his impolitic persistence did nothing to endear the organisation to the rest of the shareholders. However, SUISA regained some of its lost ground with its second and third questioners, Peter Salt and John Plumtree, two well-dressed, well-spoken and well-mannered men clearly conversant with company finances.

In the absence of McDonald, Colombotti was frequently able to deflect some of the criticism by playing his 'I was not here at the time' card. One of the main issues of dissent from the floor was the club's decision to pay off Charles Green. If, as the questioners wondered, Green had resigned as reported, why did he leave with a £107,000 cheque? According to Kevin McCabe, this was a standard termination of contract agreement, which happens all the time in business. The meeting was not convinced, and demanded that in the future if an executive failed in his task he should be sacked without compensation. Significantly, the board did not argue against this sentiment. Colombotti said that he was currently examining all the players' contracts and that no future deals would be negotiated that included a Deane and Saunders-style 'get-out clause'. He also stated that the club was aiming to reduce the wage bill to around 70 per cent of income, not the unsustainable 100 per cent it was at present. He furthermore insisted that his proposed collaboration with *Serie A* clubs was not a pipedream but declined to mention which clubs he was talking to - although he did cleverly ask the meeting if there were any top Italian clubs they would prefer he did not deal with!

The most divisive moment of the meeting was the vote for the re-election of McDonald to the board. Scarcely a hand was raised on the floor in favour of the resolution, although it was no surprise that the motion was carried massively by the board's block vote. Colombotti's explanation - a reasonable one - was that McDonald's company Texas had loaned United £500,000 and if McDonald were not re-elected he would want it back now - in cash. However, McDonald had agreed to be refunded in shares after the proposed new rights issue early in 1999, at which point he would resign. The meeting demanded that this resignation date be declared and made public. It never was. One shareholder called McDonald's chairmanship a 'disaster', another ridiculed the club's 'complete financial incompetence'. Overall, it seemed that Colombotti was somewhat taken aback by the strength of feeling against McDonald and perhaps had not been properly briefed as to what to expect. Although there were still misgivings about Colombotti's background and the source of his finances, he came across at the AGM as committed and determined to do well, and in a calculated manner. Even the most disillusioned fans would give him time – a short time anyway.

The fledgling organisation SUISA had made a most public of impressions. SUISA evolved from the perceived unfairness and victimisation felt by the Original shareholders when their previously valuable shares were rendered relatively worthless by the stock market flotation of Sheffield United PLC. Founded in the summer of 1998, SUISA claimed to have quadrupled its membership in its first six months from, in their own words, 'a small base'. It had a committee of seven: Dave Windle (chairman), Martin Brammer (vice chairman), Mark Leigh (membership secretary), Dave Rodman (treasurer), Simon Jenkins (secretary), Peter Salt (Southern representative), and John Plumtree (Original shareholders' representative). SUISA's 'mission statement', published in *Flashing Blade* and *The Red and White Wizaaard*, read: 'Since the share flotation small shareholders have taken a personal stake in the club. Individually they can be overruled by the big battalions of the board and the City but by bonding together maybe, just maybe, they can influence events. This, then, is the critical ethos of SUISA: that by joining together, independent shareholders in a democratic grouping can become a positive force for good at the PLC.' SUISA also explained the differences between it and the Blades Independent Fans' Association: 'A clear difference exists between the two organisations that we believe are not rivals but rather complementary. There is a clear divide between fans' issues and those that affect shareholders. Many people are members of both organisations and we seek warm and constructive relations with BIFA. After all, both organisations aim to achieve the same objectives, albeit by different routes.'

These 'warm and constructive relations' were endangered after BIFA held a question and answer session with Kevin McCabe at the Trades and Labour Club in October 1998, attended by around seventy BIFA and SUISA members. Dave Windle, a particularly forthright - and even abrasive - member of SUISA's committee, claimed BIFA had rigged the whole event and fed McCabe previously agreed questions to which he had prepared answers. Windle attempted to dominate proceedings by constantly asking questions, eventually forcing the chair of the meeting, Paul Blomfield, to ask him to refrain from speaking to give other people the opportunity to contribute.

Blomfield's intervention received verbal approval from many present. Windle's 'rigging' claim was vigorously denied by BIFA, which later indulged in its own bit of name-calling by accusing Windle of 'embittered paranoia' on an internet message board. The motive for Windle's attack was unclear and after this unpleasant episode the two organisations had little contact.

In the middle of January 1999 Colombotti claimed he had at last finalised the £1.9 million deal to buy McDonald's shares. He explained that a further payment would be made to McDonald on the agreed date, adding; 'People have looked at the share register, seen the shares are still in the name of Texas and assumed we have a problem finding the money. That is most definitely not the case. What I am concerned about is the share price, which went down quite dramatically while I was away in Italy last week. Someone must be dumping shares in the club at 18p. It is definitely not me. It is not in my interest that the value of the club should be reduced. We are planning an early share flotation, as promised to shareholders at the annual meeting. We still face accusations that it is our plan to own the club this way with shares at a depressed value because my company Blades Italia are the underwriters, but that is definitely not part of our plans for United.'

Two weeks after Colombotti claimed he had concluded his purchase of McDonald's shares, it emerged that McDonald was to retain a ten per cent shareholding, agreeing with Colombotti that the final £1 million instalment would be better served going into the club's coffers rather than his own. A statement from Blades Italia Ltd said, 'Blades Italia Ltd is currently raising £4 million for Sheffield United PLC. In order to assist the company further, such a sum will be increased to £5 million by the addition of monies which were otherwise payable to [McDonald's] Texas Group.' McDonald confirmed the modification from his holiday base in Switzerland: 'The bottom line is that £1 million that was coming to me is going to help Sheffield United instead. My company is to retain its shares and will not sell them to Blades Italia. Both parties believe that the money is better in the club. Basically we have called off the proposed share sale.' One of the first tasks of the reconstituted board would be to answer questions at a 'Fans' Forum', organised by BIFA, whose spokesman Andy Nicolson said that the forum would ask the board to tell fans how they planned to make United into a top-six Premier League club.

In February 1999 Colombotti found a distraction from the wrangling with McDonald thanks to the actions of a Nigerian and a Dutchman on a football pitch in north London. United were drawn away to Arsenal in the fifth round of the FA Cup and acquitted themselves well at Highbury, holding on to a 1-1 scoreline with 15 minutes remaining. When United striker Lee Morris went down injured, goalkeeper Alan Kelly kicked the ball out of play in the accepted fashion so that his team-mate could receive treatment. Then, contrary to the accepted fashion, from the resulting throw-in Arsenal did not return the ball to United. Instead, the Nigerian international Nwankwo Kanu, with his first contribution as a substitute in his first game for Arsenal, set off down the flank and crossed low for the onrushing Dutch winger Marc Overmars to score. Kelly stood perplexed, wondering what was going on. The only United player to realise this breach of etiquette was right back Shaun Derry, but he could not catch Overmars as he knocked the ball into the virtually unguarded net. There was anger amongst the Blades fans and pandemonium on the pitch as United's players protested to Kanu, Overmars and referee Peter Jones that the goal was unfair. Steve Bruce entered the playing area and threatened to call his players off, beckoning for them to do so. In the directors' box Phillip Wood was on his feet, chanting, 'Brucie, Brucie, bring them off!' much to the chagrin of the watching police commander. Two Arsenal players, Ray Parlour – who took the fateful throw-in – and goalkeeper David Seaman appeared to be arguing United's case. After an eleven-minute delay referee Jones ruled that no laws had been broken so the goal must stand. Some semblance of normality was restored but the remainder of the tie was played out in an eerie, unreal atmosphere as Arsenal went on to win 2-1.

Immediately after the game Arsenal chairman Peter Hill-Wood and vice chairman David Dein suggested to Carlo Colombotti,

Kevin McCabe and David Capper that he would ask the Football Association to annul the result and consent to having the tie replayed. The three United men agreed. Capper had already spoken to Adrian Titcombe, the FA official in charge of the match, informing him that United were considering making a formal protest. By the time the news broke an hour later the idea of a replay was reported to have been instigated by Arsenal manager Arsène Wenger - it suited Hill-Wood and Dein to let Wenger take the credit. Within hours the FA's Challenge Cup Committee had given its blessing to the game being restaged. When it was suggested that as United were only 15 minutes away from a draw and thus the replay should be at Bramall Lane, Wenger commented, 'The offer to play again means here [Highbury]. We have a fair spirit but we are not stupid.' The game was fixed for ten days later, with tickets on sale at half the normal price.

FA spokesman David Double explained that the governing body had made such a decision 'in the interests of fair play.' The world governing body FIFA still had to sanction the replay and despite its director of communications Keith Cooper saying, 'This is a magnanimous gesture of fair play by Arsenal – something we respect', only three days before the scheduled replay FIFA general secretary Michael Zen-Ruffinen said he was still awaiting clarification from the FA of the competition rules. He told *BBC Radio Five Live*, 'If we have to take a decision which is unpopular then we will have to do that. FIFA is a kind of referee in terms of the litigation which arises from the football family.' The FA's chief executive David Davies claimed there was nothing to worry about: '[Arsenal] have sold all the tickets. It's an unprecedented situation. Both clubs want a rematch.' Doubt remained with only 24 hours remaining as FIFA still hadn't confirmed its position but Capper and McCabe tried to allay any fears that the game might be cancelled at such short notice. It went ahead and United put up another commendable showing in going down by the same 2-1 scoreline. One of Arsenal's goals was scored by Overmars – legitimately this time.

After the furore surrounding the Arsenal games had died down it was back to the more prosaic matters of winning league points and, after nine months at Bramall Lane, Bruce still had no funds available to buy players. He was assured that, for the moment, he did not have to sell anyone. His and the club's resolve was tested immediately as Birmingham City made an enquiry about team captain David Holdsworth. Said Bruce, 'I don't want Holdsworth to go but everyone has a price - but it has to be right for my club.' Just two weeks later, before the transfer deadline, the picture changed again. United accepted Birmingham's £1.5 million offer for Holdsworth and also agreed a £1.1 million fee with Charlton Athletic for the transfer of Graham Stuart. Bruce did not want to sell either player and publicly discussed his state of mind, saying, 'We are heavily in debt. I cannot say I am pleased with these deals but no way will I quit and walk away but I am depressed that all the talk is of players leaving the club. After a good cup run we are in seventh spot and we should be on cloud nine, planning to beat Oxford on Friday night and then having a great Easter and reaching the play-offs. I find the situation very disappointing, to say the least.'

The two players leaving did so with both pleas and parting shots. Stuart said, 'It's a great club but if they continue to sell their best players they won't get to the Premier League. My worry is that United have become a selling club.' Holdsworth's farewell message - possibly calculated with a view to a post-playing career coaching position - was: 'You are the best set of fans in the country. It has been an honour to captain Sheffield United. I love this club, I love the people but money, politics and other issues have to be sorted out.' Before the Oxford match it took the appearance of Kevin McCabe to assuage several hundred supporters gathered in the car park, angered by the player sales. McCabe stood on one of the low dividing walls and proclaimed above the hubbub, 'Of course we want Premiership football but what all fans have got to recognise, and it's a difficult one, is that financial stability of any football club has to come in mind.' The supporters were angrier still after the game, which United, shorn of two very good players, lost 2-1 to lowly opponents[8].

After the defeat to Oxford, McCabe used the back page of the *Sheffield Star* to warn fans not to 'force out the money men'. Such men, in his opinion, did not like dissent. McCabe said, 'I met the leaders of the demonstration in private and it went well. They seemed to understand. But there were hotheads in the car park who must understand that they could strip the club of the very people whose investment has kept it going. The supporters' association must get across a more tolerant message otherwise they might end up with the club in the hands of people who don't have its best interests at heart.' The other chairman, Colombotti, also had plenty to say, reiterating what he said days earlier: 'Player sales have raised a number of questions. It is the board's view that such sales were completed having regard to several factors and a balanced consideration of the club's interests. Whilst these sales go a long way to reconfirming the financial stability of the club, the incoming players and the monies being made available to Steve Bruce must also be emphasised. The board have categorically agreed that two-thirds of the net proceeds from any player sales effected are available to him for appropriate acquisitions. Whilst offers have been received for other players for not insignificant sums, these have been, and will be, rejected. The board, together with Steve Bruce, believe they can build on the current squad with a view to achieving a play-off position this season and, if that is not achieved, certainly promotion next year. The financial position is stable.' The vocabulary used by Colombotti betrayed a legal, rather than football, background.

---

[8] At this juncture, as a result of the transfers of Holdsworth and Stuart, Ian Townsend decided to resign from the football club board. He explained; 'Although pressure of work did not leave me with as much time available to the club as I would have liked, as a director of the club I was seen to be endorsing decisions which were not discussed with me nor was I in agreement with. I decided that under the circumstances I should not retain my seat.' However, Townsend's stance was not as principled as it might have seemed as he was under pressure from other directors to leave.

Colombotti described further the reasoning for the sale of the two players in typical 'Stock Exchange language' in his chairman's statement in the company's 1998/99 *Interim Report*: 'Your board now considers that the most prudent strategy to adopt is to combine youth and experience at sensible cost whilst allowing the management team to produce a successful formula internally. Any success on the pitch will then be capitalised upon by way of growth in gates, TV revenue and commercial income. Developing a high cost-base through the recruitment of established star names does not guarantee financial or football success, as we have already seen in previous years. Our strategy should therefore ensure that losses are kept to a minimum by thorough cost-base management.' In other words, Colombotti expected the manager to produce success on the pitch at the same time as reducing costs by selling the best players and not replacing them. This was no doubt visionary – if ridiculous.

Bruce was heartened by the news that he would receive some of the £2.6 million combined transfer monies, saying, 'I have made it plain that I would rather keep both players [Holdsworth and Stuart] but the finances of the club are an absolute mess. The simple facts are that we were financially strapped but after the current transfer events it seems I now have some money available.' Ivory Coast-born defender Oliver Tebily was soon to sign from French club Chateauroux for a fee of £250,000. Two Derby County players, midfielder Jonathan Hunt and right back Rob Kozluk, were then bought for a combined £650,000. Colombotti added, 'We are not in desperate financial straits but there are confusing messages coming from the club, a situation I shall address. I do not understand the current whispering campaign.' Colombotti failed to mention that Vassilis Borbokis moved to Derby as part of the deal that brought Hunt and Kozluk to Bramall Lane and that United actually made money on the exchange, rather than spending the £650,000 quoted. That figure was the combined value assigned to Hunt and Kozluk in the swap deal, in which United were receiving £500,000, thus valuing Borbokis at £1.15 million. And maybe the 'whispering campaign' Colombotti spoke of existed because the team manager had been allowed to use the words 'absolute mess', 'financially strapped' and 'heavily in debt' as the reasons for the sales.

After giving Colombotti a cautious welcome, BIFA now rounded on him. The organisation issued a press release, announcing: 'By pressuring Bruce to sell Holdsworth the board have not only thrown our chances of Premiership football out of the window, they will lose all credibility with the fans.' The new board has failed to deliver on its major promises. It looks like fans' suspicions are being confirmed – new faces, same old broken promises. We don't expect miracles from the board but we do expect honesty and straight talking.' SUISA wanted action too – before the Oxford match they handed out leaflets detailing their 'workable and sound action plan', which, in short, was to remove the whole board and appoint a fully independent executive chairman. Whom this individual might be, where found and how the process would work was not articulated. In early April it looked as though the board might be making its first move to abide by SUISA's 'action plan'. Chief executive Phillip Wood was dismissed after only four months in office, thereby becoming the third chief executive to leave the post inside nine months. The decision followed a lengthy board meeting, attended by Mike McDonald after a 12-month absence from matches and direct boardroom activities (his adviser Laurie Turnbull had represented him). A terse club statement observed that Wood had 'stepped down' but no reason was given. McDonald appeared to be the instigator of Wood's dismissal, saying, 'I went and said my piece because I am still a major shareholder, still a supporter and I am very disappointed with the way the season has gone.' Observing the previous few months' events from the outside, McDonald decided to return to active director's duty - he was after all still the biggest individual shareholder at the club. His return made two things certain: he was ready to throw his weight around and there was going to be yet another boardroom power struggle.

As an emollient, the 67-year-old Derek Dooley was summoned out of retirement to become acting chief executive. The directors realised that he was the only man who could be trusted to maintain an uneasy peace. In his own words Dooley explained, 'I have been asked to do a job and I will give it all the time it demands. But I am not going back full time and when the post is advertised I shall not be a candidate. I have come back to mend fences and heal wounds. I will do all I can to see things run smoothly, to subdue controversy and to try to bring everyone together.' By way of response McDonald added his words of respect: 'You cannot buy experience and you cannot buy integrity. Derek has both in huge measure,' and then threatened a full-time return of his own: 'I would come back as tea lady if it meant Sheffield United moving in the right direction.' At the end of April, McDonald returned to the Bramall Lane directors' box for the first time in over six months, as he watched United's reserves play Bradford City reserves – over a cup of tea.

If not exactly welcoming McDonald back, Colombotti did agree to talk to him. The *Sheffield Star* reported that the pair were to 'thrash it out'. As was the Bramall Lane norm though, nothing was as it first appeared. The first planned meeting was postponed, reportedly due to 'travel difficulties'. Then it transpired that it did take place after all - a cabal of Mike McDonald, Bernard Procter and Andrew Laver had got together – but without Colombotti! The affronted Colombotti spoke publicly of his plan to sue his three fellow directors, Sheffield United PLC and Texas PLC alleging 'conduct detrimental to Sheffield United'. In effect, as chairman of the company, he was taking legal action against himself. He issued a statement to enlighten the perplexed: 'A meeting of directors was called for 4pm on Wednesday. At 3.30pm I met with Mr McDonald and Mr McCabe at Doncaster and we agreed the board meeting should be postponed until the following Monday. This was communicated to the other two directors, Mr Procter and Mr Laver, who agreed. Despite this, I understand that McDonald, Procter and Laver purported to hold a board meeting behind my back at which they attempted to pass certain decisions. Since my appointment as chairman I have not been supported by my co-directors. Rather than assist in my efforts to seek further finance they have sadly acted in a manner which I believe to be detrimental to Sheffield United. I was angry when I discovered the three of them had had a meeting. I have never been placed in such a situation. It is clear that they want to get rid of me.'

Bernard Procter responded, stating that there were inaccuracies in Colombotti's statement but did not want to enter into a public debate. The board meeting, in Procter's opinion, was properly constituted and those at the meeting were not trying to get rid of Colombotti. News of the legal action forced the share price down to 17p. The Monday board meeting referred to by Colombotti did go ahead, before which McDonald said, 'At the end of the day the club is run by the supporters; their backing is paramount. As far as today's board meeting is concerned, the proposed deal with Mr Colombotti has not been concluded.' The outcome of the five-hour meeting was that Colombotti was to withdraw his threat of legal action. It was a truce of sorts, with all directors now said to be backing Colombotti's proposed rights issue, which was to go ahead 'by May 21 at the latest'. To outsiders it seemed merely a case of papering over the cracks.

In late April Steve Bruce received another bombshell when he was informed he would not be able to recruit over the summer - not even free transfers - as United looked to cut the wage bill by £1.5 million after interim PLC results showed a loss of £1.9 million in the second half of 1998. The stunned manager said, 'I feel totally frustrated. I've reduced the wage bill drastically and raised £4.5 million; now I've been told by the PLC that isn't enough. Despite it all we were on the verge of the play-offs.' Typically, conflicting information emanated from a different source, as the company's December 1998 *Interim Report* quoted Colombotti as saying, 'Where possible, we will invest in the playing squad at all levels.' Clearly, something had caused the situation to change. When asked if he was considering resignation, Bruce answered, 'That's not an avenue I want to go down.'

In an effort to recover some of the ground and trust lost by the club, United decided to resurrect Reg Brealey's idea from years before of publishing a free newsletter to supporters, containing information about all aspects of the club. The eight-page pamphlet, called *Cutting Edge*, was intended, in the words of its front page, to bring 'supporters of the Blades openly up to date with events at Bramall Lane.' Issue 1 began: 'The boards of both the football club and the parent company recognise that communication with their supporters needs to be improved and this newsletter is the first publication that we intend to circulate on a regular basis.' Additionally, 'Fans' Forums', attended by directors and executives of the club, were to be held regularly throughout the season to ensure that everyone could have the opportunity to raise questions and give advice on their ideas for the betterment of Sheffield United. The newsletter went on to describe some of the details of the 'refinancing' that took place in November 1998. Readers further learned: 'Cash flow statements incorporated within the 1998 accounts and the December 1998 *Interim Report* show that the group has had significant cash outflows before accounting for the loans received during these periods. At present trading levels and without net player sales, Sheffield United PLC will continue to be cash negative on an ongoing basis. Accordingly our player trading must be managed in line with the club's income and banking facilities.' In summary, without selling players, expenditure would outstrip income for the foreseeable future.

The next section detailed the players bought and sold and their accompanying transfer fees. The press, the newsletter said, 'more often than not misquotes the amounts of fees paid and received. We have, therefore, printed below the definitive breakdown of all transfers that have occurred since the club achieved its listing on the Stock Exchange in January 1997 [a period of just over two years].' How the press was supposed to publish accurate transfer figures when the club never released or confirmed them was not explained. The accusation of 'false information appearing in the press' was rather rich when information coming out of the club was conflicting. The tables of players' transfers, into and out of the club, were said to 'show clearly that the expenditure on players during the overall period exceeds the income from sales by around £1 million'. The relevant overall numbers were £9,564,000 out and £8,597,000 in. Salaries for the following season could not continue at the same level as they had done, because: 'In order to ensure that financial stability of our club is restored, we are looking to aggregate the football wage budget for 1999/2000 at around £4.5 million. Naturally, as and when further income is secured for the club, then this would permit us to increase the budget.'

Information regarding the proposed development of leisure, retail and business facilities at Bramall Lane was then itemised, followed by details of the personnel on the board and their financial involvement. There was a chance for a few words of vitriol: 'From comments passed - idly or otherwise - there have at times been accusations that "directors line their pockets" through their involvement with the club. These accusations are grossly incorrect and both damage and frustrate all board members, as it is based upon mis-information. It is noted that pre-contract planning on Blades Leisure Park commenced over three years ago and has very much been sponsored by the efforts of board members. It should be recognised that none of the directors - either personally or via their own companies - have or will directly benefit (other than during the normal course of business on commercial terms) from the club's development activities.'

Next, another oft-asked question was answered; where had the money from the FA Cup and play-offs gone? The answer given explained how the net gate receipts to the club from the play-off appearances in the 1997/98 season were £114,000 and the net gate receipts from eight FA Cup ties in the same season were £735,000. In each case the funds were utilised to meet spiralling players' wage costs and only delayed the inevitable disposals of players, as operating expenses greatly exceeded income. *Cutting Edge* continued, 'We genuinely strive to achieve harmony and openness between the supporters and your boards, and that this will go some way to bridging the gap which previously existed.' The newsletter was an admirable attempt to correct any misinterpretations, rectify falsehoods and clear up misunderstandings, but if all this information had been presented in this manner as and when it happened, all the arguments, accusations and broken promises that followed could have been avoided.

After the end of the season, with the failure of the team to reach the play-offs, McDonald took advantage of the falling share price as their value dipped to 12.5p to buy another two million.   Kevin McCabe also purchased 400,000 shares. McDonald called it 'the bargain of a lifetime,' adding that he wished to take a more active role in the running of the club. Surprisingly, Colombotti did not welcome the offer, saying, 'I think I will have to buy out Mike and I am working on it. The boardroom division has gone on far too long and once the fund-raising issue is resolved there will be a clearer picture. Having 13 per cent of the shares doesn't give anyone control.' True, but such ownership could irritate those seeking control.

Then, instigated by reports that Steve Bruce was contemplating his future at the club following the 'no signings' ultimatum he was given, McDonald remarked, 'I have talked with Steve and I know he's been made promises that haven't been delivered. Of course he's unsettled and we need to sort this out quickly.'   Colombotti was publicly pleading with Bruce to stay: 'I very much hope he doesn't go but one cannot hide the fact that he is unhappy about not having a direct chain of command. Too many people interfere. I have told him that I want him to stay and he has gone away to think about it.'   Bruce's words of response were not encouraging, as he told reporters, 'I have got fed up of being told one thing and then being told another' and spoke of there being 'too many interferences, too many fights, too many battles which stem from the top'. He complained; 'Until we end the bickering we are going to muddle along like we have all season. It's utter frustration.'

Next, and after ten years' service, almost exactly a year after commercial manager Andy Daykin was forced out of the club, club secretary and board member David Capper, one of the signatories to the establishment of the Premier League in 1992, resigned.   With manager Bruce also on the verge of leaving and the post of permanent chief executive still vacant, vacuums in three of the top positions within the club existed. Capper would make no comment on his departure other than to confirm that he wanted discussions about a termination package 'at the earliest opportunity'. McCabe did not seem surprised by his departure: 'The loss of Mr Capper is a huge blow and a major disappointment to me. It is a great pity that circumstances prevail that persuade him to leave.' Capper was tired of the controversy and infighting that had taken place in his years at Sheffield United, none of it his fault. He was a decent man who conducted his duties with integrity. Such qualities were not always appreciated by all those who held power at Sheffield United. The fact that Capper didn't have another job lined up only added to the view that he had simply had enough. He had been particularly frustrated by the influence McDonald exerted during his ostensible year 'away' from affairs. Furthermore, despite Charles Green being no longer officially connected to the club, he was doing McDonald's bidding in terms of trying to buy and sell players without the knowledge of the directors and the manager, thus undermining their work. McDonald was still the major shareholder and it appeared that if he couldn't do what he wanted he would make sure no one else could either. As club secretary Capper was legally responsible for all football matters; his resignation clearly indicated he could no longer accept the way things were being run. Only Kevin McCabe offered him real support from the boardroom at this time.

A few days later Bruce followed Capper by confirming his own resignation. In a public statement Bruce said, 'This is the saddest day of my football life. To take an action like I've done shows how strongly I feel about the situation. I never like to walk away and leave a job unfinished. There are a lot of reasons why I'm leaving but I hope that my leaving will persuade the warring factions to sort themselves out. Unless you have one person in charge who the staff can go to there will always be a problem.' The principled actions of Capper and Bruce could even be said to have helped save the club. Their resignations brought to a head the divisions in the boardroom, allowing McCabe the opportunity to raise his profile and place himself on an equal footing with Colombotti and McDonald. McCabe was to comfortably outlast both of them.

The three main directors were well aware of the problems Bruce had faced. Colombotti lamented, 'The board clearly needs to get its act together in the interests of the club because his departure is genuinely regretted. At the moment there isn't unity.' McCabe added, 'The coincidence of both Bruce and Capper quitting within a few days of each other, both stating reasons of intolerable interference, means the board will immediately have to sort out its own reorganisation to prevent such an occurrence happening in the future. I want a 24-hour cooling-off period before I say any more because I am angry and frustrated at the situation.' McDonald's view was: 'Steve came to see me last week and told me he was very disappointed. I am really sad he feels he has to go. He asked my advice and I couldn't give him any. I told him he knew all the facts and must decide, although I expressed the hope that he would stay. It is not just the loss of the manager that distresses me. The situation is just a shambles. I fell for the five-card trick some time ago when I was led to believe that new people would bring in new money but it hasn't happened. The tragedy is that Sheffield United is such a super club with no big debts. I would come back tomorrow if I had the full support of the people who matter; directors and fans.' Such careful words from all concerned – but who carried the can?

After a couple of days to appraise the situation, McCabe laid it on the line. 'There is no other way out of our current mess; certain directors must go. If we cannot sort it out in the boardroom, by a show of hands if necessary, I will sponsor and pay for a meeting of all shareholders and let them vote for directors. If they vote against me, then so be it. That is a risk I am willing to take.' Ten per cent of the total shareholding was required to call a Special General Meeting. McCabe held just over six per cent but knew he could easily gather together enough support to reach the threshold. The *Sheffield Star* conducted a phone-in poll on the subject of whether Colombotti should resign. Eighty-four per cent voted yes. But no way was Colombotti going to resign. In fact he was going on the offensive. 'It is incredible that he [McDonald] could leave me, a new chairman, with a loss of £6 million and go into press calling the club a shambles. And it is even more astonishing that he should allow publicity in which he claims to be a close friend of Steve Bruce. The truth is quite the opposite. Steve would not be leaving if I was in control. The

McDonald group have exercised incredible interference with Bruce and his players. He and Mr Laurie Turnbull have managed to gain an extraordinary influence over other non-executive directors and created an impossible situation. I have reached the end of my tether and it is time the supporters realised what is going on. I do not like airing boardroom difficulties in public but too much has been said.' Despite this major public criticism of his rival, Colombotti still insisted they could work together. BIFA doubted that was possible, as chairman Andy Nicolson said, 'We don't trust any of the directors but somebody has to take responsibility, and that has to be the chairman. Carlo Colombotti has failed to deliver any of his promises. In three days' time he's going to fail again to raise investment via a rights issue. He should now do the honourable thing…. resign.'

Nicolson was correct about Colombotti failing to raise further investment. Colombotti's self-proclaimed deadline for the long-awaited rights issue of May 21 was fast approaching. When that day passed with nothing happening, he claimed it wasn't really a deadline after all and that the delay was procedural: 'We have not been able to hire a broker so we cannot go ahead with the rights issue as we had hoped.' A London stockbroker speculated why that might have happened, suggesting; 'Brokers may not want to get involved with Sheffield United for historic reasons, not least of which is the fact that their last broker resigned after a dispute with the club.' The broker in dispute, Collins Stewart PLC, claimed it was owed £25,000 in unpaid fees. Colombotti refuted the claim. In a bid to bring some order to the disarray, an emergency board meeting was held towards the end of May. Strangely, it was held without the PLC chairman, Colombotti, but he was 'present' - on the end of a phone line. He protested that he could have attended any day but that day, but the other directors went ahead with the meeting anyway. Senior director Bernard Procter was asked to chair the meeting, at which it was agreed that McDonald would become the spokesman on all football matters until a new team manager was appointed.

A further board meeting was to be held on June 7, which Colombotti could attend in person, at which the formal strategy for the club was to be endorsed. In advance of the meeting McDonald manoeuvred himself into a position to get Blades supporters on his side. Fans were going to have a say in who should be appointed as Steve Bruce's successor, no less. Said McDonald, 'I am absolutely determined to end all the bickering and divisions at Bramall Lane and give us a united United again. And to this end I want an input from the official Supporters' Club, from the shareholders and the Blades Independent Fans' Association. All will be involved in our deliberations. The final choice [of team manager] will come from the board but we will definitely consider any views and opinions our fans might have.' True to his word, representatives of BIFA, SUISA, the Supporters' Club and the Senior Blades were called to meet with McDonald at Bramall Lane to discuss the process by which supporters could become more involved in decision-making. All parties present were required to sign a confidentiality agreement so that the identities of applicants for the manager's job could remain secret and McDonald could talk freely about developments at the club without fear of such comments entering the public domain. That none of the subjects McDonald discussed with the fans' organisations made it into the press proved that they could indeed be relied upon. At the meeting, McDonald outlined his reasons for wanting to 'sort the board out', namely to protect both the investment of his company Texas Group PLC and his reputation in the City. He was adamant that he wanted the Consultative Committee to succeed and pointed out that it was he who appointed Richard Caborn MP as its chairman. McDonald was cognizant of the fact that most fans did not trust him and he wanted to change that situation, which he felt could only happen with the backing of the supporters' groups. Having said his piece, those present were allowed to see the CVs of some 100 applicants for the manager's job, albeit the final shortlist of four had already been decided by the United board. The supporters' organisations were asked their opinions of each of the four and declare which one they favoured. According to BIFA's minutes, the 100 applicants included 'some big names and many nutters'. One applicant was Neil Warnock. It wasn't certain which of the two categories he fell into.

Another interesting point that came out of the meeting was McDonald admitting allowing Charles Green too much leeway. McDonald said he never wanted Green to be appointed as chief executive but was outvoted in the boardroom. All he wanted to do was bring in Green to get the John Street stand built and then move him on to sort out another part of McDonald's business empire. These statements contradicted other accounts from within the club, which claimed that Green's appointment was entirely McDonald's idea. One of McDonald's major gripes was Tony Pritchett's coverage of the club's affairs in the *Sheffield Star*. McDonald was to accuse Pritchett of 'stirring things up' at Bramall Lane and even making up stories in pursuit of a headline. This was a serious allegation. Pritchett was the only avenue the majority of supporters had into what was happening at the club and more often than not his reports were believed. This, though, was McDonald's problem, not Pritchett's - the only way he could get his version of the truth printed in the papers was by releasing press statements and refusing to bite, as was his wont, whenever Pritchett rang him and confronted him with what Colombotti was supposed to have said about him.

The public relations side of the club was in need of a complete overhaul. This was supposed to be the area of United's media officer Andy Pack but nothing much was ever heard from him. This was not his fault; he could only release the information he was given, which probably wasn't much at all. Others in higher positions at the club meanwhile could not restrain themselves from making public pronouncements that often did not have the blessing of their colleagues. One such was McDonald's declaration that he did not wish to be involved with United 'in the long term' and the information that the agreement he signed with Colombotti in November included a clause that obliged Texas to support Colombotti and the board, which meant that McDonald could not vote against anything with which he disagreed. This agreement expired on May 21, probably not coincidentally the day of Colombotti's deadline for the finalisation of the new share issue. Once this day passed McDonald could make his move, relying on the backing of Bernard Procter and Andrew Laver. There was, however, a snag. McDonald explained publicly that Colombotti could not simply be voted off the board as he would demand the immediate repayment of his £750,000 loan and might sue the club for damages. McDonald's preferred approach was, in his words, to 'gradually ease him out'. He claimed that any money promised to Steve Bruce was of McCabe's doing, not his own, which was an outright contradiction of what McCabe had told BIFA. He also said that Bruce had wanted to sell David Holdsworth from the beginning of the season, a statement that contradicted everything Bruce had ever said.

In this contrast of truths, McDonald was fighting McCabe, whom he believed was siding with Colombotti. He was also singing his own praises, when he was to brag about the quality of the players he had brought to the club [Brian Deane and Vassilis Borbokis were two cited], compared to those bought by various managers. Another example of his self-confessed ability to spot good footballers when apparently more-qualified personnel could not came when he said, '[Marcelo's] scoring record is second to none. Nigel Spackman didn't rate him. He had him for seven weeks and in the end it was me and Charles Green who signed him.' Marcelo scored 19 goals in the 1998/99 season. The boasts continued. McDonald claimed; 'Every player I have been involved with we have made money on.' Then the boasts did not quite add up. McDonald said he was so serious about bringing the Colombian Hamilton Ricard to United that he even proposed his company pay for him and lease him to United. This proposal was voted down by the board, so McDonald explained he decided to broker the deal for Ricard to join Middlesbrough. Months earlier McDonald had publicly stated that Middlesbrough were never contenders for his signature. None of McDonald's sweet-talking of fans impressed Colombotti, who fumed, 'It cannot be right for one director, off his own bat, to call the factions together and discuss the future of the club. God knows what he said to them. They even discussed the appointment of the next team manager.

This meeting was not authorised by the board. He had no mandate to call it and none to issue a statement on behalf of the club. Things are coming to a head and, as chairman, I am not willing to sit by and allow Mr McDonald to paint himself as a white knight riding to the rescue of the club. There is a board meeting on Monday, which is building up into a battle. The situation at the club is becoming ludicrous and I will not allow it to continue.' The upcoming board meeting would bring things to a head.

Amazingly, the subsequent board meeting saw Colombotti and McDonald come to an agreement, and a highly unusual one at that. The pair were to be 'joint chairmen' of the PLC. Colombotti's role would be to concentrate on fund raising while McDonald would oversee all football-related matters. They did not, however, appoint a new manager. This would be done a week later. McDonald insisted that whoever was appointed manager, he would be able to make his own decisions on players: 'There will be no interference from the boardroom and whoever stays or goes will be down to the manager.' McDonald's promise that he would involve supporters' groups in selecting the new manager proved not to be hollow. Representatives of BIFA, SUISA, the Supporters' Club and the Senior Blades met with McDonald, his business colleague Laurie Turnbull and United's new managing director/chief executive John Thurman. The business of the meeting was to interview one of the final four candidates, which turned out to be former Manchester United player and Macclesfield Town manager Sammy McIlroy. What McIlroy - and his agent - thought of this arrangement is not known and although McIlroy impressed everyone, the former Stoke City, Everton and Burnley player Adrian Heath was the favoured choice of both the fans and the board, mainly because he had been a player at United in 1996 under the successful managership of Howard Kendall. Heath declined the opportunity to undergo the same interview process that McIlroy endured but this didn't hinder his chances of getting the job. Those at the meeting also learned that another of the candidates, former Wimbledon, Coventry City and Wales national manager Bobby Gould, had withdrawn from the running, walking out after being unhappy that his interview was held in the crowded lobby of a Cardiff hotel.

It was the third year running that Sheffield United had found it necessary to change their manager during the close season. The next manager would be the club's fifth in two seasons. In that same period the club also mislaid several directors, the company secretary, a few chief executives, a commercial manager, a kit man and a physiotherapist. The club was in a big mess. The fans didn't trust, nor like, the chairman. McDonald realised this and to make his task at United a success he attempted to get the fans on his side. He also knew that in support the fans would strengthen his position in the boardroom as he lined up against Colombotti. Therein lay the rub. The many cynical and sceptical Blades fans felt that McDonald was more interested in boardroom contests than running a successful football team. He would counter by saying that a successful team needs a stable board and club administration but the problem was that every time another player was sold or another administrator resigned the chances of United having both a successful team and club diminished. For this McDonald got the blame, thus relinquishing any support he may have previously gained. It was an insuperable balancing act, but then again some would say he brought it on himself. Moreover, the political infighting between McDonald and Colombotti was simply not understood by many ordinary fans, who were not really concerned who came out on top ('They're all as bad as each other' was a phrase commonly expressed). The fans simply wanted a decent team to watch.

Chapter 13

Heath In, Heath Out
Followed By McDonald

Away from the fractious boardroom, disruptions were evidenced in other departments of the club. A new club secretary, John Howarth, who had worked at Burnley and Blackburn Rovers, succeeded the departed David Capper, who weeks after resigning from United joined Hull City to be alongside Stephen Hinchliffe and United's former commercial manager Andy Daykin. Soon after, Promotions Office manager Mick Rooker announced that after over 12 years working at United he too was leaving - to join Hull City. Rooker was a smaller cog in the Bramall Lane wheel but his was the first face most supporters saw when they walked into the club offices, and it was always a smiling one. His personality was infectious and it was impossible to find anybody who had a bad word to say about him. One of his many tasks was to organise and look after the matchday mascots, all of whom regarded him as benevolent uncle. Rooker was someone who would probably have worked for the club he supported for nothing, so his departure was another indication, if any more were needed, that there was deeply embedded unrest at Bramall Lane.

On June 15 the 38-year-old Adrian Heath was duly appointed as United's new manager. He had scarcely had his name painted on his office door when the first outgoing transfer was announced. The Ivorian defender Oliver Tebily was sold to

Celtic for £1.25 million, bringing United a profit on the player of around £1 million in just a few months. Heath said of the deal, 'I assure our fans I am not selling the lad without giving him a chance. We had him at Sunderland [where Heath was assistant manager for a spell] for about two months so I know all about him. I am certainly not under pressure to sell. This is my decision all the way.' Not everyone believed this claim. A few days before Heath's appointment, McDonald was present at a BIFA committee meeting at the Railway Hotel on Bramall Lane, at which he informed the gathering that Tebily was on his way to Celtic. Heath clearly had no say, unless he agreed to the sale before he was appointed. Heath then rebuffed reported interest from Derby County for United's 19-year-old striker Lee Morris, stating, 'I am not saying the boy will never be sold. It would be ridiculous of me to say he is not for sale at any price, but at this moment the furthest thing from my mind is to sell him to anybody. The money talked about now does not tempt me. But you cannot replace 19-year-olds who can score goals.' Soon, bids were coming in for other United players. A Premier League club (believed to be Birmingham City) made an offer for Marcelo. This was turned down by McDonald, who declared, 'First they offered £1 million and that was rejected. Then they said, "If £1 million is not enough then what is?" I just said he is not for sale.' Aberdeen and Blackburn Rovers were then reported to be interested in goalkeeper Alan Kelly, who eventually went to the Lancashire club for £600,000. Again Heath insisted, 'The decision was entirely mine. I just felt it was in the best long-term interests of the football club.' It was hard to believe that Heath wasn't being forced to say what his employers wanted him to say.

As the club continued its endeavours to keep suspicious fans onside, an interview appeared in the *Sheffield Star* with the club's newly-appointed managing director John Thurman. A full-page advert in the same paper, signed by Thurman, thanked supporters for purchasing season tickets. The article informed readers that the Derbyshire-born Thurman, aged 42, had studied at St Andrews University and spent time in the Royal Marines, where he saw active service in the Falklands, Northern Ireland and the South Pacific before moving into business. In his own words, his field of expertise was 'sorting out a mess, financial and operational'. He was now the man charged with the task of reviving the fortunes of Sheffield United, a business that had lost its way on the pitch and had lost the trust of its customers, the fans. It was a financial and operational mess. Thurman stated, 'I get my job satisfaction from picking up a situation with obvious potential and sorting it out. Money isn't particularly important to me; what is is identifying problems, rolling up sleeves, leadership and making things happen. I bought a business, revitalised it, sold it, made money and then looked for an area that was of interest to me. And I believe I have found it. The commercial opportunities in football are limitless. The top clubs are pulling away from the rest and I know enough about Sheffield United, after just ten days, to understand that our public want us to join them, not be envious of them. We have excellent facilities here; the club is virtually a hotel without bedrooms. We have a first-class location, a wonderful site and it is under-utilised. If you have a successful football team it is easier to succeed but a club cannot be reliant on success on the pitch. We have to diversify and guard against those times when the team might not do so well. We have to get into a position whereby if results are not good they are not followed by a dire financial situation. I have been over to the club shop and mingled with customers; some rough and ready but the salt of the earth; others elderly gentlemen, but they all crave the same thing. I have inherited letters and have telephoned the writers and they were absolutely stunned that someone in authority at Bramall Lane should take the trouble. As much as I tried to persuade them to come back, they wouldn't do it. They reserved judgement until they see which way the playing side is headed.'

Another club official who decided it was a good idea that he should have more contact with the supporters was Mike McDonald. One of his first jobs as co-chairman would be to meet the fans or, as he so tactlessly put it, 'take them on, face to face'. He said, 'I have received a lot of letters from disappointed fans who say they won't buy season tickets until things improve and ask what I am going to do about it. I have decided that the best thing to do is to listen to their complaints and put our side of the story. I am absolutely convinced the club is on the right lines now and I hope to persuade them to stay with us. This is my style; to listen and to involve the fans all the way. If the dissidents have anything to say let them say it to my face.' McDonald then tried to raise the hopes and morale of the supporters by stating that Adrian Heath could strengthen his squad, adding, 'I've had 12 months where I've sat outside of the club and decided that something had to be done. I realised in my 12 months away that the club is owned by the supporters and should be run by them.'

His words still seemed somewhat implausible and his motives were - as ever - viewed with suspicion. McDonald was acutely aware that many Blades fans blamed him, despite his protestations, for selling Brian Deane and Jan Åge Fjørtoft, therefore costing United promotion and pushing Nigel Spackman into a corner, thus forcing his resignation. He was also a highly contradictory character, one moment declaring that the club belonged to the fans, the next claiming that they would be the ruin of it because there weren't enough of them attending games. He often spoke of 'drawing a line', 'starting afresh' and 'forgetting the past'. Those words were easy to say but were far more problematical to put into practice. At the same time McDonald wanted Colombotti out but was not able to force the issue because of the money Colombotti had invested. It was therefore very doubtful that the boardroom arguments and unrest had ended but McDonald was now the most powerful man in there and had the backing of at least two other directors.

Finding people willing to back the club financially was proving a problem. Shortly before the start of the 1999/2000 season United's new team strip was revealed. For the first time since 1979 the shirt did not carry the name of a sponsor. This anomaly was not entirely United's fault as Ward's brewery, the incumbent sponsor, had closed down earlier in the year and there was - if excuses need to be found - little time to arrange an alternative. There was, of course, the belief that the situation wouldn't have been allowed to get this far had United had a competent commercial manager. However, instead of holding off for a while and continuing discussions with parties that might be interested in a part-season sponsorship deal, the club announced what can only be described as a botch job. In what was declared as a 'Fan Forum Initiative' between the board, the Supporters' Club, the Shareholders' Association, BIFA and the Senior Blades, fans could donate £5, £10, £50 or £100 and companies £1,000 in return for various packages. The shirt sponsorship scheme was heralded under the puerile banner: 'You've Got To Wear It To Share It'. The new shirts would sport the logo 'Blades United' and the club's crossed cutlasses emblem across the chest. Elaborating on this strategy, McDonald explained; 'It is exciting that the club is being run by the supporters and that is endorsed by the shirt.' The excitement was somewhat limited. Less than £20,000 was raised by this initiative, making it probably the lowest shirt sponsorship deal in the whole of the Football League. It was entirely the wrong time for the club to ask supporters for yet more money; there was simply no faith in the people in charge.

Out of the blue, just before the start of the season and in order to preserve top-class football in the city, John Thurman kicked up a storm by advocating a merger between United and Sheffield Wednesday. In response to the annual survey of football finances by financial analysts Deloitte and Touche that revealed that United and Wednesday lost more money than any other clubs in the 1997/98 season, Thurman suggested that the city was not big enough for the both of them. Speaking before fully considering the enormity of what he was about to say, he remarked, 'If we are both in the Premier then great. If not it's going to be a disaster. If City analysts are saying that then it is something both clubs must consider. People must ask themselves whether they want to watch Carlisle or Luton or Manchester United or Real Madrid in the future.' But to the fans of both clubs, that wasn't the point - they would rather see their own team playing against Carlisle or Luton than a made-up one playing against Real Madrid.

In the ensuing storm played out in the *Sheffield Star*, Wednesday chairman Dave Richards played down the merger talk: 'I cannot imagine what a merger would be like. It's just impossible to make anything like that work. Does anyone believe I would relinquish Wednesday's power? No way. This club has written part of the history of football. It is one of the oldest clubs and one of the most highly regarded. We don't want to give our heritage away.' Richards denied that any discussions on the subject had taken place. 'We have had no contact with Sheffield United over a merger. We had a board meeting yesterday but the subject was not mentioned. It's just not an issue. If United fans want to watch Premiership football and they want Sheffield to be a real, major power, they can come and support us!' The fact that Thurman, a novice in football administration circles, should allow his private thoughts on the future of United to leak out into the public domain proved that he hadn't yet entirely grasped the concept of football supporting. The fact that he could make such a pronouncement without considering the opinions of the board of directors he answered to suggested a naïvety in management.

Thurman put his foot in it again soon after by articulating the familiar refrain that the Bramall Lane attendances were too low. The crowd for the first home game of the season against Walsall numbered 12,581, with around 1,500 away supporters present. Thurman was provoked to remark: 'If gates stay the same as they did on Saturday then that's serious. We are looking for an average of 16,000 - any less means more player sales.' A few days later Thurman tried to get people on his side by admitting that one of the reasons the crowds were not high might just be because it was too expensive to attend. He suggested that the admission price on the kop should come down. It had risen £3 to £14 for the 1999/2000 season. Said Thurman, 'We have alienated the working man and we have got to do something about that. Portsmouth's kop was packed for the first game of the season and it was a wall of sound. It was worth a goal to them. There is no reason why we can't emulate that and get the kop full. We know the only way we can do that is by offering value for money so working people can watch the team they love.' Consequently, kop prices were to be dropped to £10, which pleased uncommitted supporters but alienated season ticket holders who had paid their money - and therefore got the cheaper deal over the course of the season - up front. Thurman was becoming a figure of ridicule amongst Blades fans, who wondered why the club had appointed to such an important position a man who had no experience whatsoever in sport, never mind football. He had mentioned in the past one company he had revived and unsubstantiated stories that did the rounds claimed it was a supermarket. He therefore mockingly became known in some Blades circles as the 'Baked Bean Man'.

Despite threats of having to sell players because of poor attendances, McDonald was at the same time bragging about which players United were going to buy. Once more fans were hearing contradictory messages from the club's leaders. At the start of the season McDonald stated that the club was now financially stable. Then Adrian Heath was reportedly on the verge of spending £1 million on a striker. Then fans learned that United might have to sell and yet again it was the fans' fault for not turning up in sufficient numbers. After what had gone on in the last couple of years with managers resigning and the quality of the team decreasing, whoever budgeted for average crowds of 16,000 was at this juncture in the club's history deluded.

On September 6 a meeting at Bramall Lane, arranged by the Fan Forum, saw supporters invited to question McDonald and Heath. Around 200 attended. The next day the *Sheffield Star* reported that the club had invited offers for Lee Morris and Marcelo and at the same time printed some of the answers and statements from Heath and McDonald. When asked about the likelihood of players being sold, McDonald told fans, '[Marcelo] is the highest-paid player at the club and he knows he can earn himself up to £3 million. That's the package he is looking for and that's above what we can afford to pay.' Heath added, 'We are trying to keep him but it is very difficult. If Marcelo wants to go back to Portugal [where his wife was born and where they owned a house] then we can offer him all the money in the world and he will still go. Sometimes it is better to get £1 million because that's better than nothing.' Heath conceded that he would be tempted to sell Lee Morris if offered 'the right price'. Readers were also to learn that McDonald justified earlier player sales and possible future ones by claiming, 'This club is a selling club and that's what we've had to do. Having a wage bill of £4.5 million and an income of around £7 million means players like Tebily had to be sold. Even gates of 25,000 wouldn't be enough. Gates of 16-18,000 mean we've got to find the money from somewhere else.' When asked about the sale of goalkeeper Alan Kelly, McDonald replied, 'That was probably the finest business deal in my time at the club. He had injuries and was soon to be out of contract. Did he want to leave? The answer is yes. We offered him a tremendous deal, then his agent got involved.' This version of events was refuted by Kelly, who uniquely in the history of Sheffield United players used an internet message board to tell fans that he wanted to remain at Bramall Lane but club finances dictated otherwise. Heath answered questions about why Greek international Traianos Dellas had been allowed to leave for nothing by saying, 'He made it quite clear he wanted to go back to Greece. I think there were 127 games he could have played in when he was here and he was picked for 27 of them. With the wages he was on I didn't try to stop him leaving.' Five years later Dellas, the player Heath was happy to see depart for no fee, starred for Greece as they lifted the 2004 European Championship trophy. At the time he was playing for top Italian club AS Roma and his value was estimated at around £10 million. Kelly, meanwhile, helped Blackburn regain their place in the Premier League in 2001. The club's evident problem remained the wage bill. United had paid players lucrative contracts but could not make it into the Premier League. Later in the month McDonald explained, 'There are a few players who are not good enough and are on too much money.' The weekly wage bill for the playing staff was near £90,000 - just who was it, fans asked, who offered the players those contracts? The answer was Mike McDonald either first-hand or via his side-kick, Charles Green. For all his other faults, one thing that the much-maligned Reg Brealey never did was criticise the level of support. Indeed, he often praised Blades fans for their fervour and passion and never blamed a shortage of money on the fact that attendances were not large enough. It could be argued, though, that McDonald was only following on from the United chairman preceding Brealey. In 1975 John Hassall spoke of his 'continued disappointment at the poor level of support both numerically and vocally at home, and the pathetic following at away games. I am thankful for the existing support, but the players are conscious of the situation. I quote two examples for comparison: 1) When both Birmingham City and Middlesbrough played at Bramall Lane it sounded as if their supporters were the home crowd; 2) The population of Burnley is 78,000 - average gate 17,000. The population of Sheffield is 500,000-plus; average Lane gate 21,000. Are we not entitled to ask the reason why? Gates of 30,000-plus would enable us to compete in the transfer market.' Hassall had good reason to moan - this was during United's most successful season since the War, when they finished sixth in the top division.

Meanwhile at Bramall Lane, Marcelo refused to commit himself to either staying or going. A frustrated Adrian Heath exclaimed, 'I don't want this dragging on throughout the season. If Marcelo decides he wants to leave, then let's do it now.' The player quickly decided he did wish to leave, going to Birmingham City for £1 million, only a few weeks after McDonald supposedly told Birmingham he was not for sale. He was followed soon after by Lee Morris to Derby for a fee of £3 million. Heath said he was 'expecting to get around two-thirds of the money to bring in at least two, and possibly four, new players.' Heath did spend a portion of the money and made the best decision of his short time at the Lane, signing striker Marcus Bent from Port Vale for £300,000. Further incoming activity saw Portuguese midfielder Bruno Ribeiro bought from Leeds United for £500,000. United had therefore brought in £5.85 million from Tebily, Kelly, Marcelo and Morris and spent £800,000; far short of the two-thirds of the proceeds expected by Heath.

Blades fans were confused and annoyed. McDonald stated that Marcelo wanted to leave United for more money, Heath claimed he wished to return to Portugal. The move to Birmingham - which is not in Portugal - suggested that McDonald was closer to the mark. McDonald then somewhat incredibly insisted that he was serious about bringing Georgian international and former Manchester City star Georgi Kinkladze to Bramall Lane on loan from Ajax Amsterdam on wages of £20,000 per week. Days later he admitted; 'At the moment the figures are too high. There is

not a club in the First Division that could afford that package.'
Negotiations with Ajax to sign Kinkladze were apparently on
the go for weeks.   The fact that Kinkladze was said to be
overweight at the time didn't appear to trouble McDonald,
who seemed to believe that if he mentioned Kinkladze's name
often enough Blades fans would be won over.   While Ajax
denied that United had spoken to them about taking Kinkladze
on loan, the player himself was quoted as saying, 'I would like
to return to England and if there is no interest from a
Premiership club then Sheffield United would be fine.'

McDonald did not explain, though, how the club could
trumpet the fact that they were on the verge of signing all sorts
of international players when they had no money.   Ghanaian
striker Artur Moses was then about to sign 'within the next
few days'; Nigerian defender Kingsley Obiekwu was on
seemingly permanent trial.   More names mentioned as possible
signings were former Blade Mitch Ward, now at Everton,
Glasgow Rangers midfielder Derek McInnes, Bradford City
central defender Darren Moore, Sunderland midfielder Kevin
Ball and Norwegian striker Rikhadur Dadason.   No more
players arrived after Bent and Ribeiro.   The plug was finally
pulled on the pursuit of the plump Kinkladze when McDonald
fell back on his usual refrain, saying; 'We had lengthy
discussions but the feeling was we would need an 18,000 gate
to make it pay.'

The Consultative Committee then fell apart.   SUISA named
differences with John Thurman as the reason for its resignation
from the 'Fan Forum'.   Its chairman Dave Windle said, 'We
believe that there are certain people at the club who do not
support the forum and that as a result it is not getting the
benefit from it that it should be.   The one person who in our
opinion is not behind the forum is [Thurman].   We get the
impression he wants to do the job himself and views the
people on the forum as unqualified.   It has turned into more of
a talking shop rather than something that is going to produce
results.'   Windle believed that Thurman did not possess the
necessary expertise to run a football club and added that he
had 'a total lack of understanding of the psyche of the average
fan'.   Windle's opinion was correct.   BIFA's view on the 'Fan

Forum' was voiced by Andy Nicolson: 'The forum represents a huge leap forward in terms of communication with fans' organisations and a number of positive initiatives have resulted, but there needs to be some change to make them more focused and productive.' Nicolson was repeating in more diplomatic terms the valid opinions expressed by Windle; the forum, though an indicator of improved communications between club and supporters, was not achieving the results hoped for by many fans.

Some respite from the disenchantment came from rumours of big money arriving at Bramall Lane. In early October a London-based consortium with American backing was reported to be considering buying United. Another group, apparently 25-strong and from Sheffield, was also apparently interested in taking over but neither McDonald nor his now largely silent co-chairman Colombotti would comment. McDonald continued to talk about being 'disillusioned' and having to 'protect his investment'. Then an Icelandic group entered the picture but McDonald played down the possibility of an imminent takeover, saying, 'We have got through the nonsense period. Now we have got to be a sound business. We don't want any crackpots. We want people who are going to invest in the club. There is room on the board for anyone who wants to come on.' SUISA argued that McDonald was, in the short term at least, the best man for the job and continued to work with him to pursue commercial revenue even though it had withdrawn its membership of the 'Fan Forum'.

At the football club's Annual General Meeting in mid October 1999 neither of the PLC's co-chairmen was present. The football club chairman Kevin McCabe told the meeting that all talk of a merger with Wednesday or moving to a shared stadium was nonsense; 'Bramall Lane is our heritage and our home. It is our lifeblood and one of the oldest stadia in the world. There is no intention of selling Bramall Lane either at PLC or football club level.' McCabe lost one of his allies at this AGM when Bernard Procter resigned from the board citing as the reason 'lack of enjoyment and satisfaction'. One long, drawn-out episode finally came to a conclusion when the remaining Original shareholders voted to accept the club's offer of a free season ticket until 2021/22. From now on there would also be just one AGM, that of the PLC.

There was soon to be further boardroom activity. In late October the *Sheffield Star* reported that United had repaid PLC joint-chairman Carlo Colombotti £800,000 [his £750,000 loan plus interest] to quit Bramall Lane. A piqued Colombotti explained to the newspaper that, 'Either McDonald had to go or I did. The club is not being run properly.' During the period since the two men had been appointed 'joint chairmen', McDonald and Colombotti had just about got along in an uneasy peace. Now they had finally fallen out and Colombotti was to return to London to concentrate on his legal firm. Colombotti faxed a three-page press statement about his departure to the *Sheffield Star*, whose sister paper the *Green 'Un* invited McDonald to respond to each point. It would have done McDonald's image some good if he had declined, but typically he could not avoid getting into a good old slanging match:-

Colombotti: 'From the time of my acquiring 1,785,714 shares in Sheffield United PLC and advancing a loan of £750,000 to the company, Mr McDonald continued to remain involved in the running of the PLC in his capacity as director, albeit mainly through his alternate director, Mr Laurie Turnbull. Additionally he appeared to be able to exercise considerable influence on two other directors, Andrew Laver and, for a while, Bernard Procter. It was most unfortunate that during my time as sole chairman it was impossible for me to implement my strategy for the club given his direct or indirect interference and activities generally. He never actually left the club following my appointment as chairman. I consider my endeavours to have been totally frustrated.'

McDonald: 'The people he is slagging off, Bernard Procter and Andrew Laver, are the ones who agreed to pay him off. If I had my way he wouldn't have got a penny for all the damage he's done. No one else who didn't keep his promises would have got his money back. Sheffield United have been more than generous because he came and didn't deliver. The two directors he names are strong characters – no one influences them. They are from families who have given magnificent support to United. Without them the club would be down the river without a paddle.'

Colombotti: 'Blades Italia, my company, was at all times ready, willing and able to perform its obligations under an agreement made on November 21, 1998 in respect of proposed rights issue and I presented evidence both to Mr McDonald and to the club of the monies available for this purpose. Despite his somewhat aggressive expression of doubt, this was an accurate position. Given these doubts, he expressed quite firmly to the board that he had substantial monies available for this purpose and clearly intimated that they would be so made available and injected into the club, which clearly had urgent need thereof. At that stage no broker had been appointed and there were considerable differences within the board as to what might be an appropriate price for the rights issue.'

McDonald: 'The deal fell through because he didn't do what he said he would. Everyone knows that.'

Colombotti: 'As a result of [McDonald's] desire to step in and "sort" matters out, we agreed that he become joint chairman with myself and would take over responsibility in particular for all footballing matters. His functions have clearly extended beyond this during the past four/five months. The running of the club and its activities have not been at all satisfactory and he has imposed a number of unsatisfactory ideas: (a) Contrary to his promises, he has failed to inject any monies whatsoever into the club; (b) He took it upon himself to adopt a somewhat unusual format for the management of the club by experimenting with the introduction of shareholders/ supporters in this activity. I did not agree that this was either a feasible or proper function for shareholders/supporters, even for a football club. And I do not believe that his meetings with the Shareholders' Association have proved all that productive, nor do I accept that these associations represent the true supporters of the club.'

McDonald: 'A football club is not owned by private individuals. It is owned by the fans and he has got to realise that. The injection of money was never an issue. We didn't think it was right with the share price as low as it was. That was the board's decision, not mine.'

Colombotti: 'The morale at the club is abysmal and the attendances at matches even more so.'

McDonald: 'I think that has been brought about by his reign.'

Colombotti: 'He has adopted a totally dictatorial attitude to the purchase and sale of players without proper consultation and without any apparent strategy for the improvement of the team on the field. To take but one example, perhaps he could advise us as to what has happened to Traianos Dellas, for whom we paid £400,000 and who has left for nothing. The company took up its 12-months option on his contract and therefore he should not have been a Bosman transfer.'

McDonald: 'The company didn't take up the 12-month option. The manager was asked if he figured in his plans and he said no, so we let him go. The decision was made to save £200,000 in wages so the manager could spend that on other players.'

Colombotti: 'The commercial activity generally and the usage of areas such as the banqueting room are beyond depressive description and being dramatically left more under-utilised than last year, when my own colleagues were more closely involved.'

McDonald: 'We have brought a new man in on the commercial side. He must be given a chance.'

Colombotti: 'There appears to be no plans whatsoever for the proper funding of the club in the absence of his injecting any money. The only funding appears to be selling players.'

McDonald: 'I've said all along that our strategy is based on income stream. The current wage bill is in excess of £4.5 million. Dellas, Kelly and Marcelo were all players whose contracts were coming to an end and we did what we thought was best for the club and give Adrian Heath the money to go forward.'

Colombotti: 'The construction of the hotel is overdue, as is the Enterprise Centre. It appears from what I can assess that he [McDonald] is obstructive on both aspects, which is not in the interests of the club. Kevin McCabe has worked assiduously to put together a programme for the immediate development of Blades Enterprise Centre and the Fitness Centre. Both could commence forthwith. If the contract is not placed for the construction of the Enterprise Centre, the grant money will be lost and the relationship established with the Sharrow community will be heavily damaged. There is no reason whatsoever for the board not to see the merits of this programme and immediately approve the same. There appears to be no direction or decision on these very important matters.'

McDonald: 'Once the board is happy that it is in the best interests of Sheffield United to proceed financially then we will do so. If we feel there is no benefit in general then the project will not go ahead. We want to be sure it is viable – there's no point in building a hotel if it's going to be empty.'

Colombotti: 'No shirt sponsor was effected and was simply replaced by a very ambitious alternative of the Blades supporters. Not an appropriate commercial decision. It is well known by the board that my colleagues in Blades Italia had the possibility of a substantial sponsorship with well-known branded companies.'

McDonald: 'The only offer we got was from Carling and there was no agreement in time for the start of the season. We are negotiating a new sponsor for next season.'

Colombotti: 'My proposal for a link with an Italian team along the lines now concluded by Charlton [Athletic] with Inter were not accepted or progressed by the board. I am still in touch with two Serie A teams whereby this could possibly be resurrected in the interest of the club, who could earn monies *on transfer fees for players sent to the UK, this quite apart from footballing ability on the field.'*

McDonald: 'He was in charge and he didn't deliver anybody.' [One player, 19-year-old Francesco Meacci, did come over from Italy on trial in March 1999 but nothing more was heard of him].

Colombotti: 'This highly unsatisfactory situation should not be allowed to continue. Mr McDonald should: a) Answer these specific points to the Sheffield public; b) State categorically his plan for the immediate and urgent funding of the club, his reasons for obstructing the hotel and Enterprise Centre, his remedies for the commercial sector and infrastructure of the club generally; c) Otherwise resign. Sheffield United is a major football entity with a very considerable potential and it should be properly exploited and not end up as a Third Division club.'

McDonald: 'I have made it quite clear that I don't want to be here. It's a matter of sorting things out. We are looking to strengthen the board and bring in a non-executive chairman. I would step down tomorrow once things are put right. My record stands up to be shown and in the last 18 months the club has gone backwards at a rate of knots. I don't attend the games and my situation at the club has not changed. I just want people to see what is going on.'

One former United director (possibly Bernard Procter) who did not wish to be identified was quoted as siding with Colombotti: 'I don't particularly like Carlo Colombotti but everything he said is true. There are only two people on the football club board now and a number of Sheffield businessmen have been approached, but no one is willing to join because they know the situation. They know they will have no control. It was McDonald who brought in Colombotti in the first place, through Phillip Wood, because they wanted his money. The deal was that Wood would be chief executive but he only lasted a few months. I am also convinced the money to pay him off did not come from the bank.' McDonald couldn't resist making a final derisory swipe at the departing Colombotti: 'Empty vessels make the most noise. Carlo Colombotti is a piece of history that should never have happened. He is gone and he is yesterday's news. If he is full of sour grapes, then I'm disappointed. Colombotti failed to come up with the goods. He's had his bottom smacked, and he's been sent back to London and he doesn't like it.' Colombotti then disappeared from the football scene until he mounted a failed bid to buy Italian *Serie A* club Siena several years later.

Meanwhile, the struggling United team, having lost several players, was being linked with many others. After failing to sign Kinkladze, Moses and Obiekwu, McDonald had to do something to convince the fans that he was trying to buy good players, so the name of Bradford City defender Darren Moore gained prominence. It was reported that Moore was available for around £600,000 but that United had offered half a million. McDonald refused to up his bid, insisting that Bradford should do what he had to do with Marcelo: 'I valued Marcelo at £2 million but we had to let him go for almost nothing. Our problem is the wage bill. We have got to get below 30 players and we have 37. Buying players is not a problem, never has been and never will be. We are OK at the bank and we can buy so long as we can work within the wage structure.' Just why United's problems should force Bradford to lower their asking price for Moore was not evident. Heath was becoming increasingly frustrated and in a 'clear the air' meeting with the board was told that he could bring in Moore but would then have to sell before signing anybody else. After the board meeting the club issued a statement, saying, 'The board is backing Adrian Heath's judgement on what is immediately required and United have gone back to Bradford with another bid for Darren Moore.' However, Bradford City chairman Geoffrey Richmond poured scorn on the supposed improved offer by commenting sarcastically, 'Sheffield United have made a statement saying they have made a new bid. This comes as a surprise to me. I suppose I will have to play hell with the postman.'

It came as no surprise to Blades fans that Bradford did sell Moore - to Portsmouth. An unnamed 'club insider' said in the

Sheffield Star, 'I think for a while Adrian was quite confident he would get the money he needed [to buy Moore]. But in recent days his demeanour has changed as it has become obvious to him that there have been problems.' *Sheffield Star* reporter Martin Smith continued the theme: 'Nigel Spackman left when he saw what the club was becoming. Steve Bruce brought £4 million into the club before he realised the cash flow was strictly one way. Now Adrian Heath is beginning to realise what he has taken on. At least two local businessmen have been approached to join the board but have declined to do so while Mike McDonald is in charge.' BIFA followed SUISA by pulling out of the 'Fan Forum' arrangement and demanded that McDonald resign, claiming that promises had not been delivered and that fans did not trust him.

As usual, McDonald went on the offensive, defending his record and deflecting the blame elsewhere: 'It's like watching people commit suicide. They want someone else to come in but no one else would put up with it. I have said before that I would walk out of here tomorrow if someone will come and take over. The way I feel today they could have it for nothing. [Trust] has always been a problem at Sheffield United. However, I don't believe I have been anything but honest, even to the point of upsetting the fans. I am not a yes man and speak my mind rightly or wrongly. The truth is the wage bill was over £6 million a year when I came back to the club. It's now around £4.5 million and we budgeted that we could afford that on crowds of 16,000 and we aren't getting that many. If they don't turn up for games we can't buy players.' Spoken from the heart no doubt, but confusingly these words came only days after he had said that buying players was not a problem. McDonald also gave his version of the 'Darren Moore affair'. 'The board felt that £500,000 was a fair price, notwithstanding he is free under the Bosman ruling in six weeks' time to sign for any club he wishes. The fact is that the player was asking for a wage that would have undone the work currently taking place at Sheffield United and taking us back to well over the £4.5 million required to balance the books.'

The attendance for the game against Bolton on November 14 was just 10,013. United lost 2-1. A few dozen stayed behind to protest, chanting, 'Sack the board!' and 'Where's the money gone?' but now even the protests were half-hearted. One Blades fan joked, referring to McDonald's favourite club, 'If this was a proper club like Manchester City there'd be thousands of fans protesting, not just fifty!' Once more McDonald, who hadn't been at the match, denied all responsibility: 'Any further unrest, I believe, will take this club into the Second Division. The unrest at both Sheffield United and Sheffield Wednesday is driving both clubs downwards. I cannot perceive that anybody will invest in Sheffield United until they can see that their investment has the support of the people.' These words were redolent of Reg Brealey when trying to dispose of his shares in 1994/95.

Heath was gradually letting his feelings be known to a wider public. He appeared resigned to his fate, sounding ominously like Nigel Spackman and Steve Bruce before him. 'I fully understand the supporters' reaction to continually seeing the better players sold,' he said. 'We have got to soldier on and stick together. I will keep going as long as I can.' McDonald still insisted that none of the difficulties were his fault: 'I want out of this club as soon as possible. People at Texas are urging me to leave. The fans don't want me and I have had enough of this abuse. All I hope is that the next time Sheffield United supporters get a Mike McDonald they treat him better than I have been.' And in a strange mirror of the boardroom differences, SUISA now found itself divided. Three of its committee resigned when they disagreed with the organisation's decision to propose a vote of no confidence in the board at the forthcoming PLC Annual General Meeting. A faction, led by Peter Salt and backed by Martin Brammer, wanted the board to resign, believing that the club would be better run by a legally appointed administrator. Those who disagreed, including chairman Dave Windle and John Plumtree, argued that administration would only bring closer the possibility of assets being sold and, subsequently, a merger with Sheffield Wednesday. Windle and Plumtree resigned their positions. United director Bernard Procter appeared to sympathise with the faction headed by Salt and Brammer, stating, 'There isn't a problem with directors resigning.

Nobody is happy here. But if we step down, then who will take over?'

The fateful day of Bramall Lane resignations - November 23, 1999 - was growing ever closer and little Port Vale were the unwitting catalyst. On this day the two men who held the top posts at the club quit. The *Sheffield Star* reported on its back page: 'A routine finance meeting before tonight's visit of Port Vale now becomes the potential dawning of a new regime.' At the meeting, directors Kevin McCabe, Bernard Procter and Andrew Laver asked McDonald to step down; if he refused they had resolved to vote him out of the chair, and McCabe would take over. The newspaper reported there were at least two Sheffield businessmen waiting to join the board – but only if McDonald was gone. The PLC annual accounts had just been published, showing a loss for the year of £4.2 million, a reduction in turnover of almost 25 per cent, and a drop in average home attendance from 17,946 to 16,243. One ray of light was profits on player transfers of £2.4 million.

Without a win in seven games, United hosted one of the few teams below them in the Division One table. The attendance was just 8,965. Despite taking the lead, United were awful and surrendered to a miserable 3-1 defeat. Not many of those present knew that McDonald had resigned before the match and a bigger shock greeted them soon after the final whistle – manager Heath quit too, after only five months in charge. He therefore became the fourth consecutive Sheffield United manager to resign. Both the ex-chairman and the ex-manager expressed regret the following day. McDonald said, 'I felt that my tenure was over and I am now looking to pastures green. I don't want to put financial pressure on them [by asking for his £500,000 loan back] or sell players. I wish them all the best for the future.' Heath explained his departure: 'It was not an easy decision. I think the majority of supporters think that I came with Mike McDonald and would probably be happier if I left. The players are finding it increasingly difficult to play here so maybe a fresh start would be better. The decision is entirely mine. This job is not a poisoned chalice; I would recommend it to anyone. But I did think the "outside interests" would not have affected the job. Clearly they have.'

Heath had once told a BIFA meeting, 'I will leave this club by getting the sack. I will not walk out unless I am not told the truth.' One could only assume, therefore, that he had not been told the truth.

A policy of selling a string of Premier League-quality players (Tiler, Ward, Deane, Fjørtoft, Taylor, Hutchison, Holdsworth, Stuart, Saunders, Marcelo, Morris, Borbokis, Dellas, Kelly) in under three years could only lead to only one thing. McDonald kept reminding everyone that the club couldn't survive paying wages of £7 million in 1997 and £6 million in 1998, and that a salary budget of £4.5 million had been set for 1999/2000, based on an expected average crowd of 16,000. However, what neither he nor his colleagues seemed to grasp was that better players are usually the higher earners, thus when they are sold to reduce the wage bill the quality of the team diminishes, the results get worse, the attendances start to drop, the wage bill has to be reduced still further because you can't afford £4.5 million any more, so you sell a couple more of your better players, the team gets worse, the results get worse......

The average football supporter accepts this logic, and McDonald's beloved Manchester City apart, what other club anywhere in the country had seen attendances rise as the team worsened and plummeted down the table? The only person able to put a brake on this downward spiral was McDonald himself. He may very well have ended up with a financially secure Sheffield United PLC, but it would have been at a footballing standard several levels below the lower reaches of the First Division, as it was then. Many people felt that McDonald was deliberately bringing the club down to make a merger with a similarly financially-stricken Sheffield Wednesday all the more easy, and his veiled comments, when he often mentioned in the same sentence the situations in which United and Wednesday found themselves, lent weight to that view. Fans of both teams were disgruntled at events on and off the field and McDonald judged that they might be open to his idea.

Even after he had left the club, McDonald wouldn't let drop discussion about a possible Sheffield merger. In February 2000 he positioned himself in the headlines when interviewed on BBC Television's *Money Programme* and in other media. He wanted to keep the merger (and no doubt himself) in the forefront of people's minds. He said, 'Currently we are doing feasibility studies to find out the cost. If we can sell the two grounds and have one new stadium near the M1 and the new airport, that would be the way forward I believe. There is plenty of support. There are a lot of people in the city who want to play at the highest level and do not want to be fighting relegation every season. There is a lot of financial support for a merger but there is no appetite for investment in Sheffield Wednesday or United in their current state. Sheffield United is the first result I look for and there is nothing I would like better than for United to go up and Wednesday go down, but you have to look at what's good for Sheffield. The way forward is to form one club that can have a go at Manchester, the French and the Italians. If I had my way I would put the clubs together, play in red, white and blue and get on with it. I see Sheffield as the place where football started and it could be the place where football changes. If [the fans] sat down for half an hour and thought about the good points and the bad points then they would see I am right.'

However, Sheffield Wednesday secretary Alan Sykes' response was to state that a merger would never happen. 'We have no plans to merge with Sheffield United and we believe both clubs can maintain their own identities and be successful in their own right. This city is big enough to support two big teams.' The newly appointed United football club chairman Derek Dooley agreed: 'As far as I'm concerned the merger is a non-starter and I know of no interest from Sheffield Wednesday. The club itself is not involved in any feasibility studies about a merger.' BIFA held meetings with the Wednesday Independent Supporters' Association (WISA) and the two organisations agreed that a merger could never take place. A few weeks after raising the subject, McDonald eventually saw sense and conceded that his idea for a United/ Wednesday merger was a non-starter, stating, 'If the supporters don't want it, then so be it. The will of the people has been decided – they have come back and said they don't want it. The voice of the people has spoken. It is sad really. I was never pursuing it anyway. We just needed to let people know the options.' Despite no longer being a director, McDonald was still United's biggest individual shareholder with around 14 per cent and with a £500,000 loan to the club still in place. He had 'influence' over 20 to 30 per cent of the total shareholding because of shares held by his wife, his associates and his companies. He maintained regular contact with the Bramall Lane board because, he said, 'I don't want to see what I have built undone.'

Meanwhile, as a further move towards stability and to strengthen the communications between the football club and the PLC, Derek Dooley was invited by the other directors to join the PLC board. He immediately denied that a prompt re-payment of McDonald's loan would force distance between the former chairman and the club, arguing, 'He would still be the major shareholder and as a result entitled to pursue whatever plans he wants. But he is not on either board and at the moment paying him back is not a high priority.' Dooley's next move was to approach former Promotions Office manager Mick Rooker to attempt to entice him back from Hull City. The club had been sadly lacking in the fund-raising and commercial departments since the departures of Rooker and one-time commercial manager Andy Daykin. It didn't take much inducement for Rooker to agree to return now that McDonald had left. With Colombotti and McDonald gone, the club was now slowly embarking on the road to getting back to its tradition of being run by local men, fully aware of the heritage of the club and the particular demands of Sheffield's football supporters. Sheffield-born Kevin McCabe, Andrew Laver and Derek Dooley were now in charge, and were soon to make a decision that would come to have a great bearing on the events of the next few years, with the appointment of a Sheffield-born lifelong Blade as the manager.

Chapter 14

All The Sheffield Men
Back On Track

After the resignations of Heath and McDonald, Derek Dooley had once more stepped into the breach and took over as 'caretaker chairman'. His first big task was to find a new team manager. He defined what he was looking for: 'We need somebody who has been there and done it. I think that was one of Adrian's problems – he had very little experience of management. There are some good coaches out there – and I think Adrian is one of them – but they don't always make the best managers.' Then, transposing a common aphorism in reference to the team's performances, he amusingly added, 'I think the booing of individuals is just pouring oil on troubled waters.' Just over a week later, on December 1, 1999, Neil Warnock was appointed as manager, on his 51st birthday. It was well known that Warnock was a born-and-bred United fan and he had now been given the job he had reportedly craved his entire career. A year earlier, when manager of Bury, after a 3-3 draw with United at Gigg Lane he famously wore a Sheffield United tie to the televised post-match interview.

Speaking in the third person upon his appointment, Warnock was to say, 'I don't think Neil Warnock would have been in for it if the club had been in a healthier situation. Results-wise it's been disappointing and there are some horrendous fixtures coming up. But at last I think the club is together and that is the most important thing. The boardroom now has unity and the fans have got to realise that. I am a fan as well, which helps, and my job is to try and get the players believing as passionately as I do in the club. I remember the day, as a fan, when they sold Brian Deane and Jan Åge Fjørtoft. It was like when President Kennedy got shot – that's how deeply I felt. I know there is no money available. Everybody knows that and it is a difficult situation and we've got to rectify that as soon as possible. But I have done a 15-to-20-year apprenticeship to be here. It is a job that has always been at the top of my list. My objective is to make sure they [the fans] come back and I need to put number 12 on my team-sheet as the crowd. I want them to influence officials and other teams. I believe that when the United crowd are on song they are worth a goal start. They have got to forget their differences with the players and if a player has a nightmare now they've got to get behind him. If anyone thinks it is going to be an easy job staying up they've got another thing coming. I want them to help me fulfil my long-term ambition to be the best club in Sheffield, in the Premier League.'

Warnock also held an interview for United fanzine *Flashing Blade*, in which he said, 'It's taken a long time [to come here] because I think they've always wanted big names, and the fans have as well. It's up to me now to make sure that I get the right response from everybody for whatever period I'm here. I want to work for the next five or six years and I want to work with Sheffield United for that length of time, but results will determine that. I have ambitions to manage in the Premiership before I finish and I hope it's with us.' Despite never being officially connected with the club, Warnock displayed a sound knowledge of what had been happening at Bramall Lane. He admitted being a shareholder, and said his son attended every home game. When asked whether the club's financial situation would have put him off taking the job the previous summer, his response was light-hearted: 'Actually, after the Port Vale game my son rang me up and said he thought I would be daft to come here. I did write to McDonald after Steve Bruce was appointed, asking him to keep an eye on me, even though he didn't know me, when he came to choose the next one. I didn't even get a response, so I wasn't optimistic about getting the job while Mike was here.'

Warnock was never shy of self-promotion and knew what fans liked to hear. He claimed to be receptive to the new board, glad that they were now all Sheffield men and all fans of the club, but remarked at the same time that the fact that they were fans may have clouded their judgement in the past. With them, though, he knew where he stood: 'If they tell me I have to raise money they'll give me enough time to do that and it would be up to me who goes and when.' The obvious difference between this policy and what went before, when McDonald seemed to have more influence over such matters than the manager, was not lost on Warnock. In fact, he knew he had to both generate money and cut the wage bill and this was the reason behind his immediately placing Portuguese midfielder Bruno Ribeiro and leading scorer Martin Smith on the transfer list. Circulating the names of other players, he realised the wages they were on made it difficult for other clubs to sign them. Aware of where such contracts came from, Warnock seethed, blaming Charles Green for the situation. 'Charles Green….. he's got summat to answer for,' he fumed.

He then made a cutting comment about the state the club had got itself into regarding the salaries it paid. When Don Hutchison moved to Everton, part of the deal brought Everton reserve defender Jon O'Connor to Bramall Lane. O'Connor played as little in United's first team as he had done in Everton's and yet Warnock exclaimed incredulously, 'Jon O'Connor….. he's on more than me!' (Warnock's first contract at United earned him a basic £102,000 per year). Strengthening links between the club and the community was also high on Warnock's list, as he cited the visit to the training ground the day before of a young boy who had had two heart transplants, although he admitted such things would have to wait until he had a bit more time to get them organised. 'I'd like to take the players out to one or two companies and factories but I just haven't had time. It's something we'll be doing next season.' This sort of thinking had been completely lost to the club over the previous few years.

At the same time that Dooley came back, Bernard Procter was persuaded out of retirement to become the PLC chairman. This meant that, with the additional resignation of Manchester-born Stewart White from the football club board, Sheffield United was entirely back in the hands of Sheffield men, both in the boardroom and the manager's office. Another boost came with the news that Cayman Islands tax exile United fan Martyn Burke had bought £250,000 worth of shares. Burke last became involved with the club when McDonald bought out Reg Brealey in 1995. However, he pulled out unexpectedly a few days later, clearly finding something he didn't like the look of. Now, four years later, a similar situation arose; United soon repaid Burke his £250,000 and he returned to the Caribbean. The reason for the split was given by the *Sheffield Star* as Burke's 'remoteness' from Sheffield, but discord with other board members on future transfer policy was also suggested. The differences with other directors were reported to revolve around Burke's wish to tighten the purse strings further. It was also rumoured that he had had a stand-up row with Dooley after Burke asked, 'How much money have you ever put in the club?' Another reason for Burke's disappearance was that he was astounded at the club's failure in the area of corporate hospitality: the income from this source was only £88,000 in the year to June 30, 1999. The previous year the figure had been £497,000, emphasising the destructive effect of Andy Daykin's departure.

It was the third time Burke had been close to playing a part in the running of the club, and the third time he had walked away. He was never linked directly with Sheffield United again. He became a successful racehorse owner, his affections for the Blades being revealed in the name of one of his horses, Essyoueffcee, which was good enough to win a Listed race. Burke's best result as an owner came when his horse Guinea Hunter won the 2001 Stewards' Cup at Goodwood at odds of 33/1, netting prize money close to £100,000 and a lot more in winnings if Burke placed a bet on his own horse.

United meanwhile made pledges to Blades supporters in sentences never seen before. The second issue of the club's new newsletter *Cutting Edge* was published in December 1999. It was headlined 'New Chairman's Call to Arms'. Dooley, back for a third spell in charge, called for supporters to forget what had happened and pull together for future success. The newsletter highlighted some of the achievements and objectives of the new-look football club. Furthermore, under an article headed 'A Fresh Start' Bernard Procter wrote, 'It is paramount that directors and executives take time out to communicate with all supporters. However, we would hope that media interest in filling column inches within their newspapers reporting matters other than team affairs recedes.' Early the following year United issued its 'Customer Charter Code of Practice', which detailed the values and responsibilities adopted by the club under headings such as 'Accessibility', 'Consultation and Information', 'Community Activity', 'Staff Conduct' and 'Customer Care and Service'. The directors laid out their aspirations: they would be 'Open', 'Responsive', 'Unrelenting', 'Positive', 'Inclusive' and 'Professional'. After years of seemingly continuous controversies, arguments and name calling, this was a club trying its hardest to re-invent itself.

The club's finances were certainly on the turn. In January 2000 United announced a profit of almost £1.7 million thanks to player sales. Not long afterwards, following the further sales of Martin Smith, Petr Katchouro, Aidan Davison, Shaun Derry and Jon Cullen, the wage bill was reduced to manageable levels. Remarkably, Warnock had done this at the same time as pulling the team out of relegation trouble. When Warnock took over, the annual wage bill for the playing staff was over £4.5 million; it was now under £4 million. Director Andrew Laver stressed it wasn't all good news: 'We still have an overdraft and I don't like paying interest to anyone. We still have got significant loans owed to directors and I'm not particularly comfortable about that.'

The newly constituted board was committed to developing young players as it was aware that paying big transfer fees and wages for experienced players was out of the question. It endeavoured, therefore, to press forward with its bid to gain Youth Academy status from the Football Association for its Abbeydale Grange training facilities, despite the 1998 failure to secure National Lottery funding to assist with the project. However, United's plans were jeopardised when Sheffield City Council announced that it was going to evict the club, through the courts if necessary, from the grounds. The Council claimed that the club had not fulfilled its obligations to develop the site as a Regional Football Academy in line with Football Association guidelines. Bemused by the statement, United said they knew nothing about such a decision. Flabbergasted by the Council's decision to end the lease and denying that they had even been informed about it, United threatened to occupy the site on a 24-hour basis to prevent their removal. Managing director John Thurman asked for written clarification of the Council's decision and said, 'The club is submitting its business plan for the Academy to the Football League. It states that Abbeydale Grange will be the site of the Academy. Our expectation is that we will get approval from the Football League because the site meets the parameters they have set.' Council spokesman Phil Andrews answered, 'We accept that the club is saying that their interpretation of the talks which led up to this is different to ours. We will have to agree to differ. Officers will now talk to the club about bringing the tenancy to a conclusion and we will try to do it amicably.'

The Council's threat to evict United was welcomed by some of the residents of adjacent Carterknowle Road and Springfield Road who had long objected to the development plans. Not only were they unhappy at the proximity to houses of the proposed Academy, neither did they like the players' invective! The *Sheffield Star* spoke to a few people in the vicinity of the training ground. One local, Albert Needham, said, 'I work on a few houses in Springfield Road. What upsets the old ladies round here is the language. You can hear them swearing from the garden. This is supposed to be a residential area.' They also complained about the traffic and parked cars. Another man allowed to opine said that it wasn't all bad. Joseph Cotterill of Springfield Avenue remarked; 'Since the club has been here they've put a fence and some gates up, which has stopped the gangs of youngsters hanging around in the park.' John Thurman attempted to defend the club's position, saying, 'I have checked and we have had two formal written complaints. They related to parking and access, with people complaining about cars parking across drives. Usually our players and visitors drive into the ground and use the car parking next to the pavilion, not access roads.' And in what sounded like a tongue-in-cheek response to the swearing issue, he added; 'If we had [used bad language] I'm sure Neil Warnock would have had something to say about it. He's very strong on discipline.' Warnock was famous for using 'industrial' language and a few years later a *Sky TV* documentary with Warnock as the subject was liberally strewn with 'bleeps' to blank out his expletives.

Arising out of the problems with the Abbeydale Grange training facility, United appointed Alan Bamford as a director. For 17 years Bamford had been a director of the Henry Boot construction company. He was tasked to seek out and consider other possible locations for an Academy. There were three or four sites United had in mind. Soon after Bamford's appointment United revealed they were to abandon the Abbeydale site and pay £2 million to buy the 19 acres that was the former Sheffield Forgemasters sports ground at Shirecliffe, an area north of the city centre that was generally regarded as home to Sheffield Wednesday supporters. Derek Dooley admitted that this purchase would make even less money available for new signings, saying, 'Fans may say the money could be spent on buying players but the club is firmly committed to a strong, successful youth policy. It does mean we won't have any money to buy players, but we need to develop our own players.' When complete, the Academy would house several full-size pitches, indoor and outdoor synthetic pitches, a variety of other training facilities and educational units. United applied for full planning permission early in 2001. Academy status for the new complex was granted in April of that year. The news was confirmed by the Football Association's Sheffield-born technical director Howard Wilkinson. Neil Warnock's brother John, a former teacher at Sheffield College and one-time coach of the British Universities football team, was then appointed as Academy director. Originally brought into United's youth set-up by Dave Bassett, Warnock spoke of his dream of taking the club back to the 1960s, when 'our first team [was] filled with high-quality players from the Yorkshire region'. Around the same time Ron Reid, who had worked as the assistant to Neil

Warnock at Bury and Oldham, was given the role of youth team manager.

Final planning permission for the Academy was sanctioned by the City Council in August 2001. The objections of many local residents, mainly regarding traffic problems, were quietly resolved. Work to construct the indoor arena and to upgrade existing pitches and facilities began in February 2002. In November 2002 United received a grant of £838,000 from the Football Foundation[9] to assist in making the Academy fully functional for the use of the 'local community'. The Football Foundation's chief executive Peter Lee commented, 'This superb new facility is providing the next generation of footballers with some of the best facilities in the country.' The official opening of the Academy took place in early December 2002. The ceremony, performed by Blades fan (and former director) and by then Minister of Sport Richard Caborn, saw the Mayor of Sheffield, Marjorie Barker, in attendance. Director Alan Bamford was quoted as saying, 'We have a wonderful relationship with the local community and they will have full usage of the indoor and outdoor pitches, along with the other facilities, including tennis, netball, bowls and the social club. This will ensure the project becomes a commercial and viable proposition, therefore justifying the commitment to funding by the PLC board.' Neil Warnock added, 'It would have been easy to have pumped all that money into just buying players. But then if we'd gone down that route we could have ended up with [financial] problems. Instead we were brave, looked to the long term and decided to put our money into that. We decided a long time ago that this was the best way forward.'

Over the next few years the Academy produced many players who made Football League appearances, albeit often when on loan at other clubs. Not all the Academy protégés made good

---

[9] Replacing the Football Trust in 2000, the Football Foundation is a body dedicated to providing funding to grass-roots football and community projects. Its annual budget of over £50 million comprises grants from the FA Premier League, the Football Association, Sport England and the Government.

business sense. In August 2005 young striker Billy Sharp was sold by Warnock to Scunthorpe United for £100,000, only to be re-purchased by Bryan Robson, his successor as manager, two years later for £1.6 million, then was sold again in 2010 to Doncaster Rovers for £1.15 million. Stephen Quinn, Nicky Law, Kyle Naughton, Kyle Walker, Matthew Lowton and Jordan Slew played league football for United's first team, while Kevan Hurst (£200,000 to Scunthorpe United), Jonathan Forte (£100,000 to Scunthorpe United) and Jacob Mellis were sold on. The deal for Mellis was unusual as he never made a first-team appearance for United. At the age of 16 he moved to Chelsea for what would be a maximum fee of £1.3 million, based on what he achieved as player. He proved to be a regular in the Chelsea team that reached the final of the FA Youth Cup in 2008. Several more Academy graduates (including Evan Horwood, Ryan Cresswell, Adam Chapman and Jamie Annerson) were allowed to join other clubs without a fee but with a 'sell-on' clause included in the deal so United might benefit financially from any future sale. The biggest coup for the Academy came with the sale of the two Kyles - Naughton and Walker, both of whom had progressed as far as to the England Under-21 squad - to Tottenham Hotspur in the summer of 2009 for a combined fee of £8.6 million, which, if certain attainment (playing) criteria were met, could rise to £10 million. United's 2009 *Annual Report and Accounts* stated that since 2000, twenty Academy graduates made appearances for United's first team and another 41 played elsewhere in the Football League. The report valued at £24 million the players produced by the Academy, which in the opinion of the authors, seemed rather generous. The calculation, however, was not explained. The objective in building the Academy was that it would be self-financing by the use of its fitness centre, which was open to the public, and its hiring out of facilities. Any money accrued by selling players could then be assigned to strengthening the senior team.

Backing up his stated commitment to promote young players to the first team, Neil Warnock introduced three who were to become mainstays of his period in charge at Bramall Lane. The trio, Nick Montgomery, Michael Tonge and Phil Jagielka, progressed through United's youth set up before the establishment of the Academy and played important roles in Warnock's ever-eventful term as manager. The three had arrived at United at the age of 16 after being released by Leeds United, Manchester United and Everton respectively. Montgomery and Tonge were signed by Steve Bruce and Jagielka by Kevin Philliskirk in his position as youth team manager. The Academy was apparently a fruitful environment for the Warnock family. Gary Armstrong was a member of the Academy board for a six-month period in 2003-2004 that coincided with the appointment of John Warnock – Neil's brother – as its director, a position that was not put out to a competitive interview process. Armstrong resigned from the Academy board for a variety of reasons but whilst on it was to argue, unsuccessfully, that anyone in the position of Academy director should be answerable to the board, not voting on it. The regular presence of Neil Warnock's son, James at the facility in his role of football agent with the Leeds-based agency Hayden Young did not apparently concern the club's directors. Unsubstantiated stories circulated around Blades fans suggesting that the Academy was a source of supplementary income for Neil Warnock as well. One year, a Christmas 'bash' was held for Academy boys from the age of nine upwards and their parents. The guest speaker was the first-team manager – Neil Warnock – who agreed to attend and speak but, according to his critics, wanted £500 cash to do so. Innuendo surrounding Warnock's penchant for money-making was commonplace in the stands, in pubs and on internet message boards. For this reason a sizeable section of United fans never accepted Warnock and took any opportunity to accuse him of impropriety. The authors have found no evidence to support such claims.

Others might say any such monies would have been small reward for his achievements. After taking United clear of relegation when he joined the club in the 1999/2000 season, Warnock gradually improved the team until it was able to make a challenge on three fronts in 2002/03. All three ventures were ultimately unsuccessful as the Blades were beaten 3-0 by Wolves in the play-off final at the Millennium Stadium in Cardiff and lost two cup semi-finals: to Arsenal,

1-0 in the FA Cup at Old Trafford, and 3-2 to Liverpool on aggregate over two legs in the League Cup. The previous season had provided an occasion that nearly cost Warnock his job. This was the match that became known as the 'Battle of Bramall Lane'. In March 2002 promotion-chasing West Bromwich Albion were the visitors to Bramall Lane and took advantage of the early sending off of United goalkeeper Simon Tracey to build a 2-0 lead. Midway through the second half Georges Santos and Patrick Suffo, both United substitutes, were red-carded for violent conduct, after which Albion scored a third goal against the eight men. The double dismissal arose from a dangerous challenge by Santos on Andy Johnson, which propelled the Albion midfielder into the air. Probably not coincidentally, the same two players had been involved in an incident a year earlier, when Johnson was a Nottingham Forest player, in which Santos suffered fractures to his cheekbone and eye socket. After the West Brom game Santos insisted his challenge on Johnson was not motivated by retribution but the visual evidence did not support his claim. The brawl that erupted following the foul saw Suffo headbutt Albion captain Derek McInnes. Both United men were sent off without touching the ball. Then the departures from the field of the injured Michael Brown and Rob Ullathorne, with all three substitutes already deployed, left United one short of the minimum permitted quota of seven players. With eight minutes remaining, referee Eddie Wolstenholme had no option but to abandon the game. The fall-out proved almost terminal for Warnock's reign at Bramall Lane.

Albion's Sheffield-born manager Gary Megson claimed he had overheard 'an unnamed person on the United bench' instructing Brown to leave the pitch. In so doing the match would have to be called off. Some were to infer that the 'unnamed person' was Warnock. Sports Minister Richard Caborn, present at the match and apparently within earshot of the United bench, backed Megson's view. He said, 'Neil Warnock's behaviour appeared to be an absolute disgrace. He seemed to be encouraging players to go down.' Warnock denied giving such instructions, though he did admit to telling Brown to come off if he was hurt as, with the match already lost, he reasoned there was no point in aggravating an injury by his carrying on and risk missing the game against Millwall the following Tuesday. 'Some of the accusations being put in our direction are totally out of order,' said Warnock. 'It's totally ridiculous to say we did this deliberately.' The fact that Brown had groin surgery and did not play again that season and Ullathorne missed the next four matches was proof - surely? - that their injuries were not faked, as some had claimed. Warnock added that he knew nothing of the 'six-man abandonment' rule, which was an odd comment considering he was a qualified referee. Wolstenholme supported Warnock's position - his match report did not include 'any remarks from the technical area' and explained that he had been informed in advance by the fourth official that Brown would be coming off. However, the actions of United captain Keith Curle before Ullathorne was injured were highly suspicious. Already booked, Curle indulged in a series of reckless challenges, including one where he as good as rugby tackled an Albion player. It may have looked to some neutral observers that Curle was attempting to get himself sent off, acting either on his own volition - or was it on instruction from the United bench? - as he knew, with only six remaining players, this would result in an abandonment. Referee Wolstenholme was possibly wise to Curle's intentions, and chose to ignore the verbal abuse directed at him from Curle, showing what seemed like deliberate leniency.[10]

Despite Warnock's strenuous denial, the clamour rose amongst some Blades supporters and sections of the national press for him to be sacked. In fact, Warnock was removed from his position 45 minutes after the conclusion of the match, following an emergency meeting of United's board. However, a lengthy telephone conversation with PLC chairman Kevin

---

[10] Following the end of his playing career Curle went into management first with Mansfield Town, where he was sacked in 2004 after allegations of bullying a youth team player (though he was awarded damages when he took Mansfield to court over his dismissal) and then Chester City. Following his departure from the latter, he was offered the position of assistant manager – to Neil Warnock – at Crystal Palace. He kept the same status when Warnock moved to Queens Park Rangers in March 2010.

McCabe – McCabe's planned quiet evening in a Scarborough pub was ruined – enabled Warnock to talk his way back into the job. Football club chairman Derek Dooley then came out in Warnock's defence, telling *Look North* the following Monday he was 'convinced' that Warnock didn't cheat but, should the Football League enquiry find Warnock guilty, 'his job would be in jeopardy'. The directors were divided over Warnock's position but outwardly supported him, at least until the outcome of the League's investigation. In the meantime, the Football League announced that the 3-0 scoreline would stand and there would be no replay. Following the enquiry no charges were brought against Warnock or the club over the abandonment but Santos and Suffo were charged in relation to their dismissals. Keith Curle received a charge of using 'insulting and abusive words to a match official'. The club was charged with the offence of 'failing to control its players'. The only charge levelled at Warnock was one of 'improper conduct', which related to his leaving his technical area without permission, for which he was fined £300. The Football League's report concluded; 'No independent evidence was forthcoming to indicate that there was a deliberate attempt by any Sheffield United player or official to force the match to be abandoned.'

Warnock's job was safe, for now, but he came under increasing pressure in the coming years as United failed to build on their 2003 promotion near-miss. He was also to preside over a disgruntled backroom staff. Circumspect in what they revealed, a number of them were to discuss in the presence of Gary Armstrong how the game was being ruined by player agents. Whilst this conversation progressed Warnock was in an adjacent hotel room – with a player agent. Warnock apparently had few friends outside the playing staff at Bramall Lane but crucially he had the support of chairman Kevin McCabe, even though the two were not friends. When Warnock took the microphone at the Sheffield Town Hall 'Welcome Home' party after United's failed promotion bid at the end of the 2002/03 season he failed to mention his assistant Kevin Blackwell. In the summer of 2003 Blackwell departed to become assistant manager to Peter Reid at Leeds United (Blackwell later became Leeds' manager when Reid was sacked). Warnock felt betrayed by Blackwell - they had worked together for over a decade – and sarcastically commented; 'Leeds haven't come in for the cleaner yet but I'm waiting.' After this break-up, the relationship between the pair remained strained for several years. Shorn of his trusted right-hand man, Warnock didn't achieve a play-off position in 2003/04 or 2004/05.

Good in television interviews with his 'spontaneous' quips, Warnock also gained a reputation for falling out with people. Some in the game publicly loathed him. Fellow managers Gary Megson and Stan Ternent, with whom he had a long-running feud, could not find a good word for him. Former Blades manager Dave Bassett was not shy in his public pronouncements as to his dislike of how Warnock conducted himself. Two years after the 'Battle of Bramall Lane' Megson said he had been asked to write his autobiography, in which, he claimed, the truth about the events that day would 'come out'. Warnock retorted that such a book would be 'good news for people who suffer from insomnia', adding, 'I take everything he says with a pinch of salt.' Once, when manager of Burnley during a game at Bramall Lane, Ternent accused Warnock of instructing one of his staff to listen at the visitors' dressing room door to Ternent's half-time team talk. After the game, which United easily won 2-0, Warnock laughed off the claim, saying, 'It doesn't take much for him [Ternent] to get into one of those moods.' More generally, Warnock fell out with referees, supporters (both opposition and Blades), his own players (one of his former players, Peter Swan of Bury, publicly called him 'a prick') and even his chairmen – Ken Marsden at Gainsborough Trinity, Derek Pavis at Notts County, Terry Fisher at Huddersfield Town and Dan McCauley at Plymouth Argyle all felt the sharp edge of Warnock's tongue. Referees in particular were frequently on the receiving end of his invective and post-match tirades. He was a figure much disliked by many fellow professionals and referees. To such people, Warnock was a charmless man for whom self-doubt and self-reflection were not strong points. His nickname throughout English football was 'Colin Wanker', an anagram of his name. In contrast to this side of Warnock's personality, he sometimes elicited unusual loyalty from his players, such as when United won the two games immediately following the 'Battle of Bramall Lane'. After beating Millwall 3-2, striker Paul Peschisolido remarked, 'Some of the things people have been saying about him [Warnock] are disgraceful, totally out of order. We just want everybody to know that as a team we're fully behind him. People should really show the gaffer a bit more respect.' There were occasions, too, when Warnock showed reciprocal loyalty and respect to United supporters. Once, during a pre-season tour of Devon and Cornwall, Warnock was speaking to a small group of Blades fans before one of the friendly games at Torquay United's Plainmoor ground and, wanting to offer them more comfortable surroundings to watch the match after their long trip, instructed them to follow him into the players' entrance and then to the directors' box. 'If anyone asks,' he said, 'tell them you're guests of Neil Warnock.' Warnock then invited them to a barbecue that night at the Warnock family home in Cornwall, at which the United players and officials were to be present. There were no easy public transport options available and taxis proved too expensive, so the fans didn't attend. A few days later, at another game, Warnock saw them again and asked why they missed the barbecue. They explained the transport difficulties, to which Warnock replied, 'Why didn't you say? You could have jumped on the team coach.'

Players who fell foul of Warnock were ostracised, some never to progress in the game. In 2001 Paul Devlin and Shaun Murphy were banished from the squad when they wanted improved contracts but were later forgiven and allowed back into the fold. Warnock complained of 'things going on behind the scenes', blaming a couple of bad team performances on the distractions caused by Devlin's demands. He said he would 'root out those who aren't 100 per cent red and white.' After more than a month on the sidelines Devlin accepted he would not get a new contract and returned to the first team. Murphy was placed on the transfer list and sent out on loan, before realising he was better off staying at United. He then became an important player for United over the next couple of seasons. Warnock's hard-line stance with both players proved to be justified.

Central defender Danny Cullip suffered too. When signed from Brighton for £250,000 in December 2004, Warnock described Cullip as the on-field leader his team needed. However, after making just 15 appearances Cullip mysteriously disappeared from the first-team squad, went on loan to Watford and then signed for Nottingham Forest on a free transfer. In his autobiography *Made in Sheffield – My Story*, Warnock described the Cullip incident, writing that he thought he had signed a 'talker' but soon discovered that Cullip 'didn't say the right things. He talked for effect. Nothing was ever his fault. I told Danny he didn't fit in with us and ought to go. He went ballistic.' This seemed a trivial reason for dispensing with an expensive player after so short a time. Even more expensive was Geoff Horsfield, signed from West Bromwich Albion for over £1 million in January 2006. He found himself relegated from the first team a month after arriving, without satisfactory explanation. When he asked Warnock why he had been dropped, he learned that the manager 'wanted me in January but didn't want me now. Then he told me he didn't want me near his club and to train at home.' Horsfield never played for Warnock again; after spells on loan at Leeds United and Scunthorpe United he was eventually transferred to Lincoln City on a free transfer.

Warnock divided United fans. Following failure to make the play-offs in 2004/05, he was subject to verbal abuse from the stands as he and the team walked around the pitch acknowledging the supporters after the final home game, a poor 1-0 defeat to Millwall. He contemplated his resignation, whilst the United board considered his dismissal. The directors were split again but Kevin McCabe's casting vote tipped the scales in favour of giving him one more year. This was an astute move. Warnock was given a one-year contract with the option of another year. The chairman then took the decision to make funds available to Warnock, the like of which he had never previously enjoyed. The policy proved successful as Warnock brought in experienced former Premier League players (Craig Short, David Unsworth and Neil Shipperley) on high salaries and achieved promotion to the Premier League after over six years in the job. Promotion came at a financial cost, as United announced a loss of £6 million for the financial year, a debt reflecting the club's increased spending on wages, transfer fees and the bonuses paid to players and staff for achieving promotion.

The promotion challenge was threatened in late November 2005 by a calculated act of brinkmanship by Warnock, designed to inveigle an improved contract. Warnock became obsessive about managing in the Premier League. To this end, whilst managing United, when managerial jobs became vacant at a number of Premier League clubs he was said by sources inside the club to have contacted the respective chairmen, putting forward his candidacy. When in the final year of his current deal and with McCabe reticent to offer him an extension until the club's status was determined at the end of the season, Warnock went wandering. Portsmouth's chairman Milan Mandaric had just sacked his manager Alain Perrin as the club lay near the foot of the Premier League and his search for a new manager turned in many directions, one of which was to Warnock. According to a club statement, United 'reluctantly agreed, conditional on suitable compensation' to permit Warnock to speak to Portsmouth. It was then reported that Warnock had been offered the job and all he had to do was say yes. United defender Craig Short, a guest on *BBC Radio Five Live*, believed that Warnock had already agreed to join Portsmouth and conceded that he didn't expect to see him at training the next day. However, the next day brought a surprise – Warnock was to stay at United after all. Said McCabe, 'We are delighted that Neil Warnock's future remains with Sheffield United. It is true to say I wish the Portsmouth saga had not started but in the end the outcome in this case demonstrates the importance of the relationship between a chairman and a team manager.' Warnock cited the 'politics involved in Portsmouth' as the reason for his *volte-face*, adding, 'I don't need the hassle.' His decision was purportedly influenced by his sense of loyalty to McCabe and United. The chairman employed 'emotional blackmail' to get him to stay, he said, adding; 'I get on so well with Kevin and Derek [Dooley]. I didn't want to walk away. I couldn't.' But he could, and did, talk to at least one other club whilst ever emoting about his love for Sheffield United.

If Warnock thought McCabe would now jump to secure his manager's future beyond the end of the season he was to be disappointed. McCabe let things remain as they were – he held the right to review Warnock's contract for another year. When the contract question was raised at the December 2005 AGM, Warnock claimed it didn't bother him. 'My ability is my contract,' he confidently stated. It appeared not to bother McCabe either: he held firm and waited until promotion was won before offering Warnock a new contract. And then it was for one year only, and the sum offered made Warnock the lowest-paid manager in the Premier League. McCabe's patience with Warnock over the preceding three years and his waiting game over his contract had paid off. However, the 'relationship between a chairman and a team manager' that McCabe talked of was strained by Warnock's flirtation with Portsmouth. McCabe felt obliged to reward Warnock's promotion success with another year in charge, but appeared to do so without great conviction. Warnock took the contract but rumours persisted that he was unhappy that he was not being rewarded in line with other Premier League managers. McCabe's misgivings were displayed early in 2007 when discussions with Warnock over a new contract resulted in the manager being offered a deal that, in his words, 'was not really acceptable'. Warnock had little power in such a scenario; McCabe held all the aces.

Doubts were expressed by Blades supporters about Warnock's signings in the January 2007 transfer window. Subsequent events proved their misgivings well founded. Warnock bought five players: defender Matt Kilgallon from Leeds United for £1.75 million; striker Jon Stead from Sunderland for £750,000; Jamaican international striker Luton Shelton for £2 million from Swedish club Helsingborg; defender Mamadou Seck on a free transfer from French team Le Havre and Egyptian international midfielder Ahmed Fathi for £700,000 from Ismaily SC. None of them was the 'impact' player fans believed was needed to help maintain Premier League status. McCabe had made available a large amount of money - in United's terms - but some thought he had allowed Warnock too much leeway in how he spent it. Many felt that the £5 million-plus should have been spent on one top-class striker rather than five players with potential. Only Kilgallon was a long-term success at United. Warnock, meanwhile, spoke of the signings as 'players for the future'.

The future, however, looked bleak. In their Premier League season United won only ten games. Away from home they scored just eight goals. The team formation was changed almost weekly, such that at times Blades fans were chanting 'Four-four-two!' in anger at Warnock's implementation of a '4-5-1' or 'diamond' system. Home victories over Tottenham Hotspur and Fulham saw United ten points clear of the relegation positions in mid February 2007. Warnock spoke of his aim of taking the club into European competition (a journey predicated by a top-six finish or a cup win). Instead the club returned to where they had come from, relegated on the last day of the season. As the momentous final fixture loomed ahead, Warnock strangely raised the subject of his contract on the morning of the relegation decider, in which United needed one point to stay up and opponents Wigan Athletic needed to win. Comments attributed to him appeared in that day's Sunday newspapers, talking about his contract. Many Blades found this wrong - all his attention surely should have been focused on preparation for the match. United lost the fixture 2-1 and were relegated on goal difference. Afterwards, actor Sean Bean, a United director for the previous three years, was scathing of Warnock, angrily telling a *Calendar* television reporter: 'It would have helped if he'd kept his mouth shut and stopped mouthing off in the papers this morning about his new contract. I'm sure that must translate to the players in some way. I just wish Neil Warnock could keep his mouth shut for a change.' Warnock hit back at Bean in his autobiography *Made In Sheffield*, accusing him of verbally abusing Warnock's wife and children immediately after the game, while apparently under the influence of alcohol. Wrote Warnock, 'Sharon [his wife] had been crying and the kids knew why she was so upset. It wasn't just the football. Not just because of the result.' According to Warnock, Bean made his way from the directors' box to the corridor where Warnock's office was located. Not finding Warnock, Bean had apparently sworn at his wife and children who were in the room, saying, 'It's your fucking husband that got us relegated.' Warnock continued, 'I was never really sure why Sean Bean was on the board of directors in the first place. Celebrity supporter I suppose. I didn't have a lot to do with him and never really rated his opinion on football.' Days after the launch of Warnock's book Bean gave his widely different version of events in an interview with a national tabloid. The petulance of Warnock continued into the following season when – by this time manager of Crystal Palace – in a pre-match interview he said that somebody must have told Bean what to say in his post-match comment to the media as he couldn't have thought it up himself.

On Warnock's final day - three days after relegation - the manager and chairman spoke unconvincingly at a press conference in glowing terms of each other and their time together at the club. Warnock denied that his failure to agree a new contract was down to money. He and McCabe claimed that his departure was on good terms. Warnock stated, 'It's the right time for me and right for the club,' adding that the club was in a far better position on and off the field than when he took over in 1999. McCabe told of Warnock's 'despair' at the manner of relegation but was not openly critical of his manager. However, a week later McCabe changed his tune, conceding to the *Sheffield Star* that he might have made a mistake in allowing Warnock to lead United in the top flight. 'Hindsight is a great thing,' he said. 'Neil Warnock is a great motivator. We can reflect, now, maybe he wasn't quite right for our Premiership ambitions. I believe we should have got more points, yes.' Warnock angrily responded: 'I think he loses credibility when he makes comments like that. It makes me think he did not want me at the club for the past couple of years. I could have said a lot of hurtful things too, but I didn't. It has been obvious for a couple of years that Kevin has really wanted a Kenny Dalglish or Bryan Robson-type of manager. An ex-international sells the club when you are trying to bring in quality players.' Warnock was correct in his assessment. The former Manchester United and England captain Robson was to be Warnock's successor; Kenny Dalglish was the 'name in the frame' when Warnock was flirting with Portsmouth. On Robson's appointment, McCabe commented; 'He's got the contacts in the game, he's got regard in the game, he'll be able to encourage the players we want to come to Sheffield United, probably more than other candidates.' Warnock could have also mentioned that a 'name' manager would be beneficial to McCabe's global development plans as potential investors and even buyers would get the impression that Sheffield United, in attracting exceptional former footballers, were bigger than they really were.

The mid-morning press conference to announce Warnock's successor can only be considered a public relations debacle. In the footballing close season media sources are frequently desperate for stories, especially in the case of the 24-hour rolling channel *Sky Sports News*, which interrupted all other news to broadcast live from Bramall Lane as Robson was revealed to the audience watching in 186 countries. United director Terry Robinson said a few words predictable in their praise of the new manager. He was followed by Robson, whose equally predictable few words spoke of his excitement of joining a club with a great history and potential. Kevin McCabe spoke briefly about the club's future vision. The assembled journalists were then invited to ask questions. Only two did and each question received a short response from Robson. The questions then dried up and in the ensuing silence McCabe asked a *Sky Sports News* reporter a frivolous question about the reporter's favourite club, Wrexham. At this point *Sky Sports News* cut back to the studio presenters who, clearly expecting a longer broadcast, expressed their bewilderment at the brevity of the event. The club had missed a golden opportunity to elaborate on its ambitions to a global audience.

But these events were a year away as, in May 2006, McCabe reflected on the long-awaited promotion success, proclaiming: 'We're determined not to stand still. There are only three or four other teams who have enjoyed longer unbroken runs in the top flight than us. It was a while ago now but we spent 30-odd seasons there and we want that type of run again. We're in the Premiership and within the next four or five years we want to be in Europe. We know we need to keep on improving if we want to see this whole project through and that means spending money. However, I am absolutely determined to do that by raising new funds. We will do it sensibly and in the right manner, the manner which will give us the best chance of building upon this success.' The financial position was to be helped by plans to raise £10 million with the issue of convertible loan notes (long-term lending that could later be converted to shares in the company). Half of such monies would be invested in the team, half in commercial ventures, which were expected to bring long-term returns. This fund-raising would, in McCabe's words, allow the club to invest further in new players and improve the chances of remaining in the top flight. It would also allow new investment in 'off-pitch revenue streams'. However, this brave new world came with words never before associated with Sheffield United FC. The club was now spoken of in terms of 'revenue streams'; soon it was to be persistently referred to by McCabe as the 'product' and the 'brand'. Times had already changed and the 'football' demand of the football club seemed to be secondary to the money-making potential of the 'image'.

Initially all was good. What was significant about the club in the early years of the new century was the real sense of stability and harmony - or at least toleration - from top to bottom. Such a situation owed much to McCabe. It was quite a contrast from the constant squabbling, in-fighting and power struggles evidenced throughout the 1990s. On the field, manager Warnock was often under pressure from supporters who believed that promotion should have been won earlier but McCabe stood by him, in the full knowledge that the clubs that kept their managers for a good length of time were usually the more successful ones. After the retirement (for the third time) of Derek Dooley, Terry Robinson took over as football club chairman. Lancastrian-born, Robinson was steeped in football, having served twenty years on the board of Bury FC, where he had worked with Neil Warnock in the late 1990s. Later, Jason Rockett, who had played professional football for Rotherham United and Scarborough, was appointed chief executive. Since his retirement from the game Rockett had worked for McCabe's Scarborough Group, initially as a surveyor. Despite immediate relegation from the Premier League, between 2000 and 2010 under Kevin McCabe

Sheffield United embarked on an ambitious plan to spread the word, knowledge, influence and revenue-making potential of the club beyond the confines of South Yorkshire. Blades fans looked on bewildered for the most part as to the 'partnerships' their club now entered in to.

Chapter 15

Regeneration
And the Worldwide Football Family, 2000-2010

The United board spent the early years of the new century determined to turn round the club's financial position after the profligacy of the McDonald years. To this end they pursued a policy of reducing wages and raising money through prudent player sales. In this, they relied on Neil Warnock's acumen in the transfer market to produce a concomitant improvement from the team. It took a while, but it worked, culminating in promotion to the Premier League in 2006. A long, hard struggle to get there was required and Warnock might consider himself fortunate to be given over six years to achieve it. Then, having got to the Promised Land of the Premier League the club blew it. United were relegated on the final day of the season.

In 2000, new PLC chairman Bernard Procter warned – using that so familiar refrain - that more supporters through the turnstiles were required to prevent further player sales. Said Procter, 'The board will continue its policy to reduce football wage costs to lessen the reliance on income from transfers, while at the same time implementing measures to expand other revenue-producing activities. It would require only an extra 3,000 supporters at home games to substantially improve the club's finances and thus remove any need for player sales.' Derek Dooley continued the theme: 'We're not out of the

337

woods yet but the club is now going in the right direction. There has been an improvement and everyone has had to tighten their belts, including the football side of the club. The wage bill is still difficult to manage without more people coming through the turnstiles, or a good cup run. When you look at where we are and what we have done this season we are still only averaging just over 13,000 attendances. I would have hoped that that some of the people who have stayed away in recent years would have come back to have a look at us and see that things are on the up and up. We actually need 16,000 to break even. The only alternative is that we have to sell a player. That's not a threat it's just a mathematical fact of life. It has not been easy but we have held the club together and the board now are all born Unitedites except one!' Dooley's joke about all the board being 'born Unitedites except one' was aimed at himself; he was brought up a Wednesday supporter and played for and managed that club before defecting to United after he was sacked as the Owls' manager on Christmas Eve 1973. Eleven months later Dooley was appointed as United's first-ever commercial manager and became an associate director in 1985, becoming the club's first paid director.

Sheffield United PLC's Annual General Meeting in November 2000 was, compared to recent years, a generally equable, good-natured affair. The directors did, though, continue to emphasise the need for higher gates to avoid further player sales. Director Andrew Laver remarked to the room: 'We're constantly looking at ways of improving things and I think the situation has improved somewhat over the last year. I'm not attacking the fans at all, but in the meantime, if every season ticket holder could bring along a friend to games, just think what a difference that could make.' Moving on to the development of the stadium, both ongoing and in the future, Laver said, 'We aim [to put] facilities into place that mean people regularly use Bramall Lane on days other than when there's a match going on. That's the potential every club has to look at trying to tap.' When a question arose regarding whether United would ever consider selling Bramall Lane and moving to a new stadium Bernard Procter replied with a question: 'When you look at what's going on here, why would we want to move?' Fans took this as a 'no'.

Shareholders were informed at the meeting that the construction of a hotel adjacent to Bramall Lane had been set back because the plans of the hotel company expected to run the franchise were considered - by United - to be unworkable. The discord surrounded the hotel's 'Skydeck', which intended to overlook a corner of the pitch, with a restaurant and other corporate facilities. After the formal meeting Neil Warnock answered questions from the floor and in doing so raised doubts about his own future when admitting, 'I don't want to be dealing in Bosman free transfers two years down the line and if that's the case then I don't want to be here. It's hard to see teams like Preston and Burnley spend a couple of million because I believe we're a much bigger club than they are.' Warnock would find no comfort from interim financial results for the six months ending December 31, 2000. Operating losses had been cut from £2.5 million to £1.6 million, but they were still losses. Finances were a cause for concern; the same month the club had difficulty paying the wage bill. At that month's board meeting Warnock was instructed to raise funds by selling players following the receipt of a £350,000 tax bill. On the same day a new printer was required in a club office and had to be paid for by one of the office staff using his personal credit card. He was promised he would be reimbursed when cash flows were easier. Visiting the club that day Gary Armstrong met disgruntled staff, one of whom told him, 'Don't go to work with your credit card on you.... that's one of the first things you learn at Bramall Lane.'

Much-improved annual results came the following year. By then Bernard Procter could declare, 'The board is mindful that a combination of significant further growth of income and containment of player wage costs will be necessary before the position is reached of sufficient operating profitability to eliminate the requirement of income from player sales. The board remains committed to achieving the aim of promotion to the Premier League but within a sound financial framework, in particular the control of player wages, which is a challenge to

339

all modern professional clubs.' Andrew Laver then revealed that the wage bill was still £1 million above budget and that savings of £1.5 million had to be found from selling players and reducing salaries. He continued; 'There are two ways clubs can survive in the future: players take a significant reduction in salary or we bring on and sell players. The main thing is that we are currently in a lot better situation than we were a few years ago.' Warnock agreed with this sentiment when he wrote his opening article in the new club yearbook: 'For some - Ipswich Town and Charlton Athletic being the most recent - the key seems to have been found, and it is built on patience, continuity and good housekeeping.' The comparison to these two clubs was unfortunate. Within a year Ipswich were relegated and went into administration, while Charlton went down a few years later and also found themselves in big financial trouble. In the meantime, the manager and the board knew that although the fans demanded instant success the only feasible way forward for a club like Sheffield United was to instil a mindset of frugality. That needed time and patience, something that United supporters had precious little of.

In an interview in the *Sheffield Telegraph*, Derek Dooley reassured fans who might be worried about the possibility of the club following Nottingham Forest into having its stock market shares suspended as a result of falling share price and a £6 million debt. In doing so he handed out a warning: 'Forest's problems have arisen out of buying players and then paying them too much money - as we did [in 1996-98]. The gamble Sheffield United took on getting back to the Premier League nearly came off. But that gamble will not be taken again. We've not had the gates we anticipated. The average is 15,500, although we're not complaining because we've not exactly set the First Division alight.' Dooley also stated that United would still have to sell players to survive, even at the sensible wage levels to which they were adhering.

January 2002 was the fifth anniversary of the club becoming a publicly quoted company. Despite the many comments from the board and the manager concerning the future financial strategy, there were still complaints voiced by supporters about how the club had been and was being run. To the uninitiated, trying to understand company accounts is like reading Russian. An individual could pore over the club's accounts looking for something simple like 'How much did they spend?' or 'How much did they take in?' and it wouldn't be found straightforwardly. There was the added complication that before 1997 United were just a plain 'Limited Company' and it wasn't unknown for them to produce their accounts dreadfully late, whereas publicly quoted companies by law have to produce audited accounts within a certain timescale. In the year 1996/97 in particular (the year of the flotation) things were especially financially fuzzy. Whether pre- and post-flotation figures could be directly compared was debatable: the 1998 accounts showed the 1997 figures 'Restated', presumably meaning that a different accounting system had been used. Looking for 'like for like' figures (a phrase beloved by financial experts) that could be compared year-on-year came up with the simple statistic of 'Transfer fees paid' and 'Transfer fees received'. The 1997 accounts showed in clear terms that United had received £65,000 but spent £3,031,000 during 1996/97, which was the initial period of the 'gamble' mentioned by Dooley. Matters then got complicated. From the following year Sheffield United PLC decided to change its accounting policy, adopting expressions like 'amortisation', 'impairment' and 'permanent diminution' when it came to transfer fees. Players now became 'Intangible Fixed Assets' - they were no longer bought or sold, but assets added or disposed of.

The cumulative transfer fees paid/received each financial year (which for United was effectively a football season) showed that between 1997 and 2001 United paid out £11,429,000 and took in £13,639,000, with the biggest spending season being 1997/98 (£5,393,000) and the biggest selling season 1998/99 (£6,108,000). The company's turnover reached a peak of £12,753,000 in 1997/98 and after a sharp drop following United's two failed promotion bids, funds were only now recovering, due as much to improved commercial activities as to any success on the field. Commercial income (from sponsorship, royalties, merchandising, advertising, conferences and catering) accounted for just under half the total, the remainder garnered from gate receipts and television contracts. Wages similarly peaked when former England international Brian Deane and other highly paid players were at the club and predictably dropped after their departure. At the 2000 AGM Bernard Procter stated that it was the club's aim to get the annual wage bill down to £4.5 million. This objective looked to be attainable given the trend of the previous two years, but 2000/01 saw the wage figure climb above £6 million once more, possibly because United signed experienced players such as Carl Asaba, Robert Page, Paul Peschisolido and Peter Ndlovu to replace presumably lower-paid homegrown young players Curtis Woodhouse and Wayne Quinn, who had been sold for significant transfer fees.[11]

The 1997 accounts also gave profit and loss figures for the years immediately preceding flotation. Only once in the previous nine years had United made a profit: a mere £100,000 in the club's last Premier League season of 1993/94. In the five years since flotation there had been an overall loss of £16.6 million, although the trend was now on a steeply downward curve and the loss was only £67,000 in 2001/02. Bank overdrafts and overall debt showed that in the middle of 2000 United were in deep trouble, owing £5.4 million to the banks and £8.8 million overall, the balance mainly comprising loans from directors. By 2002 the situation had improved but the club was still in debt to the tune of £7,188,000, although less than half of that was owed to the bank.

There was one reason why United could not buy players and give them the contracts they wanted: they had not the money to do so. Those supporters who demanded that the board 'show some ambition' by splashing out on new players and paying players currently under contract what they asked for to get them to stay were unaware of the financial straits the club was in - or chose to ignore it. The expensive (failed)

---

[11] Carl Asaba cost £92,500 from Gillingham, Robert Page £350,000 from Watford and Paul Peschisolido £150,000 from Fulham. Peter Ndlovu arrived at Bramall Lane as part of a deal that took Curtis Woodhouse to Birmingham City. United also received £1 million. Wayne Quinn was sold to Newcastle United for £800,000.

promotion pushes of 1996/97 and 1997/98 had left United in a terrible fiscal position and supporters could only be grateful that something was finally being done about it, even though it did mean belt-tightening and the loss of players the manager would have liked to have kept. In September 2001 it was rumoured that Warnock was only able to bring in defender Robert Page on the proviso that he sold full back Rob Kozluk to Wigan Athletic and when Wigan's chairman stepped in to stop that deal going through it left United well over their salary budget. Consequently on-trial full back Terry Phelan could not be retained and cover players were brought in only on short-term contracts or month-long loans.

Of course there was always the grave danger that by trying to control wages and transfer expenses the club could neither keep its best players nor adequately replace them, which would lead to only one thing - a team going down rather than up the league. That is why it was so important for Warnock to sign good players on 'Bosman' free transfers and that any money available for improving players' contracts went on those who were the future of the club, such as Michael Brown, bought from Manchester City in 1999 for £400,000, and Michael Tonge, who made his debut aged 17 in 2001 and who contributed greatly to the (relatively) successful 2002/03 season. In the conditions current at the time a few other clubs were in the same position as United. Nottingham Forest had had their shares suspended, while Sheffield Wednesday, Coventry City and Bradford City were already in financial trouble and Leicester City, Ipswich Town, Leeds United and Southampton would suffer in subsequent years, all going into administration. All were former Premier League clubs.

In *Flashing Blade* No.82 (January 2002) a contributor calling himself 'Alexis' undertook an overview of the business side of the club. He wrote that the club was too small to be a public company and that the costs of holding a Stock Exchange quotation would cover a decent player's wages for a year. The motivation for flotation was to recapitalise the business, i.e. to replace bank borrowings with shares (to 'degear' the business, using the jargon) but being a commercially run business, governed by normal commercial forces, and also being a football club did not always sit comfortably together. The necessary constraints in the boardroom often conflicted with the aspirations of the fans and the manager on the field. Alexis concluded by stating that the club's future course depended on one of two things: 'We get lucky and get bought by a benevolent sugar daddy or we stay as we are: proud of our heritage, fiercely loyal, deeply frustrated, ever hopeful and a permanent fixture of the Football League.'

By the early millennium Blades fans thought they had the former in the shape of Kevin McCabe. In reality they had bought into the second scenario. The McCabe family made a perennial appearance in the upper half of the *Sunday Times* Rich List' of the one thousand wealthiest residents of the UK. In the 2000s the McCabe family ebbed and flowed up and down the 'Rich List', their highest position being 272nd in 2002, when they were worth £120 million. The family's wealth almost doubled from £125 million to £240 million in the year 2006/07 but had fallen to £175 million in 2009 because of the depressed global property market. The family stood in 322nd position in the 2009 list. However, McCabe never threw his personal fortune at his football club in the manner of Dave Whelan (Wigan Athletic), Roman Abramovich (Chelsea), Mohamed Al Fayed (Fulham) and Jack Walker (Blackburn Rovers). His investments were usually in the form of loans and share purchases.

In 2002, aware that the football club board was understrength in terms of both personnel and financial support, United wished to recruit new directors. The club issued the following statement, which effectively said nothing: 'Sheffield United PLC has been considering a variety of proposals aimed at building and advancing the business to satisfy supporters and shareholders. Positive actions have been undertaken to seek new directors for the football club board. The company hopes to make an announcement in due course concerning this matter. All directors will help develop the vision of the company, including the plans to build the north of England's best Academy for young players, who are the long-term future of the club.'

That night's main front-page story of the *Sheffield Star* reported that Hollywood actor and lifelong Blade Sean Bean was to be one of the new directors. Neither club nor actor were available for comment but a few weeks later it was announced that Bean was indeed to join the football club board. Bean was said to be making 'an investment', reported to be £100,000. Bean commented, 'It is looking very positive for the future. The club have made it clear to me they intend to hold on to their good young players. In my discussions I was impressed with the plans for the Academy. This is the way forward and I want to be associated with such a development.'

But was Carlo Colombotti about to make a dramatic return too? He admitted to meeting McCabe, adding: 'I am aware of the restructuring plans for the club. It appeals to me. I agree one hundred per cent with the plans for restructuring and I would like to be involved. I could not work with Mike McDonald when I was at United before but that is in the past now.' Colombotti's intention, along with Sheffield-born cohort Phillip Wood, a former chief executive of the club, was to buy the club with the financial assistance of former Football League chairman Keith Harris's investment company Seymour Pierce. The plan was to link up with Italian football clubs with which Colombotti claimed to have good contacts. The ultimate aim was to install former Italian international captain Franco Baresi as manager and develop an Italy/Sheffield player exchange. Colombotti talked with Bean and Gary Armstrong twice in London, all the time stressing the fact that McCabe wanted him to become involved with the club, something McCabe denied days later when asked by Armstrong. The move, if it happened, seemed certain to bring back bad memories for United fans, who remembered the turmoil of Colombotti's previous association with the club. Colombotti did not make a return. Instead, McCabe recruited to the board local businessmen Steve Slinn and Chris Steer, while former Bury FC chairman Terry Robinson was appointed to the position of 'Football Executive'. Both Slinn and Steer emphasised their Blades credentials. Said Slinn, senior partner of an industrial cleaning company, 'Like any other supporter I want us back in the Premiership. I can promise anyone who has the club at heart that we've only one thing in mind: what's best for Sheffield United. That's what we're in this for, not ourselves.' Steer, a lifelong Blade and partner at a flooring material warehouse in the Woodseats area of Sheffield, added, 'This is the start of an exciting new era for United and we want to do things the right way.' Slinn lasted less than a year before resigning to 'devote more time to his own business'.

As part of the backroom revolution, the last two of McDonald's appointments left the club - managing director John Thurman and secretary John Howarth. Their departures would save around £100,000 a year in salaries. The recruitment of Robinson had sounded the death knell for Thurman. Robinson's appointment was surprising. Known to Neil Warnock, who had managed Bury between 1998 and 1999 whilst Robinson was chairman, Robinson hardly had a pedigree for a club like Sheffield United. He also came with baggage - the investigative reporter David Conn asked questions of him in relation to transfer dealings in his book *The Beautiful Game? Searching the Soul of Football*. One such transfer concerned that of Paddy Kenny from Bury to United: Robinson refused to respond to questions seeking a breakdown of the transfer monies. Such a background was seemingly overlooked by those in charge at Bramall Lane. Why Robinson was chosen for such a role in a club the size of Sheffield United was never made public. His record at Bury was mixed; under his chairmanship this little club had struggled to attract more than 3,000 crowds and went into administration in 2002, but they also enjoyed consecutive promotions and two seasons in the second tier in the late 1990s – their first at that level for almost 30 years. For a time Robinson was also the Football League's representative on the Council of the Premier League. Those in the higher echelons of the English game saw in Robinson qualities not evidenced by some who knew him at Bramall Lane.

The early days of McCabe were exciting ones. In 2002 news broke of an imminent 'capital and financial re-organisation'. McCabe went public in explaining what it was all about: 'So many clubs in their desire to achieve league success –

including Sheffield United – have suffered the consequences of risking over-expenditure on players. In any business, substantial repeated yearly losses cannot be sustained and financial disaster confronts organisations who ignore the need to instigate change. The board is finalising proposals for a capital and financial re-organisation, which should assist in bringing long-term financial stability to the company. The fast-changing nature of the football industry, where income received from television contracts will decline in coming years and transfer activities recede largely as a result of the Bosman ruling, means that we must implement positive action. The High Court decision announced to put *ITV Digital* into administration means that its contract with the Football League is unlikely to be honoured and that [United] will financially suffer as a direct result. This will have a significant impact on our working capital and further accentuates the need to instigate our intended re-organisation to create a stronger foundation for growth. The re-organisation, together with new banking facilities presently being negotiated, should provide the company with the resources not only to see completion of the Academy, but also with it a sensible level of working capital.'

The *ITV Digital* collapse mentioned by McCabe angered everyone in English football. In 2001, possibly drunk on the success of the Premier League and its astonishingly lucrative contract with *BSkyB,* a newly formed digital television channel was set up by the independent broadcasters. *ITV Digital* offered the Football League a very generous broadcasting deal in the belief that the take-up of digital set-top receivers throughout Britain would be massive. It wasn't. This left the company with severe financial problems, which forced it into administration in March 2002. *ITV Digital's* two major shareholders, television companies Carlton and Granada, were being threatened with legal action by the Football League in an attempt to recover £178.5 million still owed under the terms of the £315 million three-year deal. Football League chief executive David Burns slammed Carlton and Granada's refusal to discuss the situation with the League, saying: 'If they wish to see a just and equitable resolution to this matter they really need to sit down with us and talk. They have used administration to put leverage on the Football League and it will not work.' There were no talks, and the Football League's legal action failed because Burns' predecessors, who had signed the deal, did so without incorporating any guarantees, meaning that by the terms of the contract Carlton and Granada were not obliged to make up any shortfall. Ultimately, no more money was available for Football League clubs. Those who had set their budgets based on the anticipated full receipt now faced grave financial trouble.

The fifth issue of the club's newsletter *Cutting Edge* was published in spring 2002. Readers learned details of the club's recent and future plans and events, including on its front page news of the impending financial re-organisation. The article informed readers that a substantial portion of the club's financial and management resources needed to be applied to youth development. Urging support for the proposed financial re-organisation, the newsletter attempted to play down fears that directors wished to 'buy the club on the cheap', as had been intimated in recent newspaper headlines. Readers were told: 'This is simply not true. Your directors are also supporters and have no desire to see the club controlled by any one individual.' To this end the proposed capital restructure would provide shareholders with an opportunity to purchase New Ordinary Shares in Sheffield United PLC. Aware that shareholders who invested when Sheffield United floated on the stock market in 1997 had seen the value of their holding reduced in recent years, potential investors were encouraged to acquire New Ordinary Shares to balance the overall value of their shareholding. One line stands out in this declaration: 'no desire to see the club controlled by any one individual'. This proved not to be the case.

The financial reorganisation was intended to raise £4.05 million by means of a share issue of 57,905,401 shares at 7p each. The issue, underwritten by four directors and, according to the prospectus, 'certain other individuals' (never specified) would help pay off £1.8 million of existing debts and develop the Academy and the Bramall Lane stadium, if it obtained the required 75 per cent majority at an Extraordinary General Meeting. In addition, Sheffield United PLC arranged a £10

348

million re-financing agreement, comprising long-term loans, with Halifax Bank of Scotland (HBOS). McCabe told the *Sheffield Star*, 'Our objective as directors and fans is to see Sheffield United re-promoted to the Premier League and we believe this programme will help facilitate the realisation of that ambition. The development of Academy facilities will attract top-level young players to Sheffield, creating a pool of home-grown talent, while the further improvement of facilities at Bramall Lane will help provide growing, long-term income streams for re-investment in the club. In my view this is absolutely vital for us. We know we can't exist in a timewarp and that you can't run a football club the way that you would have done 20 or 30 years ago.'

The Extraordinary General Meeting to vote on the re-financing plans was held in June 2002. Unexpectedly, the resolutions were all defeated, casting doubt on the financial security of the club. The votes were two to one against the proposal, although around 50 per cent of the eligible votes were not cast. The current directors were not allowed to vote due to stock market regulations, while the Texas Group, controlled by former chairman Mike McDonald, and former chief executive Ian Townsend, used their shares to vote against the plans. McCabe was angry and upset: 'This is a sad day and the board will be discussing options to come up with a revised strategy. It's back to the drawing board.' In the short term it was feared that United would have to sell players to survive. The future of the Academy was also put in doubt. McCabe also thought it necessary to immediately write to shareholders to explain what had happened. His letter read:

'At the Extraordinary General Meeting of Sheffield United PLC on 19 June 2002, Resolution One set out in the Notice of Meeting was defeated on a poll. Of the total votes cast of 15,496,576, some 5,462,127 were for the resolution and 10,034,449 against the Resolution, resulting in a majority to overturn the Resolution of 4,572,322 votes. Directors are concerned and disappointed that they did not receive the necessary support from shareholders to proceed with the proposals. The Board is currently considering further ways in

which the company can progress forward with the strategy of providing a sound base and financial security for the future.'

Having apparently disbanded in September 2000 due to internal ideological conflicts, SUISA now reappeared. Its spokesman Dave Windle stated that his organisation advised its members and Mike McDonald to vote against the share issue proposal because it placed too much emphasis on youth development and not enough on strengthening the current first-team squad. McDonald defended his decision to vote against the share issue, explaining; 'I did it to safeguard the ownership of the club. My shares are held in trust to ensure the club does not fall into the hands of a small group of individuals, which would have happened. I am supportive of [the board's] intentions but not the way they wanted to go about achieving them. I am not in favour of academies because there are no safeguards in place to keep players there. All of a sudden kids talk to a persuasive agent and they're off.' The Official Supporters' Club came out in support of the board's proposals. Its chairman Pete Whitney stated, 'I speak as an individual shareholder but also, I believe, for the vast majority of locally-based Unitedites. This represented a real opportunity to keep developing some excellent young players, but the money will now have to be found elsewhere.' BIFA added its support, stating that the association was 'dismayed and concerned about recent events' and that the organisation considered the defeated strategy as the best solution to secure the future of the club. In BIFA's opinion, SUISA's stance advocated a gamble on short-term success rather than adopting coherent long-term plans.

There were two main factors behind the failure of the proposals. The primary one, as already explained, was the decision of McDonald and his Texas group not to back it; the second was the abstention, deliberately or through apathy, of around half of the eligible voters. The opponents of the plans were entirely correct in their assertions that they did place a lot of emphasis on the Academy rather than the first team but, preferring to demolish ideas rather than create them, they were unable to offer any alternative solutions. How, one can ask, did they propose to improve the quality of the first team? To do that either a robust youth system was needed, which United were seeking to improve, or money, which United did not have, and the banks would not lend money to buy footballers. They would, though, lend money for construction projects and to develop off-field businesses. The new loans from HBOS would have put United further in debt, but they would have paid off some of the existing debts and would have been repayable over ten or more years, rather than the two or three years in which the existing debts had to be repaid. The 2001/02 PLC *Interim Report* told readers that £7,793,000 was due to creditors within the year.

It was not surprising that so many eligible shareholders chose not to vote. Some people aren't interested in elections in whatever form. The list of the company's shareholders was available to view and to do so raised questions as to whom many of them were and what interest they had in owning shares in Sheffield United PLC. The first AGM after flotation supported the view that many shareholders had obtained shares by default or inheritance; there were several present whose questions from the floor proved they didn't have a clue about football. It would be astonishing if some of these shareholders chose to vote. In addition, the share prospectus detailing the proposal stated that, 'The Offer Price (7p) is lower than the current nominal value of the Existing Ordinary Shares.' It may have been at the time the prospectus was compiled, but the statement was not valid by the time it was released - at that time the share price was 5.25p, which may have persuaded some to vote against, or not to vote at all. If an investor wanted to buy shares, why pay 7p when they could be bought on the open market for 5.25p?

Mike McDonald, as experience had shown, was not a man Blades fans would want to hold the balance of power in any situation. The reasons he stated for voting against the proposal were three-fold, all of them tenuous. The first was that he was afraid of the major shareholding falling into the hands of two or three individuals, something that, to his credit, was a view he opined several times since the club was floated. This could have occurred due to the current directors underwriting the share issue, assuming that existing shareholders did not take up enough of the new shares, but the directors continued to deny their objective was to 'buy the club on the cheap'. McDonald's second reason for voting against was that SUISA had contacted him to express the group's unhappiness at the board's proposals, claiming that it placed too much emphasis on youth development and nothing on improving the current squad. Aspects of this statement, however, didn't quite strike the right chord. If McDonald truly wanted to canvass the views of supporters, why did he not contact BIFA and the official Supporters' Club? Second, when did McDonald decide that he needed to listen to others before making up his mind? That was very unlike the obstinate, self-assured man he usually was. The money raised was not only intended to develop the Academy but also to build up alternative off-field sources of income via hotel, retail, office and leisure facilities. Those income streams were now in jeopardy. Ironically and worryingly, there was a significant possibility that SUISA's desire to strengthen the first-team squad would ultimately result in it being weakened as United might be forced to sell one or two of the better players merely to survive the next few months.

The third reason McDonald claimed for rejecting the proposals was that, 'I am not in favour of academies'. Fair enough if that was what he believed (though when he was chairman he appointed Stewart White to the board and tasked him with the founding of an Academy) but where were his alternative ideas for improving the team on the field and consequently United's chances of promotion? There were not any feasible ones. One could only conclude that McDonald voted against to promote his own interests. If the share issue had gone through, McDonald and Texas Group's holding would have been diluted by 50 per cent and his influence diminished. Undaunted, the PLC board decided to try again to push through its re-financing plans by putting it to the vote once more.

The following October Sheffield United PLC announced a loss for the year ending June 2002 of £1.8 million, up £1.4 million from the previous year. The increase was almost entirely due to a fall in player sales because of – according to the accounts

– the depressed state of the transfer market. A more cynical observer might have suggested that it was because United had no more good players to sell. The overall debt had risen to £13 million, with £4 million of this being additional directors' loans, required after the rejection of the proposed share issue. The figure was also not as bad is it sounded as United, unlike many other clubs, owned the freehold of both the Bramall Lane stadium and the Shirecliffe Academy. United had also arranged favourable banking terms with HBOS in place of former lenders HSBC, such an arrangement facilitated by McCabe's presence on the board of a satellite company of HBOS. It was also announced that the company intended to transfer from the main Stock Exchange to the Alternative Investment Market (AIM) as this was thought more suitable for smaller capitalised companies. It was also less costly in terms of administration and transaction charges.

Despite the downturn in financial performance McCabe called United 'one of the most sound and progressive clubs in the division'. He also said that the proposed share issue would be resurrected but not until after the end of the season as it might be a distraction to the efforts of the football team. He then directed a scarcely disguised dig at McDonald for withdrawing his support of the first re-financing proposals after initially intimating that he was in favour: 'The rejection of a capital and financial re-organisation of the parent company was a major setback. It should be recognised that before these proposals the company's principal outside shareholders were consulted and confirmed their support for taking the club forward both in raising new capital and the implementation of an Academy. We're puzzled too [about McDonald's stance]. We were firmly of the belief [he] would vote in favour. I suspect, and I stress the word suspect, that some people might not be in favour because unless they take up the rights they would be entitled to, then their shareholding would be diluted.'

Discussing the resurrection of the re-financing plans, McCabe said, 'No director currently has control and neither does any of us want control. We aren't concerned about the size of our shareholding. But we do not want to court controversy because that might affect what's going on on the field.' These were strange words from a man who a few years later was in total control of Sheffield United and who courted controversy to the point of going to tribunals three times to seek recompense for his relegated club. Meanwhile, to try to smooth things over with McDonald and come to an arrangement that would satisfy everybody, the former chairman was invited to a 'summit meeting' at Bramall Lane. McCabe added that the second stab at the issue of new shares now had a much better chance of succeeding as the share price had almost doubled to around 10p in the last six months. This was confirmed in May, when it was announced that another effort to raise finance would be attempted, this time by means of a rights issue. The company was to try to raise £4.9 million by issuing new shares on a one-for-one basis, underwritten by director Michael Dudley to the tune of £1.25 million. A rights issue, unlike the previous year's aborted capital reorganisation, would crucially allow the current directors to vote, giving the plan a better chance of success.

In an interview in May 2003 McCabe told the *Sheffield Star* he believed that United were now the 'standard bearer' for other clubs struggling to come to terms with the impact of the loss of about £1.2 million of the *ITV Digital* revenue. He explained the difference between the club's proposed new financial plans and those defeated the previous summer: 'This time we are not proposing a capital re-organisation. This is a rights issue. I'm confident it will get the go ahead because I can see no reason why anyone would vote against it.' Mindful of the fact that many eligible voters failed to vote on the first occasion, McCabe arranged an open day for shareholders to ask questions. 'Some didn't [vote] last time,' he said, 'because they thought that because they only had a small amount they wouldn't count. But they do and everyone should reply. This affects everybody who has United at heart. Sheffield United have become a prototype for clubs in the current climate.' Three weeks later the proposals for the new rights issue were overwhelmingly passed at an Extraordinary General Meeting, with 93 per cent of the votes cast in favour, including those of Mike McDonald. McCabe, who said he was 'pleasantly surprised' by McDonald's decision, remarked, 'This is hugely important for Sheffield United. It means we can continue the progress we made over the past few years. Importantly this will also give us even more credibility in the City as well. It means we now have a much more sensible level of borrowing. We want to generate revenue streams away from the football side of the business and that will help the club as a whole.'

The vote came between United's Division One play-off semi-final and final. Following the semi-final victory over Nottingham Forest, United were one win away from promotion to the Premier League. This fact triggered a large increase in the company's share price, by 2.25p to 11.75p. The two-legged semi-final was a dramatic affair. United gained a creditable 1-1 draw in the first leg at the City Ground, but early in the second half of the home leg found themselves 2-0 down. Goals from Michael Brown and Steve Kabba took the game to extra time, when an amazing dribble by United substitute Paul Peschisolido produced the goal that put United in front for the first time. Own goals by Des Walker and Robert Page made the final scoreline 4-3 to United, 5-4 on aggregate. However, immediately after the 3-0 play-off final defeat to Wolverhampton Wanderers at Cardiff's Millennium Stadium, the share price fell to 7.25p. Despite failure to win promotion the club continued on its chosen financial path and by the time of the company's 2005 *Interim Report* McCabe was confident enough to state, 'Financial stability has also enabled the club to rebuff interest from Premiership clubs in our best squad members. Historically player sales were forced to enable the club to continue trading; this is no longer the case and is a benchmark of Sheffield United's progress.' Such progress did not last the decade.

Further plans to increase capital arose in February 2006 when United announced they were to look to raise £10.7 million with a 'one-for-two' share issue, underwritten by Scarborough Property Company PLC, Craftglen Ltd and Green Piling Ltd, companies operated by United directors. Out of this £2.75 million would be used to finance the cost of developing a new stand in the Bramall Lane/Cherry Street corner. Another £1 million would partially fund the cost of acquiring the Thames Club, a gymnasium and health complex in Staines, Middlesex, that McCabe wished to purchase for £4 million. The balance would be applied to the cost of funding an additional investment in players' wages and for working capital purposes. Any excess amounts raised would be used to fund other business projects, including the proposed hotel development at Bramall Lane. An Extraordinary General Meeting in March approved the rights issue, after which McCabe stated it was 'a significant step forward for Sheffield United and advances further the strategy of building a property and leisure services business around a football club. We recently opened the "Impact" health club and juice bar at our Academy and stated that we intended to roll the concept out to other locations. The Thames Club will now become the flagship gym for that division'. The Thames Club was sold in 2008 for a profit of £700,000.

In November 2005 United appointed Jason Rockett, a former professional footballer with Rotherham United and Scarborough, as chief executive, thus becoming the first black chief executive in English football history. This aside, he became the club's public voice until stood down by McCabe in late 2009 and replaced by Trevor Birch. In one of his first pronouncements in the post, Rockett was to state that the additional funding would provide for 'our continued investment in the first team in order to maintain our position in the Championship and attain promotion to the Premiership'. In the company's 2006 *Interim Report* McCabe reiterated the club's business strategy: 'Recent history shows that those clubs who have over-speculated on the first-team squad with huge amounts of borrowed money so often find themselves in a position of creating a financial "black hole" which can take many years to infill and cure. Sheffield United's intention is to raise capital as appropriate to help support the club's objectives of providing the highest level of entertaining football at Bramall Lane.'

Soon after, United received approval of the long-awaited planning application to build a four-star, eight-storey, 158-bedroom hotel behind the new Bramall Lane/Cherry Street corner stand. The original plan was for ten floors but Council officials approved the scheme only after it was made 'less monolithic'. The planning permission for the construction of the hotel was the culmination of a long and arduous process – it was first mentioned in the development plans released by the club in August 1996, when its construction was identified as being one of the objectives of the stock market flotation. However, other parts of the stadium redevelopment had been going on apace. Work on the Enterprise Centre in the Bramall Lane/John Street corner of the ground began in July 2000, when representatives of the club, building contractors Mowlems and the Sharrow Community Forum[12] were present at the ground-breaking ceremony. The scheme, costing £3.5 million, involved the construction of a five-storey office block for small businesses, as well as infilling the John Street/ Shoreham Street corner with a new stand with 700 seats. Below the seats would be a community hall and offices for use by the Sharrow Community Forum. 'This is another significant step in the development of the club and its facilities at Bramall Lane,' remarked Derek Dooley. Construction work therefore began several years after plans to build the Blades Leisure Complex on land adjacent to the ground were first revealed. Tangible signs of progress were finally visible after countless delays and false starts.

In the summer of 1996 when the plans were first announced, assuming the Sheffield city planners gave the thumbs up, the project was intended to be funded largely by the stock market flotation of January 1997. Detailed plans of the complex were revealed ten days later following discussions with local residents prior to the formal application for planning permission. However it wasn't until July 1998 that drawings of the proposed complex were made available to the public, as the Town Hall Planning Department invited the lodging of objections. This was seen as a mere formality and work was expected to begin in October 1998. However, snags arose. United reported that the first part of the complex to be built would be the hotel in the Bramall Lane/Cherry Street corner, complete with its 'Skydeck' and rooms overlooking the pitch. Two factors combined to make the board have second

---

[12] A volunteer-led, grant-funded limited company and registered charity, which stated as its aim 'To improve the quality of life for people in Sharrow'.

thoughts. The first was that new hotels had suddenly begun springing up around the once quality accommodation-starved city, in particular Stakis (now the Hilton) at Victoria Quays near Sheffield city centre, and the Bristol in a refurbished office block nearby. There was a fear that United had missed the boat. The second was a boardroom personality clash. It appeared that Kevin McCabe was keen for the hotel operation to go ahead, while Mike McDonald thought it too expensive. There was also the prickly question of whether, if it were built, United would run it directly or it would be franchised. The two men favoured different options. This conflict may have been one of the major reasons behind Carlo Colombotti coming on to the board as McCabe sought support for his plans. Coincident with this was the fact that the club was suddenly forced to re-think much of the leisure complex scheme because while United dallied over purchasing the former Sheffield Works Department land on the opposite side of the adjacent Cherry Street, another party stepped in and beat them to it, despite Blades fan and local councillor Jean Cromar warning the club that this was a distinct possibility. The other party, a property developer, safe in the knowledge that planning permission had already been granted, made a firm offer to the City Council, which was accepted. The fruits of his quick actions could soon be seen in the form of new student apartment blocks housing several hundred undergraduates.

The scheduled start date for the hotel of October 1998 came and went. Despite Colombotti's proposed takeover becoming more and more protracted, somebody still had their minds on the job as detailed planning permission finally arrived in February 1999. However, by September 1999 nothing was built and the plans had changed. The hotel had taken a back seat, at least for the time being, with the Enterprise Centre and Community Hall in the corners of the John Street stand now becoming the priorities. The latter was to be the subject of local business, Government and European funding. Further details were given in Issue 2 of *Cutting Edge* in December 1999, as it was learned that 'a joint venture deal is now close to signing for the provision of a one-hundred-bed "business express" type hotel'. The likely start date was Spring 2000.

Readers were also told the Enterprise Centre and Community Hall project was proceeding on schedule. It wasn't; it was several months before it finally got underway. It was, however, finished ahead of schedule in March 2001 and six businesses moved in immediately. One of McCabe's Scarborough Group companies, Forsyth, was employed to operate and manage the Blades Enterprise Centre. Centre manager Gerry Gross said, 'We have had a great deal of interest in the centre from small and large businesses alike, and not just from Unitedites either. The idea of having offices based at a professional Football League ground really is proving an enticement.' Yunus Ahmed of the local Asian Welfare Association[13] backed the scheme, especially the community-use facilities, saying, 'This has come from the grass roots, which can only be a good thing. It wasn't a case of Sheffield United saying this is what we are going to do and this is how we are going to do it. The way things have been worked out together means it's an ideal opportunity to achieve several aims. Not only will it help create jobs for local people in the enterprise units but it also shows the club is opening its doors.'

Continuing with their ground improvement plans, July 2005 saw United officially announce their intentions to rebuild the Shoreham Street kop, increasing the stadium capacity to 36,000, and finally erect the hotel in the Bramall Lane/Cherry Street corner. The hotel had in the meantime been upgraded from 'business express' to a four-star specification - the club was now targeting the higher end of the market. Although no timescale had been put on the plans, the kop would become a two-tier stand incorporating sponsors' boxes, with the existing earth mound on which it was built being removed, to be replaced by a more conventional structure with facilities at several levels. Planning permission was granted by the City Council later that year to erect a 2,200-seater stand in the Bramall Lane/Cherry Street corner. The proposed hotel, initially to be part of the same development, would now be the

---

[13] A charitable organisation that offers advice on health, legal matters and employment opportunities to people from an Asian background.

subject of a separate planning application. The new corner stand was completed in time for the beginning of the 2006/07 season as Bramall Lane hosted Liverpool in front of an attendance of 31,726 for the first game in the Premier League following promotion. Planning permission for the hotel was granted in early in 2007. Construction began in the autumn and the four-star facility, under the guise of international hotel chain Copthorne, opened for business in January 2009. Its facilities included a high-class restaurant named '1855' (the year of the establishment of the Bramall Lane ground) and a fitness centre called 'Gym Plus'. McCabe explained to shareholders in the club's 2008 *Annual Report and Accounts* that the hotel 'provides a significant new stream of revenue'. The destination of said revenues was not specified.

The stadium plans were revised upwards in October 2008 to incorporate an expansion of the south stand to bring the capacity up to 44,500, sufficient for Bramall Lane to host World Cup matches should England be successful in its bid to stage the 2018 tournament. There would now be no sponsors' boxes in the kop design: the stand would be extended backwards with new facilities beneath. There would also be a new business centre in the Shoreham Street/Cherry Street corner. The south stand enlargement would involve removing the roof and building a second tier with executive boxes and a new roof, a scheme that would take up some of the existing car park space. Detailed planning permission for the kop plans was given in the spring of 2009 and for the south stand the following November. The planning report heralded the latter design as being an 'iconic image of the club well into the 21st century' but Jason Rockett seemed somewhat less enthused: 'Our focus remains on achieving success on the pitch and the planned stadium developments will contribute to our continued long-term strategy to drive off-the-field income for a sustainable business supporting further investment in the first-team squad.' Across the city, Sheffield Wednesday also gained planning permission to improve their Hillsborough Stadium in line with World Cup standards. They too were aiming to hold matches should England's 2018 bid succeed. The clubs joined together with the City Council in lobbying for Sheffield to be one of the host cities but were the city to be chosen, the united front would have to give way to open competition.

The Football Association announced its fifteen chosen cities in December 2009, a year before the host country was to be selected by FIFA. Sheffield was on the list but to the consternation of United and to the surprise of many, Hillsborough was named as the city's venue. Kevin McCabe told United's 2009 AGM that he was 'flabbergasted' by the decision. He added, 'We have arguably the best stadium in Yorkshire and it's a bit bizarre that the best stadium, with plans in place to expand it, plans that were submitted without the need for referring to any grants whatsoever, was for some reason refused. We will be conducting our own internal enquiry into why we failed – I do stress the word "failed". It's a great frustration. The work, the effort, the cost that we've applied to Bramall Lane to make it into a stadium worthy of the World Cup has been lost. We failed. We must find out why.' For many in football the choice of Wednesday over United had everything to do with Kevin McCabe and his historic legal battle with the Football Association, the Premier League and West Ham United (see Chapter 16). United lodged a complaint with the Local Government Ombudsman, asking for an enquiry into the way Sheffield City Council acted in its support of the city's bid. The Ombudsman would not have the power to overturn any decision but McCabe remarked, 'I expect if the Ombudsman agrees with us the council will get their knuckles wrapped.' The complaint predictably got nowhere.

By early 2006 the business side of the club was seemingly going well. The Academy incorporated a gymnasium and health club, while a new junior Academy in the Crookes district of west Sheffield was planned to encourage and develop football participation for a wider demographic than that available at the Shirecliffe Academy. Definitive plans had been published for the development of the Bramall Lane/ Cherry Street corner, including the hotel, and the long-awaited redevelopment of the kop. Jason Rockett was given the responsibility of establishing and building the property development side of the business. The PLC share price had doubled since the start of the 2005/06 season to around 20p, suggesting that a significant number of large investors shared a confidence in the club's projects. In an interview with the *Sheffield Star's* business section, McCabe detailed the club's approach to business and generating income. 'The core of Sheffield United is first-team football and the Saturday afternoon heritage,' he said. 'To make that sustainable in the long term we have to build a business and generate revenue that enables us to play at the top level. We are looking to add to those [planning] consents [already gained] by way of an application for an entertainment complex, including a big casino, but that will take a couple of years to sort out. [Our] real estate [portfolio] is quite impressive and we are trying to make the real estate assets "sweat", to make more revenue off the field that will sustain what happens on the field.' More revenue was a indeed a necessity, as on-field success - promotion to the Premier League - came at a cost, as players' salaries rose by 57 per cent to £7.7 million. In 2007, with the club operating a plausible business plan, the wage budget had only now returned to a level similar to that of nine years earlier, highlighting - again - the speculative unsustainability of the McDonald era.

The real estate portfolio was being supervised by United Scarborough Estates (USE) - later to be renamed Blades Realty - a joint venture set up for that purpose between Sheffield United PLC and McCabe's Scarborough Property Company PLC. USE announced that it had completed the sale of two properties for £9.55 million, one in the Smithfield area of London and one in Brighton. USE had also purchased eight office investments in various areas of the country. The *Sheffield Star* gave further details in its business pages. The London property was Boundary House, a multi-occupied, mixed-use building in Brentford, while the one in Brighton was located in a prominent corner, opposite the Royal Pavilion. The eight purchases were in Bristol, Crawley, Chelmsford, Egham, Leicester, Norwich and Rickmansworth, with tenants including music company EMI and insurers Friends Provident. Rockett commented, 'Following the significant returns secured in the last financial year, the two sales are another example of Sheffield United Football Club's continued determination and ability to make significant returns from non-football activities, in particular property. As a club we continue to ensure the off-the-field income stream continues to grow.' McCabe highlighted the off-field business success in his chairman's statement in the company's 2006 *Annual Report and Accounts*, writing, 'The successful transformation of Sheffield United into an exciting property, leisure and services corporation, with football at its hub, is further emphasised by the presentation of this year's *Annual Report and Accounts*.' McCabe was to add: 'In my history of supporting the Blades I reckon it is the first time that Sheffield United has not been labelled as a "selling club"!'

McCabe's mention of plans to build a casino gained prominence in March 2004, when the *Sheffield Star's* front-page headline read: 'Mr Billions'. The subject of the story was one Sheldon G. Adelson, who, with that name, just had to be American. Indeed he was, and he was also one of the richest men in the world, having made his fortune in the casino and restaurant world of Las Vegas. He was chairman and principal owner of the gambling city's Las Vegas Sands and Venetian resorts. His was the archetypal 'rags to riches' story. Born into a poor immigrant family in Boston, Massachusetts, Adelson sold newspapers on street corners to earn his first monies. He found he had the entrepreneurial touch, setting up his first business at the age of twelve. Since then Adelson had created and developed over 50 companies and in 1989 bought the Sands hotel and casino, former hangout of Frank Sinatra and the 1960s 'Rat Pack' association. He planned to open a Sands resort in Macao, China.

Adelson became connected with United after the Labour Government of Tony Blair announced that it would allow a small number of 'super casinos' to be built in England and Wales. The Sheffield United board wished to be in a position to enter the bidding. Preliminary plans were in place to construct a multi-million pound casino, leisure and residential complex that would take up almost all the area of the current south stand car park. The project, if successful, would, its publicists claimed, create more than 2,000 jobs. Said McCabe of the plans: 'With the support of the local community and a political will in Sheffield, I firmly believe that this project could not only underpin the future of this historic club, but also deliver real wealth and prosperity to Sharrow and the Sheaf Valley. We are already in meaningful consultations with the local community regarding the proposals. This has the potential to generate new revenue streams, which, if we get the green light, will go into all areas of the club. But I'm also positive that it would help us attract players here as well. They want to come to clubs that want to move forward, not ones who are content to stand still, and it all helps to create the right impression.'

Adelson's colleague William P. Weidner, chief operating officer of Las Vegas Sands, Inc., had obviously been given a quick history lesson. He was to state that 'Sheffield and its environs have a long history of innovation and success. The re-emergence of the city as one of the powerhouses of the north continues and I am delighted that Sheffield United has agreed to work with Las Vegas Sands, Inc. Together we can bring new employment and great leisure and retail facilities to the city centre. We began reaching out to football teams in the UK a year ago and we had an opportunity to meet Sheffield United. We realised how progressive they were in their thinking and ideas and how the team had been regenerating the city. It is a great partnership.' Adelson knew full well that opposition to the gambling bill would come mainly from those who predicted there would be a consequent increase in betting addiction. He was prepared for such dissension, saying, 'Addicts are victims of compulsive behaviour. There are betting shops all over the place so they don't need a casino to pursue their addiction. In the US we don't have betting shops but the UK has them on every corner so they can bet on everything and they don't have to go further than one street to do it. What is a casino going to do that isn't already being done? We are a responsible casino operator and we teach all our employees how to deal with this and to do the best they can to recognise a gambling addict and not allow them to play. We do the best we can to try to refer them to where they can get help. We don't want to carry on a business with people who are addicted; that's not responsible. My wife is a physician and treats people who are drug abusers and we fund two research facilities so we are very sensitive to people with compulsive behaviour.'

There was also the prospect of the detrimental effect the casino may have on local pubs and other businesses. The Henley Centre, a marketing company with more than ten years' experience in the gambling industry, produced a report into the anticipated economic and social impact of the proposed new gambling bill and concluded that many bingo clubs, amusement arcades and pubs could close as the casinos would take away their trade. The Henley Centre's gaming expert Ray Stone said, 'Supermarkets have had a huge impact on the way we shop but they have also had an impact on corner shops. If you develop a big casino leisure complex it is definitely going to have an impact on that area's bingo clubs, pubs and working men's clubs. The bill will allow the growth of casinos with unlimited prize slot machines and, in some cases, unlimited numbers of these machines. Machine revenue is vital to many of these [smaller] locations and therefore many will not be able to survive. Many of these closures will be rural and other community locations but some will also be in city centre locations.' Adelson argued to the contrary. 'There is no evidence that casinos take away trade. Evidence shows that business at local restaurants and pubs actually improves because there are more people coming in from outside the area. The casino becomes a centre of activity.'

Faced with opposition from anti-gambling groups, the relaxation of the bill that would allow the 'super casinos' was a long way from being passed. Second, if it did get through, the number of 'super casinos' to be permitted had not yet been decided; it was expected to be only a handful. Then, if Sheffield were selected to be one of the venues - there were other northern city bids from Manchester and Leeds - United faced competition from at least three other prospective bidders in the city. One was from another Las Vegas-based enterprise of the same standing as Las Vegas Sands, MGM Mirage, who had linked up with the British Land Company. Together they planned to build a casino complex near the Meadowhall shopping mall. Sheffield International Venues, which operated the major sporting venues in the city, was in talks with South

African gaming giants Sun International to build a casino on land adjacent to Don Valley Stadium. But perhaps the most intriguing counter-bid was to come from Sheffield Wednesday chairman Dave Allen, already owner of Sheffield's long-established casino by the name of Napoleon's, as well as nightclubs and Owlerton Greyhound Stadium. Despite being an opponent of the bill, claiming it would 'ruin a well controlled, well run and reasonably profitable industry', Allen wanted to create a huge gaming complex at Owlerton.

The Government's original plan was for around 40 'super casinos' and various other 'large' and 'small' casinos, the three designations being categorised by floor space. However, after much opposition from several sources, the number of 'super casinos' to be allowed was reduced to eight then, further, down to just one. When the Gambling Act 2005 became law, eight local authorities, including Sheffield, were on the shortlist for the single 'super casino'. It was eventually awarded to Manchester, despite Blackpool appearing to be the strong favourite, thus ending Sheffield United's hopes. Sixteen other towns and cities throughout the country were given 'large' and 'small' casinos but the situation changed again once Gordon Brown became Prime Minister in 2007. He and Culture Secretary Andy Burnham carried out a review of the policy and concluded that there was no necessity for a 'super casino' to help boost the regeneration of east Manchester, which could be efficaciously achieved by means of museums, theatres and retail, commercial and housing developments. Thus the decision was rescinded and the 'super casino' scheme dropped, although the 16 smaller casinos were to proceed.

As well as becoming involved with super-rich American businessmen, Sheffield United were casting their eyes to other corners of the globe. In 2002 they agreed a two-year sponsorship with Chinese soft drinks company Desun Fruits Technology Co Ltd. It was the first notable achievement made by returning commercial manager Andy Daykin and signalled the commencement of what was to be a significant link-up with China. 'Desun are an innovative organisation who are enjoying considerable success in China, North America and Australia,' said Daykin. FIFA-registered football agent Susan

Tham helped broker the deal. She explained: 'This is a huge opportunity for United and opens up so many possibilities. Their profile in China will be very big because of this. The market in China is huge and they are very, very interested in football. I believe this will be worth a lot to United. I can see this being the first of many similar deals in the future. This is also a compliment to United. This is the first time Desun have invested in an overseas team and they wanted to make sure they got things right.' The degree of interest in football in China was revealed when a game involving Second Division Grimsby Town, who had a Chinese international player in their team, was broadcast live on Chinese television. It attracted over 50 million viewers. However, unconfirmed reports claimed that United did not receive in full the agreed monies from Desun and the sponsorship deal was quietly allowed to lapse.

Big ideas in China and big wages for Chinese nationals followed. Around this time United – or specifically Kevin McCabe - were aiming to establish a football Academy on the Chinese holiday resort island of Hainan, which, when up and running, would apparently involve exchanges of coaches and players. The plan later went quiet and was never spoken of again. United's attempts to make inroads into the potentially lucrative Chinese football market gathered pace when they signed one of China's all-time great players, centre forward Hao Haidong, at the age of 34. It was unlikely that he would ever feature in United's first team, but more importantly he was to be a liaison between the club and its Chinese business interests. United's vice chairman Terry Robinson said that Hao was coming 'solely as a player to start with' but would learn about United's coaching methods to return to China to work at the proposed United Academy there. On an annual salary of £125,000, Hao played only one game for the first-team, as a substitute in an FA Cup home defeat to Colchester United. The deal had its apologist: Kevin McCabe said: 'We are beginning to use the Sheffield United brand [in China]. Hao Haidong is exactly the right person to be associated with. The only football they watch on TV in China is the English leagues. When we played Arsenal, 600 million people watched us in China on TV.' Effectively, Hao was paid by

United for being Chinese. The Chinese connection was extended when another player from that country, Li Tie, was signed in 2006. His salary – allegedly £6,000 a week - was reportedly paid by 'Chinese business sponsors', keen to help promote the United 'brand' in China. Li Tie, like Hao, played only once, in a cup tie against lower league opposition, and returned to China after United's relegation from the Premier League.

Improved annual results for the period ending June 30, 2005 were announced at the end of the year. McCabe was encouraged, stating that such results bore the initial fruit of the club's sustainable leisure, property and services business strategy. McCabe also announced that United were considering buying a Chinese league club. At the 2005 Annual General Meeting McCabe revealed that the Chinese club in question was Chengdu Five Bull and that Hao Haidong would act as a coach and intermediary between the two clubs. Located in the south-western Sichuan province, Chengdu was home to 11 million people, and had as its main industries food, medicine, machinery, finance, electronics and information technology. Its football club was at this time a mid-table Second Division team with a 40,000 capacity stadium.

McCabe expanded on the deal at the AGM, telling listeners: 'Contracts have been exchanged at a price which is not material to the group.' Few people in the room knew what this statement meant. He then added: 'Bringing Chengdu Five Bull into the Sheffield United fold presents enormous opportunities for the group and follows our first team's successful pre-season tour of the Far East in the summer. This does present us with a huge potential fan-base with which we can develop both the Chengdu Five Bull and Sheffield United brands. We intend to establish a leisure/football shop in the stadium, as well as a Blades bar in the city itself. The acquisition further cements our strong links with China. We have a Chinese language school at our Sheffield Academy, to enable young Chinese players to come to Sheffield to be trained by our coaching staff, whilst learning English. I can't tell you the terms but it's a hell of a deal. We've been able to pick up an interest in the club at a very small price.' The

Sheffield United 'brand' now supplied English lessons, and was to sell beer in China. Curiously, the Chinese city where a Blades bar was intended had some years earlier seen a Manchester United FC bar close due to lack of income. The Blades bar was never opened.

More details of the deal were revealed by chief executive Jason Rockett: 'Everything for us is long term with the aim of developing income from property and leisure to feed into the football club to strengthen our squad.' United duly completed the purchase of a 90 per cent share in Chengdu Five Bull, which changed its name the following season to Chengdu Blades. In the club's first full season under the Blades banner the club won promotion to the Chinese Premier League, with the help of four players brought over by United from the Ivory Coast. The Ivorian players, defenders Bamba Moussa and Souare Sekou Tidiane, striker Kamate Dramane and midfielder Kourouma Mohamed Lamine, were imported with the intention of assessing their suitability to ultimately play for Sheffield United. However, the true quality of Chinese football was emphasised when Chengdu Blades undertook a short tour of England in January 2007. They lost 3-1 to non-league Worksop Town and drew 1-1 with a United reserve side. United expected only a small crowd for the game at Bramall Lane, despite free admission, and therefore opened only the south stand. However, 10,615 people attended, forcing the club to open other stands to accommodate them. A further 400 fans were turned away as there were insufficient stewards on duty to satisfy ground safety regulations. In July 2008 Chengdu again visited England during the Chinese mid-season break, when they drew 2-2 with League Two strugglers Macclesfield Town, lost to United and Barnsley before beating non-league Sheffield FC 4-1. Before departing for Europe they were beaten 7-0 by Chelsea in Macao in a fund-raising game for victims of the 2008 Sichuan earthquake. United and Chengdu Blades (whose stadium was undamaged) offered financial and practical assistance in the affected area. Ironically, the earthquake offered McCabe manifold opportunities for new construction and property development.[14]

United's global network continued to expand with subsequent link-ups with clubs in Belgium, Brazil, Hungary and Australia. Recognising the way that Manchester United and Arsenal had set up arms of their academies across the North Sea as a way to import and develop young players from outside Europe - especially Africa - to sidestep the problems of obtaining work permits in Britain, McCabe, a resident of Brussels since 2006, used his contacts there to form an agreement with local semi-professional club Royal White Star Woluwe, of regional league Division 3B. White Star, formed as an amateur club in 1948, attracted attendances of around 1,000. McCabe attempted to explain what the deal was about, saying; 'This is not a lazy association. We are in this for the long term. Like many clubs we are keen to sign the best young talent available and because many of them cannot get work permits straight away this is the best way to do it. But everyone benefits. White Star's recent form shows that, and if [their players] continue to prove their worth then they can come to us. Likewise if a White Star player shows promise then we'll have an option but they'll benefit from a proper transfer fee.' The partnership would see five players and a coach from the Caribbean islands of Trinidad and Jamaica being 'placed' by United as full members of the White Star squad. None of the five ever made the grade in English football.

Belgian business magazine *www.thebulletin.be* described why McCabe moved to Brussels and how the contact with White Star came about. McCabe settled in Belgium for tax reasons – but, according to McCabe, not the usual ones concerning the avoidance of income tax and the capital gains tax that would come his way should he sell a football club at a profit. McCabe explained; 'Living offshore from the UK allows me to pass on wealth to my children without paying heavy

---

[14] The Chinese connection was extended in April 2009 when United agreed to sponsor the following month's Hong Kong Football Association Cup tournament, to be renamed the 'HKFA Sheffield United FA Cup'.

inheritance tax, even though the income tax is higher here in Belgium. It means the business endures beyond my lifetime.' This relocation allowed him just 91 days a year on UK territory to qualify for non-domicile tax status. It also meant that some board meetings of Sheffield United were held in Brussels. McCabe said he had not been in Brussels long enough to find his way about and didn't yet own a car, so he employed a chauffeur. It was the chauffeur who suggested he speak to White Star president Michael Farin. White Star were happy to become the shop window for a Premier League club. The *Green 'Un* reported that three Jamaicans and two Trinidadians - Matthew Bartholomew, Rafe Wolfe, Demar Stewart, Jason Morrison and Aaron Downing – arrived at White Star apparently 'scouted' by United director Terry Robinson. Boosted by their presence, White Star climbed to a fourth-place finish but were defeated in the first phase of the promotion play-offs. Season 2007/08 saw a slight improvement and a final placing of third, but again White Star fell in the play-offs. Then, without the assistance of the Caribbean players, the club ended up in mid-table in 2008/09. The partnership with White Star Woluwe also handed McCabe's companies construction and development opportunities. There were plans to build a hotel near the club's stadium, a 5,000-seater stand, corporate and dining facilities, a health and fitness centre and new changing facilities. However, by 2009 United's involvement with White Star's football team appeared to fade in favour of other ventures. Not one footballer had made it to the United first team via this route.

In late 2007 further planned associations with overseas clubs were announced. The first was fallen Hungarian giants Ferencváros of Budapest, 109 years old and champions of their country 28 times, but in July 2006 they were relegated to the second division due to financial irregularities. The club later went to court to challenge the legality of the demotion. Ferencváros won the case, the court declaring that the Hungarian Football Federation's decision was against the law. It was too late for Ferencváros to be reinstated, but an out-of-court agreement was made with the Federation. The Hungarian Government, meanwhile, had taken over the running of Ferencváros and invited tenders for the club and its adjacent empty land. Five previous attempts to sell were unsuccessful. McCabe's UK legal advisers Pinsent Masons introduced him to Hungarian law firm Gobert, Fest and Partners, which assisted McCabe in a tender for the land and club. In early 2008 one of McCabe's Hungarian-based companies, Esplanade Real Estate Kft, stated its intention to buy Ferencváros FC and its stadium for £8.45 million, pay off its £5 million debt and build a new stadium, with the aim of rejuvenating the club and restoring the team to the first division. Esplanade apparently beat off twelve other potential investors to win the contract.

Ferencváros immediately gained a strong Blades connection with the appointment of former United players Paul Shaw, Craig Short and Bobby Davison as player, player coach and manager respectively. Director Terry Robinson was sent to Budapest to manage the club's development on and off the pitch. Young United players Liban Abdi, James Ashmore, Sam Wedgbury, Matthew Lowton and Jordan Robertson also joined the club on loan, as did the Ivorian players who had previously been at Chengdu, and Trinidadian goalkeeper Jan-Michael Williams, a one-time triallist at United. Whilst Ferencváros gained promotion in the spring of 2009, they did so in front of crowds of fewer than 6,000. In the course of the previous twelve months the Hungarian economy was devastated by the world economic crisis. The property market of Europe collapsed; the implications of this for McCabe's business plans were not publicised. In mid 2009 Gary Armstrong visited the Hungarian club, where officials told of building 'plans' but could not give any date as to when work would begin.

In the autumn of 2007, continuing their bid for a global profile, United also revealed something publicised as a 'strategic alliance' with Brazilian club São Paulo FC, the club that produced world-renowned players Kaká, Cafu, Leonardo and Falcão. United director Simon McCabe, son of Kevin, was to state: 'São Paulo have been contacted about setting up something like this. They have chosen us because they want to become involved with a family club who they know they can have a close working relationship with.' What this 'working relationship' consisted of and why such a choice might be made in terms of a notion of 'family' was not explained. The great Brazilian player Pelé, himself from São Paulo, came over to Sheffield in November 2007 as part of the agreement, when a four-team youth tournament, involving São Paulo, Sheffield United, Manchester United and Porto, was held in his honour. The event took place in conjunction with the 150th anniversary celebrations of Sheffield FC, the world's oldest football club. Pelé, whose 'ears have been twitching' at the prospect of visiting Sheffield United, according to Simon McCabe, was guest of honour at a Bramall Lane dinner. The twitching ears of Pelé may well have been moving at the proposal of money. Pelé left Sheffield three days later with a £200,000 fee. Who paid him was not made public. After this, nothing was heard of the proposed 'alliance' with São Paulo, until a shareholder raised the subject at the club's 2009 AGM. Kevin McCabe explained that the lapse had occurred because of the May 2009 death of the club's Brazilian contact Harry Demitriou, the man responsible for bringing Pelé to Sheffield. However, United director David Green chipped in to say that the São Paulo link was not 'dead in the water' and that he hoped it could be resurrected 'in the coming months'.

United's next overseas link-up was in Australia, with national A-League club Central Coast Mariners. Kevin McCabe explained, 'It will mean the Blades having first choice over their best players to either play for us, join our sister clubs or to be placed in Europe with an opportunity to share the transfer proceeds. The Mariners will benefit from loan players, with some our young players from the Academy or players from our sister clubs going out to gain further experience.' McCabe expanded on the global expansion policy in the company's 2008 *Interim Report*: 'With the advancement in China recognised, the club's acquisition of Ferencváros FC is an exciting prospect. Whilst much work needs to be done to restore Fradi [the nickname of Ferencváros] to its former glory, the opportunity of combining the brands of Sheffield United with a major European club and Chengdu creates a portfolio of football brands for others to envy. Our overseas player development programme has produced new and exciting links.' This might be true - but it had not produced a footballer in the United first team. United then appointed two sports marketing 'experts' to 'maximise Sheffield United's unique international network', as it was reported on United's website. The pair were Michael Farnon, who previously worked for Manchester United, AC Parma, Atlético Madrid and the Jordan Formula One team, where he was Head of International Development, and Mike Hall-Taylor, also once with Jordan as its marketing director and who was responsible for marketing the Benson and Hedges and Silk Cut tobacco brands in the field of sports sponsorship. The former was to be given a place on the board; nothing was subsequently heard of the latter.

There were changes elsewhere too. In December 2009 Kevin McCabe relieved Terry Robinson of his duties at Ferencváros, confessing euphemistically to *BBC Radio Sheffield* about a 'blend between the Hungarians and the Brits which wasn't working'. There was an element of 'going into someone else's territory and telling them how it's done' that brought resentment, he added. McCabe took the chair of Ferencváros himself, Robinson returning to Sheffield. Manager Davison also left, for what were said to be 'family reasons', but for reasons which were a bit more salacious according to allegations on a United fans' website. Craig Short took his place as manager. Short's first game as 'caretaker' manager before his permanent appointment was a troublesome experience – the home match against Diosgyor was abandoned with third-from-bottom Ferencváros 3-1 down to the bottom side, when Ferencváros fans, unhappy about results and the way the club was being run, invaded the pitch throwing flares and fireworks. The club had to play its next three home games in an empty stadium. Short was forced to leave Ferencváros at the end of the 2009/2010 season when the Hungarian Football Federation introduced stricter eligibility criteria for the coaches of its league clubs. Short did not possess the required UEFA-approved coaching qualifications.

There was also trouble in China. United were shaken by allegations of match fixing in the Chinese Super League, which came to light in late 2009. Chengdu Blades were implicated in the investigation by a police task force, ordered by Hu Jintao, the President of China, who demanded a clean-up of professional football in the country. Football monthly *When Saturday Comes* reported that President's Hu's motive was to lift his national team, which failed to qualify for the 2010 World Cup and which was ranked 102nd in the world, to the level of success achieved in other sports at the 2008 Beijing Olympic Games. To achieve this he believed the sport must first employ what he called a 'Zhixing style', meaning 'moral uprightness'. The inquiry resulted in the arrest of two Chengdu officials and 22 people in total. Chengdu president Xu Hongtao and his deputy You Kuwei were accused of paying a bribe to the manager of rival club Qingdao Hailifeng to throw a game against Chengdu in September 2007. It was alleged that an agreement had been reached for Chengdu to win the match 2-0, which was indeed the final score. Zhang Weizhe, head coach of Chengdu Blades' reserve team – renamed Sheffield United Hong Kong – was another arrested. Investigators admitted that it would be difficult to obtain evidence to support the claims due to the time that had passed since. Kevin McCabe shrugged off the news, saying, '[Chengdu is] the only [Chinese] football club that's owned by a foreign club….. [the story] has attracted more attention than perhaps should be the case.' And that was that. The club said nothing more.

However, Lyall Gorman, executive chairman of United's Australian partners Central Coast Mariners, was not so reticent. In London to discuss the UK/Australia/China network, he told the *Sydney Morning Herald* that he had spoken to Kevin McCabe about the allegations. Both agreed that no decision would be made on the relationship with Chengdu until all the facts were made public. Gorman said, 'As of today, Chengdu are in the bucket with all of them and it may prove that they have nothing to answer for.' Gorman added that he had held lengthy talks with United's new chief executive Trevor Birch to decide 'how we can maximise the partnership' between United and Mariners. Terry Robinson was not to be part of the partnership. It was announced at the United's 2009 AGM that Robinson was to take what was unconvincingly described by McCabe as 'retirement' (in April

2010 Robinson joined Stoke City in a 'consultancy role'). It appeared that Robinson was being made to carry the can for the problems in Hungary and China. Strangely, neither the Chengdu match-fixing allegations nor the Ferencváros abandonment were deemed worthy of mention on United's website, when other news about the two clubs was plentiful.

The next development came in January 2010 when Nan Yong, the head of the Chinese Football Association, Yang Yimin, the organisation's vice president, and Zhang Jianqiang, responsible for assigning referees to matches, were taken for questioning by police investigators. The Chinese Football Association announced its findings, and its punishments, the following month. Chengdu Blades and Guangzhou GPC were demoted from the Chinese Super League, which would henceforth operate with fourteen teams, two below its regular quota, for the 2010 season. Qingdao Hailifeng, of the second division, were expelled from the league. The *Sheffield Star* reported that Sheffield United were to dispatch a delegation to China to 'help the country's clean-up football campaign'. How this would be done and what the outcome of the investigation meant for United's future involvement in the region and the club was not publicised. Chengdu Blades were re-promoted to the Chinese Super League at the end of the 2010 season.

Between 2007 and 2008 United looked to set up or become involved with football academies in China, Poland, Spain, Finland, the Ivory Coast and Malta. The small Mediterranean island of Malta was the latest on McCabe's list of countries in which he wished to establish a foothold. In August 2008 United agreed a sponsorship deal with the Malta Tourism Authority, whereby the first-team shirts would sport the logo 'visitMalta.com'. The deal was worth £350,000 per annum to United. In return, United would promote the island as a tourist destination, manage a youth football academy there and oversee local community projects. United boasted that they were the only football club 'to be sponsored by a country', a claim made by the fact that the Malta Tourism Authority was a government-owned entity. Something else unique about this sponsorship deal was that it also included a player! Maltese international goalkeeper Justin Haber signed for United as third-string behind Paddy Kenny and Ian Bennett. He never got close to a first-team appearance but, like Hao Haidong before him, he was considered a potent marketing tool in his home nation. In the summer of 2009 Haber was quietly moved on loan to Ferencváros, before being released by United in May 2010. Meanwhile, his lack of first-team games cost him his position with the Malta national team. The winter 2008 edition of United's newsletter *Cutting Edge* contained a two-page spread on Haber and Malta. Purportedly an interview with Sam Mifsud, chairman of the Malta Tourism Authority, one page was virtually a holiday advertisement. The second page held a feature on Haber and displayed a photograph of him and partner Raquel, a Maltese television sports presenter. They were portrayed as the 'Posh and Becks' of Malta. According to the newsletter, the pair were, 'Young, attractive, fashionably turned out and both in the public eye…. instantly recognisable to their fellow islanders.' A third-choice goalkeeper would not normally attract such a profile in a publication of any football club. Just maybe the fact that he was Maltese swung the issue. Soon after Haber's departure, United maintained their apparent requirement to have a Maltese player on the staff by signing striker Daniel Bogdanovic on a free transfer from Barnsley. At least Bogdanovic had some sort of pedigree at Championship level, having scored 19 goals in 49 appearances for Barnsley over the course of the previous two seasons.

There was little interest in Sheffield United in Malta. The island, which is football mad, has its football loyalties set in the duality of Italian *Serie A* and English Premier League clubs. Knowledge of the socio-political unity of Malta is required. No one at Bramall Lane had this knowledge. In truth, no one wanted to know. United's public relations consisted of slick full-page advertisements in Maltese newspapers in December 2008, wishing the population 'Merry Christmas from Sheffield United'. United played a friendly game in Malta in the summer of 2009 and held three days of public activities to promote the 'brand'. Hospitals were visited and souvenirs given out. A few items from United's 'Legends of the Lane' football museum were flown over for public viewing. The crowds did not flock.   The United 'ambassador' pairing of former players Tony Currie and Alan Hodgkinson were simply not known by the locals, having retired in the 1980s and 1970s respectively.

With such ventures, Sheffield United had become merely a subsidiary of Kevin McCabe's worldwide business empire. United were essentially a 21st century 'factory team' and, as Jason Rockett revealed in 2009, the footballing arm of an international property development company.   Many British football clubs are owned by overseas investors but, uniquely, McCabe used his football club to promote his global business interests.   The purchase of Ferencváros by one of his companies carried the admirable aim of bringing back the good times to the Hungarian club while giving young United players a broader playing experience.   The benefits to Ferencváros or United, however, were secondary to the possibilities offered to Esplanade in terms of stadium construction and retail and property development.   When Sheffield United acquired a 90 per cent share of Chengdu Five Bull, McCabe was quick to point out the 'enormous' potential for developing retail space attached to the Chengdu stadium, and the link-up with Central Coast Mariners coincided with the sale of part of McCabe's Scarborough Group to Australian-based Valad Property Group for £865 million in August 2007.

This latter part of McCabe's strategy didn't go entirely to plan. McCabe reportedly became personally wealthier to the tune of £150 million from the Valad deal but reinvested more than a quarter of the money - £42 million - in Valad and joined the company's board.   Soon afterwards, the name 'Valad' adorned United's south stand and the backs of the United team's shirts. Eighteen months later Valad was in trouble.   Its share price dropped by 44 per cent and it made a quarter of its staff redundant.   A payment of £37 million due to Valad's European Scarborough business was deferred, while part of the money still owed to McCabe was exchanged for equity, leaving McCabe owning 19.9 per cent of Valad.   The remainder of the payment to McCabe would be deferred by three years to September 2012.   Poor market conditions forced Valad to initiate discussions with banks about restructuring monetary facilities. Financial experts believed that Valad remained a 'very high risk' and would be 'very challenged to emerge from its current situation'. However, the company's future was safeguarded, if not secured, in July 2009 when a joint venture with Bank of Scotland was arranged, in which Valad handed over half its assets to the bank in exchange for a cash injection. Whether McCabe would ever receive the monies owed to him was open to question.

McCabe's relationship with Valad diminished further the following month when United signed a sponsorship deal with Dubai-based shipping and logistics company GAC Group, resulting in Bramall Lane's south stand discarding its 'Valad' regalia in favour of the GAC logo. GAC hoped to generate global business from United's connections in China, Hungary and Australia. Bill Hill, group vice president of GAC, explained how the agreement worked: 'We give Sheffield United a sum of money in direct relation to the business generated [for GAC] in return through their relationship with their customers. The more business we generate, the more cash that they will generate.' Further global-business links with the Middle East were publicised in late 2009 when a proposed friendly match between United and a club based in the Syrian capital Damascus failed to come off due to security and visa difficulties. One possible reason for United playing in Syria was that McCabe wished to use his club to promote his commercial interests or impress potential investors. After United sent a veterans' team of former players to compete in the EPL Masters Football Cup in Malaysia in November 2009, McCabe remarked, 'The very fact that we are invited to take part in events like this is because people respect us and what we are doing. In many ways our profile overseas outstrips the one we enjoy [in the UK].' This was debatable, but, more pertinent, where were the first-team footballers that such global profile was meant to produce?

The UK profile that McCabe sought saw him desperate to maintain matchday attendances at Bramall Lane. In the dark days of 1999 crowds slipped to below 10,000. In the seven seasons from 1999/2000 the average Bramall Lane home game climbed from 13,718 to 23,650. The increase was mainly down to the success of the team, but McCabe knew that maintaining that level of support would be as difficult as reaching it. He achieved it by both material and cosmetic improvements. In the summer of 2005 the exterior of the ground received a makeover, with new red and white cladding erected on the Bramall Lane stand, covering the previous shabby and crumbling rendering. Club badges and the words 'The Blades' were painted large and prominently on the south stand. They were only relatively minor aesthetic embellishments, but the ground looked the part, both inside and out. A new cantilevered roof was constructed over the Bramall Lane stand, removing the support pillars that obstructed sightlines. It all gave the impression of a club going places. New sponsors' names appeared on the stands – a firm of solicitors and a health care company at the Bramall Lane end and one of Kevin McCabe's property companies on the kop. In 2009 the John Street stand became the 'Malta Family Stand' and after the demise of the previous sponsors, sportswear retailers Streetwise, the John Street/Shoreham Street corner stand was named the 'Fortina Spa Stand' (Fortina Spa is a Maltese hotel owned by Michael Zammit-Tabona, a fanatical Manchester United fan of Maltese origin who is banned from any involvement in football in Malta). Continued ground development, particularly the infilling of two of the corners, added more seats. They had to be filled. Promotion in 2005/06 and Premier League status for a year took care of that, but how could the recently gained and returning supporters be retained following relegation?

United had over 20,000 season tickets holders for the 2006/07 Premier League season. Creative schemes had to be devised to retain them in the Coca Cola Championship. The answer was competitive pricing (United's season ticket prices for the 2007/08 season were some 10-12 per cent cheaper than Sheffield Wednesday's), alongside a promise to maintain prices for the 2008/09 season for those who paid early, even if promotion was re-gained. Inducements for young supporters were available: under-13s were given free season tickets provided they paid £10 to join the Junior Blades organisation; 14- and 15-year-olds (termed 'Teen Blades') and 16- and 17-year-olds ('Young Adults') were given scaled prices pitched between the junior and adult rates. The hope was that they would become hooked, guaranteeing their future support in adolescence and adulthood. They would also spend money in the club shop and inside the ground, which would ideally make up for the income lost by virtue of - in some instances - giving away season tickets. Finding the money for full season tickets was made easier by offering payment terms that extended for the whole season. Additionally, ticket offers were made available to the 50,000 students at the city's two universities, thousands of whom lived within two miles of Bramall Lane.

As a marketing exercise it was brilliantly executed – season ticket numbers held at around 19,000 in the three seasons after relegation (by comparison, United had 8,400 season ticket holders in the 2000/01 season). United's average attendance was the highest in the Championship in 2007/08 (25,648), the second highest in 2008/09 (26,018) and the third highest in 2009/10 (25,120). That said, 'boosterism' was ever evident. McCabe, when questioned on ticket sales, would continually use the phrases 'upwards of' and 'north of' to signify the ever-rising figures. However, most clubs, including United, publicise crowd figures as the number of tickets sold (or even given away), which is not necessarily the same as the number of spectators inside the ground, often giving a false impression of the actual attendance. Unlike in American sports where the number of 'no-shows' is identified, how many of those with tickets who don't turn up is not disclosed. Regardless of the true crowd figures, the promotion was still a major success story in terms of numbers, albeit the income generated was not big. Indeed in the 2008/09 season home games at times saw 3,000 tickets given away. Once again the attendance figures looked good but did not tell the full story as to United's 'profile' and, indeed, gate receipts.

In the summer of 2008 McCabe attempted to define and describe his hopes and expectations for the future development of all parts of the club under the mantra 'The Blades Way', which copied the 'ways' propounded a year earlier by some of the leading Premier League clubs and harked back to the 'Juventus Style' constructed by the Agnelli family at their club in the 1970s. The plan, which was not exclusive in any way to the Blades, was to establish United in the Premier League on a base of 'responsibility, determination, discipline, pride, hard work, honesty and commitment to excellence and to the community', with manager Kevin Blackwell considered the ideal personality to lead the team. When interviewed by *Flashing Blade* Blackwell explained what 'The Blades Way' meant to him: 'Sheffield United is known for hard work, integrity and it's a working man's club, it's the Steel City. No matter what happens to the industry here, that will always be a characteristic of the Blades. In Sheffield people work hard, they've always had to work hard because it's been hard graft. Determination, they've got that in abundance, loyalty, enthusiasm, all those things, so we thought how do you encapsulate that? Let's make it the Blades Way. We want it from everybody…… the car park attendant, he's bright, he's smart, he's enthusiastic. It's the Blades Way, this is ours, this is our club.'

Admirable sentiment and historically pertinent, but such words smacked too much of corporate blather. True, Sheffield is a 'northern working-class city' and Blades fans love to see hard-working, committed players, but they also dote on the unpredictability of talent and flair. For all their undoubted efforts, players such as Trevor Hockey in the 1970s and Nick Montgomery in the new millennium would not rank high on any United fan's list of the club's best-ever players. Those lofty positions are reserved for the unbridled brilliance of the likes of Tony Currie and Jimmy Hagan. The working-man's club was also a direct contradiction of the 'Family Club' cliché that had adorned club insignia since the term was pioneered by Reg Brealey in 1981. As for the bright, smart and enthusiastic car-park attendants, the club in a 2009 cost-cutting exercise dispensed with the services of half. Their Saturday afternoon tasks had seen some take home £15 a match. There was, though, a quantifiable side to the 'Blades Way'. United's network of international academies, now including one in Chengdu and another planned near Sydney, adopted what was called the 'Blades Way' of player development, which in practical terms meant they were graded using uniform technical and physical baseline measurements, comparable and transferable - in theory - between academies.

By the end of the decade the question remained whether McCabe's non-football business activities were subsiding Sheffield United, or the other way round. No players from any of United's 'sister clubs' or 'partnerships' had found their way into direct employment with Sheffield United FC. When interrogated on this subject at a question and answer session for supporters at Bramall Lane in July 2009, McCabe countered by emphasising that no money was going out of Sheffield United in connection with these businesses – rather, he, and implicitly his family – had, he said, put many millions of their own wealth into the club. The various business arrangements were sold to fans as being crucial to the future success of Sheffield United and 'diversification' and 'off-field revenue streams' became almost as common expressions as 'centre forward' and 'four-four-two'. United now possessed a 'portfolio of football brands for others to envy' so that 'international activities should add value to the company'. But McCabe admitted at the 2009 AGM that the overseas ventures weren't going to plan. He was to comment: 'I don't think we've got it right so far and that's why we've not had [players] coming through. Hungary's a bit too early, in fairness, to comment. The prospects for the academy there are very good. However, we have this dilemma of work permits. The academies themselves are very well run but maybe internationally we've just missed getting hold of the really talented youngsters. It is being re-examined. It's taking longer than we'd all wish. Maybe it needs that new blood, younger blood, to get best advantage.' The new, younger, blood was revealed in the shape of 60-year-old Ron Reid, who was to leave the Shirecliffe Academy set-up, where he had been director since its founding in 2001, for Budapest. McCabe was right to shake up the Budapest connection, especially in the light of the presence of several Hungarian players in the Premier League and the Championship. When asked at a 'Fans' Forum' at Bramall Lane in April 2010 how much money the partnerships with Ferencváros, Central Coast Mariners and Chengdu was costing United, McCabe replied, 'Not a cent. China did cost us but we have restructured and they no longer do. We have not utilised these associations enough. There are benefits commercially because we are a global brand.' McCabe later told the authors that running the Chinese operation had cost his Scarborough group of companies £2.25 million and the Hungarian interest four million Euros.

The de-listing of Sheffield United PLC from the stock market in January 2009 further strengthened McCabe's position and his ability to make decisive business interventions. The re-privatisation of the club was the culmination of several years in which McCabe steadily increased his and his family's shareholding until it reached over 75 per cent in 2008. At the time of the proposed 2002 refinancing of the club, the directors claimed that it was not anyone's desire for the club to be controlled by any one individual; six years later it ended up being that way. McCabe's Scarborough Group bought United director Michael Dudley's 14 per cent shareholding in May 2008 to reach the 75 per cent figure, at which point McCabe delivered a statement to the Stock Exchange confirming he intended to offer to buy all the remaining shares. There were several reasons for de-listing, including the post-2008 fall of the global stock markets, the inability to raise capital from investors on the Stock Exchange and the constrained ability of the company to react quickly to the requirements of a challenging marketplace.

McCabe said, 'The board has unanimously decided to recommend de-listing to the shareholders as we feel that the current economic environment means there is little benefit to Sheffield United and its shareholders in remaining listed.' Shareholders would still be able to trade their shares at an agreed price and would still be entitled to attend future AGMs. The board also offered to buy shares from shareholders at a defined price. The offer was made in December 2008. Shareholders at the AGM later that month voted in favour of de-listing the company from the AIM, a move that took place the following month.

The presence of McCabe's two sons, Simon and Scott, on the board (Simon since 2006, Scott since 2007) was another indicator of McCabe's hold over the club. Three other directors, Jason Rockett, John Burnley and Simon Capper, joined the PLC board having been previously employed by McCabe's Scarborough Group. There was in reality no room for opposition or dissent and the resignations of directors Alan Bamford in August 2005, Mark Fenoughty in June 2007 and Sean Bean in December 2007 suggested that those who disagreed with McCabe left. Bamford had fallen out with the club over expenses claims made when he was a director between 2000 and 2005. Gary Armstrong was shown documentation written by McCabe given to fellow directors detailing Bamford's exclusion from the boardroom. Fenoughty left suddenly in what was reported as a 'surprise move' but a move that probably did not surprise his godfather Alan Bamford. Bean said at the time of his departure, 'The club has come on leaps and bounds in the last five years and I'm proud to have played a small part in that. But as someone who is very passionate about his football, I know my place is out there with the fans who support the club week in, week out, whoever is in charge. I would have liked to have been more involved in the day-to-day running of the club but when your job takes you away for months at a time that simply isn't possible. I'll still get to as many Blades matches as I can. All that will change is that I won't have the luxury of a comfy seat in the directors' box.' His reasons for leaving did not sound convincing - he was said to be angry that he had been left on his own to head the delegation of Blades fans to the House of Commons to protest against the leniency of West Ham United's punishment for breaking the rules regarding third-party ownership of players (see Chapter 16). He felt that other directors should have been present too. Another version of his departure told of how Bean made one request of McCabe, which was not carried out. Consequently Bean resigned his directorship whilst keeping his six-figure investment in the club and never entered the boardroom over the following three years.

Bean's resignation meant that the number of Sheffield-born directors was reduced further. At the start of the century the PLC board comprised entirely Sheffield men (Kevin McCabe, Bernard Procter, Derek Dooley, Michael Dudley, Andrew

Laver) but at the AGM in December 2009 McCabe announced a boardroom re-shuffle that left only him of the local men remaining. Dudley moved to the football club board, while Laver stood down as a director, terminating the decades-old presence of a member of his family on the board. At the same time Jason Rockett 'retired' from the board to return to the property arm of McCabe's company, with Stephen McBride, Michael Farnon and Trevor Birch elected to join Simon McCabe, Scott McCabe, Simon Capper and Simon Argall. None of them were from Sheffield, but all were brought in by Kevin McCabe. The football club board consisted of Kevin McCabe, Chris Steer, Trevor Birch, David Green, Michael Dudley and John Burnley. Of these, McCabe, Steer, Dudley and Green were from Sheffield. Overall, the Sheffield influence had diminished, whereas the McCabe family influence had amplified.

As well as being a vehicle for his global ambitions, McCabe stressed that the club was the centre of the Sheffield 2 postal district. He continually spoke of creating jobs and opportunities for people in the Sharrow district that surrounds Bramall Lane. He insisted that the supporters were the club's greatest assets and should be treated as such. 'A football club should be owned by its community and the supporters are its family,' he said. A charitable organisation named the 'United Initiative' - headed by former United players Mark Todd and Adrian Littlejohn - was established so that the club's community involvement could be 'taken to a new level', according to the 2009 *Annual Report and Accounts*. 'Our philosophy of "Putting the community first" remains ever important,' said McCabe. But so much of this could be dismissed as corporate-speak. The fact that the cover of previous year's *Annual Report and Accounts* bore the claim 'Putting the Community First' suggested the club had to stress that which is not obvious. Such a claim is typical of politicians and corporate entities, who in their ambitions always seek – or claim – the approval of that usually mythical entity, the community. The concept of 'community' only stretched so far - amidst the financial statistics one stood out to some readers. The club's annual contribution to that listed as 'charitable donation' totalled just £29,000 in the three years

2005-2007 and strangely the recipients were not listed. Equally strangely, no such figure was itemised in either the 2008 or 2009 *Annual Report and Accounts*. Other contradictions emerged. In May 2010 the 'United Initiative' received an award from Sheffield City Council to recognise its work with more than 15,000 young people in the city, contributing to the Government's 'Aiming High for Young People' strategy[15]. At the same time the club counted among its corporate sponsors the giant Indian-based steel company Tata, which in January 2007 bought the UK's major steel producer Corus. Within three years Tata had ended 160 years of steel-making at its Redcar, Teesside, plant and made hundreds redundant at Stocksbridge and Rotherham in South Yorkshire and Scunthorpe in Lincolnshire. The incongruity of a club that 'put its community first' being sponsored by a company that made such stringent cuts to its South Yorkshire workforce would not be lost on the many Blades fans undoubtedly affected.

Despite reservations about his 'real' motives the majority of Blades supporters would probably grade McCabe as the club's best chairman in living memory. With the economic difficulties facing the world in 2009 and beyond, McCabe's task, on all fronts, remained a challenging one. Despite Sheffield United PLC making a profit of £5.7 million and reducing football-related bank debt to £2.3 million in the year to June 30, 2009, McCabe issued words of caution, warning of the erosion of real estate values and banks' lack of liquidity, also stressing the need to 'adapt to change'. According to the 2009 *Annual Report and Accounts*, one of these possible changes was deliberation over the future ownership of 'non-core assets', notably Blades Realty and Chengdu Blades. But the challenge was one promoted as ever-positive by the two public relations companies - HR Media of Sheffield and London-based Jardine International Media Communications -

---

[15] 'Aiming High for Young People: A ten year strategy for positive activities', published in July 2007, set out the Government's plans to help all young people, particularly those from disadvantaged backgrounds, to take part in enjoyable and purposeful activities in their free time.

that now handled McCabe's (and United's) affairs, the latter at a cost of around £75,000 per annum. Corporate talk and placed stories were accompaniments to the global brand of Sheffield United. Any alternative truth had to be sought in the dissenting keyboards of Blades fans posting on internet forums.

Chapter 16

'Tevezgate'
Argentinians Make Me Cry

Sheffield United were relegated from the Premier League on the final day of the 2006/07 season by a rare combination of results. The outcome echoed the events of May 7, 1994 when an injury-time goal by Chelsea's Mark Stein and unlikely results for Ipswich Town and Everton contrived to send United down from the Premier League. In 2007 United needed only a point at home to the mediocre Wigan Athletic to be safe, but West Ham United also required at least a point at champions Manchester United to be sure of saving themselves. A defeat for the Hammers would have seen them finish below both the Blades and Wigan. However, Wigan won 2-1 at Bramall Lane to go above United on goal difference and, incredibly, West Ham pulled off a 1-0 victory at Old Trafford to condemn the Blades to the drop. And just as in 1994, when rumours were rife that match-fixing took place to decide Everton's 3-2 win over Wimbledon after trailing 2-0, an element of the underhand was raised around the 2007 outcome. This time the issue had global implications for the game and the issue of player ownership. The final verdict of a protracted legal case saw Sheffield United potentially change the outcome of football results forever.

West Ham's winner at Old Trafford was scored by the Argentinian international striker Carlos Tevez. He had signed for the Hammers, along with compatriot Javier Mascherano, on the final day of the August 2006 transfer window. It was an unusual double transfer as the players were not purchased from another football club but from a company, Media Sports Investments (MSI), that owned their 'rights' and in a sense owned them. The former head of MSI, Iranian-born businessman Kia Joorabchian, had retained an investment in the two players. Joorabchian was a global football fixer. He and his family had moved to Britain following the fall of the Shah of Iran in the late 1970s. University educated in London, he became a multi-millionaire when he sold his equity company, American Capital. In 2004 he founded MSI, which took over the Brazilian football club Corinthians, paving the way for Tevez and Mascherano to leave their Argentinian sides to sign for the club, albeit they were legally owned by MSI. Following his departure and those of Tevez and Mascherano from Corinthians, the club - then managed by Argentina's 1978 World Cup winning captain Daniel Passarella and former Blade Alejandro Sabella - was relegated to the second division of the Brazilian championship.

When West Ham signed the two players on August 31, 2006, a press statement read: 'West Ham United are delighted to announce the double signing of Argentinian World Cup stars Carlos Tevez and Javier Mascherano from Brazilian club Corinthians. The pair have put pen to paper on permanent contracts with the club this afternoon. All other aspects of the transfers will remain confidential and undisclosed.' This wasn't to be. At the same time as their signing, West Ham declined to mention the fees paid, or the involvement of MSI and Joorabchian. Such omissions raised concerns in some sections of the football press, though not to the degree that would become apparent much later. Tevez, aged 22, was one of the most sought-after young strikers in the world and eyebrows were raised when he signed for Corinthians from Argentinian side Boca Juniors for £9.5 million in December 2004. Midfielder Mascherano similarly moved from Boca's great Buenos Aires rivals River Plate to Corinthians for the lesser figure of £5.5 million. It was highly unusual for such intra-continental transfers to take place within South America; top-class players from both countries were more often inclined to seek the riches on offer in Europe. It emerged that whilst they played in Brazil, Corinthians did not wholly own either player because of a 'third-party' arrangement with MSI, a practice that was both legal and commonplace in South America but against the rules in English football. Speculation in the summer of 2006 suggested that Chelsea were willing to pay anywhere between £20 million and £60 million for Tevez. Joorabchian, at the time president of MSI, had stated; 'Tevez will leave Corinthians if a team pays the contract's release clause, which is between £69 million and £83 million.' Despite the wide variety – and disparity - of the figures, Tevez's transfer value was large. There was considerable bewilderment in the English game as to how West Ham had raised such money to buy players of this stature.

Despite having two such high-quality players, West Ham spent most of the season near the bottom of the Premier League. Mascherano was not an instant success, making only five league appearances before the turn of the year. Tevez was a regular and well-liked by the fans but failed to score during the first half of the season. However, Mascherano had made enough of an impression, based more on his performances in the 2006 World Cup than anything he had done at West Ham, for Liverpool to express an interest in signing him. This presented two difficulties. The main one was that FIFA rules did not permit a player to play for more than two clubs in one year from July 1. A special dispensation for the transfer was given because of the overlap between the South American and European seasons. More problematical was the nature of Mascherano's registration with West Ham; questions regarding the ownership of the player were raised by Liverpool and brought to the attention of the Football Association and the Premier League. After investigation, the Premier League satisfied itself that the relationship between Liverpool and the player was not 'subject to third-party influence' and allowed the transfer to proceed, despite it being two weeks after the close of the January transfer window.

As a result of the Mascherano transfer, the relationship between West Ham and Carlos Tevez now attracted attention. In early March 2007 West Ham were charged by the Premier League for breaching its rules over the signings of the two

Argentinians. The Premier League was informed that Liverpool hoped to sign Mascherano on the same financial terms that he was on at West Ham. The latter then came forward with the required details, including the contractual clauses referring to MSI's involvement. The Premier League said if West Ham had submitted this information when the transfers were completed in August 2006 the two players would have been declared ineligible to play in England. The regulation broken was Premier League Rule U18, which forbade third-party player ownership of players as it was believed such ownership could potentially influence events at the club. Rule U18 stated: 'No club shall enter into a contract which enables any other party to that contract to require the ability materially to influence its policies or the performance of its teams in league matches.' Specifically, it was alleged (and even feared) that the players' representatives could determine when the players were sold and when they were selected to play. West Ham were then asked by the Premier League to provide further details of their agreement with MSI. These details were not forthcoming.

In the impasse the Premier League issued a statement, which read: 'It is the [Premier League] board's complaint that there were agreements in relation to both these transfers that enabled third parties to acquire the ability materially to influence the club's policies and/or the performance of its teams in league matches and/or the competitions set out in Rule E10. The board's view is this constitutes a breach of Rule U18. Furthermore, at the time of the transfer agreements for both Carlos Tevez and Javier Mascherano, and until January 24 2007, West Ham United failed to disclose the third-party agreements to the Premier League and/or deliberately withheld these agreements from the Premier League. The board's view is this constitutes a breach of rule B13, which states, "In all matters and transactions relating to the League each club shall behave towards each other club and the League with the utmost good faith".'

West Ham vowed to 'vigorously defend' themselves against such accusations. The club based its defence on the claim that the manager Alan Pardew had full control over team selection, so that U18 was not breached, and that any illegal agreements that may have been entered into were arranged by the club's previous owners. Since Tevez and Mascherano were signed, West Ham had been taken over by a consortium headed by Icelandic businessman Eggert Magnússon, a former president of the Football Association of Iceland. A precedent for this defence occurred in 1994 when Alan Sugar, then chairman of Tottenham Hotspur, was successful in getting a 12-point deduction rescinded after arguing that the club's offences of making illegal payments to players were committed by a former regime. This must have been known to the three-man disciplinary commission convened to hear West Ham's case, with possible punishments ranging from a fine to a points deduction should the club be found guilty. The commission comprised Simon Bourne-Arton QC (chair), Lord Herman Ouseley and David Dent. The Premier League's website gave brief biographies of the panellists. Bourne-Arton had extensive experience in all areas of criminal law, in particular white-collar fraud. Lord Ouseley was chair of the anti-racist organisation 'Let's Kick Racism Out of Football' and was previously executive chairman of the Commission For Racial Equality. David Dent began his career as secretary of Carlisle United Football Club in 1960 before moving to a similar position at Coventry City. He then served as deputy secretary and secretary of the Football League.

At the tribunal the Premier League accused West Ham of lying over the ownership of the two players. The disciplinary panel heard that the players were in fact owned by companies registered in Gibraltar and the British Virgin Islands. Tevez was owned by MSI and Just Sports Inc. (JSI) and Mascherano, prior to Liverpool acquiring him, was owned by Global Soccer Agencies, a company connected with the Israeli-born football agent Pini Zahavi. Documents outlining the third-party arrangements were given to the Premier League on January 24, during Liverpool's negotiations to sign Mascherano. At the time of West Ham's signing of the two Argentinians the club's former chief executive Paul Aldridge informed the Premier League that he had declared all relevant documentation. It was only after new chairman Magnússon bought the club in October that the other facts - unknown to him - started to emerge. As the Premier League considered the case, West Ham's former chairman Terry Brown resigned as a non-executive director of the club as Magnússon blamed him for the difficulties the club was now in.

West Ham eventually admitted breaching regulations and concealing information from the Premier League. The commission announced its decision on April 27, 2007: West Ham were to be fined £5.5 million but were not to suffer a deduction of points. In addition, Tevez was to be permitted to play for the remainder of the season as West Ham assured the hearing that any third-party agreements had been cancelled. The clubs around West Ham at the foot of the table, notably Sheffield United, Fulham, Wigan Athletic and Charlton Athletic, were appalled by what they saw as a lenient punishment. West Ham had won one and lost three of the four games immediately preceding the announcement (including a 3-0 defeat at Bramall Lane) but won 3-0 the following day at Wigan to give them a chance of escaping relegation. A penalty of even three points would have virtually sealed their fate but now they were back in it.

The Premier League published its findings on its website. The report stated: 'West Ham entered into what was called a private agreement with Mr Tevez and MSI Group Limited and Just Sports Inc. Tevez fully acknowledged that the companies had the sole, exclusive and unilateral right, upon serving written notice to the club during the transfer window, to terminate his contract with West Ham upon payment to the club of £2 million.' Further clauses in the contract reinforced the control MSI would have over Tevez's 'player's rights'. The hearing heard that Scott Duxbury, legal and commercial director of West Ham, had contacted Jane Purdon, Premier League company secretary, to confirm whether third-party clauses could be included in the contracts between the club and the players. Purdon claimed that she told Duxbury that such an arrangement would not be acceptable, due to Rule U18. Duxbury, however, claimed, 'There was no reference at all to that rule.' Amazingly for the legal and commercial director of a Premier League football club, Duxbury claimed to be 'ignorant' of U18. Duxbury claimed he spoke to Paul

Aldridge, West Ham's chief executive officer, and passed on what Purdon had said to him. Aldridge then told Duxbury he would place the fact of the third-party ownership into what he called 'side agreements', which he said he would not disclose to the Premier League. Just to be on the safe side Duxbury again checked the rules to satisfy himself that such non-disclosure would be permitted. Shockingly, the report claimed he again failed to look at Rule U18, and was of the opinion that non-disclosure was permissible.

This train of events careered off the rails on September 1, 2006 when mounting media speculation as to the nature of the deals prompted Purdon to phone Duxbury. The commission findings reported: 'She asked him if the club had entered into any arrangements with any third parties. Ms Purdon says that his answer was an unequivocal "no".' A week later Aldridge met Premier League chief executive Richard Scudamore. Scudamore wanted to know how West Ham had got the players so cheaply and whether or not there was any documentation that the Premier League had not seen. He was to receive a categorical assurance that there was no such documentation. Reflecting on this the Premier League delivered as damning a verdict as possible: 'What we believe to have occurred here is that Messrs Brown, Aldridge and Duxbury were anxious to complete the registration of these players by the deadline of August 31. They knew that the only means by which they could acquire them would be by entering into the third-party contracts. Equally, they were aware that the FA Premier League, at the very least, may not - and in all probability would not - have approved of such contracts. They determined to keep their existence from the FA Premier League.' In other words they lied.

The hearing found that West Ham United were guilty of 'an obvious and deliberate breach of the rules' - specifically 'a grave breach of trust as to the FA Premier League and its constituent members' - and 'dishonesty and deceit.' Entering into the third-party contracts was a breach of Rule U18, while lying about them was a breach of Rule B13. As the hearing noted: 'An officer of the club, its chief executive officer, told Mr Scudamore a direct lie, namely there was no documentation of whatever kind in respect of these players which the FA Premier League had not seen.' Whilst acknowledging that a points deduction was a course that it would normally consider following such a breach and that some breaches were of such a serious nature that only a deduction of points would be appropriate, the hearing managed to reach the conclusion that a deduction of points would not be proportionate punishment. The hearing gave a number of reasons for choosing a fine over a points penalty. One was that the club was under new ownership and management. This argument was contrary to company law to which, as a Public Limited Company, West Ham United PLC was subject. Among other things a company is defined as a legal entity that has a legal identity separate from its members. The 'members' included the previous regime of Brown and Aldridge and the current owners but the company had a separate legal identity from these individuals. As an example, debts incurred by a company are not wiped out when a new owner takes over. In the same way, the PLC was still the same body that was represented by Aldridge and Duxbury and was liable for any punishment it incurred from actions undertaken as representatives of West Ham United PLC. It was the identity of West Ham United PLC that was important to the case, not the persons of Aldridge or Magnússon.

A further reason given for not docking points was the delay between the discovery of the breaches and the subsequent proceedings. The commission concluded that, had the hearing been held in January, a points deduction would have been easier to bear than a points deduction in late April, which would have consigned West Ham to certain relegation. This was a curious statement considering the breaches came to light on January 24 but it wasn't until April 27 that the hearing delivered its verdict. Given the ramifications of this delay, so important that it impacted on the decision not to impose a points penalty, it could well be asked whose fault that was. The Premier League hearing was vague on this point, claiming simply that it was 'no party's fault'. The delay was in fact primarily the fault of West Ham. By covering up the third-party arrangements from August to December and then by pleading not guilty until the last minute, West Ham managed to spin out the hearing until almost the end of the season, as the Premier League explained: 'Even having submitted [the third-party clauses] West Ham United continued to argue that these agreements did not influence its policies or performance of the team and therefore were not in breach of Rule U18'. Even as late as late as April 26, the day before the hearing, Magnússon was still saying that the club would appeal if found guilty. The fact that the hearing didn't deliver its verdict until so late in the season was solely down to the actions of West Ham United. The club benefited from the delay it had caused.

It seemed that the Premier League's prime concern in reaching its decision was not to uphold its own laws but to be 'fair' to West Ham, a club it had just found guilty of 'dishonesty and deceit'. Mel Goldberg, a lawyer with sports law specialists Max Bitel Greene, admitted that he found the reasons for the penalty baffling from a legal standpoint. 'The timing of the case being presented is irrelevant,' he stressed. This showed up another glaring flaw in the hearing's judgement, namely that it beneficially took into account West Ham's guilty plea. This might be fair enough had West Ham accepted guilt and thrown themselves at the mercy of the hearing in January but Magnússon plead not guilty until the last moment, ensuring the verdict would be delivered as close to the end of the season as possible.

The hearing engaged in more questionable reasoning when it stated that a further basis for choosing a fine over a points penalty was that Carlos Tevez had continued to play for the club for three months after the discovery of the rule breaches, despite the hearing admitting that the Premier League had the power to terminate his registration. The hearing report further stated: 'For understandable reasons, they did not.' The reasons were, presumably, so 'understandable' they did not need to be divulged. Gordon Taylor, chief executive of the Professional Footballers' Association, defended the decision, saying, 'Fans of other clubs may not be [happy with the verdict] but if you need to stay in a division because another club has been deducted points it's not the sporting ethos you would want. I

397

can't believe anyone would want to stay up that way.' This opinion found little support at Sheffield United.

Perhaps the most controversial reasoning for opting for a fine over a points deduction was the hearing's contention that it had considered the position of the players and the fans, who were not to blame for the situation. This quite bizarre line of sentimental, non-legal thinking was explained further: 'The fans and the players have been fighting against relegation. They have been doing so from January to April. They have been doing so against the ever-present threat of a deduction of points. Those efforts and that loyalty would be to no avail were we to now, on what might be termed the eve of the end of the season, deduct points.' It seemed to have escaped the hearing's attention that several other clubs and their fans had been fighting against relegation from January to April. The difference was that those teams had not committed an obvious and deliberate breach of the rules to secure world-class players to help them. Sports lawyer Mel Goldberg said, 'In law, the fans have no bearing on the case. It's no good saying, "We don't want to upset the fans." What about the Wigan fans? In my opinion, there is no question about it. West Ham received favourable treatment.' In short, the hearing had admitted that a points deduction was a course that would normally follow such a breach of these rules but had instead decided to cobble together a series of spurious points in an effort to get West Ham United off the hook and cover up its own tardiness. West Ham had argued, and the Premier League accepted, that there was no evidence that third-party influence had taken place, nor was there any attempt to exert such influence. Nevertheless, this was a red herring as the offence, as laid out in U18, was not one of exerting influence but of entering into a contract that might allow it to occur. Whether any influence was then exerted was irrelevant.

Although there was no precedent for a case of 'third-party interference' there were many precedents for a deduction of points. Points deductions have a curious history in English football, becoming commonplace in recent times. One of earliest recorded cases befell Sunderland during the 1890/91 season - they lost two points for fielding an incorrectly registered player. Such an offence has resulted in many instances of points deductions over the years but in the last decade clubs entering administration has been the most common reason. Peterborough United were deducted 19 points after the end of the 1967/68 season for illegal payments to players and were subsequently relegated to Division Four; the same season Port Vale were expelled from the league for a similar offence and forced to apply for re-election, which was successful. There were two high-profile cases in the 1990s: Manchester United and Arsenal were deducted one and two points respectively for an on-field brawl and Middlesbrough had three points deducted in the 1996/97 season for failing to fulfill a fixture at Blackburn Rovers when they claimed that illness in the squad prevented them from fielding a full side. None of the above transgressions applied to West Ham, leaving the Premier League to tread new ground. So the Premier League faced a dilemma - if points were to be deducted, how many should it be? Some might argue that even a points deduction was not sufficient penalty: surely West Ham should have been automatically demoted for admitting to lying to the FA? Whatever its decision, there was little doubt that the Premier League was heading towards a legal quagmire.

West Ham claimed they had cancelled the third-party agreement. As the Premier League report put it, West Ham 'acted in a manner that is consistent with them having terminated the offensive third-party agreement'. Speaking on BBC television's *Sportsweek* and captioned as a 'Premier League Spokesman', Dan Johnson elaborated, claiming that West Ham had terminated the third-party agreement with Joorabchian and that they had presented the Premier League with written evidence of a new arrangement. That evidence, according to a Premier League letter to clubs on May 15, was: '(1) A letter from West Ham United sent to Carlos Tevez, MSI and JSI terminating the private agreement between them dated 30 August 2006 and notifying those parties that the private agreement shall cease to have any further force or effect. (2) A letter from the legal representatives of MSI and JSI acknowledging receipt of the above letter. (3) A letter confirming that the above letter had been served on Carlos

Tevez personally.' However, during the subsequent tribunal it emerged that the reply from Joorabchian's legal representatives stated; 'All my client's rights remain fully and expressly reserved.' A dissatisfied Joorabchian subsequently asserted that West Ham had unilaterally terminated the agreement and he had 'left it in the hands of my lawyer' to challenge the validity of the unilateral termination. Furthermore, when Tevez was handed his copy of the cancellation letter the tribunal recorded that he had refused to countersign it and was not prepared to acknowledge that he had received it. When *Sky Sports News* asked Eggert Magnússon to produce the documentary proof he claimed to have of the termination of the third-party arrangement, he declined.

Following the tribunal's findings, representatives of Sheffield United, Fulham, Wigan Athletic and Charlton Athletic met at Harrod's (at the time owned by Fulham chairman Mohamed Al Fayed) in London's Knightsbridge. They issued a joint statement threatening legal action against both the Premier League and West Ham over the outcome of the disciplinary hearing. Kevin McCabe stated that United began to investigate legal proceedings on the day of the announcement of West Ham's punishment: 'There was no hanging around, no grass growing under our feet. We took this course of action in an attempt to try and protect ourselves should we suffer as a consequence of this bizarre decision.' Premier League chief executive Richard Scudamore claimed that any legal action taken by the four clubs would be 'futile' and 'bound to fail'. Undeterred, McCabe retorted: 'The penalty given undermines the governance of the Premier League and invites anarchy. It is a snub to every club and their fans. This is not so much a case of gaining recompense as protecting our position in the hope that the Premier League will reconsider their decision and appoint a new tribunal.' Wigan chairman Dave Whelan demanded that the Premier League provide proof that Tevez's illegal contract was cancelled before West Ham beat Wigan on April 28, the day after the outcome of the hearing was announced.

West Ham then won their penultimate match 3-1 at home to Bolton Wanderers to set up the final-day showdown and the series of results that saved the Hammers and Wigan and relegated Sheffield United. After Wigan's 2-1 final day win at Bramall Lane their manager Paul Jewell stated to *Sky TV*: 'The wrong team went down,' while his chairman Dave Whelan called United's relegation 'an injustice'. He added that the Premier League's chief executive Richard Scudamore and chairman Dave Richards should resign as a result of 'dereliction of their duties'. McCabe immediately leapt into action, canvassing support from other Premier League clubs, calling for the Premier League to comprise 21 clubs the following season. McCabe also wrote to Football Association chairman Geoff Thompson and Minister of Sport Richard Caborn MP asking for their backing, but received no response. Sheffield MPs, including those who follow Wednesday, backed Clive Betts MP's Early Day Motion in the House of Commons protesting at the judgement. Dave Whelan again asked the Premier League to provide proof that Tevez's registration was legal. FIFA president Sepp Blatter now got involved, saying he would look into how the Premier League handled West Ham's breach of the registration rules, commenting; '[We are] watching the situation very carefully. We will look at this - and not only if we are asked, we will do it anyway.' Nothing came of his implied threat.

Just three days after relegation, United decided against pursuing legal action but instead filed arbitration proceedings against the Premier League aimed at overturning the League's disciplinary decision. International law firm Denton Wilde Sapte LLP was to handle the case on behalf of United. United's 'Request for Arbitration' was served on the Premier League under the League's Rule S4, which provided for the binding resolution of disputes between clubs and the League. United's argument was that the commission's decisions failed to meet the same general obligations as those required of public bodies, namely 'to act lawfully, fairly and reasonably'. The League's arbitration body would perform a role of reviewing the decision of the League's disciplinary commission. United were also challenging the Premier League's conduct in failing to undertake an adequate investigation into the continued fielding of Tevez after the April 27 decision despite serious questions over his eligibility, and its failure to obtain sufficient evidence as to the termination of any third-party influence over Tevez.

United were to argue that the Premier League should have cancelled Tevez's registration in the absence of such evidence and/or that further disciplinary proceedings should have been instituted against West Ham for failing to resolve their ongoing breach of Premier League rules. United were to seek: (i) a declaration that the original decision and subsequent failure to act were unlawful, and that the decision should therefore be set aside; (ii) the setting up of a new disciplinary hearing against West Ham, with the hearing to consider the issue of the club's continued fielding of Tevez; (iii) a hold on preparations for the 2007/08 season, which wrongly assumed that West Ham remained a Premier League club and that United were relegated to the Championship; (iv) an assessment of United's potential claim for damages.

Then just days after using the words 'futile' and 'bound to fail' in connection with any action United might take, the Premier League inflamed matters by acknowledging United's right to request such a tribunal but adding that, in their opinion, United were 'wasting their time and money'. When appointed, the independent arbitration panel issued its own statement: 'Sheffield United are asking the arbitration panel to determine two matters. The first is whether the decision by the independent disciplinary commission on April 27 to fine West Ham, rather than dock points, was legally flawed such as to require the issue to be determined afresh by a disciplinary commission at some point in the future. The second is whether the Premier League acted unlawfully by not de-registering Tevez.' McCabe called the original decision 'irrational', adding, 'The commission clearly say points should be deducted but because it is April and not January we are not going to deduct points but fine them. We play 38 games in the Premiership for points, not money.' The arbitration tribunal was to comprise one member selected by Sheffield United, one by the Premier League; the third would be independent. The chosen men were, for the Premier League, Nicholas Randall, barrister and member of the Chartered Institute of Arbiters and, for United, David Pannick QC. The independent chairman would be Lord Justice Sir Philip Otton. Each member was selected from an approved list of independent arbiters.

United now upped the ante by refusing to hand over their Premier League membership share to the League. A club statement read: 'Until the arbitration looking into the Tevez matter is resolved [we] remain a Premiership club. The club believes if it gives up its share the Premier League cannot be guaranteed to fulfil its promise to return the share should the arbitration reinstate Sheffield United to the Premier League.' Fulham wrote to the Premier League in support, asking whether the League's Annual General Meeting should be postponed until the arbitration process was concluded. Their letter also suggested that the original commission's decision was flawed because it took into account irrelevant factors but ignored relevant ones. Brighton and Hove Albion FC also became involved in the wrangle, asking the Football Association to clarify Tevez's eligibility to play in the FA Cup tie between Brighton and West Ham in January. The Premier League hit back, saying it might unilaterally claim back United's share at the League's AGM. McCabe responded, 'What I absolutely fail to understand is why the Premier League are choosing to fight us on this issue. Rather they should be looking to accommodate us as we have done nothing wrong. As far as we are concerned the findings of arbitration surely take precedence over those of the AGM.' However, the AGM was not delayed, though United did not attend in case their presence proved antagonistic.

McCabe then told the BBC's *Sportsweek* programme, 'I firmly believe Sheffield United will win and the previous decision will be overturned for reasons of an irrational decision that was made by the first panel. What the [Premier League] officials have said is that if the arbitration overturns the previous decision then Sheffield United should be reinstated to the Premier League.' Prior to the arbitration panel being convened, United began canvassing support for its case. In early June the *Sheffield Star's* United reporter James Shield

403

was refused entry to the Premier League's Soho Square, London, offices as he attempted to deliver a dossier containing hundreds of readers' complaints about the League's handling of the case. He had to leave the dossier at reception. Jack Nicholls, the Bishop of Sheffield, for some reason told the *Sheffield Star* he was going to pray for divine intervention. McCabe called for Blades fans to form 'a sea of red and white' protest outside Parliament to 'illustrate the depth of feeling' they held. However, after being advised by police that demonstrations of any nature outside the House of Commons were illegal, he moderated his call to arms. Instead, on June 13 a delegation of around 100 specially invited supporters aboard two coaches paid for by the club - plus club mascot Captain Blade - led by Blades fan and actor Sean Bean, lobbied the Houses of Parliament, brandishing banners and placards demanding 'Fairness in Football'. Bean said, 'We played by the rules. West Ham, by their own admission, have broken the rules.' Some of the fans met the six Sheffield MPs who signed Clive Betts MP's Early Day Motion - it was signed by 50 MPs in all - in favour of United's position. Simultaneously around 400 Blades fans, the numbers boosted by curious passers-by, attended an hour-long protest in Barkers Pool in central Sheffield. The Blades fans sang a rendition of the team anthem 'Greasy Chip Buttie' but overall the rally was a quite feeble affair. However, the most important person – McCabe, who was on business in Australia – was not present at either gathering. His absence from such a momentous event in the club's history brought sharp criticism from supporters.

Fulham chairman Al Fayed reiterated his support for United, saying he would take further action if the arbitration panel found against United. He commented, 'If any club brings in players without approval how can they just fine them, because it affects other clubs? We are going to arbitration to teach them a lesson. Why do they make favours? If arbitration fails we go to court. I am a man of principle.' Al Fayed's past suggested he was quite familiar with the workings of courtrooms and tribunals. However, McCabe confirmed that if the arbitration did not go in United's favour he would accept relegation but would then consider approaching the European Commission as he believed it would be a Human Rights issue in terms of the consequential loss of jobs and reduced salaries the staff at the club suffered as a result of relegation.

The arbitration hearing opened on June 18, 2007 at the Fleet Street, London, headquarters of the International Dispute Resolution Centre.[16]   Liverpool chief executive Rick Parry was a surprise prosecution witness. It was Parry who alerted the Premier League of contractual irregularities when Liverpool signed Mascherano from West Ham in January. The hearing concluded the following day, when McCabe commented, 'We would like to thank the tribunal. It is a very complicated case. The panel will go away and review the case and submissions. We've been told to expect a decision by the end of the month. All three parties have had the opportunity to present their case to the panel.   We look forward to the handing down of the decision from the panel.   It would be inappropriate for me to comment further until a decision is made.'

The panel's verdict was announced on July 3. It did not fall in United's favour.   In the matter of a fine being chosen over a points deduction, the tribunal had much sympathy with United, stating, 'Sheffield United have now been relegated. They have done nothing wrong to merit this outcome.   West Ham United on the other hand were found by the disciplinary commission to have been deliberately deceitful and yet they remain in the FA Premier League.'   In the second matter, Tevez's continuing presence in the West Ham side after the April 27 hearing, the tribunal found that, 'It is obvious that the possibility of the third parties' ability materially to influence was not entirely excluded.   Indeed it may still exist.'   The panel then said that United's situation was 'most unfortunate in the extreme'.   Despite such statements, it found against United on both counts.

---

[16] An independent body supported by many arbitration organisations, such as the Chartered Institute of Arbitrators, the Society of Construction Arbitrators and the London Maritime Arbitrators' Association.

The panel confirmed that United's request for arbitration was correct in these 'exceptional circumstances' and acknowledged that United would suffer considerable damage to their financial and commercial interests. It also confirmed that West Ham were 'deliberately deceitful' but concluded that it was impossible for the arbitration tribunal to find that the original decision was 'irrational or perverse', which was 'a very strict test and is very difficult to satisfy' in terms of the principles of a Judicial Review, which the panel had to apply. The findings further stated: 'It was not unreasonable for the board of the Premier League to reach this conclusion in the light of the assurances given [by West Ham] that the third parties were not able to materially influence West Ham.' The panel admitted that it would 'go as far as to say that this tribunal would in all probability have reached a different conclusion [to that of the original commission]' and deducted points from West Ham. However, the arbitration panel was not able to substitute its view for that of the original commission. United's initial reaction was subdued: 'We are pleased that the tribunal rejected the Premier League's contention that we were not entitled to challenge that disciplinary decision. We note that the tribunal decided not to overturn the disciplinary commission's decision, despite concluding that they would in all probability have deducted points from West Ham had they been hearing the case themselves.' It was a moral victory for Sheffield United, but little consolation was gained, whilst the promised support and action from Fulham and Wigan Athletic did not materialise.

McCabe would not admit defeat and considered United's chances in court. He said, 'With the information we now possess and the knowledge we had before the arbitration we are just as determined to press ahead. We recognise that if we are allowed to proceed [through the courts] then it could take months because that is the timescale involved in these sort of matters.' United did go to the High Court, which on July 13 refused leave to appeal against the arbitration panel's decision. It appeared that the only possible course of action now open to United was to pursue compensation through the civil courts. The club released a statement saying it was to sue West Ham United for damages, claiming that an important document that had recently come to light was withheld from the Premier League's initial hearing. United's statement read: 'It seems that West Ham concealed the existence of this document in order to shield its new owners.' United learned of the document in talks with Joorabchian, who made it available as he was reported to be angry about being forced to pay West Ham £2 million to release Tevez to sign for Manchester United on loan in the summer of 2007. Joorabchian had originally offered West Ham £100,000 for the release of Tevez, which West Ham rejected as they still claimed ownership. Joorabchian's companies then served a High Court writ on West Ham, which was withdrawn and the figure paid by Joorabchian raised to £2 million to allow Tevez's registration with Manchester United to be finalised before the start of the season. It was not apparent to the outsider exactly from whom Tevez was on loan, but the deal satisfied Premier League regulations. The loan agreement was made with Joorabchian, MSI and JSI and because this detail was now out in the open the tricky problem of third-party ownership was obviated. Manchester United paid Joorabchian, MSI and JSI £10 million for the one-season deal.

After the second commission's verdict, West Ham now threatened to counter-sue United for 'repeated slurs' and described the Blades' campaign as 'desperate'. Nevertheless, McCabe wrote to West Ham chairman Eggert Magnússon in a bid to ease the adversarial relationship between the two clubs, at least at boardroom level, but did not receive a reply. United withdrew their threat of civil court action in favour of petitioning for another arbitration hearing, this time to seek damages from West Ham. Having pored over the rules of the Football Association, United believed they had found an opening for further action in the FA's Rule K, which stated: 'Any dispute or difference between two or more participants….. shall be referred to and finally resolved by arbitration….. and shall operate only as the forum and procedure for a legal challenge on the grounds of breach of contract.' The rule went on to say that the 'Respondent' (West Ham) had to issue an admission or denial of the claim made by the 'Claimant' (United). West Ham did not have the option of foregoing or neglecting the claim; they were obliged to take part in the arbitration proceedings. The 'breach of contract' on which United based their claim was 'an implied contract between two members of a league'.

Accepting United's right to pursue further arbitration proceedings, the FA said the dispute would be heard 'by a private independent arbitration tribunal set up under the FA's rules. The arbitration tribunal is comprised of one member nominated by each club, plus an independent member agreed upon by the two parties.' The members of the third panel were Lord William Griffiths, a law lord and a former president of the Marylebone Cricket Club and the Royal and Ancient Golf Club; Sir Anthony Coleman, a senior judge who helped set up the Czech Republic's judiciary and who specialised in industrial disputes and arbitration law; and Robert Englehart QC, an expert in commercial, media, entertainment and broadcasting law. The FA emphasised that it did not sit in judgement on the case, it did not have any influence on the decision and did not appoint any of the tribunal members. The hearing began in early June 2008 but McCabe was not expecting an outcome until September.

McCabe was correct - the new arbitration panel announced its verdict on September 23. It found in United's favour. At last some learned men had come out on the side of the northern provincial upstarts instead of the famous London 'academy' that produced Bobby Moore, Geoff Hurst, Martin Peters, Rio Ferdinand and many more. Said McCabe, 'I can confirm that both clubs have been notified of the ruling. The matter is still legally in process so I do not wish to comment any further until we have completed that process.' According to the *Sheffield Star*, United were claiming the minutely precise sum of £38,396,897.32 in lost income, the majority of which was made up of a £21,788,795 reduction in television money. The source of these figures was not disclosed and they were neither confirmed nor denied by the club. All McCabe would admit was: 'We have put in our claim. It contains details and monies we lost because of losing our top-flight status and outlines these in a clear and meticulous way. It is totally transparent. It is an authoritative piece of work.'

United confirmed that part of the claim arose from being forced to sell England Under-21 international defender Phil Jagielka to Everton for only £4 million due to a 'relegation clause' in his contract, which, they said, was half his true market value. Who decided on such a figure in the first place was not disclosed. The remainder of the claim was based on the cost of reduced season ticket sales, sponsorship, catering, merchandising and lost business opportunities. However, sports lawyer Richard Cramer doubted that United would be awarded anything near that value as in a court of law the decision would be based on lost profits, not lost income. Others were to see pound signs. Somewhat predictably, United's former manager Neil Warnock (and less predictably ex-player Jon Stead) spoke of their desire to investigate the possibility of making claims for lost personal income brought about by reduced contracts, a move that brought derision from the press and many other observers.

The tribunal's judgement read: 'On the totality of the evidence, we have no doubt that West Ham would have secured at least three fewer points over the 2006/07 season if Carlos Tevez had not been playing. Indeed, we think it more likely than not on the evidence that we heard, that even over the final two games of the season West Ham would have achieved at least three points less overall without Mr Tevez.' Following the hearing, the Football Association and Premier League announced they were to hold a further investigation into West Ham's conduct after the original punishment was handed down. Specifically, they were to investigate allegations made by Graham Shear, solicitor for Joorabchian, that Scott Duxbury had provided Joorabchian with a verbal assurance that the third-party arrangement was still in place, despite informing the Premier League that it had been expunged.

Blades supporters rejoiced in anticipation of the millions of pounds that West Ham were to pay to United in compensation. In other quarters, however, United were heavily criticised for both their pertinacity in not letting the matter drop and for the possible precedents the decision may have set. The arbitration panel's judgement received a mainly hostile response in the national press. One such traducer was *Guardian* journalist Matt Scott, who asserted that the 'verdict rocks the very foundations of football'. West Ham vehemently refuted the influence Tevez had on their fortunes, claiming that one player could not be solely responsible for results. There was considerable weight in that argument but, in the eyes of Sheffield United, a correct decision was arrived at, eventually. However, thanks to the legal challenge it could be argued that the game is now played wherein individual contributions can be analysed and evaluated to the extent that a club can claim that its league position is not its primary responsibility.

Indubitably it had been a long, wearisome process that, to the chagrin of the Premier League, would not go away. Yet it could so easily have been prevented had the League and Sheffield United done what they should have done. The League's decision to fine West Ham instead of deducting points was unusual but it was based on reasoning and argument, however faulty some believed the reasons and arguments were. The League's real mistake was its failure to cancel Tevez's registration once West Ham had been found guilty. To allow him to play in the final three games on West Ham's say-so that the third-party contract had been cancelled was a crass error of judgement. West Ham gained maximum points from the three games. Without Tevez, those results were much less likely to have been attained. However, Tevez or no Tevez, United's fate still lay in their own hands. They should have been able to obtain the single point required from the final game at home to Wigan but did not do so. For that, Neil Warnock was culpable, choosing the most important match of the season to tinker with his line-up, producing a confused-looking team that was beaten by more determined and better organised opponents. Warnock's selections of his best central defender, Phil Jagielka, at right back for the first time that season, and of the right-footed Derek Geary, a natural right back, on the opposite flank in place of the regular left back Chris Armstrong were bewildering. Prior to kick off Warnock and his players learned of the below-strength Manchester United team selected by manager Sir Alex Ferguson to play West Ham, which only served to heighten the level of anxiety for the game ahead. However, regardless of

Manchester United's line-up, a better display by Sheffield United against a Wigan team that played the last 20 minutes with ten men after the dismissal of Lee McCulloch would have left the visitors' chairman Dave Whelan with the task of taking the tortuous path trodden by Kevin McCabe.

Once the arbitration panel had made its ruling that West Ham would have to pay compensation to United, the Football Association's Rule K5(b) came into play: 'The Award shall be final and binding on the parties.' Rule K5(c) added, 'The parties shall be deemed to have waived irrevocably any right to appeal, review or recourse to a court of law.' These paragraphs appeared self-explanatory but the 'right of appeal' statement possibly implied an appeal to the FA and therefore may not have precluded an approach to the Court of Arbitration for Sport (CAS)[17] in Switzerland. CAS's own Rule C-R47 stated: 'An appeal against the decision of a federation, association or sports-related body may be filed with the CAS insofar as the statutes or regulations of the said body so provide or as the parties have concluded a specific arbitration agreement and insofar as the Appellant [in this case West Ham] has exhausted the legal remedies available to him prior to the appeal, in accordance with the statutes or regulations of the said sports-related body.' This could be read two ways: (1) that West Ham were within their rights to appeal to CAS, or (2) the FA's Rule K5(c) prevented them from doing so.

This was by no means the end of the line. There would have to be yet another panel that would determine the level of compensation to which United would be entitled; West Ham were now the party refusing to let the situation rest. They

---

[17] The Court of Arbitration for Sport is an international arbitration body set up to settle disputes related to sports. Its headquarters are in Lausanne, with additional courts in New York and Sydney. Ad-hoc courts are created in Olympic Games host cities as required. Originally conceived by International Olympic Committee (IOC) President Juan Antonio Samaranch to deal with disputes arising during the Olympics, the body was established as part of the IOC in 1984.

quickly lodged an appeal with CAS against the arbitration panel ruling. The CAS website confirmed the news: 'A statement of appeal has been filed by West Ham United Football Club against Sheffield United Football Club with respect to the interim award of 18 September 2008 that was rendered by an arbitration panel convened by the English Football Association (FA). West Ham United requests the annulment of the FA arbitration panel's award.' CAS had still to adjudicate on whether it even had the authority to hear the appeal, but CAS's secretary general Matthieu Reeb held the opinion that it would not, saying; 'We would need agreement from Sheffield United and for Football Association rules to allow an appeal to CAS.' Before CAS made a decision United pre-empted it by seeking an injunction in the High Court to prevent West Ham's appeal going ahead. This went United's way as they were awarded a temporary injunction in late November 2008.

Lord Griffiths' independent panel was due to reconvene on March 16, 2009 to determine how much compensation West Ham would have to pay United. However, officials of the two clubs had been holding behind-the-scenes discussions to attempt to come to an 'out-of-court' settlement. West Ham were in financial difficulties after the collapse in September 2008 of their sponsor XL Airways, which had accrued debts of £143 million. Worse, the following month, Landsbanki, the Icelandic bank 40 per cent owned by West Ham chairman Björgólfur Guðmundsson, who had bought the club from fellow countryman Eggert Magnússon, was put into receivership and taken over by the country's Government. Guðmundsson was said to be £300 million in debt and looking to sell West Ham to ease his troubles. That was unlikely to happen considering the uncertainty over the club's financial commitments and it was in West Ham's interest to seek a quick solution because their auditors Deloitte told the club they would not sign off the accounts unless a settlement was reached with United.

For his part, McCabe probably felt that United would not be awarded the full amount of their claim and also desired an end to the matter. Lord Griffiths was informed that his services would no longer be required and instead United and West Ham issued a brief joint statement explaining their agreement: 'Both clubs are pleased to announce that a satisfactory settlement for compensation has been reached which brings the dispute between Sheffield United and West Ham to an end. The tribunal will not be resuming.' The next day McCabe unconvincingly and publicly stressed the amicable nature of the talks: 'We are happy and satisfied with the settlement. Throughout the finalisation of the terms of the agreement, the discussions were friendly, co-operative and in the best of spirit. We are two clubs with a fantastic footballing history who now want to move on and focus on the business of playing football. We look forward to a positive ongoing relationship with West Ham at all levels.' West Ham's Scott Duxbury added: 'For everyone concerned, the time was right to draw a line under this whole episode. We have had very positive discussions over a number of days with Sheffield United and acknowledge their willingness to resolve this in the best interests of both clubs.' Significantly, neither club divulged the agreed compensation.

Media speculation set the figure at anything between £10 million and £30 million. The *Guardian* claimed it had spoken to a source 'involved in the negotiations', who revealed that West Ham could end up paying a total of £26.5 million. The deal was said to be for £21.5 million, payable in staggered instalments until 2013, the first £1.5 million being due in May 2009. Another source claimed it was £20 million payable over five years. It was confirmed at United's December 2009 AGM that the first £1.5 million had indeed been paid in June 2009 - the only payment received so far. The remaining payments were to coincide with West Ham's major revenue streams, such as their share of television income and Premier League prize money. If West Ham were sold for more than £95m, they would have to pay a further £5 million and, according to McCabe, any sale of the club would see 'the payments to be made to Sheffield United accelerated'. A month later former Birmingham City directors David Sullivan and David Gold bought a majority share of West Ham United. At their press conference to announce the purchase, the pair revealed that West Ham had debts of £100 million, of which, they said, around £20 million was owed to Sheffield United, a figure confirmed by McCabe at a 'Fans' Forum' at Bramall Lane in April 2010. United's legal fees for the two-year fight were revealed by McCabe to amount to £1.32 million, whilst the 2009 *Annual Report and Accounts* listed a figure of £18.093 million as 'Settlement received from West Ham Football Club less associated costs'.

Now that the case had come to a conclusion it was pertinent to examine how the national football press had covered it. United's position received sympathy in the *Daily Express* and *Daily Mail* by virtue of the club employing a lobbying agency to make sure its side of the story was published. These two mid-brow tabloids were the agency's favoured outlets. One particular supporter of United's stance was the *Mirror's* Oliver Holt, who also happened to be Neil Warnock's ghost-writer for his autobiography *Made In Sheffield*. Somewhat predictably he said United had had 'an injustice… visited upon them', he belittled West Ham's legal and commercial director Scott Duxbury and supported Warnock's claim for personal compensation. He further accused West Ham of 'a whole farrago of deception' and continually called for Premier League chief executive Richard Scudamore to resign, labelling him 'a liability and an embarrassment'.

At the other end of the spectrum was Martin Samuel, at the time of *The Times* and later of the *Daily Mail*. He likened Lord Griffiths' ruling to that of the Football Association refusing to further punish United captain Chris Morgan for an elbow to the head of Barnsley striker Ian Hume that resulted in Hume suffering a fractured skull during a game in November 2008. He twice accused United of participating in their own version of 'third-party influence'. The first, in January 2007, came when United striker Steve Kabba moved to Watford and didn't play in the meeting between the teams later that season. A year later United's on-loan midfielder Matthew Spring signed permanently for Charlton Athletic, yet wasn't in Charlton's line-up for their FA Cup tie at Bramall Lane shortly afterwards. This situation was complicated by the fact that Spring's parent club Luton Town held his registration when he was at United. There were illegal contract clauses that prevented the two players playing against their former club, Samuel asserted. The Football Association investigated the Spring incident but found nothing wrong. On both occasions there was a 'gentlemen's agreement' - with nothing in writing - between the clubs that the player would not play against United. Samuel claimed that United had been 'allowed off the hook' by the Premier League over the Kabba arrangement. Kevin McCabe shrugged off Samuel's claims, stating: 'For some time now Martin Samuel has pursued a crusade against Sheffield United. As usual his reports are without foundation. I gather Martin is a West Ham supporter.'

As the compensation deal with West Ham was struck on the field, United embarked on a run that took them to the brink of promotion to the Premier League. For many, a return to the top division soon after the settlement with West Ham would have closed the circle of justice, bringing to an appropriate conclusion two years of endeavour. Following the 2007 relegation and the departure of Neil Warnock, United appointed former Manchester United and England captain Bryan Robson as the new manager. Robson had had a mixed managerial career, seeing success and failure at both Middlesbrough (whom he took to promotion - twice - and relegation, and to three cup finals) and West Bromwich Albion (whom he saved from relegation one year but failed to do so the following year) and suffering at Bradford City as, beset by financial difficulties, they fell down the divisions. Robson's appointment wasn't greeted with universal acclaim by Blades fans but McCabe believed the employment of a figure known and respected throughout the footballing world would bring attention and recognition to the club and help promote its various worldwide activities. That may have been so, but it soon became apparent that Robson wasn't suited to be Sheffield United's team manager.

His dour personality and monotone voice were in complete contrast to the effervescent Warnock. Fans found Robson hard to warm to. The players seemed to find him difficult too, as they struggled to come to terms with his preferred slower, more measured style of play. They, like the fans, had become accustomed to the fast-paced and direct approach favoured by

Warnock.   The expected promotion challenge never materialised. Rumours told of dressing-room cliques, notably the players left over from Neil Warnock's time and the newcomers signed by Robson, apparently paid more than those established at Bramall Lane. Robson's nadir came with a defeat in the derby match at Hillsborough in January 2008, before which he tried to play down the encounter as 'just another game'. After the match Kevin McCabe defended his manager, claiming there was 'still time to have a good season'. He urged supporters to 'stick together' and 'back the judgements being made', adding that it was not his intention to change the manager. However, soon afterwards a goalless draw at home to lowly Scunthorpe United, who had a player sent off after ten minutes, caused a change of mind and proved Robson's undoing.

The post-match car park demonstration by around a thousand Blades fans claimed another victim. Comically, this protest saw fans removing their shoes and waving them above their heads. These actions mimicked what is seen in the Muslim faith as an insult, where merely showing the sole of one's shoe to someone is considered rude. Shoes are 'unclean' and it is forbidden to enter a mosque wearing them. Muslims must remove their shoes before praying. When US forces took Baghdad in April 2003, opponents of Saddam Hussein hit posters and statues of the fallen Iraqi ruler with their shoes, while pictures of American President George Bush were often subject to shoe-abuse in various Islamic countries. How this practice was translated to Bramall Lane is open to conjecture but shows the never-ending creativity so evident in football fan circles worldwide.

Meanwhile, Robson lasted one more match before being removed from his post by McCabe. Offered a position in the United empire that included overseeing the development of a scouting network and player recruitment in Hungary, Brazil and Belgium, Robson turned it down, deciding that it would be better for all concerned if he left completely because the fans would not accept his remaining at the club in any capacity. He diplomatically explained; 'The role Sheffield United offered me was fantastic but it isn't what I want in my career at the moment.' Robson subsequently took on an ambassadorial role at Manchester United before taking the job of manager of Thailand in 2009.

Robson's successor was Kevin Blackwell, one-time assistant to Warnock at Bramall Lane and latterly manager of Leeds United, with whom he tasted play-off final defeat in 2006, and Luton Town, his hometown team, whom he left after the club went into administration early in 2008. Blackwell's personality and style of play were out of the same mould as Warnock's and his impact was immediate as a strong end to the season (eight wins and 26 points in 13 games) saw United finish just outside the play-off positions. Optimism for an improved 2008/09 season was high, and although United never mounted a serious challenge to the top two of Wolves and Birmingham City, another late-season surge wrapped up a play-off berth with weeks to spare, and an eventual third-place finish. Preston North End were dispatched in the two-legged semi-final as United played their best football of the season, but just as in previous play-off finals in 1997 and 2003, they were unable to carry that level of performance through to Wembley, going down 1-0 to Burnley, who ended four points behind United but had beaten the Blades twice during the regular season. Once more United had choked on the big occasion. They now had the unenviable record of losing three play-off finals. With the expiration of the Premier League 'parachute payment' (at the time an amount of £10 million paid for two seasons to clubs relegated from the Premier League but subsequently increased to £48 million over four seasons) United entered the 2009/10 season with inevitable cutbacks in terms of salaries and staff employed. The club's annual football salary level was reduced from £15.7 million to £12 million over the course of the 2008/09 season by the sale of high-earning players such as Michael Tonge and former England international striker James Beattie, both to Stoke City; Beattie for £3.5 million and Tonge for £2 million. Other big earners in Ugo Ehiogu and Lee Hendrie were later released. Kevin McCabe had warned shareholders at the December 2008 AGM that cutbacks were imminent. Making reference to the global recession, he said, 'We are not immune here [to the recession] but we have created an infrastructure

417

and a business model that should see us through when times are tough. We're not skint, we're in a better position than most but no one should be blind to the economic facts and we must cut our cloth accordingly and look at cutting wage bills.'

The departure of leading scorer Beattie the previous January provoked an angry response from fans who claimed that it proved that the club was devoid of ambition, was giving up on promotion and, despite the promises of McCabe, was once again a 'selling club'. A few days earlier McCabe was pressed during a live interview on *BBC Radio Sheffield* to explain the situation regarding Beattie, after media reports claimed he had already agreed a contract with Stoke. Three times interviewer Paul Walker asked McCabe, 'Have there been any offers for James Beattie?' and each time an unusually flustered McCabe answered, 'No deal has been done.' Eventually Walker got the reply he was looking for. There had been an offer from Stoke, McCabe admitted, but it had not been accepted. It was a few days later. United even felt it necessary to issue a press statement to explain further Beattie's sale. It signalled 'the start of a re-profiling of the squad' which would 'ensure the club is in the best position to manage any eventuality that might arise in the future'. The statement informed supporters of the difficult circumstances that would prevail with the imminent loss of Premier League parachute payments corresponding with a worldwide recession and added that 'expenditure will be realistic but [will] not put the club at risk'. The statement furthermore refuted the accusation of lack of ambition, concluding: 'Our ambitions are the same but we are not immune from financial circumstances.' McCabe had earlier claimed there was no desire to sell Beattie. He said it wasn't a question of whether Beattie would go, but whether he wanted to go. This contradicted the player's own version after he signed for Stoke. He said, 'I really wanted to see how much Sheffield United wanted to ship me out. I thought I would test the waters and it was clear they wanted me out for financial reasons.'

Immediately after the play-off final defeat manager Kevin Blackwell gave an emotional interview to *Sky TV* in which he suggested he might vacate his position. 'I'm thinking I might have taken this club as far as I can go. I know the ramifications of losing finals and the loss of parachute payments. Players will have to leave now because the wage situation will have to change.' His chairman persuaded him to stay, then outlined his plans for United, stressing a new era of austerity: 'The play-off will linger in the mind, but in a few days and weeks it erodes and everyone talks about doing better next season. We have a smaller budget - any football club who refuses to understand what is happening in the economic world is heading for disaster and you cannot go and borrow money from banks now. Banks are in more disarray than any other industry. We have had a very high wage bill over the last couple of seasons - partly parachute payments and partly money put in by [my] family. We are not going to have a high wage bill next season, but we will have a wage bill which will be amongst the highest in the division [but] we will not be paying the same amount on players' wages that we have been prepared to pay in the past.' McCabe claimed later that only the three teams relegated from the Premier League in 2009 had larger wage budgets than United. What he had not made public was that when relegated United had the Premier League's lowest-paid manager and lowest-paid Academy director.

A few weeks later McCabe answered supporters' questions at a forum arranged by the club at Bramall Lane. He said, 'Our football debt is low and the biggest one we have relates to the hotel. That position has been achieved through a combination of capital, expertise and creativity. It has not been done through bank borrowing.' When questioned about the sale of Beattie the previous January, he responded: '[Beattie and his agent] were saying that he wanted more money and a three-year [contract] extension. I replied that we would consider re-negotiating when we were in the Premiership. It could have jeopardised the finances. Sometimes, when you are chairman, you just have to say it's too big a risk.' The wages of Beattie, the highest-paid player in the Championship according to McCabe, on a reported £30,000 per week, would have claimed 35 per cent of United's 2009/10 salary budget had he remained at the club. Although the 'Tevez money' softened the blow somewhat, after two seasons with a distinct monetary advantage over many Championship clubs, United now found themselves back in a position of financial parity with their divisional rivals.

Prospects for the 2009/10 season were hindered by the sales of two of the club's best young players, a contractual impasse with one of the established players and the suspension of goalkeeper Paddy Kenny following a failed drugs test, an unwanted first in the club's history. Kenny undertook a routine drug test following the May 2009 play-off semi-final win over Preston North End. Traces of the performance-enhancing substance ephedrine were found in his sample. With no template from which to work, the United board had to quickly decide how Kenny's circumstances should be treated and had little option but to suspend him from playing and training until a Football Association tribunal heard his case. Despite the tribunal accepting Kenny's explanation that the ephedrine was innocently ingested when he took an over-the-counter cough remedy and that there was no deliberate attempt to cheat, he received a nine-month ban in August 2009 from all football activities anywhere in the world. The ban was back-dated to the day United placed him under suspension. Kenny failed to get the length of his sanction reduced on appeal. As a key player with massive experience, Kenny's enforced absence was a major blow to United's promotion chances. This wasn't the first time Kenny had caused problems for his employers. In November 2006 he was involved in a fight - with one his friends - in the early hours of the morning in an Indian restaurant in his home town of Halifax. It was reported that the 'friend' had confessed to having an affair with Kenny's wife, from whom Kenny split soon afterwards. Kenny had one of his eyebrows bitten off during the brawl, an injury requiring twelve stitches. United manager Neil Warnock subsequently forbade Kenny from going out in Halifax and when asked by reporters if his goalkeeper was 'OK mentally' to play, Warnock joked, 'I don't think so, no! But he's been like that since I signed him!' Kenny played in United's next game.

Academy products Kyle Naughton, aged 20, and Kyle Walker, aged 19, moved to Tottenham Hotspur in July 2009 for a combined fee of £8.6 million, possibly rising to £10 million dependent on playing achievements. Despite their undoubted potential, this was money that could not be turned down for young players who, combined, had made fewer then 50 first-team appearances. Walker was then allowed by Spurs to return to Bramall Lane on what was publicised as a season-long loan deal, but this wasn't as it seemed as Spurs recalled Walker at short notice in January 2010, leaving United without cover in his right-back position. The loss of Naughton was galling. After making his debut at the beginning of the 2008/09 season he had earned a place in the England Under-21 team following a series of outstanding displays at right back. He was also selected by his fellow players in the Professional Footballers' Association 'Championship team of the season'. His sale reminded supporters of earlier times when all the club's talented youngsters seemed to be sold and, following the departures of Beattie and Tonge, it appeared to signal a return to United's status as a 'selling club', three years after McCabe told shareholders that that was no longer the case. Part of the money from Tottenham was re-invested in the team - striker Ched Evans was purchased from Manchester City for a fee that could reach a maximum of £3 million based on performance criteria and midfielder Lee Williamson came from Watford for £500,000. The fee for Evans was the second-highest paid by a Championship club in 2009, bettered only by Cardiff City's £4 million purchase of Michael Chopra from Sunderland. The majority of the monies went towards what is notionally termed 'the running of the club'. Another departure was that of defender Matt Kilgallon, bought in January 2007 from Leeds United for a fee of £1.75 million, whose contract was due to expire at the end of the 2009/10 season. One of the most consistent players during the previous couple of seasons, Kilgallon felt his worth was more than United could offer him. The stalemate continued well into the season and at times affected the form of both player and team. Kilgallon was sold to Sunderland for a reported fee of £2 million during the January 2010 transfer window. Again, only a fraction of the fee was given to the manager, who bought winger Mark Yeates from Middlesbrough for £300,000. With a lengthy and continuing injury list and an over-reliance on loan players, United finished the season outside the play-off positions. Cognizant of impending budget cuts that would affect both playing and non-playing staff, manager Kevin Blackwell did not sound hopeful of an improvement in the 2010/11 season. He told the *Sheffield Star*: 'The ambition of the club while Kevin [McCabe] is in charge will be to get into the Premier League. I clearly understand that it will be done under a different guise than before.'

The Blades would have to get by without any further financial input from McCabe and his family. McCabe told *BBC Radio Sheffield* in November 2009 that over the years the family had injected about £50 million into the club, 75 per cent of which was 'straight cash', the rest being taken up by rights issues and loan notes. This capital investment was now at an end. However, he added that these investments had produced more business interests, which generated more revenue, allowing for 'better flexibility on player wages'. He did not mention where the £20 million due from West Ham would go. He said he was also looking for an 'investor partner' to put in capital so that he could 'retire and get back to being a supporter' but insisted he was not looking to sell the club outright. To this end, McCabe instigated a boardroom restructuring. Chief executive Jason Rockett was re-assigned and in his place came Trevor Birch, the man who brought together Chelsea and Russian billionaire Roman Abramovich. The Liverpool-born Birch had a minor professional playing career in the late 1970s and early 1980s at Liverpool, Shrewsbury Town and Chester City. Birch's CV also included stints as chief executive at Leeds United, Everton and Derby County - all of them, for some reason, shortlived. Birch spent just six weeks at Everton in 2004, leaving after he advised the club's board to sell young striker Wayne Rooney (they did) and majority shareholder Bill Kenwright to sell his controlling shareholding (he did not). What would Birch do for Sheffield United?

Birch's history hinted that he might be the man to unearth the 'investor partner' long sought by McCabe. In May 2007 McCabe said he intended to appoint a firm of New York-based investment advisors to perform this role. 'Americans are very creative,' he said. 'They know how to profile and brand football.' Presumably all inquiries had proved unsuccessful.

Upon his arrival Birch spoke the usual clichéd platitudes of the newly employed: 'It's a great club….. more than capable of holding its own [in the Premier League].   Kevin wanted someone with the profile, experience and professionalism to take the club forward and, hopefully, I like to think I bring that.' More tellingly, he told the *Sheffield Star*, 'Outside of the Premier League, United is one of a small number clubs that is worth a punt on in terms of its infrastructure, its support base and its chances of promotion. The people here have built a business model which is different to many others. What you would be buying into here is hope and potential without the cost of getting involved in the Premier League.' Speaking to *BBC Radio Sheffield*, McCabe said the appointment of Birch, to whom he first talked two years previously, was partly his attempt to 'pass the baton' in the running of the club. There were reports in May 2010 that McCabe was on the verge of selling his shareholding, which United denied. According to Birch, the story was without foundation. He reiterated that the club was only seeking to enhance its financial standing by bringing in additional investment. He concluded, 'As part of the process, the club has appointed an independent corporate finance and equity markets advisory firm [London-based AKUR] to help find such partner investors which would bring long-term sustainable benefits for Sheffield United.'

Clearly United faced a 'succession issue'.   McCabe, now in his early sixties, sought a back seat. He explained; 'I am not getting any younger and my personal business affairs are taking up an increasing amount of time.   Because of that, I want to be a non-executive type of chairman.'   However, he faced a dilemma; whilst wanting big-money investors he wanted at the same time to retain control. The two wants were incompatible.

In early and mid 2010 former and current members of the United board found themselves in the now familiar context of front-page headlines: one regarding alleged financial impropriety; another contesting a football-related decision that had huge financial implications.   In March 2010 a joint investigation involving the *Sunday Times* and *Channel 4's* 'Dispatches' programme followed up on the so-called 'Cash for Influence' scandal that had engulfed the New Labour government, in which three former cabinet members were exposed for talking about using their contacts to help fee-paying clients gain access to the corridors of power. The Sunday Times revealed how Sheffield Central MP and former United director Richard Caborn declared he would be prepared to trade his political contacts for cash payments. In a 'sting' operation involving a camera concealed in a handbag, Caborn was recorded conversing with a woman posing as a company executive seeking to contact senior politicians to promote the causes she represented. Caborn was captured on tape explaining how he could facilitate meetings with the Prime Minister and would be happy to meet face-to-face the (non-existent) American-based executives. His fee for such intermediary facilities would be £2,500 per day plus expenses. Days later, and upon realisation that the news of such a claim was soon to break, Caborn through his lawyers wished to make it clear that he had made no commitment to work for the fictitious lobbying company. The political fallout was not consequential for Caborn. He was to keep his position as the Prime Minister's 'Ambassador' for England's 2018 World Cup bid and in July 2010 put himself forward for the vacant role of chairman of the Football Association.

In the summer of 2010 the courts were once again the place to find lawyers representing United directors. This time the issue was the December 2009 decision to award Sheffield Wednesday's Hillsborough stadium host status should the 2018 World Cup bid be successful (see Chapter 15). In the High Court United accused Sheffield City Council of bias, asserting that it had failed to comply with planning procedures over Wednesday's plans to re-develop Hillsborough. United alleged that the council 'acted improperly and unreasonably in the exercise of its duties as a public authority' on the grounds of there having been insufficient time to appropriately consider Wednesday's scheme. United claimed consent was given without enough supporting information, such as a study of the impact on local transport, and accused the local authority of failing to provide a full explanation as to why it had granted Wednesday planning approval. However, the High Court decided there was no case for the council to answer.

United's 2009/10 season fizzled out, with fans increasingly disgruntled with the team's style of play and ever willing to boo the team and criticise manager Kevin Blackwell. Meanwhile, goalkeeper Paddy Kenny, having been paid by the club for nine months whilst banned from football for a drug offence, activated a 'get-out' clause in his contract and was sold to Queen's Park Rangers for £750,000, thereby teaming up with former Blades boss Neil Warnock. Weeks later striker Billy Sharp left for Doncaster Rovers for a fee of £1.15m. The monies received were not passed on to the manager in terms of transfer fees; the players brought in during the close season were free transfers and loans. A pre-season trip to Malta saw United play two 45-minute matches and return to England to play pre-season friendlies with a mixture of fortunes. The first league game of the season produced a spirited draw at Cardiff City but only a week later Kevin Blackwell left Bramall Lane via the now usual method of 'mutual agreement'. A midweek 2-0 Carling Cup defeat at League One Hartlepool United followed three days later by a 3-0 home defeat to Warnock's QPR were the nails in his coffin. The former match saw visiting fans rehearsing renditions of abuse intended for Paddy Kenny three days hence. They could also note that, such was the paucity of United's squad, two of the substitutes were employed as coaches and were in their forties. The Saturday game against QPR saw a United side consisting of just 14 fully fit professionals. In the squad were two young players who had yet to sign full-term professional contracts. The much-anticipated abuse of Kenny was somewhat stifled when United found themselves 3-0 down after 23 minutes. Blades fans turned their anger on Blackwell, and Kevin McCabe decided there and then that Blackwell should no longer be manager. Days before the game McCabe and Trevor Birch were in Malaysia on club-related business, primarily seeking investors. They held discussions with Vinod Sekhar, a Malaysian businessman who was the country's 16th-richest man in 2008. McCabe later told the authors he expected nothing to come of the talks, but added that the club was now in discussions with an unnamed party in India.

Blackwell was a decent, honest and hard-working manager. The 2009/10 season had seen a calamitous injury list at

Bramall Lane, forcing him to use five different goalkeepers and give United debuts to over 20 players. In his two and a half years at United Blackwell claimed to have brought some £25m into the club via transfers. He had a win ratio that made him the third-most successful manager (of those with more than a season in charge) in Blades post-war history. He reached the Championship play-off final three times in six years: in 2003 with Sheffield United as assistant manager to Neil Warnock; in 2006 as manager of Leeds United and in 2009 as manager of Sheffield United. All three ended in defeat. His critics argued that the transfer monies accrued were from players signed by predecessors Bryan Robson and Neil Warnock or had come through the academy system. Furthermore, many considered Blackwell as being over-concerned with 'playing safe' and consequently with employing an over-negative system. Blackwell was in a no-win position. He was ordered to sell players and had to replace them with free transfers and short-term loan signings. Many fans realised this and sympathised with him. In post-match interviews and when speaking on *BBC Radio Sheffield*, Blackwell was prone to be 'chippy' in his responses to questions, intimating a barely-concealed anger over his situation. His departure immediately after the QPR game was an opportunity for Neil Warnock to dance on the proverbial grave. Warnock was to gleefully tell tabloid reporters of how he had earlier in the day reminded Blackwell that for less than the £3 million United had reportedly paid for Ched Evans (a rare big-money signing for Blackwell) he had brought eight players to QPR.

Within days of Blackwell's departure United called a press conference to reveal former Blades player Gary Speed as the new manager. Holding the accolade of Wales' most-capped outfield player and at one time having the most appearances of any player in the Premier League, Speed had over the previous two years acted as Blackwell's first-team coach. This time the press conference broadcast live on *Sky TV* lasted five times longer than that for the appointment of Bryan Robson some three years earlier, mainly due to *Sky* reporter Bryn Laws' twelve questions to Speed. Thoughtful words from chief executive Trevor Birch were followed by the expected soundbites from Speed, who referred to United as 'the brand', while the Sheffield United chairman remained on holiday in Spain. Meanwhile, some Blades supporters claimed that the 'Tevez money' was being used to pay back McCabe's loans to the club - certainly there was no obvious evidence of any of it being given to the team manager. The collapse of global property markets and sizeable drop in office rental incomes had hit McCabe hard. There had been plenty of highs along the way, but by October 2010 Sheffield United were in a similar position to when McCabe took over at the end of the 1990s: at the wrong end of the Championship table and with no money.

Things change but remain the same. The deaths in 2008 of Derek Dooley and Bernard Procter meant that two of the few remaining links to the days of chaos, back-stabbing, bickering and outright comedy of Brealey, Hashimi, Woolhouse, Hinchliffe, McDonald and Colombotti were gone. And John Hassall, the man who, by inviting Reg Brealey to the club in 1980, was the unwitting catalyst to the events of the next three decades, also passed away in August 2009, breaking another connection with the turbulent past. And now with McCabe looking to step into the background while the team faltered in its bid to return to the Premier League, the immediate future of Sheffield United Football Club was – as always - in the balance.

****

To the ordinary Blades fan the club boardroom - with apologies to Winston Churchill - has usually been considered as a riddle wrapped in a mystery inside an enigma. We hope the preceding words go some way to providing an insight into the enigmas and riddles that have occupied the boardroom seats of Bramall Lane. We recognise that the history of any topic is not neutral and there are always competing 'truths' and thus realise that those reading this who recognise themselves as 'there' might have a different take on events. Similar to the boardroom of any entity, 'politics' and personality clashes are inevitable and undeniable. Things are said in the heat of the moment, words are not always meant. Decisions are made with a sub-text that is not always evident to the others around

427

the table. At times an individual's conscience will override what is feasible or profit-making. We caution against criticism or ridicule. Hindsight is great perspective for those with the luxury of never having to make consequential decisions. In an ideal world supporters want to see unity at all levels at their club; this will never be the case. The best a fan can hope for is that the directors, in a similar manner to the playing staff they employ, manifest both determination and a sense of vision, with a dose of 'team spirit'. Clarity of thought helps as well. The board of directors should, similar to the team manager, have targets to hit and a game-plan as to how to achieve them. To a greater degree than their playing staff the club's directors should recognise the duty to build an image of the organisation they control - preferably one that people of the city the club resides in will be proud of and want to be associated with. This has never been an easy task. It will not be easier in the near future.

Passion and money are integral to a football club. This couplet does not always make for the best bed-fellows. In the boardroom the cautious will disagree with the speculative, the traditionalist with the modernist and the virtuous with those less so. Unable to agree with one another the same men have then to deal with the team manager who might be a loose cannon or too often drunk. They have, on top of such possibilities, the task of reining in the demands and excesses of the dozens of players in their employ, too many of whom act as if they are a law unto themselves. The hierarchies - and in a sense certainties - that sustained football since its late 19th century beginnings were crumbling by the late 1960s and mostly ended in the late 1980s. Football club directors were no longer the feared patriarchs of times gone by. In some instances by the start of the new millennium many directors had less wealth and income than the players at their club. Whilst these internal issues are decided over, fans will forever opine of their desire to follow and in some way be part of a 'well-run club', ideally one that communicates well with its fans and shares their ambitions. But beyond these requirements comes a range of possibilities as to the much sought-after criteria of how 'well-run' is defined. This raises the following questions: Is footballing success to be pursued at all costs regardless of debts incurred? Does the source of club funds matter less than what might be achieved by such monies? Are fans happy to lose the local identity that the club was built upon and sustained for over 120 years and sell its soul to a foreign entity that has riches beyond belief but no sense of history and tradition? Can the presence of a 'sugar-daddy' chairman, whose financial largesse pays wages way above the income generated through the turnstiles, ever be considered a rational way to run a football club? If the answer to these questions is always 'No' then what level of largesse should club directors ideally give or loan? And if they do loan monies should it be free of interest costs?   There are no 'correct' answers.   It's all about opinions.   The reader, we suspect, has indulged in such debates a thousand times. The wider world, we feel, is consciously and sometimes unconsciously mediated through such controversies.   This book will not end these debates.

In the opening chapter we raised the question as to what might best describe the purpose of a football club. A simple answer is that a football club allows us to engage with something trivial that we then at times get very serious about.   As a consequence the rituals of both the game as played and those surrounding the support of a club serve a multitude of purposes. We enjoy at times the possibility the club's fortunes offer for us to collectively submerge our very being.   At an individual level football and football clubs allow us to reflect on the arbitrary nature of desire and hatred and consider - and be reminded of - the precariousness of success and failure. The game and its players offer audiences endless pantomimes that facilitate narratives on morality and deliberate on quintessentially human issues, such as character, strategic thinking, bewilderment, pity, farce and those occasions when brute force is preferable to sweet reason.   The game and its clubs mirror our existence; the football calendar offers a beacon of predictability in a confusing world.   The very certainty of the club and its position in the footballing hierarchies assists in diverting us in some way from the inevitability of death.   But let's not overstate the matter - the game is not for everyone and the passions the club once generated in an individual can recede. Some in recent years have completely fallen out of love with the game. The French can sometimes help us in these matters. Antoine de Saint-Exupé, the Gallic author of *The Little Prince*, writes in the text that: 'One sees clearly only with the heart. The essential is invisible to the eye.' Such an observation is pertinent to football supporters - reflect on the line in years to come.

We thus now stand back and ask of the men who took the reins at Bramall Lane: if not them, who? What we are asking is who might have stepped into the breach if not the men who featured herein? Such a question is pertinent because, despite the claims made a few years ago about some English football clubs' pedigrees and traditions, none has proven to be inoculated against an actual or potential takeover. Marble staircases, wood-panelled boardrooms and fine fellowship mean nothing to the men from foreign lands who arrive expending their wealth and extolling promises, usually seeking in the highest echelons of the English game a public profile they have hitherto not achieved with their wealth-making schemes and with it the potential to make - and possibly clean - monies earned from a wide variety of global operations. What has happened in the boardroom at Sheffield United over the past 30 years could have been evidenced at any one of the 92 league clubs. The fact that the Blades' story is unique - and at times plain daft - is down to chance and serendipity. The club just attracted people who saw a chance to make a difference - and money - and then had their dreams compromised and moved on. In some cases they should have gone sooner. Maybe this is where a Sheffield United angle is evident - the club had a complacent boardroom that did not see the way football was heading and thus did not know how to deal with that which is currently dismissed by its critics as 'Modern Football'. Whilst on occasion the club has attracted the mirth of the English football system, remember that over the past 20 years nearly one third of professional football clubs in England have gone into administration; Sheffield United are not on that list.

We leave off - until the next time - aware that what is 'knowable' outside of the Bramall Lane boardroom may well diminish due to the now routine contractual agreements that prevent former Bramall Lane employees from discussing the details of their engagement at the club. In the new-found silence Blades fans must take comfort when the current chairman assures questioning supporters that 'not a cent' of monies generated at Bramall Lane is subsidising associated foreign-based projects. In the present we must trust that no one making pronouncements on behalf of the club suffers from any conflict of conscience. In the absence of anyone willing or seeking to buy the club we must believe that Sheffield United is being run in a fit and proper manner.

BIBLIOGRAPHY

Books

Armstrong, Gary (1998); *Blade Runners – Lives in Football,* The Hallamshire Press, Sheffield

Armstrong, Gary with Garrett, John (2006); *Sheffield United FC – The Biography,* The Hallamshire Press, Sheffield

Armstrong, Gary and Mitchell, John P. (2008); *Global and Local Football – Politics and Europeanisation on the fringes of the EU,*Routledge, Abingdon

Bassett, Dave (1997); *Harry's Game,* Breedon Books, Derby

Bell, Matthew; Nicolson, Andy and Titterton, Kevin (Editors) (2004); *Blades Tales 2 – More memories of supporting Sheffield United,* Juma, Sheffield

Clarebrough, Denis (1989); *The Official Centenary History - Sheffield United Football Club - The First 100 Years,* Sheffield United Football Club, Sheffield

Clarebrough, Denis and Kirkham, Andrew (1999); *A Complete Record of Sheffield United Football Club 1889-1999,* Sheffield United Football Club, Sheffield

Conn, David (2005); *The Beautiful Game? Searching the Soul of Football,* Yellow Jersey Press, London

Dooley, Derek with Farnsworth, Keith (2000); *Dooley! The Autobiography of a Soccer Legend,*The Hallamshire Press, Sheffield

Eyre, Fred (2005); *Kicked Into Touch,* Pomona, Hebden Bridge

Foot, John (2007); *Calcio – A History of Italian Football,* Harper Perennial, London

Hopcraft, Arthur (2006); *The Football Man,* Aurum Press Ltd, London

Kane, Samantha (1998); *A Two-Tiered Existence,* Writers & Artists, Ahmedabad

Warnock, Neil (2007); *Made in Sheffield – My Story,* Hodder and Stoughton, London

Reports/Yearbooks/Commemorative Brochures

The Hillsborough Stadium Disaster 15 April 1989 – Inquiry by Rt. Hon. Lord Justice Taylor, Final Report, Presented to Parliament by the Secretary of State for the Home Department by Command of Her Majesty, January 1990 (published by HMSO, London, 1990)

Sheffield United FC – Portrait of a Championship, 1981/82 (published by Sheffield United Football Club, 1982)

Sheffield United – Back in the First Division – The Blades Official Promotion Story Souvenir, 1989/90 (published by Sheffield United Football Club, 1990)

Sheffield United Official Handbook, Volume 9, 2001/02 (written by Andy Pack and Kevin Cookson, published by Polar Group Ltd, Leicester, 2002)

Sheffield United PLC Annual and Interim Reports and Accounts (published by Sheffield United Football Club, 1997-2009)

The Story of Cricket at Bramall Lane – End of an Era, 1855-1973 (written by Keith Farnsworth, published by Sheffield Morning Telegraph, 1973)

Periodicals, Magazines and Newspapers

Blades News

Blades Revival News

Communiqué

Cutting Edge

Daily Express

Daily Mail

Derniere Heure

Finance North

Financial Times

Flashing Blade

Football Today

Guardian

Halifax Evening Courier

Hello!

Herald

Independent

Independent on Sunday

Lane Line Up

Mail on Sunday

New Statesman

News of the World

Red and White Wizaaaard

Sheffield Star

Sheffield Green 'Un

Sheffield Telegraph

Stockport District Advertiser

Sydney Morning Herald

When Saturday Comes

www.thebulletin.be

Yorkshire Post

Television and Radio Programmes

BBC Radio 4 'Face the Facts'

BBC Radio Sheffield

BBC Teletext

BBC TV 'Breakfast TV'

BBC TV 'Crimewatch'

BBC TV 'Money Programme'

BBC TV 'Look North'

BBC TV 'One Life: Make Me a Man Again' Documentary

BBC TV 'Sportsweek'

BBC TV 'United' Documentary

Sky TV

Sky Sports News

Yorkshire TV 'Calendar'

Other Sources

Minutes of the Blades Independent Fans' Association

Minutes of the Sheffield United Football Club Board Meetings

Historical Archives of Sheffield United Football Club

http://www.publications.parliament.uk

http://www.premierleague.com

http://www.thefa.com

http://www.tas-cas.org/

http://news.bbc.co.uk

http://www.mirror.co.uk

http://football.guardian.co.uk

http://www.dailymail.co.uk

http://sport.independent.co.uk

http://www.thetimes.co.uk

http://soccernet.espn.go.com

http://www.kumb.com

http://eccentricworlds.blogspot.com

http://www.wikipedia.org

http://www.sufc.co.uk

http://www.whitestar.be

http://www.journalisted.com

http://www.soccerbase.com